E1.
$8.95

D1279536

FACTS IN
PERSPECTIVE

TO KAY, KAY-KAY, AND E.H.K.

FACTS IN PERSPECTIVE

the editorial page
and news interpretation

HILLIER KRIEGHBAUM

*Professor of Journalism and Chairman,
Department of Journalism
New York University*

PRENTICE - HALL, INC.
Englewood Cliffs, N.J.

PRENTICE-HALL JOURNALISM SERIES

Kenneth E. Olson, Editor

Current printing (last digit):
14 13 12 11 10 9 8 7

PRINTED IN THE UNITED STATES OF AMERICA

C – 29964

Need for an understanding
of the complexities of news events, whether far away or on the
periphery of research in a nearby laboratory, has skyrocketed
in recent decades. Whether this demand is met might well be the
paramount factor in the survival of a free world. Communication and interpretation of news, ideas, and opinions is one of the
necessities for proper functioning of our contemporary society.
This book attempts to examine and assay how this is done
through printed media—newspapers, general magazines, business publications, and other specialized publications.

I have tried to present the broad picture and indicate the
problems involved in obtaining "the essential truth" of happenings in the mid-Twentieth Century. I have also given how-to-do
details for readers interested in participating in this important
aspect of present-day journalism.

Without the cooperation and enthusiastic encouragement of
dozens of editorial writers, news commentators, reporters, publishers, and journalism instructors, this book would not have become a reality.

Hillier Krieghbaum

Reproductions of editorial pages, 321–336

Life, Better Living, Richmond News Leader, The New York Times, The Milwaukee Journal, Chicago Daily News, The Atlanta Constitution, The Macon News, Bristol Herald Courier, La Salle Daily News-Tribune, Lapeer County Press, Los Angeles Mirror and Daily News, The Des Moines Register, The Louisville Times, Chicago Sun-Times, New York Daily News, Newsday

ACKNOWLEDGMENTS

THE AUTHOR IS GRATEFUL TO THE NUMEROUS INDIVIDUALS AND organizations whose cooperation made this book possible. He particularly wants to acknowledge his debt for material that appeared in *The Masthead* of the National Conference of Editorial Writers, *Nieman Reports,* and *The Quill* of Sigma Delta Chi, professional journalistic fraternity.

He also wishes to thank the following individuals, organizations, and publications for permission to use material for which they hold the copyrights:

Association for Education in Journalism; *Atlanta Constitution; Annals of the American Academy of Political and Social Science;* Baltimore *Sun;* Bell Syndicate; *Better Living;* Herbert L. Block; *Buffalo Evening News; Business Week; Chicago Daily News; Chicago Daily Tribune; Chicago Sun-Times; Christian Century; Christian Science Monitor; Cleveland Plain Dealer;* Columbia University Press; *Commonweal;* Congressional Quarterly News Features; *Cosmopolitan Magazine;* Crowell-Collier Publishing Company; Crown Publishers, Inc., for excerpt from *The Columnists* by Charles Fisher (Copyright, 1944, by Howell, Soskin, Publishers, Inc.)

Denver Post; Bernard DeVoto; *Des Moines Register* and *Tribune;* Edgartown (Massachusetts) *Vineyard Gazette; Editor and Publisher; Emporia Gazette;* Dr. Benjamin Fine; Daniel R. Fitzpatrick; General Features Corporation; Wolcott Gibbs; Greenville (Mississippi) *Delta Democrat-Times;* Harcourt, Brace and Company for excerpts from *Without Fear or Favor* by Neil MacNeil; Harper and Brothers for excerpts from *Business Journalism* by Julien Elfenbein and *The Second Tree From the Corner* by E. B. White; Houghton-Mifflin Company for excerpt from *Editorial Writing* by M. Lyle Spencer.

Jackson, Nash, Brophy, Barringer, and Brooks for editorial from the *New York World; Kansas City Star* and *Times;* King Features; *Ladies' Home Journal* and George H. Sibley for editorial (Copyright, 1952, by The Curtis Publishing Company) ; *Lapeer County Press;* La Salle (Illinois) *Daily News-Tribune;*

Life; Long Island Star-Journal; Los Angeles Mirror and Daily News; Louisville *Courier-Journal* and *Times; LP-Gas;* Macmillan Company for excerpts from *Freedom of Information* by Herbert Brucker (Copyright, 1949, by Herbert Brucker) and *Public Opinion* by Walter Lippmann (Copyright, 1922, by Walter Lippmann) ; *Macon News;* John Bartlow Martin and *Harper's Magazine.*

Materials and Methods; McNaught Syndicate; Metropolitan Life Insurance Company; *Miami Herald; Milwaukee Journal; Minneapolis Star* and *Tribune;* NEA Service, Inc.; *New Orleans Item; New Republic; Newsday; Newsweek;* New York *Daily News; New York Herald Tribune; The New York Times; New York World-Telegram and Sun; New Yorker;* North American Newspaper Alliance, Inc.; Old Greenwich (Connecticut) *Village Gazette; Philadelphia Inquirer;* Pine Plains (N.Y.) *Register Herald;* Portland *Oregonian; Power;* Prentice-Hall, Inc., for excerpts from *Makers of Modern Journalism* by Kenneth Stewart and John Tebbel (Copyright, 1953, by Prentice-Hall, Inc.) and *Design and Makeup of the Newspaper* by Albert A. Sutton (Copyright, 1948, by Prentice-Hall, Inc.) ; *Providence Journal;* Public Affairs Press for excerpt from *The People Know Best: The Ballots vs The Polls* by Morris L. Ernst and David Loth (Copyright, 1949, by Joan Ernst and Fanny Loth).

James Reston; *St. Louis Post-Dispatch;* Salt Lake City *Deseret News-Salt Lake Telegram; San Francisco Chronicle; Saturday Evening Post* and David Wittels; *Saturday Review;* Science Service; *Scripps-Howard News; Shell Progress* and John Earl Davis for editorial (Copyright, 1953, by Shell Oil Company) ; *The Sohioan; Stanton* (Nebraska) *Register; The Reporter;* Richmond *News-Leader* and *Times Dispatch;* Time, Inc.; *Wall Street Journal;* University of Chicago Press for excerpts from *A Free and Responsible Press* by the Commission on Freedom of the Press (Copyright, 1947, by the University of Chicago Press) ; *Washington Evening Star;* United Feature Syndicate.

BUT A FREE PRESS CAN DISCHARGE ITS RESPONSIBILITY TO FREE PEOPLE ONLY BY GIVING ALL THE FACTS IN BALANCE. FACTS IN PERSPECTIVE ARE VITAL TO VALID CITIZEN JUDGMENTS. . . . KNOWLEDGE OF THE FACTS AND OF THEIR INTERRELATIONSHIPS IS MORE THAN EVER ESSENTIAL TO THE SOLUTION OF HUMAN PROBLEMS. I KNOW THAT TO PRESENT THE FACTS IN PERSPECTIVE IS A DIFFICULT TASK.

PRESIDENT DWIGHT D. EISENHOWER
before the American Newspaper Publishers Association, April 22, 1954

ONE

Straight news
is not enough

AMERICANS PERSISTENTLY HAVE SOUGHT INFORMATION AND BACK-
ground on which they could build, or at least reinforce, their
opinions about what was happening in the world. Since men in
powdered wigs wore silken breeches and woman curtsied in hoop
skirts, they have asked, "What does this mean?" or the even more
demanding single word question, "Why?" when they discussed
the latest news. This attitude has been a traditional hallmark and
primary requisite of an informed democracy.

The press long has been, and still remains, a chief avenue for
obtaining both straight news and the comments on that reporting.
The term "press," as used here, lumps together newspapers and
magazines in all their assorted variations. This involves some obvious oversimplification. But the press provides a basis for building
public opinion—whether it is a weekly newspaper serving a small
village, a morning daily circulating throughout a huge metropolitan area covering parts of several states, a technical publication
providing information and comments for a specialized trade group
or profession across the country, or a nationally circulated magazine bought by a cross section of the general public. Thus it is
fair to lump them all together for some generalizing; each group,
however, has it own particular problems and one must not push
such simplifications too far.

This chapter examines why the news commentaries deserve a

king's size share of attention from today's press. (They might also be called news interpretations, background articles, or opinion writing except that special shadings of differences have grown up around these terms which might prejudice some against them.) Then an attempt is made to find some valid definitions for the channels through which newspapermen and magazine writers interpret the news and give it perspective. Finally some examples of the various types of comments are given.

Objectivity is under attack

The old journalistic god of an impersonal, absolute objectivity for news reporting has largely failed its modern believers. Assaults on the conventional presentation of events have come from two principal directions. On the one hand, understanding the complexities of the mid-Twentieth Century requires such specialization and expertness that the average man cannot hope to compete with the full-time authority. He needs help and he should be able to turn confidently to a responsible press. On the other hand, shrewd and sometimes unscrupulous men have exploited surface half-truths for their own advantage in expectation of obscuring the essential truths. The reader should feel that his paper or magazine will shine a spotlight of truth on these men if the missing facts are known.

If the newspapers still take seriously the admonition of Joseph Pulitzer to be "both a daily teacher and a daily tribune," they have responsibilities far beyond reporting surface facts. Yet the journalistic emphasis on competitive speed and on the "conflict angle" for presentation of the news remains little changed. Naked facts have been pushed at the readers with machine gun fire rapidity; too frequently they have been expected to clothe them unassisted with background, interpretation, and comprehension. Many of today's thoughtful publishers and editors agree with Pulitzer. Even those who believe that a publication's primary job is to print the news also subscribe to printing it in perspective. How can this be done? Many, although not all, feel that they can discharge their obligations through explanatory writings, interpretive articles, background features, and syndicated columns as well as the more conventional and traditional editorial comments.

John Cowles, president of the *Minneapolis Star* and *Tribune* and chairman of the board of the *Des Moines Register* and *Tribune*, stated his views before a University of Missouri audience when he discussed how daily papers should meet the competition of television:

> People will want far more interpretive news from their papers so that they can understand what is happening. People will want more background information. People will want not only the bare facts of what did happen yesterday but will want from their newspapers information on what is probably going to happen tomorrow or next week or next month.
>
> The relative importance of editorial writers will greatly increase. It will not be tub-thumping, violent, partisan editorial assertions that the readers will want, but understandable analyses of the complicated problems that trouble them.
>
> This means that we will need better reporters and better editors and must give them more latitude than most papers now do.

Mounting complexities of specialized knowledge, especially in the physical and social sciences, are demonstrated neatly by recent history. The mathematical abstractions of Dr. Albert Einstein smashed the conventional Newtonian concept of physics and thus paved the way for splitting the atom. Yet the typical newspaper and magazine reader was ill prepared for the shattering military and social impact of atomic energy. He has been almost as badly forewarned of most comparable advances in the sciences.

Before establishment of the Atomic Energy Commission under civilian control and again while President Harry S. Truman pondered an order to develop the hydrogen bomb, scientists who understood the full implications conducted frantic and belated campaigns in adult education. This work should have already been under way by the nation's press, but the atomic physicists' efforts showed that only a portion of the press had done this assignment. Those publications that printed background stories and adequate editorials stood out as conspicuous exceptions to the general performance.

Spectacular as has been the coverage in some individual newspapers and magazines, much the same sad story could be repeated for mental hygiene, the implications of an aging population, and such other social problems as race discrimination, housing, conservation, and labor-management relations. On a few occasions, all the press rallied in good fashion.

The United States' rise as a world power highlights another aspect of the increasing demands for greater knowledge and sound public opinion in this country. A century ago, when the United States spoke, its voice was weak and that of a newcomer without great influence. Now all that has changed. Thus it is important to us—and to the peoples of most far-away lands, too—that there be the widest dissemination of not only straight news reports but also of the truth behind the surface facts and the mountainous complexities which usually make an argument shadings of gray rather than pristine white or black. Reactions in the United States may extend to such distant places as Tibet, South Africa, or Argentina. Ignorance seldom has carried a heavier penalty than in the contemporary United States.

Crossing of the 38th Parallel in Korea by Communist forces in June, 1950, graphically illustrated the potentialities of a suddenly erupting event abroad having tremendous domestic ramifications. Practically all the American public, except possibly a few top officials, was unprepared for this news. Unquestionably, adequate interpretations of developments from trained correspondents at the scene were too scanty and this deficiency was not compensated by articles from other news centers, such as Washington. Obviously some of the story, such as the planning by the Communists, could only be guessed; but a great deal that might have been told was not.

Some serious students of contemporary journalism have lamented the "disappearing foreign correspondent" and claimed that the United States had insufficient reporters at potential sore spots around the world to insure the sound grounding of United States opinion. Greater coverage, these writers said, was necessary if this country's public was to be aware of undercurrents that might break out as violent news events affecting world activities. Along with reporting of the surface facts, however, the whole story with background as well as foreground is needed.

Many students of international communications are aware of these problems and are working toward a solution. For example, *The Flow of the News, A Study by the International Press Institute* (I.P.I., 1953) commented as follows:

Editors, agency executives, foreign correspondents and readers agree on the importance of interpretation in foreign news coverage. Foreign news stories should explain the meaning of the events they report, and in terms that will have significance for American readers.

The kind of writing that produces this significance is called *interpretation* by many editors. Others call it *background*. Some agency executives like the term *explanatory writing,* and that is close to what newspaper editors and others mean by either *background* or *interpretation*. But whatever term is used, it denotes the kind of writing designed to give meaning to the bare facts, to provide setting, sequence and significance. . . .

Explanation of the meaning of events reported from abroad is desired by the great majority of American editors. While only about one-fifth of the editors queried in this study volunteer "more interpretation" as the key to improvement in foreign news coverage, 130 out of 169 in answer to a specific question say they want their news agency sources to interpret the meaning of all stories requiring explanation.

It is the complexities of events abroad—politics, foreign relations—which dominate the flow of news into the United States. "Much foreign economic and political news," says an American editor, "is

5

meaningless without interpretation." "Interpretation," says another, "makes the news a vital, living incident to readers who otherwise would be only perplexed by the factual statements."

Just what is truth?

More than a quarter of a century ago, Walter Lippmann outlined brilliantly in *Public Opinion* (Macmillan, 1922) how news differed from truth. "The function of news," he wrote, "is to signalize an event, the function of truth is to bring to light the hidden facts, to set them into relation with each other, and make a picture of reality on which man can act. Only at those points, where social conditions take recognizable and measurable shape, do the body of truth and the body of news coincide."

The working press has shifted its sights somewhat since Lippmann discussed reporting. After an event has become news, there is now some obligation to print "the essential truth." Obligations of the responsible newspaper and magazine news commentator—that is, the editorial writer, columnist, opinion article writer, and author of an explanatory or interpretive story—thus devolve, in many cases, upon finding and then presenting the truth. Few journalists acted upon the implications of Lippmann's distinctions until the post-war years brought a fairly general revolt against "dead-pan" reporting. A few key statements from this post-war period will show how thinking has been shifting.

The Commission on Freedom of the Press argued forcefully for accurate and meaningful coverage of the day's events in its *A Free and Responsible Press* (University of Chicago Press, 1947). Discussing specifically international correspondence, but in terms applicable to all reporting, the commission members said:

It is no longer enough to report *the fact* truthfully. It is now necessary to report *the truth about the fact*.

As it turned out, the distinguished group of non-journalists was ahead of most of the men and women who work regularly for newspapers and magazines. The commission took a long, hard look at whether impassive objectivity furthered public understanding of the contemporary world. Perhaps the Ivory Tower made it possible to distinguish sooner the forest from the trees. Most journalistic groups, however, in the years since the Commission on Freedom of the Press reported, have spent considerable time in discussion of this topic.

When an Associated Press Managing Editors' convention devotes an entire session, as it did in 1948 and in later years, to the breakdown of objective reporting and to advocating more explanatory writing, it is apparent that something has gone terribly wrong with the goal of undiluted objectivity.

One of the keen students of the post-war press, James B. Reston of *The New York Times*, went to that 1948 APME session fresh from Washington, where he had witnessed first-hand the abuses of congressional immunity and tampering with truth by skilled propagandists. Reston told the editors that there was a great difference between "the essential truth" and "the literal truth." In language that must have sounded strange to some of the newspapermen who long had looked upon *The New York Times* as the pinnacle of objectivity, Reston continued:

The whole future of reporting depends on telling intelligently what is going on in the world. The world is getting more complicated every year. Explanatory writing is the field in which we can excel. You cannot merely report the literal truth. You have to explain it.

Authors of explanatory articles, interpretive pieces, columns, or editorials all have a responsibility to point out this difference between the literal and the essential truth. It is the job of these writers to show what is not obvious. As Reston aptly put it, the assignment involves reading the fine print for the general reader and then pointing out the dangers.

Arthur Hays Sulzberger, publisher of *The New York Times* and whose father-in-law and predecessor, Adolph S. Ochs, pledged "to give the news without fear or favor," showed how far times had changed when he told the 1952 annual convention of the Association for Education in Journalism:

Now, strange as it may sound, I do not believe that it is possible ". . . to give the news without fear or favor, without regard to any party, sect or interest involved," and I sincerely trust that this heresy will not cast me for the leading role in an auto da fe. I do not think it possible to be strictly objective or to present the news without any bias. . .

I believe further that only those who are aware that these ideals are, in fact, beyond their reach can ever truly approach them. As I see it, all of us have been acquiring prejudice from the day we were born, and we must strive constantly and consciously to rid ourselves of these prejudices if we seek objectivity. . .

Despite everything I have said about the need for interpretation of the news it does not take the place of the factual news report. It is supplementary and essential as it is, it is dangerous if not watched and done correctly and within rigid limits. The balance between opinion and interpretation is delicate and it must be preserved. The newspaperman must be imbued with the spirit of a crusader for truth and then drawing on a rich educational background, try to explain the meaning and the consequences of that truth.

How objectivity broke down was analyzed by Elmer Davis, outstanding newspaper writer, distinguished radio commentator, and director of the Office of War Information during World War II, in the 1951 Minneapolis Newspaper Guild Memorial Lecture as follows:

This striving for objectivity was in its beginnings a good thing; but it went a little too far. From holding that newspapers ought to present both sides it went on to the position that it was all right to present only one side, if nobody happened to be talking on the other; and it was not the business of the newspaper to tell the reader if that one argument happened to be phony. . .

This kind of dead-pan reporting—So-and-so said it, and if he's lying in his teeth it isn't my business to say so—may salve the conscience of the reporter (or of the editor, who has the ultimate responsibility) as to his loyalty to some obscure ideal of objectivity. But what about his loyalty to the reader? The reader lays down his nickel, or whatever, for the paper, in the belief that he is going to find out what is going on in the world; and it does not seem to me that the newspaper is giving him his nickel's worth if it only gives him what somebody says is going on in the world, with no hint as to whether what that somebody says is right or wrong.

This "dead-pan reporting" may actually lead both the newspaper and the readers to miss the essence of the story. Too frequently this new coverage has descended to what Basil L. Walters, executive editor of Knight Newspapers, called "little more than an adaptation of stenographic reporting of official handouts and official speeches." The answer, he said, was to develop "investigative reporters." Palmer Hoyt, editor and publisher of the *Denver Post*, described the job of covering the activities of Senator Joseph McCarthy as "one of spontaneous and objective search for facts, with full publication of those facts accompanied by careful interpretation thereof." He dictated a memorandum to the staff of the *Post* so that it would be possible, in his opinion, "to present news stories and headlines in such a manner that the reading public will be able to measure the real worth or value and the true meaning of the stories."

Even more sharp were these warnings before New York State editors by Dr. William P. Tolley, chancellor of Syracuse University:

Accurate reporting is not the solution for our difficulties. An accurate report of a lying official statement is still not the truth. . . . Obviously the truth that comes out of the American press can be no greater or more certain than the truth that goes into it.

So long as we have existing censorship at the source of all types of important news, the newspaper will not be able to give the public the truth. Government bureaucrats and the public relations operatives of business have established a quarantine on truth through which the press is able to break only on occasion.

Even as prominent a practitioner of public relations as Edward L. Bernays conceded that all was not well in his vocation. In his book, *Public Relations* (University of Oklahoma Press, 1952), he admitted that "society thus far has developed no legal sanctions to safeguard itself against the uninformed or unethical or antisocial counsel on public relations—only against the man who breaks the law."

This revolt against a stifling objectivity is not confined to newspapers, as may be realized by looking over representative news weeklies. A break with the conventions of objectivity in its more limited sense accounted in part for the initial popularity of these publications. A sidelight on how one group of magazines formulated its policy is told in these excerpts from instructions issued to string correspondents for the several publications managed by Henry R. Luce:

We do not believe that a lot of information necessarily equals a little comprehension. We do believe that in every case it is possible to get to the heart of the matter, and that it is our duty to take the reader quickly to it. This means that we as editors and reporters must not only report the news but say what it means. A mere recitation of the facts is not enough without an evaluation, blunt or subtle, of how the facts should be faced.

The mechanics of contemporary news reporting contribute, in a small way, to the flowering of "dead-pan reporting." While much has been said in favor of competition between news services and among newspapers and magazines, this is not an unmixed blessing. Undoubtedly the good outweighs the bad; but let us examine the liabilities.

In competing with other reporters, a press association correspondent or a staff writer for a newspaper or magazine is constantly striving to excel. One way is to get his story ahead of all rivals. That puts a premium on speed and too frequently accuracy may be by-passed in the rush. In this scramble to hurry, even highly competent reporters may miss facts that really do make a difference in public reaction. Another way to get a news story into print is to put greater weight on the public's natural interest in human conflict, whether it be in the front lines of a battlefield, a political debate in the United States Senate, or a contest for control of a gigantic financial structure. Information specialists attached to the United Nations have been particularly bitter in their criticism of the reporting, in great detail, of every Russian veto or "walk-out" and the playing down or outright neglecting of such constructive accomplishments as technical assistance to curb malaria and tuberculosis or aid in setting up modern educational systems in under-developed areas.

Most serious-minded newspaper and magazine writers and editors agree that writing devoid of all interpretations, all perspective, all opinions may not be enough to tell the real facts. A reporter's accurate reflection of the obvious surface facts too frequently has proven a sad distortion of the essential truth. Along the line, somewhere, forces have shoved the ideas and facts out of focus; the resulting distortion may sometimes be worse than no story at all. Frequently the difficulty may develop because of prejudices and bias of the reporters, copyreaders, and editors who handle the information. Again it may arise from the complicated nature of the news and the lack of training of those handling it. Other times, it grows out of the deliberate perversions of men with selfish ends to serve.

Interpretations are never easy

Even the most enthusiastic believers in the need for interpretation to make the news understandable to the general reader admit that such assignments are extremely difficult. The reason is that the author is describing, as best he can, the nine-tenths of the iceberg of a news happening that is not easily visible above the surface. The chief hazard in avoiding the admitted dangers of conventional objectivity is that the writer may fall into an equally deep hole on the other side. When he attempts to interpret, he may end up with an unsupported subjectivity mixing emotions, prejudices, or propaganda. This may happen despite recent advances in psychology, psychiatry, and sociology which will help him understand better how people tick.

Elmer Davis was fully aware of this. In his Minneapolis speech, he pointed it out as follows:

What is now called objectivity has its great and visible shortcomings; but any attempt at interpretation has its perils too—it should be undertaken only by a man who bears always in mind that famous admonition of Oliver Cromwell: "In the bowels of Christ, think it possible you may be mistaken.". . .

I am not arguing against objectivity; I am all *for* objectivity that gives the reader a real understanding of what is going on. My complaint is only that what is now called objectivity too often makes the newspaper a mere mouthpiece for pretentious phonies.

The good newspaper must walk a tight rope between two abysses —on the one side the false objectivity which takes everything at face value, and lets the public be imposed upon by the charlatan with the most brazen front; on the other, the interpretive reporting which fails to draw the line between objective and subjective, between a reasonably well established fact and what the reporter or the editor wishes were the fact. This is primary-school stuff, of course; everybody knows it, and if few people practise it, that is because practising it is very hard. It is easier to pick out the nearest exit—to fall back on the incontrovertible fact that the Hon. John P. Hoosis said, colon quote, without going into the question whether he was lying or not. . . .

To sum up—objectivity is all right if it is really objective, if it conveys as accurate an impression of the truth as can be obtained. But to let demonstrably false statements stand with no warning of their falsity is not what I would call objectivity.

When the printed statement cannot be anchored incontrovertibly, both writer and editor are subject to criticism. That is a risk that they must take if they are going to accept their full jobs as responsible journalists. During the emotional aftermath of General Douglas MacArthur's relief of his Far Eastern Commands in 1951 even the *Christian Science Monitor* was accused of interpreting the news by its own preconceived standards. As a result of these accusations, Editor Erwin Canham published a series of six articles entitled, "How to Use Your Newspaper." Included were these wise comments by one of the nation's respected editors:

News interpretation, with all its hazards, often is safer and wiser than printing the bare news alone. Nothing can be more misleading than the unrelated fact, just because it is a fact and hence impressive. Background, motives, surrounding circumstances, related events and issues all need to be understood and appraised as well as the immediate event. . . . But interpretation requires integrity and knowledge and understanding and balance and detachment.

News interpretation is all too readily misunderstood. Whenever the interpretations differ from the preconceived notions of the readers, misunderstanding is likely to creep in. Objectivity is a very elusive thing. It usually means, to the individual, agreement with his own views.

Attempting to explain why editors differed so on how successful interpretive reporting had been, the 1954 APME Red Book blamed "the very simple reason that one man's interpretive writing can be another man's jaundiced editorial prejudices." Then it so rightly commented: "The trick is to avoid the dangers yawning on either side of the tightrope trod by the interpretive writer."

Davis, Canham, and the APME pointed up the semantic fog beclouding discussions of objectivity. The very word means different things to different people. In a conventional sense and as it was used generally until the 1930's, objectivity meant being strictly non-partisan in news reporting. In more recent years, it became easier to skim the surface, as Elmer Davis has explained, and to avoid the hard work of really objective reporting, which makes the news meaningful for the typical reader. The slip-shod work was defended as "objective" while the carefully prepared, more complete presentation was condemned as opinionated.

To illustrate, a Sunday edition of *The New York Times* had a front page United Press dispatch from Vienna announcing that the Czechoslovak Communists had drastically revalued that country's currency. The various rates for exchange of outstanding Czech crowns were given, together with the Prague radio announcement that the action cut any link with the dollar, "the money of a capitalist state and a country with potential economic crises." All of this was reporting in the best conventions of traditional "objectivity" although it did have a fillip of political propaganda. But to let it go at that would have left unanswered the American readers' question: What does it mean? The United Press story did answer it in a paragraph inserted well down in the item and it aptly illustrated this business of telling "the essential truth." That paragraph read:

The reform obviously was aimed at cleaning out crowns held by anti-Communist former middle-class and wealthy Czechs and other persons hoarding crowns—since the hardest rate of 50 to 1 was aimed at cash on hand.

Frequently, it cannot be done simply in a paragraph. An entire background article may be required to explain the meaning and, on occasion, a series may be needed.

Probably this whole argument arose because journalists thought of only two categories of writing: news—pure, simple, and pristine objectivity for the front pages of newspapers—and opinion—dripping and colored subjectivity on the editorial pages. A third or possibly a fourth or fifth classification was needed. There are the chapters that have gone before—background. There are the translations needed to make clear the complexities of many events—interpretation and exposition. There are forecasts and predictions to make meaningful the significance. And there may be others.

If newspaper and magazine folk will admit that a writer may become "a partisan for truth" without committing a mortal journalistic sin or if they will possibly just recognize that they have a continuing responsibility to their readers to tell "the essential truth," then much of this semantic fog will be dispelled. In his inevitable selection of the facts to use in his news story, a reporter should discard the false; he should also *add* those *truths* that give *perspective*. So should the editorial writer, columnist, and news interpreter.

All of this does not mean that supporters of interpretation and explanation want to introduce a "press of opinion" into this country. They want, if we understand them correctly, more truthful reporting because it includes not only the obvious foreground but also the more subtle background.

Despite the admitted difficulties and dangers from news interpretation, the risks are worth the gamble for journalists who can meet the exacting requirements of "integrity and knowledge and understanding and balance and detachment." If United States public opinion is to depend upon the press as a chief avenue for both information and comment, then publishers, editors, copyreaders, and writers must put forward their greatest efforts. If this can be done, then this country will attain a real "Golden Age" for its newspapers and magazines.

New rivals enter the arena

Since 1900, major changes have taken place not only in the departments of the press and the scope of their influence but also in the world on which they comment. It may not be unfortunate that present day news commentators cannot put the clock back. They still have a key job to do: to supply the background and explanations on which readers may make up their own minds and, when the editors and publishers believe it necessary, to argue from these facts for a cause they believe just and right. Yet the changing world itself provides some of the answers for the difference in the influence of the press today.

In addition to professional changes, such as the rise of the news weekly, the role of the editorial, column, and news interpretation has been influenced by two developments which are only vaguely related to the press itself:

(1) Increasing competition for newspapers and magazines as other media sought to become rival opinion makers.

(2) A mounting level of general education.

Toward the close of the Nineteenth Century, the newspapers still dominated the scene. Except for an infrequent magazine article or a book, none challenged or contradicted what an editor had to say. The "muckrakers" were just starting to wield power in magazines. One writer might oppose another in a magazine or newspaper with violence and vindictiveness but few contestants in the arena of public opinion came from other fields.

Commentators on the news now meet competition from journalistic enterprises developed in the Twentieth Century. Technological advances brought such new media as motion pictures, radio, and television.

While motion pictures generally are considered entertainment, most movie houses show news reels and thus qualify as media for news communication. Motion pictures have progressed a long way since the flickers of the early nickelodeons and this increasing competence has been reflected in news reels. Considerably more than two-thirds of the adult American public may flock to see films in any one week. Part of their time is spent viewing pictures of news events.

Radio and television have established themselves firmly as media for mass communications. President Franklin D. Roosevelt, it was estimated, was able to reach 40,000,000 radio listeners on at least ten occasions. By way of comparison, daily newspaper circulation during those times was approximately 50,000,000. Although newspaper circulation statistics have risen well beyond that figure, radio and television audiences have grown even more rapidly. It is now possible for more individuals to hear over radio or view by television than to read a daily newspaper. Multiple readership may give the daily newspapers some margin of popularity. Both radio and television enjoy a decided advantage over newspapers in being able to present important news first. To break in with,

"We interrupt this program to bring you a news bulletin. . . ." is far easier for the radio or television announcer than for the newspaperman to make over the front page and start the press again.

Thanks to these innovations in mass communications during the Twentieth Century, the typical newspaper and magazine reader today brings a far greater background knowledge than all but the small elite in any community had a century or even a half century ago. These changes have influenced those who work for the press, their publications, and, to some extent, their ultimate goals.

As more and more individuals have been graduated from high schools and colleges, independence in forming their own opinions has mounted. Educational benefits to veterans of World War II and the Korean War made it possible for millions to attend colleges. This spurt in the number of graduates was reflected, in some degree, in the readership of the more serious articles in periodicals. When the reader has the facts, both those on the surface and those buried deep in the background, and when he thinks he has the ability to draw his own valid conclusions, he will give scant ration to dogmatic, partisan expressions of opinion. This has brought a minor journalistic revolution. Less heat is generated in an argument now and more light is shed in an interpretation. At least, that is what has happened on the more responsible newspapers and magazines.

Charles Merz of *The New York Times* discussed this as it applied to the editorial pages when he wrote:

The modern editorial page is dealing with readers who are incomparably better informed about everything that is happening in the world than newspaper readers used to be. These readers have formed the habit of thinking for themselves. And if the editorial page is arbitrary, or if its conclusions do not seem to follow the known premises in any given case, it will not move opinion.

The editor has a job

Any realistic discussion about commenting on the news and squaring this job with newspaper or magazine policy must rest on the

17

realization that, although some generalizations may be made, there is no single standard of performance. For instance, a colorful, vigorous individual in a small town, who illuminates the day's events may be quoted frequently in a half dozen countries. The standardized and spineless comments of an editorial writer may be printed in a group of daily papers appearing in a dozen or more different communities without a ripple of attention, even among the regular readers of the publications.

Comments in *The New York Times* or *New York Herald Tribune*, for example, will differ markedly from those of their New York City tabloid rivals. All these metropolitan expressions may vary from those in the small daily or weekly in a rural midwestern community, a representative of the specialized trade press, or a fraternal monthly magazine. These differences, however, need have little influence on the effectiveness of the writing. A successful writer is able to transfer his ideas to the reader. And, if effective, he will have worked out the means for doing that in any area of the press in which he is operating. That is the nearest to standardization in performance that will be found.

The extent and vigor of news comments, whether they are editorials, columns, interpretive pieces, or opinion articles, will depend largely upon the courage, the integrity, and the freedom of expression permitted by the publications and those who control them, as well as the goals they seek to attain.

Many newspaper and magazine workers can agree on the broad responsibilities and goals of the person who sets the publication's tone. *The New York Times*, for instance, once explained that its editorial page had a duty "not to shout its own opinions at its readers, or to issue commands on their social and political behavior, but to assist them in the task of reaching conclusions after reading the daily newspaper; to analyze and interpret some news stories; to pass judgment on others; to help the reader see them in proper perspective and in their relation to the rest of the news, and to help him realize their significance to him." This description might be extended to the entire field of commenting on the news.

In some respects, the commentator's role is to tutor the typical citizen who is too busy earning a living to devote his time to studying the complexities and confusions of modern life. But there still remain some occasions when the responsible newspaper and magazine worker must abandon neutrality and battle for the truth.

One of the best statements on an American editor's obligations, duties, and responsibilities also is one of the oldest credos. It appeared during the decade of the 1830's when the United States' penny press was performing the democratic function of bringing the daily newspaper within reach of the common man. Less than a month after the Philadelphia *Public Ledger* was launched as the first penny paper in that community, Russell Jarvis, who was to be its editor for years, wrote:

The post of an editor is a post of high responsibility. His purpose ought to be to instruct, to improve the world; not *to take it as he finds it,* and as he finds it, to direct it to his own views or private interest. His duty is to assail prejudices, for the purpose of correcting them; not to flatter, for the purpose of profiting by them. His duty is to hold up folly and vice to ridicule and scorn; not to treat them tenderly if they have money in their pockets, for the purpose of buying their patronage. The editor who will be frightened from his duty by the cry of *"stop my paper,"* or who will withhold one stroke of the lash from any back that deserves it, in the hope of obtaining an advertisement or a subscriber, is a venal pandar. He is in the market; his services are for sale to anybody or any cause and the highest bidder may obtain him.

What Jarvis wrote applies to an editor in the second half of the Twentieth Century. The contemporary editor has a responsibility to serve the "essential truth" not only on the editorial pages but throughout all the outlets for commenting on the news.

Some definitions may be useful

To define just what is meant by an editorial, a column, or an interpretive news article is as difficult as trying to explain what news is. And trying to define the whole field of news commentaries

19

is almost impossible; yet the trained newspaperman and magazine writer is able to sense it with canny precision.

Undoubtedly it will be helpful to look first at the various segments and then to see if we can draw a defining line around the whole.

First, let's look at editorials.

At the first National Conference of Editorial Writers in 1947, one speaker suggested facetiously that possibly the only all embracing definition would be "anything that is printed under the masthead of an editorial page." Even this generalization is unsatisfactory. A few paragraphs marked "Editorial" may be printed on the front page or in a news column adjoining the story the editor is discussing. The masthead now is being put at the bottom of some editorial pages.

William Allen White, possibly one of the last of the personalizing editorial writers in the same sense as applied to those of the so-called "Golden Age" of journalism, offered this definition in an editorial published in his *Emporia* (Kansas) *Gazette* during World War II:

What's An Editorial?

Often we are asked by intelligent people to define an editorial—a hard question. But generally speaking, an editorial is expression of opinion based upon a selection of facts which present a truth in a new light—something that everyone knows which no one before ever thought of!

The definition is made with particular reference to an editorial in the New York Times this week. The editorial calls attention to the fact that although the Germans have had victory after victory, they have no peace nor hope of peace; and that with all their victories they are further into the war than they were nearly two years ago when the war started. Here, indeed, are the facts. The truth, reflected from the facts, is set in a line which declares that the Germans can deliver blow after deadly blow but never a knockout blow. There are facts which everyone knew. There is a truth shining from the assembled facts which everyone recognizes so clearly that no one may gainsay it.

That, dear readers, is an editorial.

A conventional editorial might be defined as a critical interpretation of significant, usually contemporary, events so that the publication's typical reader will be informed, influenced, or entertained. The word "critical" is used as *evaluating* and not exclusively as *fault-finding*. In other words, it usually is a considered statement of opinion.

What about the columns that newspapers and some magazines have printed so widely in recent years?

Walter Lippmann, one-time editor of the *New York World* and more recently a dean of the syndicated columnists, described himself and others in his class as "an editorial writer who lives in Washington or spends a great deal of his time there." Then he added in an article appearing in *The Quill* (March, 1951):

I think the reason why the newspapers use columnists is that in a country as big as this one, and in an era when national and international affairs have become extraordinarily complicated and important, it is no longer possible for any staff of editorial writers to do the whole work of explaining and interpreting all the news.

Another widely syndicated Washington columnist, Marquis W. Childs, saw himself more as a reporter who filled in some of the gaps in purely "objective" reporting. Commenting on his role as he saw it, he told a University of Oregon audience:

The interpretive reporter expands the horizon of the news. He explains, he amplifies, he clarifies. Often he does this within a framework of opinion trying honestly to make the reader understand when opinion ends and interpretation and exposition begin. In my opinion the interpretive reporter is a phenomenon too little understood and explored. Since this is what I conceive to be my role, I want to talk with you about it.

And what of giving the news event perspective through explanation or interpretation or background?

The Associated Press Managing Editors' Committee on Explanatory Writing and Readability took time in 1949 to work out its own definition of what it was dealing with. This is what the committee reported:

Explanatory Writing may be anything from a word inserted to make clear the meaning of another word, all the way up to a series of background articles about a complex news situation. Its purpose is to make the news understandable to the average reader.

There is nothing really new about Explanatory Writing. Good news reporting has always called for inclusion of all the facts and background necessary to make the story clear. . . . What is new is the emphasis being placed on this important part of our job.

Lester Markel, Sunday editor of *The New York Times*, neatly broke down the various types of comments on the news this way in his roundup of wartime journalistic developments in *While You Were Gone* (Simon and Schuster, 1946):

What you *see* is news; what you *know* is background; what you *feel* is opinion.

All these definitions put the editorial writer, the columnist, and the explanatory article writer in a pigeonhole of classification with some common boundaries. Their common goal is well summed up in the Associated Press quotation as "to make the news understandable to the average reader." When conventional straight news reporting fails to do that, then other staff members move in, regardless of what department they are assigned. Then they are commenting on the news. This assignment need not always be drably sober-faced either and so the comments sometimes entertain with a light touch.

Some examples should help, too

The difference between writing opinion, as typified by an editorial, and backgrounding the news can be shown graphically by presenting these two approaches to the same event. Here are two pieces: (1) a byline story from a Sunday edition of *The New York Times* rounding up information from various sections of the United States on the pressures put on schools to discontinue study of the United Nations and its specialized agencies, especially the United Nations Educational, Scientific and Cultural Organization (UNESCO) and (2) an editorial from the *San Francisco Chronicle* on substantially the same subject. Benjamin Fine, education editor of *The Times*, supplied facts on which the reader could better make up his own mind. The *Chronicle* editorial writer, on the other hand, presented his opinions and then backed them up with what he considered factual chapter and verse references.

Pressure Is Put on Schools to End United Nations Study

BY BENJAMIN FINE

Within recent months bitter opposition has developed to teaching about the United Nations Educational, Scientific and Cultural Organizations (UNESCO) or the United Nations in the schools and colleges of this country.

Some school systems have discarded the use of teaching materials relating to the United Nations or its specialized agencies because of highly vocal minority groups. Much of the growing opposition comes from self-styled super-patriotic organizations or critical individuals.

These groups and individuals charge that the United Nations, or its educational branch, UNESCO, is subversive or tainted with atheism and communism. They maintain that UNESCO is propagandizing for world government and, through revision of textbooks, is undermining nationalism.

23

Leading educators are deeply concerned over this trend. They see in it an extension of the "thought control" found in the increased censorship of textbooks. And they are concerned lest school teachers or administrators be so intimidated by the sniping at their curriculum that they will drop all teaching materials in international relations.

Essay Contest Under Fire

The American Association for the United Nations conducts an annual essay contest among the high school students of this country. Full cooperation of school officials has always been received. This year, however, some superintendents found that suddenly the United Nations contest had become a controversial issue. They were accused of participating in an un-American project.

Several school systems withdrew from the contest or put obstacles in the way of their students entering it.

Houston, Tex., can be cited as an example of what is happening elsewhere, though perhaps not to the same degree. The Houston school board, after hearing critics voice opposition, voted on March 24 to ban the United Nations contest from the schools. Then a group of interested citizens became sponsors of the essay contest and the examinations were held in the offices of the Young Women's Christian Association.

On the West Coast, the opposition to the teaching about UNESCO or the United Nations showed its strongest force in Los Angeles. As a result of continued pressure, the Superintendent of Schools, Dr. Alexander J. Stoddard, directed the teachers in the high schools not to participate in the United Nations essay contest. As at Houston, arguments were made that somehow it was "un-American" to cooperate in a program connected with the United Nations.

Answer to Spread of Fear

According to Miss Dorothy B. Robbins, education director of the American Association for the United Nations, 2,600 schools, with 50,000 students, participated in the essay contest this year as compared with 2,700 schools in 1951. She said that the drop was caused by fear of participating in anything dealing with the United Nations.

Taking cognizance of this growing fear or distrust, the association issued a statement yesterday calling the disturbing developments to the attention of educators and lay citizens everywhere.

Because the United States is a member of the United Nations, the statement said, it is the duty of all teachers to give their students as much information about the United Nations as possible. Courses in civics and history, it added, would be incomplete without some consideration of the United Nations and its specialized agencies.

"There is a strange attitude in some communities where objections have been raised to teaching about the United Nations," the statement went on. "Such opposition to teaching about the United Nations, UNESCO and the other specialized agencies is founded on misinformation, fear and prejudice.

"Where these three menaces to our institutions exist, education is doubly needed, but we cannot expect the individual teacher to withstand the pressure of intolerance unaided.

"It is the duty of all public-minded citizens to stand behind educators in their efforts to teach young people what they should know about the United Nations if they are to help build a world of peace and justice."

Role of UNESCO Explained

The greatest opposition has developed against UNESCO. The critics warn that this agency is going to step in and tell the teachers how to run their schools. Educators answer that the main objective of UNESCO is to encourage the kind of informed understanding which will lead to international cooperation rather than conflict.

25

Having no authority over any country, UNESCO, it is explained, provides a clearing house for the exchange of ideas among educators, scientists and artists, but does not offer specific advice to a country except at its request.

The situation in Los Angeles, while not typical, is indicative of what is happening elsewhere. Two years ago the Los Angeles school officials, under the guidance of Superintendent Stoddard, prepared a scholarly teaching manual called "The E in UNESCO."

This manual received the acclaim of the teaching profession. But about six months ago charges were made that anything dealing with UNESCO was harmful to this country. In the press and on the radio the clamor became more and more insistent that UNESCO would destroy the nation's sovereignty. One speaker warned that "UNESCO is a movement greater and more dangerous than communism."

According to Dr. Stoddard, much of the criticism was based on bibliography. It was charged that some of the books listed as suggested readings were written by un-American authors and that some of the books listed in the Los Angeles manual themselves contained reading lists that were "subversive." Those opposing UNESCO objected to the inclusion of the Human Rights document in the manual, it, too, being charged with "subversiveness."

"We withdrew the teaching manual from active use about five months ago," said Dr. Stoddard. "It is now being reviewed by committees from the junior and senior high schools. We hope that the committees will report soon and that after suitable changes that may be suggested are made the manual will be returned to the Los Angeles schools."

Dr. Stoddard said that "a revulsion" had sprung up against the super-patriotic groups leading the attacks on the UNESCO teaching materials. He declared that any person who is not concerned with what is happening outside of our own borders is not a good American.

Florida Seminar Is Fought

The attacks are made on colleges as well as schools. The University of Florida is scheduled to hold a seminar on its campus on July 10-11 on teaching the role of UNESCO. This is one of five regional seminars arranged by the United States National Commission for UNESCO and the National Council for Social Studies.

At the seminar teachers are to examine instructional materials published by the United Nations and UNESCO and select those that can be used to best advantage in the schools. When news about the seminar became generally known, the question of "subversive" motives was raised. The university's board of control is now considering whether to hold the seminar.

"We feel that this is a critical issue," said Dr. Charles H. Hamblen, Professor of Education at the university and executive secretary of the seminar. "As a state university we certainly should have the right to present and discuss the United Nations or UNESCO. We are confident that we will get the support of the intelligent, responsible people of the state."

Banning of Student Club

Not long ago the principal of a high school in Pawtucket, R. I., suspended the "UNESCO Thinkers," a club of students, because, he said, he suspected that UNESCO itself had atheistic and communistic leanings.

After considerable controversy, the school committee upheld the principal, James T. McGeough, in banning the group. Additional support came from the Pawtucket Chapter of the Daughters of the American Revolution.

The American Civil Liberties Union recently condemned this action as "arbitrary and authoritarian" and termed the suspension "a blow to the education of students in world affairs." A joint committee of members of the League of Women Voters and the Pawtucket Council for Education said that it was hard to see "why a club whose purpose it is to study and discuss this [UNESCO] program should have been suspended."

Dr. Luther H. Evans, Librarian of Congress, and chairman of the United States National Commission for UNESCO, said:

"There is clearly a growing tendency to accept false charges about UNESCO and the result is a growing restriction of efforts to teach our school children about the United Nations and UNESCO.

"The deliberately cultivated misconception that UNESCO is making propaganda for world government or is a party to subversive Communistic schemes, or is trying to replace our Bill of Rights with a less liberty-giving covenant of human rights, or is trying to revise our school textbooks, or is undermining our sense of national patriotism is something we cannot let pass without challenge.

"We who know better because we have helped establish and operate UNESCO and know that nothing of the sort is the intention or the unintended fact, have a special responsibility to speak up and make the truth manifest. Otherwise, millions of well-intentioned people may be frightened by statements and beliefs they have no means of checking."

Stand Taken by Defenders

Dr. Ralph Himstead, executive secretary of the American Association of University Professors, said that "a tendency is developing to view with suspicion our support of UNESCO."

The International Relations Committee of the American Association of University Women is preparing a kit of materials on the United Nations and UNESCO for the use of the association's members in combating these attacks.

Dr. Willard E. Givens, executive secretary of the National Education Association, said that the growing tendency toward linking UNESCO with subversive groups was "almost unbelievable." Much of the criticism of UNESCO, he asserted, comes from the "lunatic fringe who just don't believe in democracy."

*   *   *

Objective: Peace
UNESCO's Attackers Distort Its Aims

Reactionary extremists, joined in some cases by individuals and institutions of isolationist leanings, have lately been stepping up a slandering and belittling campaign against the United Nations. The character of the campaign has caused concern to many, and we consider that the public in general ought to acquire some awareness of it.

In the main, this anti-U.N. movement has masked itself as flag-draped patriotism. In order to discredit the idea of international cooperation, detractors of the U. N. shed tears over the loss of sovereignty which they say is incurred in the undertaking of international obligations. They heavily exaggerate this loss.

Thus Gerald L. K. Smith, the veteran American extremist, announcing his chairmanship of a special committee to be known as the American National Committee for the Abolition of the United Nations, expresses great apprehension "concerning the trickery being employed which points toward the abolition of America's sovereignty. . . ."

Gerald L. K. Smith is but one of numerous supporters of totalitarianism and of racial and religious bigotry who have taken up the crusade against the United Nations and, in particular, against the United Nations Educational, Scientific and Cultural Organization (UNESCO), which is the U.N.'s cultural branch. For example, W. Henry MacFarland Jr., promoter of a group called the American Flag Committee, denounces UNESCO as a "subversive association" and says it is "consciously furthering a campaign calculated to pervert the teaching profession in this country." A major objective of the anti-U.N. and anti-UNESCO pamphleteers is to intimidate teachers in the public schools from dealing with concepts of internationalism.

The United States National Commission for UNESCO, headed by Luther H. Evans, Librarian of

29

Congress, recently took note of these attacks which, the Commission said, "often emanate from groups which hide their identity under titles deceptively like those of honorable organizations. The attacks distort the purpose of UNESCO, and sometimes they are directed toward control of courses of study and of contents of textbooks, the end in view being to diminish opportunities to learn the true aims of UNESCO and the United Nations."

The Chronicle certainly does not deny to anyone the right to advocate, if he chooses, the diminishment of the U.N., up to and including America's withdrawal from membership. That would be foolish, but it's a point of view to which groups like the Sons of the American Revolution are entitled. (Their anti-U.N. resolution adopted at the S.A.R. convention here last July comes to mind.)

What seems particularly objectionable, and even sinister, is the evident tactic of the out-and-out smearers of the U.N. to pick on UNESCO as their chosen point of attack. Presumably they choose to slander the aims and practices of UNESCO because it appears to them the most vulnerable body of the U.N. for their purposes of general destruction. UNESCO is by definition an instrumentality for cultural exchange. It is the intellectual, scientific and artistic forum of the world, a court of appeal to which men may go for the elimination of barriers to the freer flow of ideas.

As an example of the kind of work which UNESCO sets out to do and does with good effect, a press release of last Wednesday tells of the deposit at the U.N. headquarters of an international treaty, sponsored by UNESCO and now signed by 29 nations, providing for the elimination of customs duties on books, newspapers, magazines, paintings and sculpture, travel literature, maps, musical scores, museum materials, educational films and filmstrips, scientific equipment for school use, and so on.

"Our agreement to make easier the exchange of thoughts over frontiers will aid humanity when it travels that road," remarked Sven Grafstrom, of Sweden, at the treaty-depositing ceremony.

We find it impossible to share a sense of alarm at things like this with Gerald L. K. Smith, or the Sons of the American Revolution, or the D.A.R., or Senator John W. Bricker (who fears the U.N. is "attempting to prepare a blueprint for world socialism"). Of course, UNESCO can reach conclusions about matters which might differ from ours. Of course, it can embrace a certain number of strange birds who don't happen to think just as we do. Obviously, Communists are free to belong to it, since it is a United Nations agency with an open membership, and not a closed membership, like that of the S.A.R. and the D.A.R.

But the usefulness of an agency seeking to demolish the barriers in the way of education and enlightenment for all mankind outweighs these objections, if they are objections. We Americans, who lack for nothing in material means for procuring the tools of knowledge, hardly realize the tremendous importance of UNESCO in those less favored parts of the world where a dictionary, or a biology textbook, or a microscope, or a film with which to teach illiterates reading and writing, may be hard to come by. We tend to be unaware of the fact that UNESCO means more to people in some countries than the Security Council does. They are not so much wrapped up in the big power plays as we are; they are more concerned with grabbing the means to lift themselves out of their condition of backwardness and underdevelopment.

We haven't room here to set forth in detail the UNESCO program, nor do we attempt to defend it in every item. But we defend UNESCO in its broad purposes, just as we defend the entire U.N. program in its broad purposes. We suspect, moreover, that the ultimate object of some of those who are waging these incessant, distorted campaigns against the U.N. and UNESCO is to deprive Americans of their independence of thought and judgment, to constrict the breadth of their outlook upon the world, and to put an end to reasonableness and cooperation in international affairs.

The obvious fact is that these negative objectives happen to be also the ruling objectives of the Kremlin authoritarians. Thus the non-Communist reactionaries of the Right, though making a great to-do about their hostility toward Communism, effectively carry on its aims.

TWO

How it all
came about

THROUGH THE CENTURIES SINCE *Publick Occurrences* WAS PUB-lished September 25, 1690, in Boston, American newspapers and magazines have constantly thrown around their journalistic weight. During that period, the techniques have varied widely but have been primarily concerned with where and how the job of influencing readers was to be done. For example, even in the era of greatest devotion to the ideal of objectivity in reporting, practically all publications paid special attention to their editorial pages.

Almost without exception, journalists whose names are legendary today spent much of their time in translating the news so that their subscribers could make up their minds—or have them made up for them. Some did this through rambunctious, highly personal accounts of the world's happenings. James Gordon Bennett, Sr., or William Randolph Hearst typify this group. Others confined their efforts strictly to intellectual editorials. E. L. Godkin illustrates this. Still others blended both reporting and commenting. Arthur Hays Sulzberger of *The New York Times* serves as a contemporary example. All, however, have been concerned with moulding public opinion and providing a leadership for causes they considered desirable. Regardless of the means they used, publishers, editors, and writers have been attracted to those channels through which they felt they could influence readers.

Once the press had no editorials

The Colonial newspapers and those of the American Revolution included little material resembling the editorial as we know it. Even some basic concepts of a newspaper's functions differed then. Much of the copy for these early papers came from unpaid contributors who wrote letters of news or comment, as they desired. In contrast with his enterprising successor of today, the Eighteenth Century publisher served as little more than a printer who set in type such items or opinions as came his way. He seldom had sufficient copy to permit a choice of what to publish. He spent no time writing editorials, although sometimes he sent letters to himself under a pen name so that he could advocate his own views. Less often, a shrewd publicist would supply information as he wanted it presented to the readers.

Ironically, the first American newspaper crusade was intensely one-sided, prejudiced, and anti-social. Yet it was so popular that it established its printer's success after the early issues. Capitalizing on popular opposition to vaccination for smallpox, a disease then raging in Boston, James Franklin launched the *New-England Courant* in 1721 as a vehicle for opposing inoculation and, incidentally, for poking fun at the Puritan hierarchy which supported the scientific innovation. Chief Puritan leaders were Increase and Cotton Mather, father and son who solemnly ruled the colony. The Mathers publicly denounced the new paper, but its circulation grew as it continued to attack the two preachers and their ideas on vaccination. By the time the epidemic ended, the *Courant* was so well established that it continued an erratic career for a number of years.

One of the earliest editorials that approached present-day standards was Benjamin Franklin's comments on "the present disunited state of the British colonies" during the Albany Congress of 1754. His remarks appeared in the *Pennsylvania Gazette* at Philadelphia on May 9, 1754. They were reinforced by the first American newspaper cartoon, the "Join, or Die" snake divided to represent the various British colonies. Both cartoon and editorial were widely reprinted.

The more successful publicists of the Revolution mobilized opinion through communications to the American press and through pamphlets, which were extensively reprinted in newspapers. Reproduced from colony to colony, these articles kept readers informed of developments. Samuel Adams, John Adams, James Otis, and Josiah Quincy in Massachusetts were prolific writers and many of their articles got into print. John Dickinson, using the signature of "A Farmer in Pennsylvania" for a series of letters on taxation, was another prominent newspaper contributor before the Declaration of Independence. Although Thomas Paine's *Common Sense* was issued early in 1776 as a pamphlet, its wide re-publication in Colonial papers supplemented the other arguments that were paving the way for splitting away from Great Britain.

After the Revolution began, Thomas Paine wrote "The Crisis" letters which appeared in the *Pennsylvania Journal*. Receiving copies of this inspiring appeal the day before the attack on Trenton, General George Washington ordered it read to every corporal's squad. Starting with these now familiar phrases, Paine's words were credited with arousing the dejected Americans to achieve victory the following day:

> These are the times that try men's souls. The Summer soldier and the sunshine Patriot will, in this crisis, shrink from the service of their country; but he that stands it now, deserves the love and thanks of man and woman. Tyranny, like Hell, is not easily conquered; yet we have this consolation with us, that the harder the conflict the more glorious the triumph. What we obtain too cheap, we esteem too lightly; it is dearness only that gives everything its value. Heaven knows how to put a proper price upon its goods; and it would be strange indeed if so celestial an article as FREEDOM should not be highly rated.

Many a contemporary editor would be happy to have such writing contributed to his page!

With the Revolution won, publicists continued to express their viewpoint through the press. Otherwise little opinion got into print. Infrequently, an editor would write himself a letter under some classical pen name. As "Publius," Alexander Hamilton, John Jay, and James Madison argued in favor of the pending federal constitution in a brilliant series of letters printed in the New York *Independent Journal* and widely re-published. Collected as *The Federalist*, these comments continued to influence interpretation of the constitution throughout the years, just as they helped to obtain its adoption by the thirteen independent states.

With the rise of political parties during George Washington's administration, both Federalists and Republicans launched their own newspapers so that they could mould opinion to their partisan purposes. Alexander Hamilton and Thomas Jefferson, both cabinet members, started numerous publications for their respective parties. Hamilton was instrumental in helping John Fenno, William Coleman, and Noah Webster, while Jefferson assisted Philip Freneau, Benjamin Franklin Bache, William Duane, and James Cheetham.

Three months after President George Washington issued his Farewell Address, Bache, grandson of Benjamin Franklin, wrote this denunciation in an item headed "From a Correspondent":

> If ever a nation was debauched by a man, the American nation has been debauched by Washington. If ever a nation has suffered from the improper influence of a man, the American nation has suffered from the influence of Washington. If ever a nation was deceived by a man, the American nation has been deceived by Washington. Let his conduct then be an example to future ages. Let it serve to be a warning that no man may be an idol and that a people may confide in themselves rather than in an individual. — Let the history of the federal government instruct mankind, that the masque

of patriotism may be worn to conceal the foulest designs against the liberties of the people.

Name-calling was a chief weapon in these battles of personal and party vituperation. Bache's Republican *Aurora* described Fenno's *Gazette* as the "sink of prostitution, the British hireling Grub-Street gazette." The same paper called Noah Webster of the Federalist *American Minerva* the "jackall of the British faction." William Cobbett, writing in *Porcupine's Gazette and United States Advertiser*, called the Jeffersonian *Aurora* a "vehicle of lies and sedition." These highly vindictive and emotional comments were not from editorial columns such as might be printed in some dailies now, but from letters signed by pen names or from remarks interpolated in local news columns or clippings from other publications.

During the closing years of the Eighteenth Century, Noah Webster in the *American Minerva* and, only a few years later, James Cheetham in the *American Citizen*, began publishing comments as separate departments, usually on page two or three. These early editorials were short, generally limited to a single paragraph, and were frequently pilfered by other periodicals. Before the penny press emerged in the 1830's, the editorial had become an established part of some daily papers, but as a rule this department still was a weak one.

Joseph Dennie, who has been called "probably the first country editor of any consequence in America," set a pattern for rural journalism during the immediate post-Revolutionary years that continued as an ideal for generations. His "Lay Preacher" essays from the *Farmer's Weekly Museum* of Walpole, N.H., were widely reprinted and in 1796 he was named editor of the *Museum*. The weekly, however, was not a financial success and Dennie left for Philadelphia where he founded the weekly *Port Folio* in 1801. A magazine of literature and politics, the *Port Folio* became for a decade the United States' leading literary review, partly due to Dennie's continuing his "Lay Preacher" essays. Dr. Frank

Luther Mott, Pulitzer-prize-winning historian of the nation's press, said in *American Journalism* (Macmillan, 1950) that Dennie's writings were "probably the best periodical essays ever produced in America."

William Lloyd Garrison's *Liberator,* which was started in Boston in 1831, was so effective as an outspoken abolition journal that after a single year of editorial commenting a $5,000 reward was offered for him, "dead or alive," by the legislature of Georgia. In his first issue, Garrison wrote with extraordinary prevision:

> I *will* be as harsh as truth, and as uncompromising as justice. On this subject [abolition], I do not wish to think, or speak, or write, with moderation . . . urge me not to use moderation in a cause like the present. I am in earnest—I will not equivocate—I will not excuse —I will not retreat a single inch—AND I WILL BE HEARD.

And heard *The Liberator* was, from its initial issue until the Civil War ended. Although Garrison frankly admitted that its circulation ran only in the thousands, his paper was truly an effective editorial influence in its era.

The penny press helped change things

The innovation of the penny press a generation later did not immediately make itself felt in the evolution of editorial comments. This contrasted with the radical changes in presenting news and appealing to a popular audience. Benjamin Day of the New York *Sun* and James Gordon Bennett, Sr., of the *Morning Herald,* the pioneers who introduced the cheap daily papers, concerned themselves primarily with news. They were concerned with lively and spicy items from police courts, Wall Street, the theater, and Society (the kind with a capital "S").

When the *Herald* made its debut on May 6, 1835, Bennett outlined his general policy as follows:

We shall support no party—be the organ of no faction or *coterie*, and care nothing for any election, or any candidate from President down to Constable. We shall endeavor to record facts, on every public and proper subject, stripped of verbiage and coloring, with comments when suitable, just, independent, fearless, and good tempered.

At first, Bennett found only infrequent occasions when comments were "suitable." His preference for the pronoun "I" instead of the more conventional editorial "we" indicated the strongly personal attitude he adopted toward most events, either as news or subjects for comment. His "Declaration of Love— Caught At Last" statement to the readers when he became engaged typified his gold-fish bowl attitude. So does the following article from the *Herald* of May 10, 1836:

As I was leisurely pursuing my business yesterday, in Wall Street, collecting the information which is daily disseminated in the *Herald*, James Watson Webb came up to me, on the northern side of the street—said something which I could not hear distinctly, then pushed me down the stone steps, leading to one of the broker's offices, and commenced fighting with a species of brutal and demoniac desperation characteristic of a fury.

My damage is a scratch, about three quarters of an inch in length, on the third finger of my left hand, which I received from the iron railing I was forced against, and three buttons torn from my vest, which any tailor will reinstate for a sixpence. His loss is a rent from top to bottom of a very beautiful black coat, which cost the ruffian $40, and a blow in the face, which may have knocked down his throat some of his infernal teeth for anything I know. Balance in my favor, $39.94.

As to intimidating me or changing my course, the thing cannot be done. Neither Webb nor any other man shall, or can, intimidate me. I tell the honest truth in my paper, and leave the consequences to God. Could I leave them in better hands? I may be attacked, I may be assailed, I may be killed, I may be murdered, but I never will succumb. I never will abandon the cause of truth, morals, and virtue.

Horace Greeley and his *New-York Tribune*, founded in 1841, brought the editorial to a high point of personalized journalism. His enthusiasm for crusades designed to improve mankind at times veered toward childlike naïvete althought it must now be admitted that his goals generally have been attained. Vernon L. Parrington in *Main Currents in American Thought* (Harcourt, Brace, 1927) described Greeley as a "Yankee radical" who was "as ready to adopt new social machinery as the mill-owner to adopt a new invention." His editorial blessings went to woman suffrage, the Brook Farm community experiment in communal living, a protective tariff, government aid for constructing railroads and telegraph lines to the Pacific, the ten-hour day, scientific agriculture, freedom of speech for abolitionists, abolition of slavery, and universal amnesty for the Confederates.

In 1845, he wrote defensively of his own editorials and the *Tribune's* general policies.

> It has been urged as an objection to The Tribune that it proposed to "give hospitality to every *new* thought." Our own expression here aimed at, contemplated not every new but every *generous thought*. To that profession we shall be constant at whatever sacrifice. Full of error and suffering as the world yet is, we cannot afford to reject unexamined any idea which proposes to improve the Moral, Intellectual or Social condition of mankind. Better incur the trouble of testing and exploding a thousand fallacies than by rejecting stifle a single beneficent truth.

The *Weekly Tribune* extended Greeley's influence because it circulated across the country much as the present-day news magazines. Readers paid special attention to what the New York editor wrote because his comments covered a wide range with an enthusiasm that seldom failed to thrill the public and with a style that was unsurpassed for simplicity, clearness, and vigor. He became one of the influential personalities of his age despite his inability to make every cause he supported a popular one.

Greeley has been credited with the slogan, "Go West, young man, go West." What he actually wrote was this paragraph:

> If any young man is about to commence in the world, with little in his circumstances to prepossess him in favor of one section above another, we say to him publicly and privately, Go to the West; there your capacities are sure to be appreciated and your industry and energy rewarded.

During a tour of the West in 1859, Greeley interviewed Brigham Young in Salt Lake City for two hours and reported much of their conversation to *Tribune* readers in direct question-and-answer fashion. This was an early, if not the first, break from the paraphrased and formal manner previously used for newspaper interviews. It also allowed Greeley to emphasize his support of women's rights, thus injecting his own opinions despite the most "objective" reporting.

During the Civil War, Greeley exerted a tremendous editorial pressure on Northern public opinion. He was blamed for the defeat of Union forces at the First Battle of Bull Run. The slogan of "Forward to Richmond" originated with Charles Dana, then on the *Tribune*, but Greeley approved the idea of repeating it daily on the editorial page. This repetition built up public demand until Northern generals launched an inopportune effort to capture the Confederate capital before the Southern Congress could meet there. The editor was grief-striken after the Union debacle prevented an early end of the war. Recognizing the *Tribune's* editorial prestige, President Abraham Lincoln answered in an open letter Greeley's widely reprinted comment entitled, "The

Prayer of Twenty Millions." The editorial was a demand that the federal government free all the slaves.

Near the close of his long career, Greeley reminisced:

> He [the editorial writer] who is not conscious of having first interpreted events, suggested policies, corrected long-standing errors, or thrown forward a more searching light in the path of progress, has never tasted the luxury of journalism. It is the province of journalism to lead and to lead.

Henry J. Raymond, schooled under Greeley on the *Tribune,* started the *New-York Daily Times* on September 18, 1851. In revolt against the passionate belief that everything was either good or bad, he wrote regarding his policies for both news coverage and editorial comments:

> We do not mean to write as if we were in a passion, unless that shall really be the case; and we shall make it a point to get in a passion as rarely as possible. There are very few things in this world which it is worth while to get angry about; and they are just the things that anger will not improve.

Raymond, more than any of his contemporaries, pointed the way toward the dispassionate, impersonal editorial which has wide vogue today. When he died in 1869 while still in his forties, many ramifications of his concept of unbiased policies remained to be worked out and these developments had to wait for others to perfect them in the future.

The elder Bennett, Greeley, and Raymond all died within a few years of each other. In the decades that followed, Charles A. Dana of the New York *Sun* and E. L. Godkin of the New York *Evening Post* and its companion weekly, *The Nation,* refined the previous policies and brought them sophistication and astuteness.

Dana had a passionate feeling for certain ideas, as witness his consistent opposition to Rutherford B. Hayes, who always was labeled in the *Sun*, "the Fraudulent President," and a delightful sense of whimsy, as illustrated by his editorial page remarks blaming the office cat for some of the *Sun's* journalistic errors. His prose was generally superior to that of most of his predecessors. The *Sun's* news stories and editorials made the publication a newspaperman's newspaper, a journal to be read, studied, and imitated.

An example of editorial which combined simplicity of style with human interest appeal is Francis P. Church's classic, "Is There a Santa Claus?" Although it appeared just after Dana had retired, the editorial was in keeping with the traditions he established and illustrated why the *Sun* was so admired by rival journalists. Incidentally, the story is that Church tried to decline the task of answering Virginia's letter but finally was assigned the job that brought him journalistic immortality. It has become the most widely known editorial ever written for a United States newspaper.

This classic was printed September 21, 1897:

Is There a Santa Claus?

We take pleasure in answering at once and thus prominently the communication below, expressing at the same time our great gratification that its faithful author is numbered among the friends of *The Sun*.

Dear Editor: I am eight years old. Some of my little friends say there is no Santa Claus. Papa says, "If you see it in *The Sun* it's so." Please tell me the truth, is there a Santa Claus?

Virginia O'Hanlon
115 West 95th Street.

Virginia, your little friends are wrong. They have been affected by the skepticism of a skeptical age. They do not believe except they see. They think that nothing can be which is not comprehended by their little minds.

All minds, Virginia, whether they be men's or children's, are little. In this great universe of ours man is a mere insect, an ant, in his intellect, as compared with the boundless world about him, as measured by the intelligence capable of grasping the whole of truth and knowledge.

Yes, Virginia, there is a Santa Claus. He exists as certainly as love and generosity and devotion exist, and you know that they abound and give to our life its highest beauty and joy. Alas! how dreary would be the world if there were no Santa Claus. It would be as dreary as if there were no Virginias. There would be no childish faith then, no poetry, no romance, to make tolerable this existence. We should have no enjoyment, except in sense and sight. The eternal light with which childhood fills the world would be extinguished.

Not believe in Santa Claus! You might as well not believe in fairies! You might get your papa to hire men to watch in all the chimneys on Christmas Eve to catch Santa Claus, but even if they did not see Santa Claus coming down, what would that prove? Nobody sees Santa Claus, but that is no sign that there is no Santa Claus. The most real things in the world are those that neither children nor men can see. Did you ever see fairies dancing on the lawn? Of course not, but that's no proof that they are not there. Nobody can conceive or imagine all the wonders there are unseen and unseeable in the world.

You may tear apart the baby's rattle and see what makes the noise inside, but there is a veil covering the unseen world which not the strongest men, nor even the united strength of all the strongest men that ever lived, could tear apart. Only fancy, poetry, love, romance can push aside that curtain and view and picture the supernal beauty and glory behind. Is it all real? Ah, Virginia, in all this world there nothing else real and abiding.

No Santa Claus! Thank God! he lives and he lives forever. A thousand years from now, Virginia, nay, ten times ten thousand years from now, he will continue to make glad the heart of childhood.

Carrying forward Raymond's devotion to facts, Godkin of the *Evening Post* and *The Nation* became an influence, not because he wrote for the masses but because his brilliant interpretations and comments on the news pointed a way that others with larger followings could and frequently did pursue. His style was intellectual and often sarcastically devastating. Oswald Garrison Villard in *The Disappearing Daily* (Alfred A. Knopf, 1944) described Godkin's commentaries as "the writings of a completely educated man polished by travel and the society of intellectual leaders everywhere, who wrote only with profound conviction." Called the editor's editor, Godkin set a pattern and ideal for many other writers and thus helped to raise the intellectual tone of editorial pages in many parts of the country. Such flaws as he had grew from his inability to cotton to the average newspaper readers.

On *The New-York Times* during this period, a skilled combination of investigative reporting and editorial attacks broke the notorious Tweed Ring's hold on New York City politics. Despite an offer of $5,000,000 as a bribe, George Jones was incorruptible. The machine was smashed. *The Times*, however, did not continue its prosperity after Jones' death in 1891.

To rescue *The Times* came Adolph S. Ochs, who had won regional recognition as publisher of the *Chattanooga* (Tennessee) *Times*. In his statement of principles under a heading, "Business Announcement," on the editorial page of August 19, 1896, Ochs made the frequently repeated pledge, "to give the news impartially, without fear or favor, regardless of any party, sect or interest involved." But he also included this significant paragraph:

> To undertake the management of The New-York Times, with its great history for right-doing, and to attempt to keep bright the lustre which Henry J. Raymond and George Jones have given it, is an extraordinary task. But if a sincere desire to conduct a high-standard newspaper, clean, dignified and trustworthy, requires honesty, watchfulness, earnestness, industry

and practical knowledge applied with common sense, I entertain the hope that I can succeed in maintaining the high estimate that thoughtful, pure-minded people have ever had of The New-York Times.

Ochs was true to these ideals and his paper attracted increasing numbers of "thoughtful, pure-minded people" as "yellow journalism" rose to climactic heights in New York City.

"Yellow journalism" entered

The journalistic feud between Joseph Pulitzer and William Randolph Hearst brought competing brands of "yellow journalism," a newspaper idea of peddling sensations to attain mass circulation. This technique, some of its critics claimed, was capable of fomenting the Spanish-American War to test maximum limits for newspaper sales. Both Pulitzer and Hearst modified editorial page traditions.

Pulitzer set a fast pace by rallying public opinion against possible war with Great Britain when President Grover Cleveland backed Venezuela's demands to territory also claimed by the British, and by breaking a monopoly dealing in United States government bonds.

Frank I. Cobb, who developed a critical insight and a vigorous style under Pulitzer's insistent prodding, dug out hidden facts and struck at Democratic and Republican administrations alike. When the *World* disclosed details of how President Theodore Roosevelt "took" Panama, the chief executive was so irate that he had charges of criminal libel brought against the paper. The government lost its case. The *World*, under Cobb, showed that factual editorial writing with vigor of style could be tremendously potent. It was a major shift from the personal and partisan squabbles of an earlier generation. The targets were not rival publishers and editors but rather representatives of what Pulitzer and Cobb believed to be evil forces. The pair largely let the facts, assembled through exhaustive research by both reporters and editorial writers, speak for themselves without personal vituperation. They truly reflected Greeley's admonition "to lead and to lead." Walter Lippmann carried on in this tradition until the end of the *World*. Yet the papers never attained the enthusiastic support accorded Greeley's *Tribune* in an earlier age.

In *Makers of Modern Journalism* (Prentice-Hall, Inc., 1952), John Tebbel explained that the *World's* intellectual, liberal editorial page "was not read by the middlebrows, that body of substantial citizens who could not stomach the *World's* sensationalism and thereby missed the progressive leadership which Pulitzer was supplying on the editorial page to a rather limited minority."

Illustrative of the powerful language and logic of a Cobb editorial is the following, which was, in part, responsible for the 1912 nomination of Woodrow Wilson:

Wilson—No Compromise with Ryan and Murphy

It is too late to talk compromise at Baltimore.

Ryanism and Murphyism have created an issue that makes the nomination of Woodrow Wilson a matter of Democratic life or death.

To compromise now is for the Democratic National Convention to surrender to Thomas F. Ryan.

To compromise now is for the Democratic National Convention to surrender to August Belmont.

To compromise now is for the Democratic National Convention to surrender to Charles F. Murphy.

To compromise now is for the Democratic National Convention to surrender to Wall Street.

To compromise now is for the Democratic National Convention to surrender to Tammany Hall.

To compromise now is to send a Democratic ticket into the campaign shackled to bossism and plutocracy.

To compromise now is to give Theodore Roosevelt the supreme issue that he needs.

Compromise was possible until the Ryan-Murphy conspiracy was fully revealed and the Tammany boss carried out the terms of his bargain with the Clark managers by throwing New York's ninety votes to Champ Clark. Compromise was possible until Mr. Bryan was compelled by the inexorable logic of events to repudiate Champ Clark's candidacy and vote for Woodrow Wilson. Compromise was possible until it became apparent to every intelligent man that the Ryan-Murphy-Belmont-Hearst coalition had set out to strangle progressive Democracy, destroy Mr. Bryan politically and prevent the nomination of Woodrow Wilson at any cost.

Compromise is no longer possible. There can be no Democratic harmony, there can be no Democratic unity, there can be no Democratic integrity, until the convention overwhelms this shameful alliance between corrupt finance and corrupt politics.

It is the duty of Mr. Bryan to stand fast in his support of Gov. Wilson, and it is the duty of true Democrats to stand fast in their support of Mr. Bryan. Whatever their differences with him in the past, he is fighting today the battle of honest Democracy, he is fighting the battle of the American people, and he is fighting it manfully and magnificently.

The Ryan-Murphy coalition will now accept anybody except Wilson. If the convention yields to the plea for a compromise candidate, it will be a Ryan-Murphy victory.

A thousand Roosevelt orators will be thundering from the stump their denunciation of Democracy's surrender to Wall Street.

A thousand Taft orators will be thundering from the stump their denunciation of Democracy's surrender to Wall Street.

The issue that is vital to Roosevelt's compaign for a third term will come to his hand ready made. The Democratic party might as well retire from the contest as to go before the country with the Ryan-Murphy taint upon its ticket.

This is no longer a question of Woodrow Wilson's political strength, great as that is. It is no longer a question of his ability, undeniable as that is. It is no longer
a question of his availability, self-evident as that is.
Ryan and Murphy have left honest Democrats no choice.
Ryan and Murphy have left honest Democrats no alternative. Ryan and Murphy have made Wilson's nomination the crucial test of the Democratic Party's fitness to
live.

As Stephen A. Douglas once said, "There can be no
neutrals in this war—only patriots or traitors."

Arthur Brisbane, first with Pulitzer on the *New York World*
and then shifting to Hearst, simplified his writing style until his
comments served as primer English texts for immigrants. He freed
the editorial page from the typographical conventions that made
it an ocean of gray. He moved the page to the back of most
Hearst papers so it would have greater readership. Brisbane visualized his assignment with a strange combination of contempt for
the mass mind and a simplicity of style particularly adapted to it.
He once described editorial writing as "the art of saying in a com-
monplace and inoffensive way what everybody knew long ago,"
yet he insisted another time that better editorial writers might
hope "to make the reader think for himself." Brisbane brought
editorials back from the intellectualism of Dana and Godkin but
he vulgarized them by trying to wield them as a force upon the
millions that bought the "yellow" journals. In his declining years,
he wrote an opinionated comment column, entitled "Today,"
which Hearst papers printed on page one. A recurring topic for
his consideration was what might happen if a human athlete were
matched against a gorilla. He certainly knew what would provoke
popular discussions but he failed to contribute much enlightenment in the process.

Throughout his long career, Hearst himself frequently wrote
signed editorials and then had them printed in large type on the
front pages of his papers from Boston to California. As he aged,

what liberalism "The Chief" had in his younger years turned bitter and sour. Few were the issues on which his papers, over his decades of activity, did not switch sides. He and his associates, however, always claimed that they were serving the interests of the mass readers.

While New York City journalism paced developments within the profession, other successful editors were exercising journalistic influence in their communities and regions. Some of them were more rewarded than their metropolitan contemporaries.

In Louisville, Kentucky, Henry Watterson, of the *Courier-Journal* wrote widely-copied editorials in a rhetorical style that occasionally developed apt, quotable phrases that illuminated a whole philosophical approach for most of the nation. During World War I, for instance, he helped popularize the saying, "To Hell with the Hohenzollerns," and thus reflected the general feeling toward the German ruling family.

Illustrative of his vigorous style is this final paragraph from his rather long "Vae Victis" editorial, which was written after the United States entered World War I and which helped win him the Pulitzer prize:

> First of all on bended knee we should pray God to forgive us. Then erect as men, Christian men, soldierly men, to the flag and the fray—wherever they lead us— over the ocean—through France to Flanders—across the Low Countries to Köln, Bonn and Koblens—tumbling the fortress of Ehrenbreitstein into the Rhine as we pass and damming the mouth of the Moselle with the débris of the ruin we make of it—then on, on to Berlin, the Black Horse Cavalry sweeping the Wilhelmstrasse like lava down the mountainside, the Junker and the saber rattler flying before us, the tunes being "Dixie" and "Yankee Doodle," the cry being, "Hail the French Republic—Hail the Republic of Russia—welcome the Commonwealth of the Vaterland—no peace with the Kaiser—no parley with Autocracy, Absolutism and the

divine right of Kings—to Hell with the Hapsburg and the Hohenzollern!"

In Chicago, Victor Lawson's talented staff on the *Daily News* demonstrated that literary competence could contribute to editorial attractiveness.

In Kansas City, Missouri, William Rockhill Nelson graphically lived out the slogan, "Anybody can print the news but the *Star* tries to build things up." In building things up, the *Kansas City Star* was involved with parks, boulevards, a municipal auditorium, and better city government.

In Emporia, Kansas, William Allen White won national fame during the 1896 presidential campaign with his personal, sarcastic "What's the Matter with Kansas?" that continued to be quoted for half a century. Although atypical to extreme, he was the country editor most widely quoted in the United States. Although he later reflected a more progressive philosophy, White's editorial did demonstrate the power of his writings:

What's the Matter with Kansas?

Today the Kansas department of agriculture sent out a statement which indicates that Kansas has gained less than two thousand people in the past year. There are about 225,000 families in the State, and there were about ten thousand babies born in Kansas, and yet so many people have left the State that the natural increase is cut down to less than two thousand net.

This has been going on for eight years.

If there had been a high brick wall around the State eight years ago, and not a soul had been admitted or permitted to leave, Kansas would be a half million souls better off than she is today. And yet the nation has increased in population. In five years ten million people have been added to the national population, yet instead of gaining a share of this—say half a million—Kansas has apparently been a plague spot, and in the very garden of the world, has lost population by ten thousands every year.

Not only has she lost population, but she has lost money. Every moneyed man in the State who could get out without loss has gone. Every month in every community sees someone who has a little money pack up and leave the State. This has been going on for eight years. Money has been drained out all the time. In towns where ten years ago there were three or four or half a dozen money-lending concerns stimulating industry by furnishing capital, there is now none, or one or two that are looking after the interest and principal already outstanding.

No one brings any money into Kansas any more. What community knows over one or two men who have moved in with more than $5,000 in the past three years? And what community cannot count half a score of men in that time who have left, taking all the money they could scrape together?

Yet the nation has grown rich, other States have increased in population and wealth—other neighboring States. Missouri has gained over two million, while Kansas has been losing half a million. Nebraska has gained in wealth and population while Kansas has gone down hill. Colorado has gained every way, while Kansas has lost every way since 1888.

What's the matter with Kansas?

There is no substantial city in the State. Every big town save one has lost in population. Yet Kansas City, Omaha, Lincoln, St. Louis, Denver, Colorado Springs, Sedalia, the cities of the Dakotas, St. Paul and Minneapolis and Des Moines—all cities and towns in the West have steadily grown.

Take up the government blue book and you will see that Kansas is virtually off the map. Two or three little scrubby consular places in yellow-fever-stricken communities that do not aggregate ten thousand dollars a year is all the recognition that Kansas has. Nebraska draws about one hundred thousand dollars; little old North Dakota draws about fifty thousand dollars; Oklahoma doubles Kansas; Missouri leaves her a thousand miles behind; Colorado is almost seven times greater than Kansas—the whole West is ahead of Kansas. Take it by any standard you please, Kansas is not in it.

Go east and you hear them laugh at Kansas, go west and they sneer at her, go south and they "cuss" her, go north and they have forgotten her. Go into any crowd of intelligent people gathered anywhere on the globe, and you will find the Kansas man on the defensive. The newspaper columns and magazines once devoted to praise of her, to boastful facts and startling figures concerning her resources, are now filled with cartoons, jibes, and Pefferian speeches. Kansas just naturally isn't in it. She has traded places with Arkansas and Timbuctoo.

What's the matter with Kansas?

We all know; yet here we are at it again. We have an old mossback Jacksonian who snorts and howls because there is a bathtub in the statehouse; we are running that old jay for governor. We have another shabby, wild-eyed, rattle-brained fanatic who has said openly in a dozen speeches that "the rights of the user are paramount to the rights of the owner"; we are running him for chief justice, so that capital will come tumbling over itself to get into the State. We have raked the old ashheap of failure in the State and found an old human hoopskirt who has failed as a business man, who has failed as an editor, who has failed as a preacher, and we are going to run him for Congress-at-large. He will help the looks of the Kansas delegation in Washington. Then we have discovered a kid without a law practice and decided to run him for attorney-general. Then for fear some hint that the State had become respectable might percolate through the civilized portions of the nation, we have decided to send three or four harpies out lecturing, telling the people that Kansas is raising hell and letting the corn go to weeds.

Oh, this is a State to be proud of! We are a people who can hold up our heads! What we need is not more money, but less capital, fewer white shirts, and brains, fewer

53

men with business judgment, and more of those fellows who boast that they are "just ordinary clodhoppers, but they know more in a minute about finance than John Sherman"; we need more men who are "posted," who can bellow about the crime of '73, who hate prosperity and who think because a man believes in national honor, he is a tool of Wall Street. We have a few of them —some hundred and fifty thousand—but we need more.

We need several thousand gibbering idiots to scream about the "Great Red Dragon" of Lombard Street. We don't need population, we don't need wealth, we don't need well-dressed men on the streets, we don't need cities on the fertile prairies; you bet we don't! What we are after is the money-power. Because we have become poorer and ornerier and meaner than a spavined, distempered mule, we, the people of Kansas, propose to kick; we don't care to build up, we wish to tear down.

"There are two ideas of government," said our noble Bryan at Chicago. "There are those who believe that if you just legislate to make the well-to-do prosperous, the prosperity will leak through on those below. The Democratic idea has been that if you legislate to make the masses prosperous their prosperity will find its way up through every class and rest on us."

That's the stuff! Give the prosperous man the dickens! Legislate the thriftless man into ease, whack the stuffing out of the creditors and tell the debtors who borrowed the money five years ago when money "per capita" was greater than it is now that the contraction of the currency gives him a right to repudiate. Whoop it up for the ragged trousers; put the ragged, greasy fizzle who can't pay his debts on the altar, and bow down and worship him. Let the State ideal be high. What we need is not the respect of our fellow men, but the chance to get something for nothing.

O, yes, Kansas is a great State. Here are people fleeing from it by the score every day, capital going out of the State by the hundreds of dollars; and every industry but farming paralyzed, and that crippled, because its products have to go across the ocean before they can find a laboring man at work who can afford to buy them. Let's don't stop this year. Let's drive all the decent, self-respecting men out of the State. Let's keep the old clod-hoppers who know it all. Let's encourage the man who is "posted." He can talk, and what we need is not mill-hands to eat our meat, nor factory hands to eat our wheat, nor cities to oppress the farmer by consuming his butter and eggs and chickens and produce. What Kansas needs is men who can talk, who have large leisure to argue the currency question while their wives wait at home for that nickel's worth of bluing.

What's the matter with Kansas?

Nothing under the shining sun. She is losing wealth, population, and standing. She has got her statesmen, and the money power is afraid of her. Kansas is all right. She has started in to raise hell, as Mrs. Lease advised, and she seems to have an over-production. But that doesn't matter. Kansas never did believe in diversified crops. Kansas is all right. There is absolutely nothing wrong with Kansas. "Every prospect pleases, and only man is vile."

In the neighboring community of Atchison, Kansas, Ed Howe wrote iconoclastic, sharp paragraphs that were re-published from coast to coast.

In a dozen or more communities, E. W. Scripps brought cheap afternoon dailies dedicated to a democratic faith in the so-called "little man." He believed his papers should crusade on the local scene instead of concentrating on editorial guidance for distant capitals.

In San Francisco, Fremont Older fought against a corrupt municipal political machine that resorted to kidnapping and shooting before it was smashed.

While "yellow journalism" was booming in newspapers, the "muckrakers" brought new vitality and enthusiasm to magazines that were growing up just before and after the turn of the century. Ida M. Tarbell, Lincoln Steffens, Ray Stannard Baker, Burton J.

Hendrick, and others demonstrated that interpretive reporting of brutal facts could be mobilized into powerful social forces. Despite the crusading of a few newspapers, such as the *New York World*, the daily press generally waited at least a generation before it applied the lessons that might have been adapted from the successes of the "muckrakers."

Shortly after World War I, two Yale graduates with a few years of newspaper reporting experience, Henry R. Luce and Briton Hadden, launched a new type of magazine journalism. *Time* was first published March 3, 1923. The founders described their publication in a prospectus which concluded:

> *TIME* is a weekly news-magazine, aimed to serve the modern necessity of keeping people informed, created on a new principle of COMPLETE ORGANIZATION.
>
> *TIME* is interested—not in how much it includes between its covers —but in HOW MUCH IT GETS OFF ITS PAGES INTO THE MINDS OF ITS READERS.

Journalism that admitted built-in prejudices and acknowledged opinionation, as *Time's* editors did from the beginning, was both new and old. It was new in that it broke through the shallow objectivity then so highly regarded by newspapermen, and it was old in that it strove to attain Greeley's advice "to lead and to lead." All of it *Time* did with sophistication and in an individualized style.

A *Time* editor of a later era described his magazine as "a conscious attempt to bridge the gap between the scattergun technique of the newspaper and the slow fire-at-will of the magazine."

Time competed successfully against the well-established weekly *Literary Digest*, which summarized the news and quoted extensively from editorials and opinionated articles of newspapers and magazines. The *Literary Digest*, losing ground to the newer style weekly that more successfully met the public demands for interpretation of events, floundered after its 1936 pre-election poll picked Alfred M. Landon to defeat Franklin D. Roosevelt for the presidency. Landon carried only two states.

Like most successes, journalistic or otherwise, *Time* was not without imitators. Within a few years, *Newsweek* and *United States News* (originally founded in 1926 as *United States Daily*) were providing a comparable type of news blended with interpretations and opinions. Both added new devices in making world history meaningful to their readers.

Impressed with *Time's* success, some newspaper publishers and editors experimented with news-in-review sections to meet the weekly's competition. In 1930, the *Cincinnati Enquirer* started such a feature and in 1933, the *New York Sun* began such a department. In 1935, *The New York Times* launched a Review of the Week section after a long campaign by Lester Markel, who became Sunday editor, for such a departure from the more conventional news reporting of daily events around the world. Other papers' weekend or Sunday editions began carrying such summary and interpretive sections during the 1930's and 1940's. These innovations marked an indirect admission that the then-current version of objectivity had its flaws. While this implied need for change did not bring other modifications in most news reporting and commenting immediately, it demonstrated for those with the perception to see a chink in the generally approved practices.

The columnists and interpreters came in

During the depression and initial recovery of the early New Deal years, the personalized approach toward events again was provided newspaper readers, this time by opinionated columnists. Editorial writers generally in this period confined themselves either to providing conflicting statements and statistics and then allowing readers to take their choice or to repeating threadbare platitudes that added little to public enlightenment. Some papers, of course, stood out for their intelligent perspective and vigor but they were few. Too many publishers and editors decreed that news columns must be kept pure from opinion, background, and interpretation even if this sterile kind of reporting gave readers a completely distorted impression. Against rampant objectivity of this narrowest sort, the columnist launched a revolt.

Up to the 1930's, the "colyumnists," as they were called, had collected humor, verse, or bright little essays. Sometimes these were strictly their own writings but more frequently they came from contributors. Then the grim, depression-bred demand for explanation of economic and social complexities and for background to fill gaps in the typical reader's knowledge changed all that. A new brand of column writing was born. Two general types of Washington columns grew up. One translated the complicated news into understandable, meaningful language; the other applied "dope and gossip" writing to political Washington.

Pioneers of the political columnists included Walter Lippmann, who shifted to writing news interpretations for the *New York Herald Tribune* after the sale of the *World* in 1931 cut short that outlet for his editorials; David Lawrence, whose New York *Evening Post* dispatches were syndicated in 1916 and later distributed by his own organization; and Mark Sullivan, who followed Lawrence on the *Post* and then was distributed nationally. Others who joined in this more serious column writing were Raymond Clapper, former United Press Washington bureau chief who died in a World War II airplane crash in the Pacific; Marquis Childs, trained on the *St. Louis Post-Dispatch;* Thomas Stokes, another United Press alumnus; and the irrepressible Dorothy Thompson.

Two pugnacious correspondents, Drew Pearson and Robert S. Allen, set a pace for gossip reporting in a racy, irreverent book, *Washington Merry-Go-Round* (Horace Liveright, 1931). When Pearson and Allen were identified as the authors of the anonymous volume, both were eventually fired from their newspaper jobs. They turned to syndicating a daily column of chit-chat material. After a slow start, their syndication picked up momentum until theirs was the most widely published Washington column. During World War II, Allen left to serve in the Army, lost an arm, and then returned to split up the partnership.

Competing with Pearson and Allen was Paul Mallon's "News Behind the News." Among eventual rivals were Peter Edson, the Alsop brothers, and Ray Tucker.

Professor Kenneth Stewart, co-author of *Makers of Modern Journalism* (Prentice-Hall, Inc., 1952), summarized column writing from Washington this way:

The new personal journalism of the syndicated columnist, here at least, seemed to be recapturing some of the high old flavor of invective and vituperation that marked the old personal journalism of the nineteenth-century editors.

With a few notable exceptions such as the *New York Times, Christian Science Monitor*, and *Chicago Tribune*, scarcely a daily newspaper in the country with 25,000 circulation or more fails to print the writings of one or more of the syndicated columnist from three to six times a week. The *Times*, the *Monitor*, and the *Tribune*, of course, give their readers a similar service through the opinions of their own writers like Arthur Krock, and Roscoe Drummond, and Walter Trohan.

Not all editors were content to abdicate the bulk of newspaper influence in favor of columnists. Events at home and abroad which brought the rise of these syndicated innovations forced some dailies to re-assess their policies. Enormous stakes were involved and some publishers and editors felt they had to stand up and be counted for democracy. Some sought to revitalize their editorial pages and to introduce their own opinion articles. Others used news column interpretations to make events more understandable. A few pioneered with previously untried techniques.

During the 1930's, first United Press and then the Associated Press began what Frank Luther Mott in *The News In America* (Harvard University Press, 1952) called "a modest job of explaining the bald facts." Then during World War II, Kent Cooper, general manager for the Associated Press, told his staff to do "the direct, factual, and wholly objective news reporting that digs below the surface and tells the true story."

Illustrative of how the trend was developing was the selection of the title, *Interpretative Reporting*, by Professor Curtis D. MacDougall of Northwestern University for a 1938 revision of his earlier text, *Reporting for Beginners* (Macmillan, 1932) along with a complete re-orientation of viewpoint that set a new pattern in reporting textbooks.

Supreme Court Justice Felix Frankfurter, in his opinion on the Associated Press case during 1945, pointed out that the press' business was "the promotion of truth regarding public matters by furnishing the basis for an understanding of them." His discussion brought to the foreground again John Milton's concept, "Who ever knew Truth put to the worse, in a free and open encounter?" That part of the decision had special meaning for some publishers, editors, and writers because they already had concluded they might have paid too high a price for an objectivity in reporting that dwelt only upon surface aspects.

What was happening on some of the conservative but responsible newspapers was shown by changes in *The New York Times*. Up to Ochs' death in 1935, that daily had deliberately tuned its editorial tone for the quiet of the Ivory Tower. In that attitude, it was widely copied. But as dictators threatened the free world, it undertook an editorial crusade.

On June 15, 1938, *The Times* printed a summation of its whole philosophy, entitled "A Way of Life." This editorial concluded with this prophetic statement:

> No remoteness from the scene of a potential European conflict can isolate the United States from the consequences of a major war. No Neutrality Act can prevent the American people from favoring their natural allies. In any ultimate test of strength between democracy and dictatorship, the good will and the moral support—and in the long run more likely than not the phy-

sical power of the United States—will be found on the side of those nations defending a way of life which is our own way of life and the only way of life which Americans believe to be worth living.

Arthur Hays Sulzberger, Ochs' son-in-law and successor as *The Times'* publisher, agreed with other staff members that a choice of sides was then required if editorial page influence was not to be completely dissipated and faith in the power of the press betrayed. In editorial policy, *The Times* became more aggressive. It vigorously championed such causes as freedom of the press and of speech, Negro rights, anti-discrimination laws, a liberal immigration policy, and President Harry S. Truman's civil rights program in 1949. It called those proposals "one of the most courageous acts of his Administration." While *The Times* denounced Communism without let-up, the paper warned of undermining the American people's own privileges. In 1949, an editorial warned, "In defending ourselves against the international threat of communism our country can ill afford to curtail its own precious and hard-won liberties." *The Times* was in the vanguard of the newspaper critics of Senator Joseph McCarthy, Wisconsin Republican.

To prevent a return to an Ivory Tower atmosphere, Sulzberger sent editorial writers to many parts of the world to freshen their viewpoints and staff members in other departments were encouraged to contribute comments on subjects they covered as reporters.

The Times, its metropolitan competitor, the *New York Herald Tribune*, and the *Christian Science Monitor* in Boston all added national subscribers who desired extensive interpretations, explanations, and background pieces as well as editorials. These three papers maintained Washington and foreign bureaus where their own correspondents could dig below the surface facts and put the news into better perspective.

New York City also was the site for an experiment in crusading journalism that broke forcefully with the conventional standards of "pure" objectivity. Marshall Field, as principal backer, and Ralph Ingersoll, as editor, developed *PM*. Series after series of investigative reporting and opinionated interpretations during the 1940's highlighted the nine-year life of that tabloid and its short-lived successor, *The Star*. Although the experiment eventually failed, the influence of *PM* "do-gooders" on other newspapers has been freely admitted. In Chicago, for example, Marshall Field followed a more traditional style on his *Sun* and later *Sun-Times* but the *PM* pattern was never forgotten completely. Other papers also remembered that they too could still crusade. The short-lived *New York Compass* went beyond *PM* and tried "spot editorials."

Under Eugene Meyer's ownership, the *Washington Post* became one of the brilliantly-edited dailies in the country. The wife of the publisher, Agnes Meyer, who once had done social work, turned reporter to write several notable "case history" series for the *Post*. Typical were her stories of a tour of the British home front and wartime America, later published in book form as *Journey through Chaos* (Harcourt, Brace, 1944), and a group of human interest dispatches telling how coal miners lived. Meanwhile the *Post's* invigorated editorial page attracted some of the profession's top writers.

Ralph McGill, one of the South's distinguished editors, won a Rosenwald Foundation fellowship in 1937 for European travel and study, partly because of his investigative series on share-cropping and farm-tenancy. After McGill became editor of the *Atlanta Constitution* in 1941, he established a signed, outspoken editorial column in the tradition of an earlier *Constitution* editor of the 1880's, Henry W. Grady. Even after the *Atlanta Journal* and the *Constitution* came under common ownership in 1950, McGill remained to edit the *Constitution* and the influence of his personal column continued to grow.

Another editor who advanced his own viewpoint through a personal column was John S. Knight. The *Miami Herald, Chicago*

Daily News and *Detroit Free Press* in the Knight group printed "The Editor's Notebook." Here he frequently discussed his political and social philosophy as he analyzed the news of the week or some outstanding event and occasionally such personal prejudices as his aversion to double-feature motion pictures and martinis with too much vermouth.

The New Orleans *Daily States'* running battle against the political machine of Huey Long included not only editorials but hard-hitting news column exposes of corruption. The combination brought prison terms to some of Long's "heirs" and a Pulitzer prize to the newspaper staff.

In the Midwest, two newspapers carried on the crusading tradition to a greater degree than most of their regional contemporaries. In Louisville, Kentucky, the *Courier-Journal* forcefully demonstrated that monopoly in newspaper ownership need not be bad for a community, as some critics insist is always true. In St. Louis, Missouri, the *Post-Dispatch* so brilliantly carried on the Pulitzer crusading tradition that many working newspapermen regarded it as "just about the best all-around newspaper there is."

Directing the *Courier-Journal* have been Barry Bingham, whose preparation for managing the paper he inherited included personally investigating Kentucky's hospitals for the insane and writing a series that brought state-wide reforms, and Mark Ethridge, a believer in democracy who is "constantly alive to the responsibilities which freedom of the press implies." Together, they combined professional competence with outstanding courage to fight for the right as they saw it. As a result, the *Courier-Journal* won distinction, as *Fortune* (July, 1950) noted, for its "editorial protein" of extensive reporting of national and international affairs, highly cultured, staff-written columns of comment, and strong-voiced editorials.

Of the *St. Louis Post-Dispatch*, Roger Butterfield wrote in *Collier's* (Dec. 16, 1950):

Its news coverage of the entire country is superb; its editorials hit hard and speak plain, yet remain completely civilized in their language and world outlook; its cartoons (by the celebrated D. R. Fitzpatrick) are famed for draftsmanship and power; its photographs and features compare favorably with the best in the leading national magazines. . . . But what really makes the Post Dispatch great is the deadly thoroughness and generally high purpose with which it fights. In an age when too many well-meaning newspapers are either too proud or too timid to "crusade," the P-D—as St. Louisans call it—is frankly a crusading paper.

In Minneapolis, Minnesota, John Cowles pioneered with typographical innovations of editorial page make-up which increased readership and attracted attention and imitators from his fellow publishers. Some of pollster George Gallup's first surveys were for the Cowles-owned *Des Moines Register* and *Tribune*. The Cowles brothers applied his reports on readership to all departments of their growing newspaper and magazine empire.

In Denver, Palmer Hoyt, who helped to modernize the Portland *Oregonian,* moved to the *Post* in 1946 and revitalized both editorial and news pages. "So the People May Know" became the editorial page line, reflecting a sincerity unkown under ex-bartender Harry Tammen and promoter Frederick G. Bonfils. Hoyt's assignment was to bring respectability to the *Post* while retaining much of the color and vitality of its pioneering days. He succeeded, too. The *Denver Post* could truthfully boast that it was the "Voice of the Rocky Mountain Empire."

In San Francisco, energetic, red-haired Paul C. Smith made the *Chronicle* one of the West's worthiest and most respected dailies. Printing articles in 1935 under the heading, "It Can Happen Here," the *Chronicle* focused national attention on the fascist-like tactics used to stop a strike of Salinas lettuce workers. After service in both the Navy and Marines, Smith returned to the paper following World War II to develop editorial writer-reporters— men sent out to gather the facts on the scene and then to write their comments. He left the *Chronicle* in 1952 and joined Crowell-Collier.

Another Pacific Coast editor who built his opinions on a firm basis of facts was Elias Manchester Boddy of the Los Angeles *Daily News*. His signed, daily "Thinking and Living" column exhibited much the same receptiveness to new ideas that Horace Greeley had shown a century earlier. Like the *New York Tribune* editor, Boddy defended himself against charges of instability. He explained:

> I doubt if anything I advocate, urge, promote or espouse makes much difference. But I am a firm believer in Fact, the Dictator.

Most small daily and weekly publishers and editors were preoccupied with mounting production costs and encroaching competition from big city rivals. But some conspicuous exceptions stood out. Among them were John Gould and his weekly which circulated to subscribers far from Lisbon Falls, Maine; Henry Beetle Hough and the *Vineyard Gazette;* Houston Waring and the Littleton (Colorado) *Independent;* Jonathan Daniels, who carried on his father's work on the Raleigh (N. C.) *News and Observer;* Hodding Carter, who won a Pulitzer prize in 1946 for an editorial on tolerance in race relations which appeared in the *Delta Democrat-Times* of Greenville, Mississippi; and the *Whiteville* (N. C.) *News Reporter* and *Tabor City* (N. C.) *Tribune*, which shared the 1953 Pulitzer award for "disinterested and meritorious public service" with a campaign against the Ku Klux Klan which culminated with the conviction of more than 100 Klan members.

Magazines, too, sometimes surprised their readers by turning enthusiastically to investigative reporting. *The New Yorker*, for instance, eliminated all its regular departments in one issue to print the book-length text of John Hersey's *Hiroshima* (Alfred A. Knopf, 1946). With newspaper-trained editors and writers in the post-war period, *Collier's* returned to startling reporting of social problems and to inquisitive poking into dirty corners of national life. The *Saturday Evening Post* found an editor with midwestern newspaper experience, Ben Hibbs, who was not afraid to spotlight a social problem after careful research showed it to be an evil. These two mass circulation publications set a pattern that was followed by others with fewer readers. The over-all effect was to print more factual magazine articles than ever before.

The opinion function was exercised most vigorously by the idea magazines, such as *The Nation, New Republic, Commonweal, Christian Century, America,* and *The Reporter.* Less objective than most magazines, and committed to causes, this group extended its influence far beyond the limited number of subscribers. But probably the most influential of all were the numerous trade and business journals that had grown up during the present century. They numbered in the thousands and practically every one of them had some semblance of prestige and ability to persuade readers. Many could wield powerful forces in their trade or profession.

Some journalists greeted these changes with gravest misgivings; others rejoiced. Charles Merz, editor of *The New York Times,* offered an explanation of why the partisan editorial of the so-called "Golden Age" of daily newspapers had been replaced by more factual commentary. In the *Annals of the American Academy of Political and Social Science* (January, 1942), he wrote:

A reader who now turns back to the editorials of the early giants —Horace Greeley, for example—will be impressed by his discovery of how much of them consists of mere rhetoric and invective. There is little approaching the reasoned argument and the careful documentation that one expects today. There is a good deal that one can only regard as sheer rant.

It is a fair statement that the reason why Horace Greeleys are not writing editorials today is not the scarcity of Horace Greeleys but the difficulty of finding people who would read them. . . Where Mr. Greeley thundered, Mr. Greeley's successor is forced by the circumstances of his own generation to try to create some light.

And the light is being shed not only by less partisan editorial writers but by syndicated columnists and news commentators who do not appear exclusively on the editorial pages of newspapers and magazines. Background, interpretation, and explanation appear in the news columns and all help to shed some light.

THREE

What's the

matter with

editorial writing?

"Nobody reads editorials these days."

"Who cares, editorials haven't any influence anyway."

That is what a lot of people say. Both statements have some truth but both are oversimplifications, too. There are all sorts of editorial pages and at least a few of them will justify any comment. One cannot talk glibly about THE editorial page, as if all were like so many peas in a pod. Few of even the baldest comments apply to all of them. As Charles Merz, editor of *The New York Times*, put it, "There are not so many different kinds of editorial pages as there are different kinds of quadruped, but there are certainly a good many." In brief, you should not generalize too frequently about THE editorial page. Yet when critics of contemporary newspapers and magazines start complaining, one fertile field for their attention is THE editorial page.

A newspaper has an opportunity to be more than a "word factory," something more than a "common carrier" for information. That opportunity is to exercise a positive force in its community. And how does it do that? By carrying out Joseph Pulitzer's advice, still printed under the masthead of the *St. Louis Post-Dispatch*: ". . . always remain devoted to the public welfare; never be satisfied with merely printing news." And editorial pages still remain a chief way for doing that despite the shift toward interpretation and background and despite all the criticism that is dumped about the declining power of the press.

Editorials are widely used

First, let's see how widely used editorials are.

Among daily newspapers, those without editorial pages are about as common as inhabitants of the tropics who live in igloos. In all the United States, there probably are only a few dozen daily papers that omit editorial comments. This is not surprising since it is in this field that publishers, editors, and writers openly bring to bear what pressures they can upon public opinion.

Among the weeklies, the figure of those without editorials is somewhat larger. One survey of 40 weeklies from Maine to Nevada showed 34 with editorials, according to *The National Publisher* (October, 1951). Some weekly paper publishers wisely decide that since their comments cannot shed real light on an issue because they and their staff members haven't the time to think topics through, they will not contribute solely heat—or worse, confusion. However, the overwhelming majority of weeklies do carry editorials. Some publish ready made reprints or hurriedly-dashed-off platitudes. Other country papers can match any product of the better known metropolitan dailies.

Among magazines, the number without editorials is still larger. Tardier deadlines and different objectives account for part of this.

In the mass circulation magazine field, the primary emphasis is on entertainment. A study of the 20 most widely circulated magazines recently showed that five had editorials of the conventional variety. Five others had neither editorials nor any substitute in opinionated comment. The rest had columnists or editor's short commentaries which chiefly told about articles or fiction in the present or future issues but occasionally they also contained a bit of advice or opinion. This certainly is the least impressive attempt among publications to exercise editorial influence.

Among the idea magazines, as pointed out in a previous chapter, the opinion-moulding function comes to full bloom.

With employee or house magazines and with business and trade publications, the story is in marked contrast to that of the mass circulation group. A survey of a representative group of business journals showed all but two of the 33 studied printed editorials. This meant that 94 per cent of these publications attempted to exert influence through editorials. Several of the group had not only editorials but also comment columns signed by the editor or publisher.

A 1948 study of 399 employee publications by the Policyholders Service Bureau of the Metropolitan Life Insurance Company showed 108 used editorials and 66 carried messages from company executives. The figure for editorials was almost double that reported in a 1942 study. Reader-interest surveys cited by the Metropolitan Life report showed that a sizable percentage of employee publication readers liked editorials and columns by ranking executives and would have preferred even more than they were receiving.

Publishers and editors who seek outright influence on their readers' opinions are trying to wield that pressure through editorials in dailies, weeklies, and magazines. All of them, however, also exert influence by what news they select to print, how they tell that story, and where in their newspaper or magazine they print the article. In publications where entertainment is paramount, the editorial function has been allowed to shrivel or actually to slough off.

The mere fact that a publication prints *an* editorial does not, of itself, signify that it is truly exercising its responsibilities as a medium for shaping public opinion or providing needed information or interpretation. A syndicated editorial may be so watered down to meet the greatest common requirements that it fails to do more than say, "Yes, but on the other hand no." Many of the smaller dailies and weeklies too often use "canned" editorials supplied by a nationwide syndicate or, even worse, by an interested lobbying or promotion group.

Louis M. Lyons reported in *Nieman Reports* (July, 1948) that 59 newspapers with 390,000 circulation had printed a "prefabricated editorial" distributed by a concern "on behalf of power interests, especially in opposition to Federal power." Then he added, "This outfit has discovered that there are editors either too lazy to write their own editorials or venal enough to present the paid-for propaganda of special interests as their own views."

Lyons raised a further question which must bother many readers around the country who are not sure that the editorials they read really are the thoughts of their publication's editors:

What would be the readers' judgment of an editor who farmed out his editorials to some one else without letting them know? Suppose this some one else was an anonymous person not resident in their community or within a thousand miles of it—some one not working for the interests of their community or even the interests of their newspaper—but working for some special interest with an axe to grind of which the readers are not told.

Surveys show there are readers

Readership surveys show that other sections of newspapers and magazines are more widely read than editorial pages. Obviously, this might have been expected. After studying available statistics, the reader may draw some logical conclusions instead of just crying emotionally, "The editorial page is dead," as some critics of today's press have a habit of doing.

While the process of questioning readers may not yield an infallible answer any more than any other type of polling, readership surveys provide one measuring rod that will give some clues of considerable value on how many and what type of readers turn to editorial pages.

First, is it possible to find out how many readers, on an average, give even a passing glance at editorial pages? Possibly they only look hurriedly at the cartoon, an inquiring reporter column, or some other feature deliberately printed on these pages with the idea of increasing potential readership. The Bureau of Advertising of the American Newspaper Publishers Association and the Advertising Research Foundation have surveyed readers of newspapers, large and small, in all sections of the United States, to find out how many read each item. On the basis of 142 surveys, these *Continuing Studies* show that 83 per cent of the men and 79 per cent of the women looked at some item on the editorial pages. That does not imply that they read the editorials, as will be evident later. But it does mean five male readers in six, and four women in five, stopped to glance at something on the page. With more than 50,000,000 copies of newspapers sold daily, this readership mounts to an impressive total.

Obviously, great differences in readership exist among various papers included in these surveys. For instance, the most popular editorial page attracted 96 per cent of the men readers while the most poorly read had 50 per cent. For women, the figures were 96 per cent and 43 per cent.

Just as readership of different editorial pages varied, so did the number of persons who picked out a particular feature to read. The *Continuing Study's* summary of 138 newspapers gave these median percentages for editorial page features:

	MEN:	WOMEN:
Some editorial page item	83	79
Editorial cartoon	64	56
Some editoral	43	27
Best read editorial	36	22
Lead editorial	34	22
Letters to the editor	32	30

Even in competition with the comic strips, editorial pages need not take a back seat. Among both men and women, the median figure for some item on the editorial page was slightly ahead of the comics in these *Continuing Study* summaries. This was not, it should be pointed out, true of the editorials themselves. Generally the leading editorial page feature was the cartoon, itself an adaption of the comics technique to an editorial topic. Other times, it was a syndicated columnist who ranked first. So the editorial writers should not claim too many bows in this contest for popularity.

The National Publisher's survey of 40 representative weeklies showed readership of editorials varying from 87 per cent to 27, indicating that country editorial writers need not feel self-conscious and inferior among their big city brethren.

In a recapitulation on results of 24 carefully-documented surveys of weekly newspaper readership, Dr. Wilbur Schramm and Merritt Ludwig of the University of Illinois reported in *Journalism Quarterly* (Summer, 1951) that "local editorials are better read, on the average, than half the other content categories in a weekly." The mean readership percentage for all 24 surveys was 38.3. These studies showed men's readership was "significantly higher" than women's. This was in keeping with the findings for readers of urban dailies.

As Miss Gertrude Stein might have put it: A good editorial is a good editorial is a good editorial.

Practically all readership surveys confirm the greater interest of men than of women in editorial pages. Perhaps this is just another reflection of the assertion, "It's a man's world." Or it might arise from men editors' selecting subjects that interest them rather than the women readers. Of course, editorial comments in general women's magazines are edited primarily for women and are written by women. Dorothy Thompson and Eleanor Roosevelt have been popular women's magazine contributors and both have exercised extraordinary influence on readers.

Readership of editorial pages also is related to age of readers. Almost without exception, the surveys agree that teen agers are not yet concerned with the opinion-makers' conventional, sober discussions of national and world affairs. For example, a University of Minnesota survey of the *Minneapolis* (Minnesota) *Star-Journal* for May 15, 1945, showed a 20 per cent increase in editorial page reading among readers more than 21 years old as compared with those 12 to 20. Dr. Wilbur Schramm found during studies of two Iowa weekly newspapers in 1946 and 1947 that editorial page readership doubled after the age of 20. Another survey by Dr. Schramm disclosed mounting numbers of readers of editorials in an Illinois evening newspaper until a peak was reached between 50 and 59 years for men (47.6 per cent) and between 30 and 39 for women (36.3 per cent). A study by Eugene Liner of the University of Illinois revealed that editorial readership was 40 per cent higher among people who grew up before the development of radio than it was among people who listened to the radio during their youth.

Economic status and occupation also seem to have a direct relationship to reading of editorial pages. In the *Continuing Study's* 138-newspaper summary, investigators reported a steadily declining percentage as they went from executive and professional people, to junior executives, skilled workmen, and finally unskilled laborers. Dr. Schramm's research confirmed this same trend.

Discussing his own and other readership studies, Dr. Schramm concluded in *Journalism Quarterly* (June, 1949):

If the results of this study are representative, some of the already written obituaries of the editorial had better be rewritten. The editorial comes out of this study with an impressive index of readership. The significant fact is *where* it plays its most important part in reading groups—with older age groups, more highly educated groups, and higher economic groups. These are opinion-making groups. On the other hand, it is worth asking whether the editorial's effect in these places is likely to be reinforcement or change. People tend to read what they agree with. The majority of editorials are written by representatives of these very groups where editorial readership is highest, and their editorials may be expected to represent the viewpoints of their own groups. That may help to explain the locus of high editorial reading.

Dr. Schramm has put his finger on a matter of policy of major importance: To whom should the editorial be addressed? Some editors, especially those on the more respectable dailies that are cited as showpieces in a journalistic display, aim primarily at the opinion-moulders. They are carrying on Godkin's appeal to the intelligentsia a century ago. Others turn their backs on this approach and write for the mass reader. The effect is noted in choice of subject matter, writing style, and whole philosophy. In New York City, this conflict is exemplified by *The New York Times* and the New York *Daily News*.

In times of crises, more and more readers turn to editorial pages. The *Continuing Study* 138-paper summary showed that readership of both editorials and other editorial page items increased during World War II and then declined after the defeat of Germany and Japan. If sufficient readership studies for the 1920's and 1930's were available, they undoubtedly would indicate an upswing during the depression years and the initial New Deal period. Many editors recall that readers followed editorials and the new commentators—the columnists—with increasing interest during that period.

The *Continuing Study* added two other clues on readership. Both men and women exhibit less interest in editorial reading during the three-month period of July, August, and September. Since this is the time of summer vacations, possibly people postpone most of the serious things in life until cooler weather. An analysis of the volumes in the *Continuing Study of Newspaper Reading* brought out significant variations for geographical regions. The pattern indicated greatest editorial readership in the Middle Atlantic area and least in the South, which was less than three-quarters of that in the leading region. Interestingly, comic strip reading was high where editorial readership was low.

What conclusions can we come to about editorial page readership? The following seem to be supported by a wide variety of surveys:

1. The editorial page is more widely read than many people believe.

2. The editorial cartoon is the most popular feature on the page; the columnists and then the editorials follow in popularity.

3. More men than women read editorial pages.

4. Older and more prosperous groups—the opinion-makers—lead in readership of editorial pages.

5. Editorial readership is highest in times of crisis.

What happens when editorials are absent?

During July, 1945, a strike of newspaper deliverers in New York City prevented most residents of the metropolitan area from buying their regular daily paper. The ANPA Bureau of Advertising tested the public reaction and came up with some fairly impressive findings about readership of editorials. The survey questionnaire included the query, "What do you miss most of what you usually get from your newspapers?" Out of 1,017 interviews, 201 cited editorials and 145 listed columnists. These figures compared with 144 mentions of comics and 133 for sports news.

Newspapers of St. Louis had a similar carriers' strike starting on August 16, 1945. The question asked New Yorkers was put to 537 persons in the Midwestern community; 17.9 per cent of the St. Louis readers mentioned editorials, compared with 19.9 per cent of those polled in New York.

A walkout of newspaper mailing-room employees on Pittsburgh newspapers in the fall of 1950 provided another chance to find out what readers missed most. A national advertising and public relations agency, which made a survey, reported that men put columnists in seventh place and editorials in eighth. Women readers did not put either among their first eight. Comics did better with both sexes.

Forrest W. Seymour of the *Des Moines Register* and *Tribune* did not feel badly about this showing. He wrote in *The Masthead* (Winter, 1950–51) as follows about the Pittsburgh findings:

Why, hell's fire, they ought to go around with chests as big as blimps if male readers put the editorial page in seventh or eighth place. Then they ought to settle down and fight like wildcats to get their readership into sixth or fifth place.

This could be done, incidentally, if editorial pages regularly had something to say that was as interesting and exciting as the sports page, the comics, the markets, and other sections. I do not say that any editorial page could beat out the *front* page—it *shouldn't*. The news itself is a darned sight more important than anything else. In fact, the sports page and the market page are also *news* pages—and they ought to come first.

And what about editorials' political influence?

After the presidential elections of the 1930's and 1940's, many people declared that the daily and weekly newspapers were declining in influence. They gleefully claimed that voters again had repudiated the press and had demonstrated anew that newspapers and magazines could not "deliver" political victory. In each of these five elections, ever increasing numbers of dailies editorially supported the Republican presidential nominee. Each time, the Democratic candidate won.

Then came 1952 when Dwight D. Eisenhower won, with nearly 90 per cent of the daily press supporting him. His Democratic opponent, Adlai E. Stevenson, in a speech at Portland, Oregon, said he was "considerably concerned when I see the extent to which we are developing a one-party press in a two-party country."

But let's go back and look at what critics said after some of these elections.

After the Republican debacle of 1936, crowds swept past the arch-Republican *Chicago Tribune's* tower shaking their fists in defiance. An editorial in the *Christian Century* (November 18, 1936) voiced a prevailing viewpoint when it warned publishers:

Hundreds of thousands of American citizens rejoiced in the catastrophe which has overwhelmed you. They obtained a deep emotional

77

satisfaction from the fact that you have not merely been defeated but that you have been smashed.

Four years later President Franklin D. Roosevelt dramatically shattered the third term tradition despite the opposition of a large section of the press. Secretary of the Interior Harold L. Ickes attacked newspapers at a press conference the morning after the election results were tabulated. He issued a statement that concluded:

This [declining Democratic newspaper support] reveals an unprecedented and progressively perilous situation requiring public consideration. Although we are fortunate in having free communication over the air, I am convinced that our democracy needs, more than ever before, a truly free press that represents no class or economic group and that will rewin the confidence of our citizens because it is worthy of rewinning that confidence.

After the unexpected re-election of Harry S. Truman in 1948, Morris L. Ernst and David Loth in their book, *The People Know Best* (Public Affairs Press, 1949), cautioned:

The laughter and the jeers will be wasted if they lead only to a cynical belief that the press and the radio are not to be trusted at all. If we preserve these great institutions only for their entertainment values, for their comic strips, their tips on etiquette, their air-borne dramas and comedies, we will have lost our First Freedom. Men do not sacrifice and fight and die for a principle in which they have lost faith. The day that Americans feel freedom of speech is not worth the effort of preserving it, the concept upon which our civilization is based will have been destroyed.

Granted then that during the 1930's and 1940's the majority of the United States dailies failed to support editorially the winning nominee for president. Does that mean that the press was without influence? Does it mean that the press, at least temporarily, lost a power that it once wielded with magic effectiveness? What did the Eisenhower victory in 1952 prove? Did it mean that all the unheeded editorial endorsements of five earlier presidential campaigns had finally been obeyed? Is a newspaper's function to win elections?

Let's try to answer these questions by asking two more:

(1) Did the newspaper editors ever deliver the people's votes?

(2) Is political influence a major function of present-day editorial writing?

Dr. Frank Luther Mott, then dean of the School of Journalism at the University of Missouri and an outstanding historian of American newspapers, carefully studied the power of the press in presidential elections and reported his findings in *Public Opinion Quarterly* (Fall, 1944). He found that the papers had been beaten more frequently than they had triumphed. Only once in United States history—from Grover Cleveland's second election through William Howard Taft's victory—have editors supported the winning presidential candidate for five successive elections. That period counterbalances their misses during the 1930's and 1940's.

Dr. Mott's study showed that newspapers consistently have been a conservative influence. In the times of Jefferson, they supported the Federalists. In the age of Jackson, Whig newspapers dominated the scene. Abraham Lincoln failed to obtain the support of a majority of newspapers until his second campaign, when he was a favorite of Northern publications. After 1872, papers were fairly evenly divided between Democrats and Republicans for several decades. Grover Cleveland, however, got majority press support during his turbulent campaign against James G. Blaine. He continued to have a majority during the two succeeding contests, one of which he lost. During the three-cornered contest between Theodore Roosevelt, William Howard Taft, and Woodrow Wilson in 1912, no candidate had a journalistic majority. From that time onward, the Republicans have won the majority of editorial page endorsements during each presidential campaign.

On the basis of his analysis, Dr. Mott concluded that "there seems to be no correlation, positive or negative, between support of a majority of newspapers during a campaign and success at the polls." So Harold L. Ickes' "unprecedented and progressively perilous situation" may be taken with several grains of salt. The press apparently never has been able to bring in the necessary votes for its favorite candidates for any long time. That does not, however, sweep aside all the implications of the charge of a "one-party press." Marshall Field in *Freedom Is More Than A Word* (University of Chicago Press, 1945) claimed that a majority of newspapers consistently supported "our greatest presidential protectors of vested privilege."

Presidential election returns in recent years may simply validate spectacularly that front page news is more impressive than inside page editorials. After the 1948 election, Dean Kenneth E. Olson of the Medill School of Journalism, Northwestern University, explained it this way:

Elections are decided, not in editorial columns, but in news columns. Many newspapers may have opposed Roosevelt all through these years in their editorial pages back on page 12 or 16, yet everything that Roosevelt said or did, pre-war and during the war, was NEWS with capital letters on page one. It was the same this time. Even though newspapers may have attacked the President's blundering foreign policy and his inept handling of domestic affairs on their editorial pages, nevertheless everything President Truman said or did was NEWS. Even those who opposed him most bitterly printed his speeches in full, even his attacks upon them. And somehow this game little man with a fighting heart, punching away almost by himself, but given the opportunity to tell his story, persuaded a majority of our people that he was right.

Whether the news columns themselves have been perverted to help elect the political candidate favored on the editorial pages has been increasingly debated in recent presidential election campaigns and long after each one. When Professor Nathan B. Blumberg of the University of Nebraska studied 35 dailies which he claimed were "a representative distribution of newspapers on the basis of editorial political preference in the 1952 election," he concluded that "there was slanting in the news columns during the 1952 election, but it was not as widespread as some critics have maintained." Six of the 35 papers examined, he found, provided evidence of partiality in their news columns. His full report is printed in *One-Party Press?* (University of Nebraska Press, 1954).

When twitted by his fellow newspaper editors over the *Kansas City* (Missouri) *Star's* initially unsuccessful attempts to unseat Boss Tom Pendergast, Roy Roberts, the paper's managing editor at that time, denied that a newspaper's primary job was to win elections. Rather, he said, it was to print the news. Then he suggested, "If it is a matter of winning elections, then I say you ought to add an election department to your newspaper, set yourself up (like a political machine), put in your precinct workers."

Other editors, however, believed that the press did lose face as a leader and guide for public sentiment when its candidates lost.

Virginius Dabney, editor of the *Richmond* (Virginia) *Times-Dispatch* and a Pulitzer prize-winner, took this attitude. In the *Saturday Review of Literature* (February 24, 1945), he wrote:

> In defending our press from the attacks which were made upon it following the November (1944) election, some of the apologists offered extraordinary arguments. One of the most frequent was that no newspaper wants to exercise a decisive influence in elections, anyway, and that when it has carefully weighed the issues and expressed its views, it is not concerned with whether these views are accepted. Poppycock! An editor who urges his readers to support Candidate A cannot possibly remain indifferent when he sees his advice totally disregarded, and his readers stampeding into the camp of Candidate B.

During a panel discussion at the 1952 Sigma Delta Chi convention, J. B. Mullaney, editor of the Editorial Page, *Cleveland News*, and then National Conference of Editorial Writers chairman, made much the same point:

I want to be fair, not to any candidate or to any cause, but to myself and my readers. I believe in being very wary of "on the other hand" kind of editorial. I think when we support a man or a cause we ought to fight to win, and when we don't succeed, then we ought to go lie down on a couch and not necessarily call in a psychiatrist but ask ourselves what was the cause of the failure, whether we did know what we were doing and what we were trying to do.

When editors do contemplate the returns for state, district, and local elections, as Mullaney has suggested, they uncover much to encourage them. Such studies as have been made (admittedly they are sketchy) demonstrate that a newspaper endorsement is not a political "kiss of death" but rather something sought by most candidates.

There is the non-political side

But politics are only part of the picture. The editorial writer has a good many other things to talk about. The job of reporting and commenting on what elected officials are doing during the many months between campaigns may be more important than plus-or-minus evaluations made during the actual appeals for votes. Beyond politics and government, a whole world awaits the editorial writer. If the press has influence here, it can easily justify its claims to social responsibility.

If newspapers and magazines are powerful to sway opinion, a large part of their effectiveness comes from comments on the editorial pages. Prominent display of a news story or an illuminating explanation or background article may help a community make up its mind, but the editorials are the focal point of any publication's most deliberate effort to create or mould public opinion. Most effective, of course, is a combination which provides not only ready-made opinions but also the information, the interpretation, and the background against which the facts rest.

What do we find when we examine this non-political aspect?

A local newspaper, either daily or weekly, can mobilize generosity for "The 100 Neediest Cases" as *The New York Times*, for instance, does at Christmas time each year, or raise money to finance summer camps for underprivileged children, as the *New York Herald Tribune* does.

It can uncover inefficiency, corruption, and maladministration which go beyond government into other fields. The *Chicago Daily News* and the *St. Louis Post-Dispatch* shared the 1950 Pulitzer prize for exposing that a number of Illinois editors had accepted state jobs and salaries without contributing much besides favorable comments on the state administration.

It can expose brutality by the police or in mental institutions or homes for juvenile delinquents. Newspapers across the country have played an important part in having adopted a more enlightened attitude by the public and their elected officials.

It can fight intolerance and make its community a better place in which to live. New York City, Detroit, St. Louis, and other dailies have exposed the roots of prejudice which cause racial rioting in their localities and then fought editorially for their elimination. A Pulitzer prize in 1946 to Hodding Carter of the *Delta Democrat-Times* of Greenville, Mississippi, showed that recognition could come to a small paper as well as the metropolitan ones.

It can support civic projects to build up a better citizenry. Thousands of worth while programs have received an editorial pat-on-the-back which inspired the leaders to go on when they might have otherwise been faint-hearted.

It can help puzzled readers to find their way through confusing economic developments and baffling statistics. The *Wall Street Journal*, for instance, does a commendable job here which attracts readers other than those interested in strictly business activities.

It can promote international good will. The *Christian Science Monitor* and *The New York Times* repeatedly have illustrated how this can be done.

It can become the articulate voice of a region, such as the *Denver Post*, *Des Moines Register* and *Tribune*, Portland *Oregonian*, and other dailies have become.

In a phrase, a local newspaper can throw its weight on the side that it believes right. The editor of such a paper can win attention and fame, as he certainly should, and possibly a Pulitzer prize, too.

Unlike most daily papers, some country weeklies and most specialized periodicals still carry on the tradition of personal journalism. Editors of these publications wield power on local or specialized issues reminiscent of the so-called "Golden Age" of journalism when readers accepted their opinions more because they respected the writers than because of the impressive arrangement of facts, background, interpretation, and explanation. However, some struggling editors are willing to bow to the threat of advertising boycott or subscriber protest. Others, overworked trying to cover the straight news and to collect advertising and subscriptions, willingly abandon their opinion-making assignment. Some accept syndicate-tailored editorials because they have neither the time nor the energy to write their own.

That editors of the better business papers accept the responsibilities of leading their subscribers' thinking is shown by Julien Elfenbein in his text, *Business Journalism* (Harper, 1947). Discussing the editor and his job, Elfenbein said:

> On his editorial page the businesspaper editor integrates news and trends, discusses, analyzes, interprets. Here issues are joined, defined, clarified, illuminated, so that readers may reach convictions, make *decisions*. Here, too, the editor not only guides and advises; he also persuades, urges action.

Magazine editors, too, duplicate these performances in public service. As pointed out earlier, the small-circulation idea magazines do it more blatantly but many a mass-circulation journal has highlighted a social problem. Present-day "muckrakers" get into print in widely circulated magazines but their tone is not as shrill as their predecessors of Theodore Roosevelt's days.

What critics say about editorial pages

Newspapermen and magazine writers familiar with the routines of news and editorial departments frequently criticize more caustically than ordinary readers do. Since they have a practical knowledge of the inside operations, let's look at what they have said.

Here are a few typical comments:

H. L. Mencken, brilliant Baltimore *Sun* editor and critic of much Americana, called the editorial page the newspapers' "grandest and gaudiest failure" when he appeared before the 1937 sessions of the American Society of Newspaper Editors. Ten years later he repeated almost the same accusation before the first National Conference of Editorial Writers.

Another Baltimore *Sun* editorial page staff alumnus, Gerald W. Johnson, told the 1951 N.C.E.W. that "I find the factual editorial the dreariest reading in the paper, not excluding the legal notices."

Felix Morley, a Pulitzer prize-winning editorial writer who later left journalism, in the 1940 Don Mellett Memorial Lecture called the editorial "just another rather dull accessory" among the press' gadgets.

Alan Barth, former Nieman Fellow and editorial writer on the *Washington* (D.C.) *Post*, wrote in the *American Mercury* (May, 1946), "The editorial page, once the heart of any newspaper, has become far too commonly, a mere vermiform appendix. Still part of the organism, it has in many cases, lost almost all organic functions."

Oswald Garrison Villard, once called "the dean of editorial writers on American metropolitan newspapers," lamented in an article for *The Masthead* (Autumn, 1949), "The worst sins of American editors are their ignorance, their lack of courage and their failure to expose and censure their own misdeeds."

Virginius Dabney, Pulitzer prize-winning editor of the *Richmond Times-Dispatch*, found "convincing evidence" that editorials are not the force in American life that they were a generation or two ago and that they ought to be now.

Jack Kilpatrick, editor of the Richmond *News Leader*, told a 1953 Columbia University audience that vast numbers of editorials are written by men who neither read nor write nor even think. And he added, for good measure, that "all too many editorial pronouncements still trudge into the public print in dull dress, camouflaged under dull heads, and hung with a veil of dull type."

Most drastic proposal of all made in recent years was that of Dr. Douglas Southall Freeman, editor of the Richmond *News Leader*, top-ranking military historian, and Pulitzer prize-winning biographer. He advocated abolition of his paper's editorial page in a plan that "seeks deliberately to break down the barrier between the editorial writing and the news reporting." Although dated October 28, 1935, a memorandum to his publisher did not come to light until after his death and it received general publicity only when published in the Spring, 1954, issue of *The Masthead*.

In his efforts to establish "a modern newspaper, a newspaper that informs and interprets," Dr. Freeman proposed "that the editorial pages as a separate part of the paper be abolished in the *News Leader* and that interpretation and comment be directly related to the news." Then he went on:

Editorial and interpretative comment (it is significant that both words have to be used) would take one of two forms.

(1) To the average story, if the facts did not fully explain themselves, or lacked background, there would be appended under a 5-em dash a paragraph or two headed "Interpretative Comment" or "Editorial Comment." The material that followed this would be an attempt to supply the background or interpret the happening for the reader who was unfamiliar with it.

(2) In those instances where a general situation had to be summarized and interpreted as important to the reader or to the general public, an article would be printed on the front page or on the local page plainly marked "Editorial." This would usually be in a two-

column measure and would be an expression of the opinion of the
paper. The same treatment would be given crusading activities of
the paper, as, for instance, on automobile casualties.

Editorial writers, it should be plain, may be as hard on their
colleagues as any other group. They at least should know what
they are talking about.

Adverse comments may be broken down into three general
groupings: (1) Content and policies, (2) Style or composition,
and (3) Make-up.

Summarized here are some of the criticisms voiced about present-day editorial policies and about the contents of editorial
pages:

(1) Editors roar like lions regarding distant situations that readers have no interest in but they act like lambs about near-by problems that might bring reprisals from local enthusiasts.

(2) Editorial writers in one-newspaper towns—and that includes more than nine out of every ten communities with dailies—
either try to be all things to all men or go to the other extreme and
throttle ideas that the paper disapproves.

(3) Too many commentators live in Ivory Towers.

(4) Insufficient editorial attention is paid to the "significant
silences" in the news and so editorial comments generally are
confined to the noisy events.

(5) Editorials reflect the big business attitudes of publishers
and their interests in protecting their investments.

(6) Editorial-page favors are sold to the highest bidder.

Let's examine each of these in more detail.

Jenkin Lloyd Jones, editor of the *Tulsa* (Oklahoma) *Tribune*,
used the word "Afghanistanism" to describe editorial fervor for
a cause far enough away to prevent possible retort from irate
advertisers or outraged subscribers.

Reporting on a survey of Midwestern editorial pages in a talk
before the American Society of Newspaper Editors in 1948, Jones
said:

The tragic fact is that many an editorial writer can't hit a short range target. He's hell on distance. And there's a lot that's comfortable about this distance. It takes guts to dig up the dirt on the sheriff, or to expose a utility racket or to tangle with the Governor. They all bite back, and you had better know your stuff.

But you can pontificate about the situation in Afghanistan in perfect safety. You have no fanatic Afghans among your readers. Nobody knows any more about the subject than you do, and nobody gives a damn.

Jones pointed out that even the editorials on local subjects might be neat evasions of controversy. He cited one newspaper that had eight editorials on local and state subjects compared with six on remoter fields. That breakdown looked satisfactory. But Jones pointed out:

There's a big battle on around this town. The city wants to drill more artesian wells to care for its growing population. The surrounding ranchers fear they will be ruined by the subsequent lowering of the water table. The community is obviously divided. The scrap provides front page stuff every day.

And those eight local editorials? Damned if they don't attack juvenile delinquency!

It is easy for an editorial writer to be against things remote from his local community where those attacked will not "bite back" but it requires courage to hit out hard against local abuses. An editor may have to consider himself "expendable" as did Kenneth Dixon of the Lake Charles (Louisiana) *American Press* when he decided to hit out at local gambling and the public officials who permitted it. He defended himself and four staff members against charges of defaming 16 officials and three gamblers. The newspapermen's acquittal in 1952 brought him the acclaim and praise of his fellow journalists. The Pulitzer prize awards and the Sigma Delta Chi annual citations record in elequent fashion some of the crusades by newspapers, large and small, that have won recognition by hitting out at local people who may "bite back." Many other examples are known only to editors, their readers, and other interested newspapermen. During informal N.C.E.W. "critique" discussions of individual pages, the men who form policies have displayed it in their own dailies. Yet some editors, as Mr. Jones accurately pointed out, play it the easy and comfortable way. For many papers, however, "Afghanistanism" is not as valid a sweeping criticism as it once was.

Just to keep the record straight, however, there is a word of caution about "Afghanistanism." Foreign affairs can be important as Francis P. Locke of the *Dayton* (Ohio) *Daily News* pointed pointed out in *The Masthead* (Fall, 1953):

I know local's vital. I know it's where our muscle really counts for something, immediately and proximately. I know that society must be sound at the grassroots. At the same time, I know that whether Russia takes over Iran (that's almost as far out as Afghanistan) will one day be a lot more important to the people of Dayton than whether the city commission takes too long to make up its mind to enforce the rules against off-hours trash burning.

I also suspect that the exact level of the municipal tax rate is going to mean less in the citizen's life than whether his home is hit by an H-bomb or his business goes bankrupt in another depression. . . .

It cannot be disputed that the immediate impact of an editorial is in proportion inverse to the distance of the target. All glory to those of us who can pound the typewriter with enough authority to drum the city into enforcing the trash-burning ordinance. But some glory also to those of us who merely add one tiny drop to the ocean of public opinion as it forms on such issues as continuing the reciprocal trade treaties or carrying the war to the Chinese mainland. For if editorial diffidence, or sense of futility, dried up all the drops, there would be no ocean.

One-newspaper towns create special editorial problems. Now more than nine out of every ten communities with daily papers have only one. In many localities, common ownership of the daily and the radio station simply strengthens a local news monopoly. Editors in these towns have an uneasy time. They may try to play it safe. Their writing may become so spineless that they lose their readers' respect—and deservedly so. Or, at the other extreme, they may support one viewpoint so vigorously that their opponents do not have a fair chance in the "arena of ideas."

The Commission on Freedom of the Press included a recommendation in *A Free and Responsible Press* (University of Chicago Press, 1947) that "the agencies of mass communication accept the responsibilities of common carriers of information and discussion." It is unquestionably true that when a newspaper throws its editorial support against a cause, those favoring it can create events which reporters will be forced to cover or they may turn to other communication channels. But the Commission, and many other critics, argue:

> Those agencies of mass communication which have achieved a dominant position in their areas can exert an influence over the minds of their audience too powerful to be disregarded. We do not wish to break up these agencies, because to do so would break up the service they render. We do not wish to have them owned or controlled by government. They must therefore themselves be hospitable to ideas and attitudes different from their own, and they must present them to the public as meriting its attention. In no other way can the danger to the mind of democracy which is inherent in the present concentration be avoided.

At best, this assignment will require exacting patience. Some editors, certainly, will fail. Yet, if this goal cannot be achieved by at least a hard core of influential United States newspapers and magazines on their editorial pages, then the editors face the sad choice of being so inoffensive as to be ineffectual or of maintaining an intellectual balancing act that surpasses anything yet seen on a circus tightrope.

Advice on how the problem may be resolved came from Herbert Brucker, editor of the *Hartford* (Connecticut) *Courant* and a former Columbia University journalism teacher. In his book, *Freedom of Information*, (Macmillan, 1949), he said:

Objectivity in opinion is achieved not by emasculating editorials, but by directing every possible ounce of missionary zeal and hellfire to the service of the entire community rather than merely to a part of it. A news story is made objective by weighing both sides of a controversy. An editorial is made objective by weighing both sides of a controversy with a broad perspective and a deep understanding before deciding which side to fight for. Editorially, a newspaper should be objective only as to purpose. Once it has determined what is right in a given issue, it should pull no punches. . . . Too many newspapers now get too many of their opinions first, and then look for facts to bolster them. It is the deepest obligation of newspapers in a really free world to get the facts first and let those facts determine their opinions.

A third criticism of present-day editorials is that too many writers pick their subjects as if they lived in Ivory Towers. They appear untouched by the realities that affect everyday men. Topics are neatly chosen according to pre-conceived notions of what will interest the "masses" and these topics fail to change even if subscribers' interests shift. Such are the arguments.

D. M. Richardson, chief editorial writer for the *Christian Science Monitor*, wrote some years ago that too many editorial writers had a "desk chair viewpoint" toward the news and failed to keep vital contacts outside their offices. Neil MacNeil, then assistant managing editor of *The New York Times*, conceded in his *Without Fear or Favor* (Harcourt, Brace, 1940) that too many editorials have "the atmosphere of the cloister." The 1949–50 Nieman Fellows at Harvard complained that too many editorial writers "sooner or later acquire an Olympian complex about their own fund of knowledge" and "feel it would be an admission of weakness to consult a local reporter or Washington correspondent for his views or inside information."

Some newspapers have tried to evict their editorial writers from

Ivory Towers. For example, the *Christian Science Monitor* kept an editorial writer in Washington to write firsthand comments on the national scene for five war years and several afterwards. During the San Francisco conference at which the United Nations was born, the *Washington Post, Christian Science Monitor,* and *St. Paul Dispatch* and *Pioneer Press,* among others, sent editorial writers to work directly from the meeting hall. Every four years, presidential nominating conventions attract editorial page staff representatives as well as regular news correspondents.

Since World War II, an increasing number of editorial writers have been assigned to tour the countryside, consult staff reporters, or look up basic documents in search of the facts; then they have written their conclusions. Less and less do they rely on second or third or fourth hand sources. Notable examples of this trend have been the reporter-editorial essayists of the *San Francisco Chronicle* and *Birmingham* (Alabama) *Age-Herald* and the wide opportunities which the *Wall Street Journal* and *The New York Times* have given editorial writers to travel across the country and abroad in order to recharge their mental batteries, so to speak, by contacts with new faces and new places. Oswald Garrison Villard, editor of the *New York Evening Post* before World War I and for many years publisher of *The Nation,* proposed "a Cook's tour in the hearts of plain America" for editorial page staff members.

Students of newspapers and magazines emphasize that too much attention is given the sensational rather than the significant, the interesting rather than the important. Although public demand is not as important in selecting topics for editorials as in picking stories for page one display, it does influence editorial writers as well as news editors. On the one hand, comments in daily papers are geared generally to the news of the preceding 24 hours, or at least the previous few days. The pressure for timeliness is only slightly less strong for editorials than for news items. On the other hand, this concern over what the public wants results in too much emphasis on the noisy events that attract attention and news space and too little on the "significant silences" in world happenings. Frequently some little-publicized sub-surface development—for example, an item on page 13 dealing with biological warfare research—may have more real significance for the reader than a noisy, front page spread on the latest maneuver in a long drawn out debate over appropriation bills in the House of Representatives. A union meeting to discuss the possibilities of a strike at which issues were brought out clearly may have more significance for the astute editorial writer than an outbreak of violence on the picket line.

Nine out of ten reporters polled by Leo C. Rosten for *The Washington Correspondents* (Harcourt, Brace, 1937) agreed that "comparatively few papers give significant accounts of our basic economic conflicts." And that comment still is true of editorial pages.

Although he won a Pulitzer prize for a spectacular campaign that put the names of all Republican presidential aspirants on Nebraska's 1948 preferential primary ballots, Raymond A. Mc-Connell, Jr., editor and managing editor of the *Nebraska State Journal* at Lincoln, Nebraska, does not feel papers pay enough attention to non-political subjects. In *The Masthead* (Summer, 1949), he warned that many editorial writers spend nine-tenths of their time on "subjects to which not even the erudite editor and his wife, let alone the boys in the back shop, devote a tenth of their conversation time among themselves."

Of course, editorial writers cannot cut themselves off completely from the news executives and front page display. If they do, they may end up supplying interpretation and background in editorials for which the readers have no foreground in straight news reporting. Some papers do make this mistake. Others coordinate news and editorials. All should try. But they must, to be most effective, include comments on the "significant silences" of the news.

Few, if any, informed students of contemporary newspapers,

magazines, radio, and television deny that these agencies of mass communication have become big business. To some, this is an object of pride; to others, it is a badge of shame. The transition from the days a century ago, when a printer with ideas and a cheap press could start his own newspaper, to the present time, when millions are required to launch a metropolitan daily or tens of thousands to buy a successful weekly, brought some not-so-subtle changes in editorial vigor.

Virginius Dabney, editor of the *Richmond Times-Dispatch*, described the shift from an emphasis on public service to an emphasis on property. In the *Saturday Review of Literature* (February 24, 1945), he wrote:

Today newspapers are Big Business and they are run in that tradition. The publisher, who often knows little about the editorial side of the operation, usually is one of the leading business men in his community, and his editorial page, under normal circumstances, strongly reflects that point of view. Sometimes he gives his editor a free hand, but far oftener he does not. He looks upon the paper primarily as a "property," rather than as an instrument for public service. There are brilliant and honorable exceptions to these generalizations, but an American editor was disconcertingly close to the mark when he spoke not long ago of "the blinker-wearing stupidity of publishers as a class—men with the vision of soap manufacturers and the souls of oysters because almost all of them come from the counting room." . . .

The fact that the average American publisher is not only conservative, but frequently reactionary, and the further fact that he often imposes his views upon his editor, is the greatest single reason why the American editorial page has declined so sharply in influence. Instead of letting trained newspapermen conduct the paper, an art and mystery about which many publishers know little or nothing, they insist upon inflicting their prejudices and predilections upon the entire staff. It is in the realm of editorial policy that this interference produces its most appalling results. The publisher who is imbued with blind preconceptions concerning social and economic questions, preconceptions which stem from no particular study, but merely from the fact that he associates almost entirely with people entertaining similar notions, is hardly the sort of person to formulate an editorial policy which is fair to all classes in the community.

Alan Barth, former Nieman Fellow and editorial writer on the *Washington Post*, voiced similiar sentiments when he wrote in the *American Mercury* (May, 1946) that most newspapers were started by men who had something to say but now were printed by men who merely had something to sell. He added that editorial writers frequently were "merely grammatical mouthpieces for the boss, translating his prejudices into more or less coherent literary form."

These two criticisms from editorial writers paint a dark picture, indeed. But both Dabney and Barth, as well as other critics, have not abandoned hope. We should not either. Leadership will come, as Dabney said, if the editorial pages are "dedicated to the welfare of all the people, not merely to the interests of one exclusive and fortunate class." And Barth admitted that the fortunate editorial writers work "under a publisher who is willing to give weight to the views of his professional people on the subjects on which they are supposed to be expert." Even severe critics admit the picture has its bright side in the "honorable exceptions."

Criticism is frequently made that editorial pages, even more than news columns, are for sale. Advertisers usually are mentioned as the chief offenders against an untrammeled press. Although occasionally an authenticated case of such influence makes some readers suspicious of all press comments and opinions, it is not a serious threat to journalistic freedom. For example, after a careful study of the editorial policies of 75 newspapers in the Midwest, one publisher found that just one publication had a recent reputation for auctioning its editorial support to the highest bidder. Then Jenkin Lloyd Jones, editor of the *Tulsa Tribune*, added, "I know of no group of 75 preachers in which 74 would refuse to publicly bless the scoundrel who filled the collection plate."

Editorial policy, then, is seldom for sale. The overwhelming majority of editorial writers condemn such practice, not only publicly but privately, too. Venality is uncommon in journalism, less common probably than in most professions. Yet some editors who would throw out of their offices anyone who offered them a bribe in return for support sometimes are bribed by the money in their own pockets. Men of wealth themselves, they believe that other rich men can do little wrong. They have what William Allen White of the *Emporia Gazette* used to call the country club complex. Newspaper owners and their chief executives may be unconsciously influenced by those with whom they associate.

Then there are criticisms of style

Here are the most common criticisms of editorial style:

(1) Editorials are in too much of a hurry, both in arriving at opinions and in writing.

(2) Editorial writing is bookish, prosy, and pontifical.

(3) Editorials are ineffective because they are unsigned and institutional.

Tired minds are slow minds. This well known psychological axiom can be demonstrated by experiments. Yet some newspaper and magazine owners expect their editorial writers—or even worse, their single editorial writer—to fill two or three columns daily with profound remarks on a wide range of subjects. It just cannot be done—except by an occasional genius.

A fresh approach to an editorial topic requires time for research, time for thinking, and time for writing. A really profound discussion of a complex development on the other side of the globe—for instance, new economic regulations in India— may require hours, if not days, of researching. And then more time is needed to write an editorial that will be lucid enough for the hurried reader to grasp. A reader is entitled to hurry, but an editorial writer can do so only at his peril. He needs ample time for research, thinking, and writing.

While he was editor and general manager of the *San Francisco Chronicle*, Paul C. Smith said that "too much half-cocked expression on complex and important subjects" was printed and too many writers commented editorially before they were properly prepared.

After studying the nation's editorial pages for three years, Professor Roscoe Ellard of Columbia University concluded much the same thing. He found that "the principal reason why the best editorial pages are worth reading is because their writers make a business of informing themselves about the background and integration of the news."

How an editorial writer on one influential newspaper informed himself was discussed by Charles Merz, editor of *The New York Times*, in the *Annals of the American Academy of Political and Social Science* (January, 1942):

> If he is alive to his responsibility, the editor studies the news more carefully than any possible reader of his paper. He puts together items that are seemingly not linked, and looks for trends that are not always evident on the face of the day's news. He reads a good many books, talks with as many informed people as he can, uses his personal contacts for enlightenment. He tries to equip himself to interpret the news just as an architect equips himself to interpret buildings, a physician to interpret what he sees under a microscope in a blood smear. He takes it as his duty to tell his readers what, in his opinion, the news signifies. . . . He does not always succeed, even within the limited scope of his own opportunity. But he tries in a large enough number of cases to establish a pattern of effort.

The harassed editorial writers on understaffed papers certainly do not have the time to follow this advice and the results too often are the "half-cocked expression" cited by Smith. How big the editorial page staff should be is discussed in detail in Chapter Seventeen.

As if poor choice of material were not enough of a handicap, some editorial writers use an obtuse style. To write clearly and stimulatingly is always a difficult assignment. The high caliber of the men and women on those newspapers and magazines whose opinions are studied and respected is repeatedly shown by their good writing.

Stylistic transgressions and the reasons for them vary. Some writers take refuge in the obtuse because they have neither time nor initiative for lucid, simple prose. Some pontificate on the news because it is easier to write that way than to dig up the facts and conclusions and then to allow the case to rest on the evidence. Some resort to clichés that obscure the meaning and they weasel through a tight spot without having to think through to clearer conclusions. Some are intellectual snobs who relish writing for the few, including, of course, their fellow editorial writers. This group hopes to impress by a historical illusion, an unusual reference, or such elegantisms as "men of the requisite outlook of intelligence." "the distaff side," and "penned."

Harry M. Ayers of the *Anniston* (Alabama) *Star* wrote in *The Masthead* (Autumn, 1949) that he considered the "worst" editorial page the "one in which its editors are wont to parade their French, Latin or other esoteric words and phrases that cannot be interpreted by the fellow on the other side of the railroad tracks." He also lamented those pages "given to polysyllableism or orotundity and therefore, as was said of Dr. Johnson, 'make their little fishes talk like whales.' "

Paul Bellamy, then managing editor of the *Cleveland Plain Dealer*, told the American Society of Newspaper Editors in 1929 that editorials, with few exceptions, were "terrible jobs of writing." Nearly 20 years later, Virginius Dabney of the *Richmond Times-Dispatch* found the criticism still valid. For every outstanding editorial page, he claimed there were dozens of others whose editorials were "flat, jejune, and without sparkle."

Some critics of the press would sum this up in a single word:

dullness. Many a reader feels better after he knows the opinions of his favorite journal, but, admittedly, he would prefer to have them expressed in sprightly fashion. Editorial writing style will be discussed at greater length in Chapter Sixteen.

Editorials have been condemned as "anonymous private opinions." Curtis D. MacDougall, Northwestern University professor who earlier edited the *Evanston* (Illinois) *Daily News-Index,* contributed a personalized editorial column instead of formal, unsigned editorials. In his first column in 1935, he said that readers rejected editorials because "they are like a telephone conversation in which the anonymous person at the other end of the line bawls you out, throws in an occasional compliment, threatens, hints and praises himself and then hangs up before you have a chance to answer and without disclosing his identity."

The tradition that editorials reflect the opinions of the publication and not those of the individual writer is still strong. Several papers have tried to compromise by identifying all or some of their editorial staff members. The Louisville *Courier-Journal,* for instance, listed its editorial page staff members in a two-column masthead. The nine Nieman Fellows who wrote *Your Newspaper* (Macmillan, 1947) proposed signed editorials for their ideal daily paper. Ralph McGill, editor of the *Atlanta Constitution,* contributed a daily signed article for the editorial page until it was moved to the front page to enhance its popularity. Royce Brier of the *San Francisco Chronicle* did a bylined news interpretation that appeared variously on page one and the editorial page. Dents have been made in the customary wall of newspaper editorial anonymity but it is unlikely that signed editorials will soon carry the day. Some magazines, especially among the business and trade journals, have signed comments that are more influential because of the prestige of the writer. When an outsider contributes an editorial to the *Saturday Evening Post,* the article appears with his name and, frequently, his identification.

Make-up is a problem, too

Here is what the critics usually find wrong with the make-up of editorial pages:

(1) Editorial pages are the dullest looking part of the paper.

(2) Too many editorials are buried on a catch-all page.

For several generations, front pages have been splashed with large headlines, red ink, and pictures. Some magazines have livened up their covers and non-editorial pages. But many editorial pages still look as though they might have been made up during the Civil War. They resemble gray oceans of print, unrelieved by illustrations, charts, maps, attention-getting headlines, or boldface type. An editorial page cartoon is often the sole concession to readership. Is it any wonder then that so many readers look at the cartoon and skip the editorials?

Increasingly during recent years, editors and publishers have experimented in ways to attract attention to editorial pages. This is all to the good—if the editorials are worth reading. Little need for a beauty parlor treatment for a journalistic hag!

Barry Bingham of the Louisville *Courier-Journal* remodelled that newspaper's editorial page. The traditional masthead was replaced by four lines of type, set double column in wide measure, which listed the name of the paper, its executives, and its entire staff of editorial writers. This arrangement directed readers' attention to the lead editorial. Illustrations have been used within the editorials themselves and in connection with letters to the editor. Each comment has an attractive headline, large enough to attract the readers' eyes.

Discussing his innovations, Bingham told the 1945–46 Nieman Fellows:

We have tried to make the editorial page as readable as possible, working on the theory that it helps to make it attract the eye of the reader. There used to be a theory, as you know, that a girl who was intelligent had necessarily to be plain. I think that theory is exploded. So we have tried to convert the editorial page, which has been more or less the bluestocking of the press, into a more attractive product so that readers will inadvertently turn to it and maybe read one, two or three editorials. We have done that largely by changing the format of the page. We have increased the column width so that it's five columns to the page, which makes the editorials look considerably shorter. It's much more likely to attract reader's attention. It is more like a magazine technique.

Study of newspapers of today and of only ten or twenty years ago will show that considerable concessions have been made to better typographic display. The *New York Herald Tribune*, a paper which won three F. Wayland Ayer cups for excellence in make-up, moved its masthead to an insignificant place at the bottom of the editorial page in 1952 and thus gave its lead editorial an even stronger eye-catching position. Increasing numbers of dailies and weeklies have followed the good example of the better magazines in recent years, but there is still room for more improvements.

Editorial pages, particularly those of small dailies and weeklies, have been long used as a dumping ground for the columns, advertising, and features that are crowded off other pages. Under the pressure of wartime newsprint shortages, some editors surrendered space adjoining editorials to the general news department. Several years after the close of World War II, even as large a newspaper as the Baltimore *Evening Sun* was printing news items in three columns of its editorial page. Complaining of the use of editorial pages as "a catchall for all the junk in the paper," Irving Brant, then editor of the *St. Louis Star-Times*, counseled, "The editorial page needs more room for the genuine editorial function, a little less space for the cure of constipation."

Newspapermen who write for the editorial page and who know it best bitterly condemn the make-up of many present-day pages just as they criticize content and style. Yet every honest critic can easily name many publications whose comments are carefully read, studied, and heeded—regardless of their typographical trimmings. They might be even more effective, however, if their editors were to give editorial pages a face-lifting treatment.

Years ago one writer asked, "Are editorials worth reading?" *Editor and Publisher* answered, "Yes, when they are worth reading." The reply still stands.

FOUR

Where to get ideas and information

AN EDITORIAL WRITER TAPS THE SAME SOURCES FOR IDEAS AS A RE-porter in search of a news story or feature article. However, the editorial writer uses an Alice-in-Wonderland, topsy-turvy approach in marked contrast to the reporter's. As Professor Leon N. Flint of the University of Kansas pointed out years ago, both reporter and editor depend upon conversation, observation, experience, reflection, and reading. He listed them in that order of descending importance for the reporter. The arrangement for an editorial writer, according to Professor Flint, shifted to reading as most frequently used, followed by reflection, conversation, experience, and finally observation.

What sources do editorial writers tap to get ideas and to what reference books do they turn to obtain information needed after they have picked an idea?

Sources for ideas are everywhere

Geoffrey Parsons, chief editorial writer of the *New York Herald Tribune*, declared in *Late City Edition* (Henry Holt, 1947), "Nothing human is alien to an editorial page." Editorials have been written about everything that gets into other columns of a publication—and about some things that do not get into print elsewhere. For instance, comments on the beauties of fall sunsets, the excitement over a lake's freezing over, or the blossoming of the first spring tulips are seldom found in regular news columns. Yet they are stock items for editorials in some papers.

Current news events are a primary source for material on which to write editorials. So are comic strips, beauty hints, letters to the editor, syndicated columns, and even advertisements. Anything that interests a publication's typical reader is a potential topic. The greater the number of individuals who share an interest, the greater may be the expected readership for an editorial on that topic. Naturally, writing style has something to do with how many persons read any newspaper or magazine item, be it news, feature, column, or editorial.

From time to time, surveys have been made of the subject content of editorials. Some typical ones, spaced over the decades since World War I, offer guideposts for trends. The selections were made by Professor Flint from several metropolitan newspapers and representative rural papers during the fall of 1919; by Dr. Norval Neil Luxon from 12 large city dailies during January and February, 1936; by Milton and Hortense Gabel from ten Texas dailies during September to December, 1945; by Hillier Krieghbaum from *The New York Times* and the *San Francisco Chronicle* during March, 1947; by Frank A. Clarvoe of the *San Francisco News* from 100 West Coast dailies during January and February, 1948; by Dwight E. Sargent from three dailies during January, 1952; and by James Saxon Childers of the *Atlanta Journal* for January through June, 1954.* These studies showed the following distribution by geography for the number of editorials:

---

* Those who wish to read fuller reports on these surveys may consult:

Leon Nelson Flint, *The Editorial* (D. Appleton and Company, 1920), page 58.

Norman Neil Luxon, "3,206 Newspaper Editorials Studied," *Editor and Publisher,* Vol. 69, No. 15, April 11, 1936, pages 7, 42.

Hillier Krieghbaum, "Editorial Viewpoints Alike in N.Y. and S.F." *Editor and Publisher,* Vol. 80, No. 24, June 7, 1947, pages 46, 50.

Milton and Hortense Gabel, "Texas Newspaper Opinion I," *Public Opinion Quarterly,* Vol. 10, Spring, 1946, pages 57-70.

Frank A. Clarvoe, "Editors Want to Serve Their Readers—Clarvoe," *Editor and Publisher,* Vol. 81, No. 18, April 24, 1948, pages 21, 108.

Dwight E. Sargent, "The Mid-Winter Mail Critiques," *The Masthead,* Vol. 4, No. 1, Winter, 1951-52, page 4.

James Saxon Childers, "No Ivory Tower for Editorial Writers," *I.P.I. Report,* Vol. 3, No. 6, October, 1954, pages 8-9.

DATES AND PAPERS	LOCAL	REGIONAL AND STATE	NA- TIONAL	FOR- EIGN	GENERAL OR MIS- CELLA- NEOUS
FALL 1919					
Metropolitan	8	4	75	8	5
Rural Papers	20	10	45	16	9
JAN.–FEB. 1936					
12 City Dailies	28	10	48	13	–
SEPT.–DEC. 1945					
10 Texas Dailies	11	5	31	27	26
MARCH 1947					
New York Times	26	7	32	35	–
S. F. Chronicle	13	10	40	37	–
JANUARY 1948					
100 West Coast Dailies		48.6	34.6	16.8	–
JANUARY 1952					
Dayton Daily News	24	7	38	21	10
Louisville Courier-Journal	17	33	25	14	11
Philadelphia Bulletin	23	18	18	23	18
JAN.–JUNE 1954					
Atlanta Journal	26	26	21	16	11

Much generalizing about trends for the whole press, based on these scattered returns, would rest on a shaky foundation. But we may safely conclude that at least the geographical distribution for editorial subjects has followed general reader interest at the time. During the decades covered by these surveys, interest in foreign affairs has taken hold and expanded. Consequently, the increase in attention to foreign or international material is not surprising. This shift has taken place at the expense of national affairs although that field remained a favorite for editorial comments by some editors.

Of course, variation between papers is tremendous. Some of the surveys cited showed this, and details of others do, too. For instance, Professor Luxon found that the *Cleveland Press* had 64 per cent local and 22 per cent national editorials while William Randolph Hearst's *Chicago Herald-Examiner* had only 13 per cent local and as much as 70 per cent national comment. The Gabels' survey showed that the Hearst-owned *San Antonio Light* carried not a single municipal, Texas, or regional editorial during the entire period while the *Dallas Times Herald* printed 61 municipal and 16 Texas editorials and used 73 on national and world affairs.

Professor Luxon also reported that the 3,206 editorials he studied veered most heavily (35 per cent) to political subjects. Social subjects were second with 21 per cent; economic was next with 17 per cent. This dominance of political comment in the second quarter of the Twentieth Century reflects the traditions of a century earlier when publishers and editors were concerned almost as much with political power and favors as with circulation and advertising. Present day newspaper and, less frequently, magazine executives are still fascinated by political topics. But such discussions simply drive a large group of readers away from editorials—that is, except at election time.

Raymond A. McConnell, Jr., of the *Nebraska State Journal*, Lincoln, Nebraska, who won a Pulitzer prize for getting all possible presidential candidates entered in the 1948 Nebraska primary preference election and thus establishing the voters' real choices, lamented this traditional overemphasis on politics. He wrote in *The Masthead* (Summer 1949):

Somewhere along the line the editors seem to have assumed that most men and women spend most of their time discussing politics, when actually—although this is strictly unscientific observation—they spend most of their time discussing themselves, their stomachs, their sleep, their children, their labor pains, their arthritis or their gray hairs. . . .

The ordinary problems, the ordinary sorrows, the ordinary triumphs, of ordinary living by ordinary people—or are they really ordinary?—are, in fact, the things people talk about. They are the things newspaper editorial pages must discuss if they want to be widely read.

That is sound advice for an editorial writer who wants to reach a wide audience regardless of whether he is on a metropolitan newspaper, a small town weekly, a trade publication, or a mass circulation magazine. If the editorial writer considers himself different from his publication's typical reader, then he should make a greater effort to find out what interests his audience.

Quite apart from anything the publisher, editorial writer, or make-up man may do to an editorial page, the very issues that demand discussion have become complex. During the so-called Golden Age of editorial writing, only scant, if any, attention had to be paid to such complexities as the economics of foreign trade, the gold content of the United States dollar in relation to world trade, the administrative costs of old age pensions, the sociological influence of racial prejudices, and the delicate shadings of international diplomacy in an Atomic Age. A globe with wireless, radio transmission of pictures, and a world-wide newsgathering set-up has forced almost everyone to become his brother's keeper. Keys to world differences concern economics, sociology, psychology, and political science. These can be duplicated again on the national, regional, and local levels. Out of these complexities, editorial writers must build their copy. In the modern world, to comment intelligently has thus become a mental exercise.

Editorials follow the news

Since much of the public buys newspapers and news magazines primarily for their news and feature content, it is not strange that front-page stories or featured articles provide much of the grist for editorials. Morning papers may exploit a special time advantage in that some of the events their editorial writers may wish to discuss—such as events in Europe—have taken place before the writers reported for work. Afternoon newspapers more frequently have to wait until the following day to comment on events mentioned on today's front pages. The Baltimore *Evening Sun* and the *Chicago Daily News* are among the few afternoon dailies that replate the editorial page from edition to edition to keep it as current and fresh as page one. While this approach offers readers an up-to-date comment, it may foster a tendency to print hurried, uninformed opinions that have little value except their immediacy. It is much better to be a day later and say something worth while than to rush into print with a trite editorial.

One survey of weekday editorials in *The New York Times* during a typical week showed the dominant emphasis on front page news. Of 36 editorials published Monday through Saturday, 19 dealt with news printed on the front pages. Ten editorials concerned news that appeared on page one of the issue in which they were published; eight covered front-page news of the previous day; one was based on a page-one story of two days earlier. Of the 36 editorials, 16 (or not quite half) were based on news items printed in the same edition as the editorials. Besides the 10 editorials dealing with front page stories, six discussed dispatches on inside pages. Four of these dispatches were follow stories for earlier news that had been printed on page one when the news broke. Since newspaper staff assignments for weekends force Sunday editorials into a different pattern, these were not included in the study.

Asked how recent an idea should be for an editorial, Walter Lippmann, then editor of the *New York World*, replied that it could be anywhere from two hours to 2,000 years. As a matter of record, an editorial writer with a flair for dramatizing and a wealth of background did draw enthusiastic approval from readers with a discussion of Julius Caesar's outlook on life.

Although time pressure is less acute for an editorial writer on a weekly, a trade publication, or a general magazine, lack of staff in many cases may more than offset the gain in time. Time to think, not hours filled with other duties, is needed for successful editorializing.

An editorial writer sometimes tries to hit not only "while the iron is hot" but while it is at its very hottest—that is, at the peak of popular interest.

Geoffrey Parsons of the *New York Herald Tribune* cited that paper's editorial endorsement of Wendell Willkie to illustrate how timing may be used in spectacular fashion. The *Herald Tribune* had long been friendly to Willkie but it held off its endorsement until the most effective moment. During the jockeying as the convention opened, the editors' temptation to shoot the works for Willkie was almost overpowering. But they held off. Then it became clear that the 1940 Republican convention delegates would not pick Thomas E. Dewey. In the edition of June 27, after the nominating speeches were all made, the *Herald Tribune* printed an editorial headed "Wendell Willkie for President" in three columns at the top of page one. Argued the paper: "Such timing of the man and the hour does not come often in history. We doubt if it ever comes twice to a political party." As the delegates picked up the *Herald Tribune* that morning, emotional tension was at its peak. Late that night Willkie was nominated for president. Parsons wrote later that his paper's front page editorial, thus timed, was credited with being "a considerable factor in gaining the day for Willkie."

In contrast, the *Herald Tribune* endorsed Dwight D. Eisenhower months before the Republican convention and approximately a year before the 1952 election. Here the paper was trying to channel public opinion so that the general's nomination would be inevitable.

During consideration of revisions for the Wagner labor-relations law during the spring of 1947, the *San Francisco Chronicle* devoted its entire editorial page on two consecutive days to a historical study of labor legislation and then to the paper's own recommendations for new laws. Reprints of these pages were mailed to each member of both Senate and House of Representatives. Although the same information had been available for months, it was not rounded up and printed until labor law revisions were due to come before Congress.

On election days, dozens, if not hundreds, of dailies print their recommendations on how the electorate should vote. Frequently, they even reproduce marked ballots, to make their views as clear as possible.

Although he needs to read the news as reported in his own publication, the editorial writer who depends solely upon such information eventually becomes at least intellectually inbred, if not downright sterile. Consequently, he should spend much time reading current periodicals and recent books. Although serious articles and books probably should predominate, a sense of humor also fits into an editorial writer's kit of qualifications and equipment.

One source for up-to-the-minute material that is sometimes neglected is the discarded interpretation or background articles sent out by the press associations or syndicates to which the publication subscribes. Too often these are crowded out because of lack of space and thus the information is completely fresh if adapted by the editorial writer. Not only do these articles frequently stimulate ideas for future editorials, they also supply completed research work that would take the editorial writer hours to dig up on his own time.

The same advantages apply to dailies that specialize as newspapers of reference. Among these are *The New York Times*, *New York Herald Tribune*, *Christian Science Monitor*, *Washington*

Post and Times Herald, and *St. Louis Post-Dispatch*. Sunday or weekend editions of these papers are even more fertile ground than the daily editions. One danger, however, is that some readers of the editorial writer's own publication may also have seen this source material. Thus he can not "borrow," so to speak, with too heavy a hand.

Twenty-five editorial writers at the 1947 seminar of the American Press Institute at Columbia University were asked what magazine sources they used. Here are their replies:

Time, Harper's, United States News—8 each
Business Week—7
Atlantic, Fortune, Newsweek—5 each
Life—4
New Republic, National Geographic, Reader's Digest—3 each

Dean Gordon A. Sabine of the School of Journalism, University of Oregon, questioned 23 editorial writers on Oregon's 21 daily newspapers during 1950 and found that two-thirds of them saw some non-Oregon daily regularly and all but two read a national news magazine weekly. *The New York Times* was the most popular non-state daily and *Time* lead the news magazines. These editorial writers read an average of five magazines each, two of them for entertainment, three for serious information.

Of course, editorial writers should read professional journals to learn what is going on in other shops. Of special interest is *The Masthead*, started in 1949 by the National Conference of Editorial Writers and dealing with their own special field. The weekly *Editor and Publisher* and the quarterly *Nieman Reports* are also on their "must" reading list. *The Quill*, monthly publication of Sigma Delta Chi, professional journalism fraternity, and *Journalism Quarterly*, published by the Association for Education in Journalism for teachers, from time to time contain articles that stimulate ideas and explain new techniques. The *Saturday Review* in recent years has paid special attention to journalism and some excellent discussions of editorial writing have been printed there.

Current books that an editorial writer may profitably read vary widely, depending on the background required for his job. A newspaper staff member might read the latest autobiography of a correspondent in Europe with the hope of untangling some interwoven strands of diplomacy that would help him write more informedly on international affairs. On the other hand, an editor on a trade publication for grocery-store owners might study a recent volume from the United States Department of Commerce about retail distribution problems. Specialization, which has grown up among reporters during recent years, also is reflected among members of the editorial page staff.

Always retain the human touch

People are essential to a successful editorial writer. His personal experiences often yield material upon which he can comment. One metropolitan newspaper staff writer, for instance, put real understanding into his editorials on a fuel oil shortage after the tank in his own home ran down to its last few gallons before new supplies arrived.

Conversation, as Professor Flint pointed out, is one key way in which an editorial writer may find out what other people are thinking. On his way to work, he may overhear a discussion of a proposed change in the community's school system or a bitter condemnation of the current price of head lettuce. The waitress at the counter where he buys his morning cup of coffee may complain on the smallness of tips since meal costs increased. The elevator boy in his office building may voice glowing approval of the changing length of women's skirts. Obviously, it would not be possible to shift all this chit-chat into editorial page comments. But it may start a writer thinking about a change of pace editorial for tomorrow's issue in contrast to his traditional bit on the Washington political scene or the outlook in foreign affairs.

One caution, however, is necessary. The editorial writer should be careful not to confine his conversations to his golf club associates or his luncheon companions. They generally represent the successful, conservative viewpoint, a stand that is not likely to square for long with the typical reader's outlook.

Hobbies can yield editorial ideas as well as recreation. A semiprofessional weekend hiker through the rural countryside might supply nature editorials with a ring of authenticity. A stamp collector could write with knowledge and possibly with humor on the appearance of the latest commemorative issue. An avid motorist might gather ideas for a human-interest piece while caught in a Sunday traffic jam.

Letters to the editor, one of the most popular departments on the editorial page, also indicate what appeals to readers. The intelligent editorial writer not only comments occasionally in his columns about a letter printed in adjoining space but he uses them, including those that do not get into print, as his own private public-opinion poll on what readers are thinking.

The formal editorial conference, which will be discussed in detail in Chapter Nine in connection with formation of editorial policy, may generate ideas for comment as well as supply an arena where the whole editorial page staff can wrestle with a topic.

Typical of the non-metropolitan dailies is the Raleigh (N.C.) *News and Observer*, whose operation was described by Jonathan Daniels as follows:

I suspect that our short-handed and informal approach to the editorial page applies to the great majority of newspapers throughout the United States. I supervise both the editorial and the news departments of the paper, and my two associates, the Associate Editor, who works with me on the editorial page, and our Managing Editor, are located so that we can holler at each other when any idea comes to any of us. Of course, we get together when important questions arise on a more formal basis, but generally we just talk as something pops into our minds.

How one conscientious editorial writer on a large paper gathered his facts and put them together was told in *The Masthead* (Spring, 1950) by Reed Sarratt, then on the Baltimore *Evening Sun.* He wrote:

Presumably an editorial writer brings to the assignment in hand some prior knowledge of the subject with which he is dealing. He may know all there is to know, or all he needs to know, without any research. Otherwise he has a digging job ahead. It is not enough to read a news story, then to dash off one's immediate reactions to it.

The least that the conscientious editorial writer can do is to check facts given in one newspaper against reports on the same event in other papers. That might guard against factual error, but news reports often omit facts which are essential to accurate judgment. Recourse to the material in any good newspaper library should supply much of the required information. If there still are gaps, they often may be filled at the public library. Nothing can take the place of going directly to the people who make the news, if that is possible. Facts collected in the office and from libraries sometimes take on an entirely different light after interviews with those who are dealing with the real situations involved. If time does not permit a personal visit, a telephone call may suffice.

These things an editorial writer can, and should, do in preparation for a specific assignment. If he does not have all the facts necessary for the drawing of sound conclusions, and if he hasn't verified his information, it is better that he wait a day or two to write than to rush half-baked opinion into print. Of course, the process of informing himself generally in the fields in which he regularly writes is never-ending. Everything he reads—in books, magazines, official reports—and everything he learns from whatever source become part of his background, upon which he can draw as the need arises.

At the 1952 Sigma Delta Chi convention, Robert White, associate editor of the *Mexico* (Missouri) *Ledger,* had this to say about how ideas for editorials germinate:

I believe good editorials are not written when you sit down at a desk with a typewriter on it, put your paper in it and then stare blankly into that paper and ask yourself, "Now, Bob, what am I going to write an editorial about today?"

No, good editorials, gentlemen, are written in those last few minutes before you go to sleep at night. Good editorials are written when you are driving to work in the morning. Good editorials are written when you are raking the lawn, maybe, or cutting the grass, or when your two-year-old daughter is sitting on your lap and happily putting bobby pins in your too-short hair. . . .

I think good editorials are the result of steeping yourself, day after day, every waking hour, not only with the facts that go into editorials but also that great factor that we in America are accused by all Orientals of forgetting—we the occidental world—the factor of the human angle. . . .

I think that human angle is tremendously important because I think it lies right down at the root along with accuracy and this well stocked mind, the root from which good editorials spring, the root of conviction. Conviction, to me, is the key to good editorials.

You know, it isn't true at all that all big papers don't have that. There are innumerable examples that can be cited of really great editorials which don't come from anybody reaching up on a shelf and pulling down a thick book full of fine print, picking up these very important, of course, details, and making notes on them and studying them, then writing the editorial. That kind of research is tremendously important, but don't forget the human angle.

Here are some cautions

In spite of a wide open choice of subjects on which to write, an editorial writer had better proceed with caution on some topics. With these subjects, it is wise to regard them as we would the highway signs of "Men Working—Proceed at Your Own Risk." A writer should not necessarily avoid discussing the points outlined below but he should weigh the costs carefully before he begins.

1. *Every news story does not merit editorial comment.*

Frequently editorial writers are tempted to comment on some page one story because of, as Robert Lasch, then on the *Chicago*

Sun-Times, called it, "the time-honored practice of writing an editorial on a news subject just because an editorial on that subject seemed to be called for." Most better editorial writers try to resist the temptation unless they really have something to contribute to the public understanding. As Lasch wrote in *The Masthead* (Winter, 1950), "A big news story is not an editorial unless it generates an editorial reaction of some sort." What is the use of concluding that the latest step in foreign relations may point the way to lasting peace or "may be as unavailing as all of the documents with the same objective which have gone before it"? For the same editor to take both stands in a single editorial hardly generates "an editorial reaction of some sort."

   2. *Avoid "trial by newspapers" but do not duck a fight.*

   This caution cuts both ways. Some publications rush in to convict a person in the news before any judge has rapped a court to order for the first hearing. This was especially true of many large circulation papers during the late 1940's and early 1950's. Other newspapers and magazines fear a battle so much that they hide behind this caution when an exceptional situation does require mobilizing public reaction. This applies particularly if a judge gives indications of being corrupt or if a prosecuting attorney is suspected of covering up important facts. In other words, "trial by newspapers" is to be avoided generally but a responsible editor will not hesitate to risk criticism if standing by his principles demands that he take that chance.

   3. *Beware of "Afghanistanism."*

   The dangers of "Afghanistanism" were outlined in Chapter Three. One editorial writer formulated it this way: "The strength of editorial conviction increases by the square of the distance of the topic from home." If an editorial writer's advice and conclusions are valid on foreign affairs, about which the publication's typical reader can do little, why should not comments on local and regional issues be many times more important because here at home the reader can act?

Intelligent, progressive editorial writers are fully aware of this problem and are trying to localize their editorials. For instance, one localized editorial praised at a recent National Conference of Editorial Writers meeting was a discussion of living costs that started off with figures from the local markets. It is generally agreed that almost any editorial could be given a local twist if its writer took the time to think about it. Of course, every editorial does not need this "Anti-Afghanistanism" treatment. In this age when events abroad can have such impact on Americans' lives, there is obviously a place for comments on foreign affairs without a local angle—if these are not just an escape from topics at home that might bring irate subscribers and annoyed advertisers into the office.

4. *Proceed with caution regarding the "Three R's:" Rumor, Race, and Religion.*

A generation ago few editorial writers dared to comment on rumors, race questions, or religious problems. Current staff members, however, not infrequently cross their fingers and print an editorial on any one of these subjects. Changing conditions have made some publishers and editors willing to brave the threats of pressure groups. Many times this is all to the good because necessary comments and suggestions need to be made. An editorial writer on a public service newspaper can hardly escape such topics. But it should never be forgotten that appeals to prejudices can be explosively dangerous.

Here's where to get information

Once the idea has been selected for an editorial, the hardest tasks remain to be done. They are: (1) gathering the background and (2) writing the article. A suitable idea may well be strangled either by inadequate research or by poor writing style. This section is concerned with where to obtain the necessary factual information and background.

As mentioned earlier in this chapter, sources of ideas may carry much of the needed research material. For instance, the copy of an interpretive article that comes over a press association wire or from a syndicate and is not printed in the writer's publication because of lack of space may contain all the information the editorial writer needs before starting to write. This is not usual, however, since a careful writer will make at least a fast check to confirm the essentials cited in the copy. A magazine article or a book also may carry its own factual background, again information that may require checking.

An editorial writer should learn as much as possible about the persons who handle the news, the organizations as well as individual reporters. The peculiarities of a news agency may explain why a particular item was written the way it was.

The "Big Three" in United States press associations are the Associated Press, United Press Associations, and International News Service. Among the newspapers that sell their own news dispatches, the more widely known include the *New York Daily News-Chicago Daily Tribune*, *The New York Times*, the *New York Herald Tribune*, the *Chicago Daily News*, and the *Des Moines Register* and *Tribune*. Among the syndicates that supply news items, feature articles and, in some cases, editorials are King Features, Newspaper Enterprise Association, United Feature Syndicate, Western Newspaper Union, North American Newspaper Alliance, and Bell Syndicate. Others serve special regions or groups of papers.

The "Big Three" press associations follow a news policy that will please as many of their hundreds of clients as possible: impartial reporting of the world's happenings in perspective. Clients of the large news agencies include a gamut of publications with almost all political, economic, and social attitudes. When stories from the major press associations conflict with an account sent by a special correspondent for one paper or magazine, the chances are better than nine out of ten that the press association is right. The same rule applies for most of the syndicates. Critics, of course, may cite those rare instances in which individual publishers and editors have ordered the news tailored to their prejudices. But that is certainly not common.

What columnists and news interpreters say is important, too. Their comments are evaluated by an editorial writer in the light of their past performance. He remembers, as Quincy Howe, a radio commentator, pointed out in *The News and How to Understand It* (Simon and Schuster, 1940), that "experienced reporters and news agencies are not being scooped day after day by gossip merchants, rumor artists, and purveyors of inside stuff."

Yet, despite all these possible aids, the editorial writer usually has to do his own research instead of grabbing it, cafeteria style, ready for use. What does he do? He uses all his ingenuity to obtain as rapidly and efficiently as possible every bit of information that he will need. Reference books generally and newspaper or magazine "morgues" in particular are geared for this speedy checking.

What are the standard reference books? The 25 editorial writers at a 1947 seminar of the American Press Institute listed their favorites and came up with the following:

General references:

> *World Almanac*—19
> *Who's Who in America; Congressional Record, Quarterly*, and *Directory* (the three as a group); and *Editorial Research Reports*—13 each
> *Encyclopaedia Britannica*—10
> *The Encyclopedia Americana, Facts on File*, and *World Report*—7 each
> Webster's dictionary—6

Statesman's Yearbook, and Bartlett's *Familiar Quotations—*
5 each

*Bible and Concordance—*4

*Annals of the American Academy of Political and Social
Science,* and *Information Please Almanac—*3 each

The old standbys, general (number of votes not listed):

The writer's own clippings, the newspaper library, beat reporters, public library, press agents and releases, *Dictionary of
American Biography,* local yearbooks, state code, state legislative
manual, municipal histories, *United States Official Postal Guide,
Editor and Publisher International Year Book,* N. W. Ayer's
Directory of Newspapers and Periodicals, United States Constitution, *Encyclopaedia of the Social Sciences* (and all such specialized works), Roget's *Thesaurus,* United States census reports,
Foreign Policy Reports, atlas, Stevenson's *Home Book of Verse,
Dictionary of American History, Statistical Abstract of the United States,* Hart's *The American Nation,* city directory, phone
book and *International Yearbook.*

And now a road map for references

Reference books may be classified according to what facts they
contain; this is probably the way most editorial writers think
of them. Helpful to the beginner should be this grouping, which is
far from complete:

1. GENERAL INFORMATION.

(a) *Almanacs and Yearbooks.* Many newspapermen and
magazine writers regard the *World Almanac,* published annually
by the *New York World-Telegram and Sun,* as the best single
reference book. Librarians commonly call it the "Bible of reference books." It is cheap and piles fact on fact, statistic on statistic.
This almanac certainly would make poor vacation reading but for

digging out information it is excellent. The *Information Please Almanac*, containing much the same in the way of dry facts, also has summary discussions of the year's outstanding events in fairly readable style. The *Statesman's Yearbook* includes descriptive and statistical information about the world's various governments. The *Yearbook of the United Nations* has a wealth of material on this world organization, its specialized agencies, and its member governments. The *Congressional Directory* specializes in names and facts on the United States government. Nearly all the states and many of the larger metropolises publish annual yearbooks. These are invaluable sources of information about governmental organization, historical background, and names and titles of individual office holders.

(b) *Encyclopedias.* These compendiums of knowledge try to answer all the common questions that you might ask. They range from the single-volume *Columbia Encyclopedia,* issued by the Columbia University Press, to the multi-volume *Encyclopaedia Britannica,* now printed under sponsorship of the University of Chicago. Some students prefer the 11th edition of the *Britannica* to the current one because it included signed articles and a somewhat more scholarly treatment of some topics dealing with England and Europe. The *Encyclopedia Americana, Collier's Encyclopedia,* and the *New International Encyclopedia* are widely used. Of special value in research on social questions is the specialized *Encyclopaedia of the Social Sciences,* which contains signed articles. Some of the encyclopedias publish annual supplements or yearbooks, which are extremely valuable references. Three that librarians rate high are the *Britannica Book of the Year, The American Annual,* and *Collier's Year Book.*

2. GEOGRAPHY. The definitive and authoritative reference on place names in this country is the *United States Official Postal Guide,* which lists every post office in the nation. Numerous atlases are on the market and most of them are satisfactory. Map

changes in recent turbulent years created difficulties that carto-
graphers have trouble resolving.

3. STATISTICS. In addition to the almanacs mentioned earlier,
sources for statistics include the *Statistical Abstract of the United
States*, a standard reference for information about this country;
and specialized handbooks of the United States Departments of
Agriculture, Commerce, and Labor. The Department of Labor's
Bureau of Labor Statistics compiles a cost-of-living index that is
frequently cited.

4. BIOGRAPHIES. Best single reference on the so-called "Very
Important Persons" in the country is *Who's Who in America*,
published every two years. It contains approximately 50,000 short
biographies of individuals most likely to get into the news. Variations of the "Who's Who" idea have been adapted to regions and
professions, such as *Who's Who in the East* and *Leaders in Education*. One of the most useful of these is *American Men of Science*.
Current Biographies, issued monthly and cumulated annually, offers information on a limited number of persons in a far more
readable form. These accounts are written in narrative style with
some human interest and incident illustrations included in addition to statistics and listings. State and municipal handbooks and
local city directories provide information at the community level.
The *Congressional Directory* includes biographies of members of
Congress and cabinet members. *Who's Who* is a British publication and includes only those United States citizens who have
special interest for foreign readers. For famous Americans of the
past, two references are *Who Was Who in America*, which
covers the period since 1900, and *Dictionary of American Biography*, which runs to almost as many volumes as an encyclopedia.

5. WORDS. To select the correct word, you may turn to either
a dictionary or a thesaurus. Bartlett's *Familiar Quotations* is helpful in locating the exact wording for a quoted phrase.

6. CURRENT FACTS. An editorial writer *must* have the latest information. That is one reason he studies his own and other newspapers so diligently. Even a yearbook, a few months out of date, may be obsolete as far as he is concerned. For instance, the cabinet of the country one is interested in—France, for example—may have changed, giving way to a whole new group of officials. To keep abreast of this parade of transitory information, one depends on current periodicals. *The New York Times Index*, issued fortnightly and cumulatively, tells when and where any given news item was published in that daily. To locate the most recent magazine article on a subject, one may turn to the *Readers' Guide to Periodical Literature*, the *Industrial Arts Index*, and the *Public Affairs Information Service*, all published cumulatively.

Other publications that deal particularly with current topics include *Editorial Research Reports, Facts on File, Foreign Policy Reports*, and *Public Affairs Pamphlets*. While most of them try to take up a subject as it breaks into the news, only *Facts on File* attempts to present a comprehensive roundup of all the news week by week. The *Congressional Record*, printed daily while House and Senate are meeting, is a transcript of capitol sessions and is consulted to obtain the official text of a member's remarks.

7. CURRENT BOOKS. Obviously an editorial writer can only read a few of the approximately 10,000 books published annually. Yet he should know about the contents of many of them. To do this, he may subscribe to the book review section of *The New York Times* or *New York Herald Tribune* or to the *Saturday Review*. The *Book Review Digest* provides a more tardy source for summaries of contents or for a comprehensive background of older books.

The effective editorial writer also needs an exceptional knowledge of recent American history. If he has lived through the past decade or two working on a newspaper or magazine, well and good. If he has not, he might well turn to some of the historians of the years since World War I. He might, for instance, read:

Only Yesterday (1918–1929) (Harper, 1931; also Bantam); *Since Yesterday* (1929–1939) (Harper, 1940); and *The Great Change* (1900–1950) (Harper, 1952) by Frederick Lewis Allen. The first two provide a running story of what happened between two world wars in highly readable style; the third rounds up the first half of the century.

The Age of the Great Depression (1921–1941) (Macmillan, 1948) by Dixon Wecter. A comparable account with more attention to science, culture, and the arts.

Postscript to Yesterday: America: The Last Fifty Years (1896–1946) (Random House, 1947) by Lloyd Morris. A synthesis of American life from the bicycle built for two to the atomic bomb, with two chapters (8 and 9) on newspapers and magazines.

While You Were Gone (1941–1945) (Simon and Schuster, 1946) edited by Jack Goodman. The United States of World War II years reported by various authorities.

Roosevelt and Hopkins (Harper, 1948) by Robert Sherwood. The wartime relationship of the President and his aide told by a dramatist of renown and based on Harry Hopkins' personal papers.

Inside U.S.A. (Harper, 1947; revised edition, Harper, 1951; also Bantam) by John Gunther. A combination of background, recent history, and geography for all 48 states.

The American Mind: An Interpretation of American Thought and Character Since the 1880's (1880–1950) (Yale University Press, 1950) by Henry Steele Commager. A report on the cultural progress of the United States with an especially good summation on America at the middle of the Twentieth Century in the final chapter.

The modern reference department, or "morgue" as it is called around newspaper and magazine offices, is of special service to editorial writers. Like reporters covering a news story, they can gather background on a topic with a minimum of effort by consulting the files. They simply check out the clippings on a designated subject; then they may be sure they have not only what has been published in their own paper but also, in most cases, additional facts from other publications.

So important do some editorial-page staffs consider a good "morgue" that the writers, either individually for the topics on which they specialize or collectively, maintain their own clippings. One daily that does this is the *Los Angeles Times*. K. W. Smith, editorial page editor, explained the set-up this way:

In addition to our regular morgue and reference library, we maintain a separate editorial file containing some 2,000 folders. These contain news, editorial, magazine, etc., clippings, pamphlets and other data on local, state, federal and foreign topics. Editorials of the nation's leading papers on major topics, pro and con, are also included. These folders give the writers (1) a quick review of the paper's past stand, (2) a refresher on background, and (3) such statistical or factual data as they might wish to use. As the topics in the folders sometimes overlap, frequently a half dozen folders will be used for reference in preparing an editorial.

A well-kept "future book" can tell an editorial writer what anniversaries and other set dates and events are coming up. A "future book" may be kept in conjunction with other departments of the publication or by the editorial-page staff alone.

Since World War II, more and more publications have recognized the partial validity of the criticisms that editorial writers tended to live in Ivory Towers; as a result, more and more publishers have approved plans for staff members to travel. That meant that an editorial writer, like a reporter, had a chance to observe on the spot and talk first hand to persons involved in the news. When such a trip was impossible, the editorial writer turned to the telephone—if the business office approved. In recent years, more and more bills for editorial writers' long distance telephone calls, sometimes totaling hundreds of dollars a week, have been approved.

Beside these channels, an astute editorial writer consults the reporter who was on the spot. Correspondents around the state, in Washington, or abroad are not infrequently asked to send long memos for the editorial writers' consideration. Few papers follow the horrible example of one writer who started his editorial on a series of exclusive articles in his own publication with the phrase, "If newspaper accounts are to be believed . . ."

FIVE

Building an
editorial

BUILDING AN EDITORIAL IS MUCH LIKE ANY OTHER CONSTRUCTION
work: it may be done routinely or with originality. In either case,
however, certain basic rules and traditions are followed.

In this chapter, an attempt is made to outline what many of
these are and how editorial writers use them. First is a discussion of
the common parts of an editorial and then some blueprints of how
these parts are put together.

Editorials may have four parts

The four traditional parts of an editorial are, in the order the
reader encounters them:

(1) Title.
(2) Lead or introduction.
(3) Body.
(4) Conclusion, summary, or appeal for action.

At the outset, it may be well to point out that, unlike problems
in mathematics, journalistic assignments may be handled in more
than one acceptable way. This is particularly true in editorial
writing. That one newspaper or magazine handles a certain subject
one way while a second does it differently does not mean that one
is right and the other wrong. Both ways may be satisfactory—
or both may be incorrect.

Although these four parts are essentials of most editorials, a writer may achieve the desired effect by omitting one, or even three, of the parts. Only one part is truly essential; the barest skeleton of an editorial has a body, if one will pardon the metaphor. An editorial would not be an editorial if it did not at least cite an event or occasion and present an editorial reaction. Without that, it would be an essay. That is why an editorial writer starts with his main theme, then works into the introduction and conclusion, and finally picks his title.

Here is a reconstructed case history that may tell how an editorial writer works. The event was the first public demonstration of an atomic battery which converted atomic energy directly and simply into sufficient electricity to make a transistor produce audible tones.

Brigadier General David Sarnoff, chairman of the Board of the Radio Corporation of America, who displayed the atomic battery to reporters in his offices in Radio City, New York, early in 1954, explained, "This development, though still in a pioneer stage, may prove to be the beginning of a new and basic chapter in man's efforts to utilize some of the enormous untapped energies within the nucleus of the atom for peaceful purposes and for the enrichment of human life rather than its destruction." He mentioned as a comparable earlier chapter in the history of scientific progress the production of electric current when Michael Faraday rotated a copper disk between ends of a magnet 120 years previous.

Suppose that an editorial writer decided to write on this event. What were some of the basic questions that confronted him as he sought background information? Here are a few:

(1) Just what is atomic energy? How does it differ from electrical energy, for example? (A standard text or reference book might answer this. Possibly there would be clippings from newspapers or magazines in the publication's morgue that gave such background.)

(2) Where does this news fit into the historical development of atomic energy? How does it compare with the initial nuclear chain reaction at the University of Chicago in 1942? The explosions of the first atomic and hydrogen bombs? (The Atomic Energy Commission has released numerous reports on the beginnings and progress of atomic research and all of these have been popularized in newspaper and magazine articles. This knowledge would provide a backdrop against which the newest progress could be placed.)

(3) What is the scope of the current program of the Atomic Energy Commission? (The Commission makes semi-annual reports and from time to time news stories and features round up its multitude of activities in all sections of the country. Many of these should be in the publication's morgue or in the clippings filed by the editorial writer for his own special use.)

(4) What was the importance of Michael Faraday's demonstrations? What others fall in the same top-bracket category? Did Thomas A. Edison's electric light, for instance? (Again the editorial writer would have to consult standard reference books such as popular encyclopedias and possibly text books on the history of science.)

After the writer had adequate general or basic background information, he would examine the immediate event in the light of this general knowledge. For example, he might ask himself these further questions:

(1) How did the R.C.A. scientists develop their atomic battery? For instance, what radioactive material did they use? (The press association or New York reporters' news stories or the R.C.A. press releases would provide much of this information. Otherwise questions would have to be directed to staff members with scientific training or to other experts, such as faculty members at nearby universities or local industrial research specialists.)

(2) Could this be tied in with President Eisenhower's "atoms for peace" proposals? (Clippings on the President's speech on

this subject should be in the newspaper or magazine morgue and the editorial writer would have to re-read the speech and make his own conclusions, with possibly an assist from statements in Washington follow stories.)

(3) What potentials does the atomic battery hold for the future? Is it the answer to the problem of finding a small-scale, home-model nuclear "furnace"? (Some of the answers to these questions were included in the news stories and in the R.C.A. press releases. The wise editorial writer, if possible, would check the speculations against the knowledge of the paper's science writer or that of someone with a wealth of scientific background. This "someone" might be an acquaintance of the editorial writer or he might be an expert whom the writer would telephone in the interest of greater journalistic accuracy.)

The editorial writer recalled that Dr. Karl Compton of Massachusetts Institute of Technology told the 1953 National Conference of Editorial Writers in Boston that using heat from an atomic pile to convert water into steam was extremely expensive. The R.C.A. demonstration indicated that this barrier may now be short-circuited and that it was possible, in a crude way, to convert atomic energy directly into electricity, a dream of scientists for more than half a century.

With both general and specific information assembled, the editorial writer then would decide what he wanted to comment. Here was an admitted milestone in the application of atomic energy. It might possibly rank with the great inventions of all scientific history. It might, in truth, revolutionize the ways in which we live.

An editorial writer could decide to utilize this milestone aspect as the central theme of his editorial. Then he might summarize the editorial reaction into this single sentence statement: "The R.C.A. atomic battery demonstration, which may one day rank with Michael Faraday's production of electric current, opens up a whole new vista of potential applications of atomic-induced electricity."

He would have to give up the ideas of educating his readers on many of the technological aspects of atomic energy that did not directly tie in with the atomic battery demonstration. He also would have to abandon the opportunity to discuss President Eisenhower's "atoms for peace" program. Being a competent editorial writer, he would realize that he must keep constantly on his target, even if it meant forsaking some of his previous research findings.

He then had to decide whether to mention the news event immediately or more or less to back into his topic by giving a general statement and then applying that to the atomic battery demonstration. Either would be correct. After thinking it over, he favored the news peg lead paragraph. The conclusion, he determined, should be a summary and reiteration of the possible future applications.

All this research and preliminary thinking-through done, the editorial writer would turn to his typewriter. After he had pounded out his copy, he would think about a title. Since he wanted to include the word "milestone" to attract attention and set the general tone, he hit upon "Electronic Milestone."

The final product in such a case history would somewhat resemble this one, which did appear at the time:

Title:
Label Head

Electronic Milestone

Event: News Peg.
Demonstra-
tion of first
atomic battery

A milestone in scientific history as important as Faraday's discovery 120 years ago of the current-producing potentialities of a moving wire in a magnetic field may have been reached by Radio Corporation research experts. Certainly the announcement by Board Chairman Sarnoff of RCA that small amounts of electricity have been generated by direct utilization of radiated electrons will stimulate the imagination of those who have dreamed of such an "improbable" development. It is hard to keep a checkrein on the imagination when the possible significance of the RCA feat is pondered.

Faraday's wire, cutting the lines of force of a magnetic field, became charged with a current. He could not foresee that his crude device would revolutionize the power industry. Yet it was the forerunner of the giant dynamos which today light great cities and keep the machinery of industry moving. It is possible that the crude electronic "battery" displayed by General Sarnoff in a New York demonstration may lead eventually to obsolescence of the dynamo and its replacement by a small, cheaply operated generating plant powered by atomic energy.

Production of electrical power by means of atomic energy has been possible in the past only through a wasteful and costly process utilizing conventional steam turbines and dynamos. Heat from an atomic pile was used to convert water into steam, which turned the turbine, which turned the dynamo. Dr. Karl Compton, chairman of the Massachusetts Institute of Technology, told the National Conference of Editorial Writers in Boston last fall that this roundabout method of obtaining electricity from atomic fuels made commercial use of the system "uneconomical" as long as coal and oil remained in ample supply. Only in such special applications as submarines and other ships has the expensive system been regarded as feasible now.

But a whole new vista of potential applications of atomic-induced electricity has been opened by the RCA experiments. The so-called battery used in the demonstration employed a small quantity of radioactive strontium to energize a transistorlike wafer of silicon crystals. It was explained that electrons emanating from the strontium (a waste product of atomic piles) in some way caused multitudes of electrons to flow from the wafer over attached wires, in the form of electrical current. The amount of cur-

Explanation:
Editorial's body
(a) Comparison
with Faraday's
work

(b) Significance
of atomic
battery
demonstration

Reaction:
Potentialities for
future which
make demon-
stration a real
"milestone"

rent thus created was extremely small—but the principle involved apparently could be used in developing larger power plants. It may take years of further experimentation and development to bring into being commercially practicable generators. But the long-nurtured dream of scientists for direct conversion of atomic energy into cheap and useful electrical power is no longer as fantastic as it once was.

—*Washington Evening Star*

Let us dissect some editorials that have appeared in newspapers and magazines around the United States in an attempt to find out further what writers are trying to do and how well they do it.

Since the first thing that an editorial writer does after he picks a possible topic for comment and does his research is to think about developing the subject, it might be well to start with the body of an editorial.

The body of an editorial may range from one sentence to a number of columns. It provides the explanation or reason for the editorial reaction. Sometimes these reasons are so self-evident that all the writer has to do is put the two or more events together and they generate an editorial reaction, as the Boy Scout starts a fire by rubbing two sticks together. The *New York Post's* comments on President Dwight D. Eisenhower and his press conferences, reproduced on page 144, illustrate this. In other cases, the reasons may be complex and involved, in which case the editorial may require so much space that it is split into parts run on consecutive days.

Effective editorials generally have sections that can be plainly marked as information and reaction. This may be done by giving background, explaining a complex situation, predicting the future developments as a result of some action, or generally adding up the significance of some event. Other editorials add a third element of argument or deliberation. Here the editorial writer definitely is trying to sway public opinion in the direction he thinks it should move.

Even change of pace editorials, which certainly do not rate as "heavy think stuff," present an event, a situation, a trend, an idea, a quotation, or a theory and give the editorial writer's reactions. To repeat what has been said earlier, it is this reactional aspect that distinguishes the editorial from the news story and feature article, on the one hand, and the entertaining and informative essay, on the other.

After he has planned the general approach for his editorial, the writer turns to the introductory paragraph. If it is unattractive, the reader may turn away without reading the rest. A writer has the widest possible latitude in picking a satisfactory beginning. Several common lead patterns follow:

(1) *News Peg Leads.* This is the most commonly used type and, in most cases, the most effective way to handle the introduction. The editorial writer presents in summary what he is going to discuss. It may be a speech by the President; it may be passage of a tax bill by the state legislature; it may be an automobile accident, or a football game, or a murder, or any one of a thousand news events that have been reported in recent issues of the publication.

Here are two examples of news peg leads linked to specific events, the first to a single event and the second rounding up several recent developments in allied fields:

> By a 23-to-1 vote, the Board of Aldermen has legalized prefabricated steel houses, and the Lustron porcelain-enameled house in particular, for construction in St. Louis. This vote has the effect of ratifying some progressive thinking in two quarters which have not always thought progressively in the past.
>
> —*St. Louis Post-Dispatch*

The announcements of two new synthetic drugs, one to cure seasickness and the other for alcoholism, within a few days of each other serve as a reminder of the rapid advances made in recent years in chemotherapy —the technical word for using chemicals to treat or prevent disease.

—Baltimore *Sun*

A news peg lead may also refer to a continuing situation, such as a bill that is pending before the state legislature or a housing situation that needs attention. In most instances, even these editorials are linked with some recent action in the news, something more direct or specific than the importance of the general situation. The following example, however, does not mention such a spot news development in the entire editorial, although it alludes to pending bills needing action by the state legislature:

There are before the Georgia Legislature two local bills affecting Fulton County and the City of Atlanta about which there is no dispute.

These bills concern the water supply for expanding County population.

—*Atlanta Constitution*

2. *Inverted Leads.* In variation of the news peg lead, a writer sometimes offers his editorial reactions first and then in the body of the article refers to a fairly recent event on which his opinion is based. Two examples follow:

It is often said that one of the chief satisfactions in a teacher's life is that of preparing the next generation to do a better job in the world than its predecessors. It might also be said that one of the chief interests of any parent is to make the world a better place for his children. In the larger sense, therefore, the inner motives of both teachers and parents who make up the public, are parallel. It simply happens that teachers

135

are the experts to whom the parent-public has delegated major responsibility for training tomorrow's citizens.

[The editorial then argued for wage increases for District of Columbia school teachers as provided in a bill pending in Congress.]

—Washington Post

Nowadays, as everyone knows, Government is very much big business, not only the Federal Government but state and local government too. Like any other big business, government desperately needs a supply of able administrators. Unfortunately, such men are scarce. Even the government executives who would honestly prefer to appoint an able man than a political crony don't know where to look.

[The writer went on to suggest that governments follow the example of the Commonwealth of Pennsylvania in appointing a retired military man.]

—Saturday Evening Post

A major variation of this technique is when the author of an argumentative editorial presents his general statement of the argument to be proved in the introductory paragraph. This fairly limited practice is illustrated by the *Philadelphia Inquirer* editorial entitled, "For a Better Philadelphia Government," reproduced in part on pages 148-149.

3. *Generalization Leads.* Some nature, change-of-pace, and other miscellaneous editorials have no direct tie-in with current news. They are discussions of the eternal verities of life and nature. Some editorial writers disapprove of such generalizations because they feel that the editorial reaction is too weak. However, some of the most highly regarded United States newspapers run such editorials regularly. General editorials often require an unusual type of lead. Here is the lead from an editorial on the coming of spring:

The year holds one moment, which may last for a week, when tree and bush and vine are on the breathless verge of leafing out. It is then that you stand on a hillside and look across the wooded valley and see the scarlet and orange of maple blossoms like the touch of pastel crayon across the treetops. You see the greenish yellow in the tops of the wine-glass elms, and the amber green fountain that is the big weeping willow beside the brook.

—*The New York Times*

When the editorial writer comes to the final section of his work, he almost always sums up what he had in mind. It may be a straight-away summary, a well-turned quotation, or an appeal for action. If it does not do this, it falls into what William T. Polk of the *Greensboro* (N.C.) *Daily News* called the "long weak end." Warning against this type of conclusions, he said in *The Masthead* (Winter, 1950):

This is an editorial that has an end which is long and weak, but it is an end and you know it is because it concludes with a period and is followed by another editorial head or the bottom of the page. Sometimes the end is merely a fact dragged in as an afterthought, such as, "Nearly a million men will be idle if the coal and steel strikes materialize." This is all wrong. Facts should precede conclusions. No self-respecting bee would sit down on anybody without leaving a sting behind.

Here are some examples of editorial endings:

1. *Straight-Away Summary:*

This newspaper firmly believes that $4 billion more in taxes is asked, not for debt retirement or even for budget balance, but to make spending look respectable. It is convinced that as a budget balancing or debt retirement measure, this tax lift would defeat itself.

—*Wall Street Journal*

137

2. *Quotable Ending:*

This community has enough teen age problems with-out adding teen age beer halls.

—*Milwaukee Journal*

When the taxpayer sits down with his records he should keep in mind that along with the high cost of living it is possible to enjoy the satisfaction of comparatively low cost of giving.

—*News-Times*, Forest Grove, Oregon

3. *Appeal for Action:*

It would be well, therefore, for retailers, in view of the possible emergency ahead, to give greater attention to forward buying, especially of basic lines they know they will need. This will justify manufacturers' increasing their supplies of materials and be in a better and more prompt position to meet the delivery requirements of retailers.

—Arthur I. Millin, signed editorial,
Luggage and Leather Goods

With this information at hand, it occurred to us that the P.T.A. is ideally situated to sponsor such a project for the coming year—or years—in Madison.

—*Messenger*, Madison, S.C.

To pick the right title is a demanding assignment. An effective title should attract attention and thus draw the reader toward the editorial. It should also tell what the topic is. It should be in harmony with the editorial itself so that there will be no clash in tone between the parts.

Most editorial pages have no more than two lines for headings and many of them use a single line—although this may be set over two or more columns. Thus requirements for editorial titles are far more exacting than those for most news headlines.

Although a wide range of classifications for editorial titles might be worked out, no hard and fast groups are used by a majority of writers and students of the editorial. The following types and illustrations, however, may point out what publications are doing:

1. *Label Heads*. This group includes those that use a simple phrase to give the subject of the editorial. Usually it is not a great attention-getter but it does inform the reader what the editorial discusses. Some examples are:

Spiritual Revival
—THINK
Problem of the Aged
—RICHMOND TIMES-DISPATCH
Air Travel Milestone
—LOS ANGELES TIMES
The Climate of Freedom
—SATURDAY REVIEW
Thanksgiving, U.S.A.
—NEW YORK POST
This Day and Our Heritage
—WASHINGTON EVENING STAR

2. *Summary Statements*. Here the writer attempts to compress into a single sentence the message of the entire editorial. Illustrations include:

It's the Legislature's Responsibility
—ATLANTA CONSTITUTION
Farmer and City Man
Should Know Each Other
—LOUISVILLE COURIER-JOURNAL
The Governor Defaults
—Now It's Up to the People
—DENVER POST
Parking Receipts Are Up;
Fines and Complaints Are Down
—FALMOUTH (MASS.) ENTERPRISE

3. *Striking Statements.* Editorial writers frequently try to come up with a striking statement. Examples of interest-arousing phrases and sentences are:

> *God and Lucifer*
> —BALTIMORE SUN
> *God Hates a Coward*
> —OMAHA WORLD-HERALD
> *Hurry Up and Wait*
> —WALL STREET JOURNAL
> *The Right to Talk Back*
> —CHICAGO SUN-TIMES
> *Bloomer Girl Regulators*
> —BOSTON HERALD
> *Weather Reports*
> *Via Truckdrivers*
> —WARD COUNTY INDEPENDENT, MINOT, N.D.

4. *Descriptive Phrases.* Some label headlines have a descriptive touch that adds color or flavor. They are included in this grouping. Illustrative are:

> *Hybrid Cows*
> —MINNEAPOLIS STAR
> *Magpie's Nest*
> —YACHTING
> *Angelus at Midnight*
> —NEW YORK HERALD TRIBUNE
> *The Man Who Took Mom*
> *Out of a Mother Hubbard*
> —LOUISVILLE COURIER-JOURNAL
> *Questionnaires for Preachers*
> —BOWLING GREEN (MISSOURI) TIMES

5. *Quotations.* A quotation may describe the subject better than anything the editorial writer may think up. In that case, he does well to use the quotation, either within quotation marks or not. Examples of this are:

Lest We Forget
   —COLLIER'S
"I Am The State"
   —WASHINGTON POST
"Their Finest Hour"
   —THE NEW YORK TIMES
"The Next Three Years"
   —LIFE
Batten Down the Hatches
   —POWER
The Lord Helps Those Who Help Themselves
   —LOUISVILLE COURIER-JOURNAL

6. *Parodies and Literary Allusions.* A parody on a well-known phrase or an allusion to a widely known quotation may be effective. Here are some examples:

Focusing the Far East Picture
   —SAN FRANCISCO CHRONICLE
On the Fine Art
Of Name-Calling
   —BALTIMORE SUN
Answer to the Bureaucrat's Prayer
   —NEW YORK HERALD TRIBUNE
The House Cuts Itself a Piece of Cake
   —RICHMOND TIMES-DISPATCH
What This Country Needs—
More Afghanistan Editorials
   —SIDNEY (N.Y.) RECORD-ENTERPRISE

7. *Alliterations.* Alliterations or other plays on words may lend a light touch to some editorial titles and summarize others. They certainly attract attention and amuse the reader. Some typical ones are:

Crisis in Caracas
—THE NEW YORK TIMES
Cussed and Discussed
—DENVER POST
Billion Dollar Blight
—HARTFORD (CONNECTICUT) COURANT
Highway Horrors No. 2
—TULSA (OKLAHOMA) TRIBUNE
Toward Totalitarianism
—SAN FRANCISCO EXAMINER
Those Blankety Blank Blanks
—ELMER (N.J.) TIMES
Careful Cocktail for Kansas
—ST. LOUIS POST-DISPATCH
The Lorelei Song for Lower Prices
—PRODUCT ENGINEERING

8. *Questions.* The reader's interest may be aroused by a question as a title for an editorial. This device should not be blunted by overuse. Examples include:

A New Melting Pot?
—CHRISTIAN SCIENCE MONITOR
Free Speech For What?
—WASHINGTON POST
Who Clutters Our Doorstep?
—PELLA (IOWA) CHRONICLE
Who Cares About a Soldier?
—LADIES' HOME JOURNAL
What Makes a Good Doctor Good?
—LIFE AND HEALTH
Which Came First
Kentucky or Bluegrass?
—LOUISVILLE COURIER-JOURNAL
Must Propaganda
Be The Monopoly
Of Our Leftists?
—SATURDAY EVENING POST

9. *Direct Address*. A direct appeal to the reader may be a successful approach for some editorials. For instance, here are some titles of that sort:

Vote Tomorrow
—MIAMI HERALD
Kill the Ragweed Now
—PHILADELPHIA INQUIRER
Beware of Age Categories
—LIFE
Time to Watch Public Budgets
—DES MOINES REGISTER
This Is Your Aviation Market
—AVIATION WEEK
Let's Chop Off Those Tax Dodgers
—DENVER POST
They'll Try to Light Again, Sheriff
—ATLANTA CONSTITUTION

10. *First-Person Statements*. Infrequently a publication may want to emphasize its own policy or its viewpoint by making a first person statement. Some examples are:

We Make Our Own Trouble
—CONSTRUCTION METHODS AND EQUIPMENT
We Must Be Ready to Sell
—GAS AGE
We Will Not Be Intimidated
—RICHMOND TIMES-DISPATCH
Through the Red Cross
We Plan for Emergency
—SATURDAY EVENING POST
Our Schools Are What
We Make Them
—LADIES' HOME JOURNAL

Here are some blueprints of editorials

The various parts of an editorial may be combined in any number of ways. For instance, there may be a single event with a simple editorial reaction. Or a writer may pick a series of recent happenings and try to connect them or to find a common feature in them. Again, he may pick the latest event in a complicated sequence and attempt to explain its relationship to what has gone before or what will come in the future. Or he may select an occurrence and advocate a public reaction. All these possibilities—and many more—are available to the editorial writer.

One way to learn how to write editorials is to study those that get into print in the better-edited pages around the United States. A blueprint or outline of an editorial may help us to understand how the writer built that particular article.

Here are some editorials, arranged in increasing degree of complexity, together with their blueprints:

1

Title: Label Head

The Press and the Pressure

Events: News Peg. Quotations from Associated Press dispatches

WASHINGTON, May 20 (AP)—President Eisenhower won't hold a news conference this week, White House Secretary James C. Hagerty said today.

Asked why the President was passing up the weekly session with reporters, Hagerty said Eisenhower has a long schedule of other engagements.

* * * * *

Reaction: Implied, not stated

WASHINGTON, May 20 (AP)—President Eisenhower left the White House at noon today for his usual Wednesday round of golf at Burning Tree Country Club in near-by Maryland.

—*New York Post*

2

Title: Label
Head
Event: News Peg.
Quotations from
Washington
Evening Star

The Wreckers

From a news report from our contemporary, the *Evening Star*, on the ticket line for the Toscanini concert May 25:

First arrival was . . . He is a student at American University and a Government employe.

Asked where his Government job was, he said, "State Department," with obvious embarrassment.

"This is going to be investigated," said someone in the line and everybody laughed.

Reaction:
Quotable Ending.
One sentence
conclusion

To us, and we may be very simple, this is equivalent to a soldier being made ashamed of his calling in time of a shooting war.

—Washington Post

3

Title: Descriptive phrase
Events:
News Peg.
(a) Israeli delegate's word,
"peacelessness"
(b) Campbell-MacDonald feud settlement

Reaction: Summary conclusion.
"Peacelessness" need not
be eternal

This Peaceless World

An Israeli delegate to the U.N., Aubrey S. Eban, has just coined a word to describe the state of affairs in the Middle East. It is "peacelessness." This would seem to tick off the situation just about everywhere in the world. It would be mighty discouraging if it were not for some hot news just in from Scotland, where the clans Campbell and MacDonald have patched up a 250-year old feud. The Campbell-MacDonald rift ended with a simple handshake at a veterans' reunion, which proves that "peacelessness" is not necessarily an eternal phenomenon.

—Life

145

4

Title:
Label head.

Event:
News Peg.
Georgia-Pacific
Plywood ac-
cepted by New
York Stock
Exchange

Explanation:
Editorial's body.
(a) Importance
and size
of concern

A Georgia Success Story

Georgia's small number of companies on the "Big Board" of the New York Stock Exchange (three, we believe) yesterday was increased by one when the Georgia-Pacific Plywood and Lumber Company formally was accepted by the Exchange.

Behind this appearance is a Georgia and Southern success story in the American pattern and tradition. The concern's headquarters are in Augusta and that means that this East Georgia city is the nerve center of a business which has five large plants on the Pacific Coast and eight in the South, with assets of $20,000,-000 and employees and representatives in 51 countries.

The story is one of those which, multiplied many times, best illustrates the development of this country whose factories now produce half the total supply of the world's goods.

(b) Story of
its founding

Twenty-one years ago Owen R. Cheatham, with a self-taught knowledge of the lumber business, founded the Georgia Hardwood Lumber Company in a one-room, plank office in Augusta on $12,000 borrowed capital. It is that company which today has grown into an internationally known company with the world's largest productive capacity for plywood. Cheatham, who follows a daily routine of 12 hours in his office, has a simple success formula: "Hard work, the right to produce, buy and sell in a free market, due regard for the rights of others, and an abiding faith in Divine providence."

Reaction: Sum-
mary conclusion.
Congratulations

We hail this evidence of Georgia and Southern achievement with appreciation and join in congratulations.

—Atlanta Constitution

146

5

Title: Question

Event:
News Peg.
Dr. Harris' book
appears

Explanation:
Editorial's body.
(a) Summary of
the book's
contents

(b) Possible les-
sons from
Nazis' expe-
rience

More College Graduates Than Graduate-Type Jobs?

Harvard's runner-up economist-to-the-popu-lace-at-large (the universial and prodigious Slichter is top Harvard man in this category) has done a chilly little book on the higher education. Dr. Seymour E. Harris, something of a liberal on general balance, is not at all happy about the liberal zeal to put every child in America—or almost everyone—through college, if not through graduate school.

The way Dr. Harris sees it, this drive to get everybody through college may well lead to a "frustrated intelligentsia." He figures that most people who go to college expect to get top-drawer jobs, mostly in the professions. In 1940, there were about 3,000,000 college graduates, but by 1968, under the various new drives to put people through college, there will be from 10,000,000 to 14,000,000 college graduates.

To maintain the present portion of professional jobs among college graduates, there would have to be some 5,000,000 new jobs at these aerated levels for the new A.B.'s and B.S.'s. But Dr. Harris can't see anything like this boost and he recalls that the increase from 1910 to 1940 was only some 1,800,000 professional jobs.

The problem of a vast surplus of college graduates who can't get jobs of the traditional college-graduate type is something our society has never had to cope with. But one of the most perceptive biographers of Hitler, Herr Heiden, attributed the rise of the Nazi movement to the frustrated intelligentsia type of person in post-1918 Germany. Probably nothing as ruinous as Hitlerism would develop from a state of widened education in America. And there is a way of

147

guaranteeing that widened education would be a positive good.

(c) Positive good possible in U.S.

That is simply to get away from the fallacious notion that a college diploma is a guarantee of economic status. It is false pride, after all, which makes a degree-holder ashamed to work with his hands or at the order of others.

A knowledge of Plato or the physics of atomic energy does not unfit a man for work as a postal clerk, a garage mechanic or a policeman. On the contrary, education ought to improve the citizenship of men at every level in the economic pyramid.

Reaction: Combination of summary and appeal for action

To guard against a frustrated intelligentsia, the colleges ought to educate away the misconceptions about education which feed the frustration. That is not easy, but Dr. Harris makes it clear that something of the sort will have to be tried if present universal-education schemes are followed through.

—Baltimore *Sun*

6

For a Better Philadelphia Government

Title:
Label head
Reaction:
General thesis of editorial's argument is given

Most Philadelphians, we are convinced, are dissatisfied with conditions at City Hall because they are not getting first-class, efficient municipal government.

Events:
News peg.
Recent activities that tie in

The exposures of theft, incompetence and waste in various city departments made by the Grand Jury and the Committee of Fifteen are symptomatic of an advanced stage of deterioration in city administration.

Obviously, a wholesale housecleaning and a comprehensive change-over in our system of local government are in order.

Explanation:
Editorial's body.
What needs to be done?

But just what can be done? Citizens have a right to ask that question. Critics of existing conditions have a right to furnish a constructive answer.

(a) Generalizations in answer to question

The Inquirer is sure there is an answer. There is no reason why Philadelphia cannot be rescued from its present state. There are certain things to be done. Among them is consolidation of the city and county, the granting of a new City Charter and a complete change in top personnel at City Hall.

(b) Eleven specific points in reply

We submit, in brief, the following program to make over Philadelphia:

[Then followed 11 points in the program.]

(c) More points could be added to the list

The above list, which could be amplified, shows what can be done, now, to rescue Philadelphia's city government. If conditions are not to grow worse, each of these reforms will have to be instituted. The people are going to demand them, and the Republican Organization now in control at City Hall had better recognize that fact before it is too late.

Reaction: Conclusion. Appeal for action with slogans

Good government is more than a phrase or a campaign slogan. It is something the people of this city want, something they do not now have and something they are determined to get. They can get it by means of the forward-looking program outlined above.

It must be adopted.

—Philadelphia Inquirer

Regardless of how the editorial writer does it, his chief concern always is to put his editorial together so that it will generate a reaction on the part of the reader. With originality and ingenuity, he may use practically any technique.

SIX

Editorials that

inform or explain

PIGEONHOLING EDITORIALS BY TYPES, AT BEST, INCLUDES A BIT OF blindman's buff. There is little agreement on methods for grouping the wide variety of comments that appear in newspapers and magazines or on places where a specific example belongs once a classification has been set up. Every series of categories that has been devised has its limitations. Yet some more or less artificial divisions do serve to illuminate the problem and possibilities for a versatile editor.

Among these classifications are:

By purpose: To inform, to influence, to entertain.

By form of composition: Narrative, descriptive, expository, argumentative.

By appeal: Emotional and intellectual.

By content: Political, social, economic, historical, scientific, aesthetic, humorous.

By geography of subject matter: Local, state, regional, national, international.

By source: Full-time editorial writers, other staff members who specialize in certain news coverage, free-lance contributors, syndicates, non-journalistic organizations that desire public support of their viewpoint.

For this book, the grouping by purpose was chosen. The next three chapters will discuss the three classifications of this group:

(1) Informative, (2) Argumentative, and (3) Change of Pace or Miscellaneous Editorials.

Informative editorials are supposed to inform

The editorials that we are classifying as informative have been called by a whole series of other names, among them the interpretive, the explanatory, and the expository editorial. Whatever may be the name, its chief purpose remains to inform the reader.

To the busy reader, much of the news is a fast-moving kaleidoscope in which events are constantly changing positions and apparently never falling into designated places for long. He has too many demands on his time to spend hours in a library looking up background material or talking to experts who might supply some answers. So the editorial writer attempts to do this work for him. In the informative editorial, the writer helps his readers understand the complexities of the news without trying to force his own conclusions, prejudices, and opinions. When supplying information, the editorial writer should not load the facts to grind an axe. His comments ideally should be as unbiased as the traditional, straight news story of a reporter. Admittedly, this ideal is not always attained.

A century ago, as pointed out in an earlier chapter, editors considered it their duty to tell subscribers what opinions to hold and frequently readers accepted them with only the slightest questioning. Now, many readers make up their own minds, although they appreciate help in unravelling background, perspective, and interpretation. As a result, styles in editorial writing have shifted, too. More and more writers have turned to the informative editorial, with its wealth of backdrop material against which to evaluate news events.

Dean M. Lyle Spencer of the School of Journalism, Syracuse University, some years ago stressed the importance of this type of editorial. He wrote in *Editorial Writing* (Houghton Mifflin, 1924):

The interpretive editorial offers writers their greatest opportunity for service and influence, because readers always stand ready to be informed about problems in which they are interested, but which they cannot solve. Instead of being argued with, they want to know —know what has occurred, why, and how, and what the effect is going to be on their personal lives. For this reason the editorial of interpretation ought to stand highest in the estimation of writers.

A somewhat less exalted view was expressed by the 1949–50 Nieman Fellows although they still held this type of editorial to be of considerable value. Writing in *Nieman Reports* (April, 1950), they concluded:

> There is a proper place for editorials that do not insist on taking a stand, but rather probe informatively behind or ahead of the news in a way background reporters could not safely do without dealing dangerously in opinion. There is nothing immoral about an expository editorial once in a while, and it can often be a highly useful addition to the editorial page.

John L. Hulteng, editorial writer on the *Providence Journal* who helped draft the group statement just cited, supported a much more enthusiastic evaluation of the informative or expository editorial when he wrote in *Nieman Reports* (January, 1950):

> The expository editorial seeks to probe behind the facts of news, and sometimes ahead of them. Its success rests upon the experience and skill of the editorial writer. Ideally it should develop the news from two- to three-dimensional depth. At its worst, of course, the expository editorial becomes merely a clip-and-paste filler for a dull day or a lazy typewriter.
>
> But when properly used the expository piece gives a strength and reader value to the editorial page that could not be achieved in any editorial room guided by a rigid rule that every piece must "take a stand." There are many subjects in any day's news budget that do not lend themselves to pro-con editorial comment, but which could be treated to the reader's clear profit in an expository editorial. And there are many days when the news is altogether barren of developments on which the paper could plausibly "take a stand."

What do working editors think?

An overwhelming majority of editors on 40 representative daily newspapers in all sections of the United States polled in the author's survey agreed that a conspicuous trend existed away from the opinionated editorial and toward the informative or interpretive type.

Louis LaCoss of the *St. Louis Globe-Democrat* reflected the opinions of a large group when he wrote:

Editorials today I believe tend more to the informative than the dictatorial. That is, our readers may be guided by our way of thinking but primarily they wish to be informed and then draw their own conclusions. And my experience is that the light, sometimes whimsical editorials frequently cause much more comment than the profound, two-story stuff.

Virginius Dabney, editor of the *Richmond Times-Dispatch*, put it this way:

It is hard to document this, but it seems to me that there *is* a trend toward less opinionated writing. This may not be true, but I believe there is more of a tendency to give full background treatment of subjects, and to argue one's position on its merits, rather than to make dogmatic statements in editorials which offer little in the way of facts to back them up.

F. J. Cainsway, managing editor of the *Jersey Journal*, Jersey City, N.J., the daily with editorials having the highest readership of any in the *Continuing Study of Newspaper Reading*, approved the less opinionated editorial approach "because I think the readers get the impression that you are talking directly to them and not over their heads." A. T. Burch, associate editor of the *Chicago Daily News*, said his editorial page staff aimed "to reach firm conclusions but not arrogantly." Mark F. Ethridge, publisher of the Louisville *Courier-Journal* and *Louisville Times*, pointed out, "After all, putting a few facts in does calm down dogma."

153

Conscious of the responsibilities of a daily without competition, Herbert Lewis, editor of the *St. Paul Dispatch* and *Pioneer Press*, said:

> We use on occasion "strong" editorials, but we are mindful of our position as the only newspaper in St. Paul. We therefore usually avoid the highly opinionated type of editorial, and engage in few crusades . . . We try to avoid the essay type of editorial and emphasize comment on current situations and events.

Jenkin Lloyd Jones, editor of the *Tulsa* (Oklahoma) *Tribune*, warned against informative editorials degenerating into spineless essays:

> I believe and hope that editorial writers in the future will increase their judicious objectivity without, of course, losing their punch. An editorial is, after all, opinion. If it is completely neutral it is not an editorial.

Philip H. Parrish, editor of the Portland *Oregonian* editorial page, said that while the trend on his paper was away from opinionated editorials, "when I or one of our writers, after sufficient research, is thoroughly aroused, anger is welcome."

In his book, *Freedom of Information* (Macmillan, 1949), Herbert Brucker, editor of the *Hartford* (Connecticut) *Courant*, expounded at length on the proper use of anger. He argued for an "objective" editorial policy where a newspaper staff's collective mind "will not be largely made up in advance on political issues, political candidates, economic disputes, or anything else." But he said that once the facts determined the publication's stand, it should pull no punches.

Although the informative editorial serves a need in providing background, information, and interpretation, some editors may use it to avoid a plus-and-minus stand. Just as the intense opinionation of Greeley and Dana was unsatisfactory, so informative editorials with little courage and no aggressiveness may be a weakness today. The informative editorial can contribute tremendously to the contemporary editorial page but it should not be used to dodge taking sides on important issues about which the newspaper or magazine should speak its opinions.

An amusing satire on how one Washington, D.C., newspaper might, as some critics say the press does too frequently, "sit on the fence with both ears to the ground" is given in the following "Variations on the Theme of Mary's Little Lamb" from *The Masthead* (Summer, 1950):

The Homey Touch

"Mary had a little lamb," says an Associated Press dispatch from Atlanta, Ga., which we are certain will delight all our little readers. "Its fleece," the dispatch goes on to say, "was white as snow. And everywhere that Mary went, the lamb was sure to go."

What a wonderful picture of life in America this conjures up. What a tribute to the American home. Every Mary, and every Sue and Jane and Elizabeth too, we hope, has her little lamb, in addition to her little father and her little mother and her little vine-covered cottage beside the dreamy little Potomac.

What a picture of purity. "Its fleece was white as snow." Not a dab of dirt, not a speck of soot, not a stain or spot to sully the pristine whiteness of its coat. A perfect companion for Mary, herself as pure. It is sometimes said that the dog is man's best friend, but for a small female child we do not believe you can beat a lamb. Dogs get dirty sometimes. Mothers are even better for small female children than lambs, though, and they sometimes get dirty, so the issue is a slightly mixed one. Anyhow, we are for the American Home, dirty or not.

To get out of the American Home and back to Mary's lamb, note that it was sure to go everywhere Mary went. What companionship. How monotonous. Summing it all up, we would say that the sweetness, the purity and the companionship of Mary and her lamb represent all that is best in this great nation of ours. To some, this little story from Atlanta, Ga., may seem trivial. But to trivial people it won't, you betcha. Every Senator and every

155

Representative and every President himself will do well to pause and reflect on the story of Mary and her lamb. It is their responsibility to see that Mary keeps her lamb and vice versa. That is what Democracy is for.

Types of informative editorials are many

Successful informative editorials answer questions that an intelligent reader has about some event in the news. For instance, one that supplies the historical setting for a current happening answers such questions as "What's been happening?" or "What's the background on this?" An editorial breaking down the issues attempts to reply to the query "What's this all about?" whereas one predicting what may happen in the light of certain developments answers "What does this mean?" In fact, all the informative editorials may be visualized this way: answering questions for readers.

Repetitions in history or historical parallels fascinate editorial writers just as they do many other students. Does the past hold a pattern for the present and the future? Not as frequently as many would have you believe, perhaps, but nevertheless often enough to give value to the historical-setting editorial that may help readers understand a current event better.

Here is an example of how an editorial writer dug up information about the Egyptian royal family that would interest the typical reader when the republic was proclaimed:

Dynasty and Old Tradition Pass in Egypt

Surprisingly little interest and concern seem to have been manifested in Egypt over the proclamation of a republic. FAROUK, the exiled former king, his infant son who was to have become King FUAD II, and the long history of bloody reigns which preceded them—these are politically unimportant today. What is important is the power and competence of General MOHAMED NAGUIB, who seized power just a year ago and who is now the first president of the new Republic of Egypt.

Thus there ends, temporarily at least, the dynasty

which began with that able, extraordinary and fero-
cious man, MOHAMED ALI, great-grandfather of FA-
ROUK. MOHAMED was the ambitious young Albanian
soldier who rose to power in battle with the Turks,
whom he ultimately expelled from Egypt. His daughter
married a French officer, brought by MOHAMED ALI to
reform the Egyptian Army. The Frenchman became a
Mohammedan, took an Arab name and bequeathed to
his descendants a part at least of the striking beauty
which made the sisters of FAROUK famous for their good
looks.

MOHAMED ALI possessed a ruthless efficiency that
made him complete master of Egypt under a gentle old
Sultan. He killed rivals without compunction, over-
taxed and oppressed the helpless peasant, expropri-
ated land for his own, and at the same time restored
order to the ravaged country, improved the educational
system, courted the warlike Bedouin tribes, founded
factories and fostered the cultivation of cotton.

The Great Powers watched the rise of MOHAMED ALI
with qualified approval. When he sought to intervene
to defeat the war of Greek independence and attacked
Syria, he was made to understand that continuing
power depended on his willingness to confine his ambi-
tions to Egypt. In return, Egyptian rule was made he-
reditary in his family, and his nephews, sons and
grandsons have reigned since. The unlucky FAROUK
was ninth in a line of rulers, none of whom inherited
the force and ruthlessness of their ancestor.

FAROUK'S grandfather ISMAIL brought the British
actively into Egypt by selling the controlling share of
Suez Canal stock to the British government. Misman-
agement and extravagance had brought ISMAIL'S government close to ruin, and the necessary reorganiza-
tion permitted the British to intervene actively as advisers, a role they maintained until FAROUK came to the
throne.

FAROUK himself was looked upon for a time as a
worthy successor to the great MOHAMED. Grimly tu-
tored from babyhood in English, French, Arabic, history, geography, chemistry, physics, mathematics, gym-

nastics, fencing, boxing and tennis, his education was supervised by British advisers, and at 15 he was taken to England. A handsome boy in his teens, he was described in the popular press as "the most perfectly brought-up boy in the world."

The perfect upbringing did not succeed in making FAROUK the sort of king Egypt badly needed. The condition of the peasants did not improve, poverty and discontent remained widespread and FAROUK'S self-indulgence became daily more obvious to a population exposed on every hand to the pressures of civilization and the mutterings of revolt. The ancient land of Egypt has not, after all, had so much for which to thank its kings. The world may hope that a new rule and a modernized form of government will bring peace and a measure of stability to a people who have had little of either.

—Louisville *Courier-Journal*

Original treatment is possible with almost every editorial subject. Historical backgrounding, although it would seem to cry out for conventionality, is no exception. Consider, for example, William A. Korns' "What's Justice?" from the *New Orleans Item*:

What's Justice?

Question: Does crime pay?

Answer: It all depends.

Proof: The case of Frank Baggott.

Let's look at the record.

Feb. 6, 1946: Fire Department Captain Baggott charged with attempting to vote more than once in the January 22nd primary election, and with supplying false information to election officials.

Dec. 9, 1946: Tried and found guilty.

March 10, 1947: Sentenced to eight months in prison, $300 fine, and loss of right to hold public employment for four years.

April 29, 1947: Conviction appealed to the state Supreme Court.

Dec. 15, 1947: Case remanded for new sentence minus job ineligibility provision, which was ruled to be unconstitutional.

Jan. 12, 1948: Rehearing denied by Supreme Court; sentence upheld.

March 9, 1948: Granted 45-day reprieve by Governor Davis, in order to enter plea for pardon.

April 23, 1948: Pardon denied. Entered Parish Prison to begin sentence.

May 12, 1948: Granted 90-day reprieve by Governor Long and released from prison after 18 days served.

August 10, 1948: Granted another 90-day reprieve by Governor Long.

Oct. 14, 1948: Filed another appeal for a pardon.

Dec. 17, 1948: Pardon recommended by State Pardon Board to the Governor, who on May 18, 1948, said of the convicted man, "He wasn't any more guilty than others who were not convicted."

Summary: Almost three years of litigation, but a total penalty of 18 days for vote fraud (drunks get 30 days).

Conclusion: Does crime pay? It all depends—on who you are.

—New Orleans Item

When this editorial was reprinted in *The Masthead* (Spring, 1949), Frank Hawkins of the *Pittsburgh* (Pennsylvania) *Post-Gazette*, in a critique, called it " a very sharp piece" that left him "more envious than critical." Then he added:

Unlike 999 out of 1,000 editorials, it has received unique, and I think effective, treatment.

To have cited the court record in any form other than that employed by Mr. Korns could easily have resulted in a tedious muddle. As it is, the record is set forth in succinct chronology. And the quick, simple introduction and conclusion are all the framework the piece requires.

In brief, as Mr. Korns has been, he has wrapped up a rather involved case with a minimum of rhetoric and confusion and has made

159

his point with telling effect. What more can you ask of an editorial than that?

One assignment that eventually comes to every editorial writer is to comment when a prominent citizen dies. Often it is someone who has had a high standing in the community or in his profession; in such cases, the editorial reaction simply expresses the publication's condolences and extends sympathy. In other cases, the editorial writer attempts the more difficult task of realistically appraising the individual's place in history or, at least, in his own community.

Barry Bingham of the Louisville *Courier-Journal* warned that the writer of an obituary editorial, conscious of the adage, "Of the dead let no evil be spoken," should also shun "the high-flown flattery of the old-time country funeral oration." To illustrate how full of verbal booby-traps such editorials may be, Bingham recalled how one self-made community leader at the time of his death was praised for his "homespun virtues" only to have his widow voice rage and indignation. She felt that "homespun" reflected on her social position.

When its founder and long-time editor died in December, 1951, *The New Yorker* writer captured the poignant feelings of its staff members. The editorial ranks with William Allen White's tribute to his daughter, Mary, as one of the truly great obituary comments. It may be read in the December 15, 1951, issue of *The New Yorker*.

Rare indeed are the times that an editorial writer says out loud, with real candor, anything derogatory that many have felt about the dead. One such editorial that has become a classic is William Allen White's single paragraph summing up the career of Frank Munsey, whose consolidations had thrown thousands of newspapermen out of work. Here it is:

> Frank Munsey, the great publisher, is dead. Frank Munsey contributed to the journalism of his day the great talent of a meat packer, the morals of a money

changer and the manners of an undertaker. He and his kind have about succeeded in transforming a once great profession into an eight per-cent security. May he rest in trust!

—*Emporia Gazette*

The rise of the United States as a major world power and the resultant interest in what is going on everywhere have brought to the forefront an editorial type that was almost unknown several generations ago. This is the geographical editorial which answers the question, "Where is it anyway and why is it important?" Writers may serve an especially useful purpose through these pieces by catching the first news break in a story that will mount in importance and then providing the background of geography on which readers may better follow developments. Some editors have made it a custom to print maps and diagrams to supplement their words.

An example of this sort of anticipatory geographical editorial was printed by the *New York Herald Tribune* when difficulties between Hyderabad and India started appearing as front page news. This editorial was published well in advance of the eventual occupation of Hyderabad and thus readers were informed before the climactic event took place:

India and Hyderabad

The princely state of Hyderabad lies in the heart of the Dominion of India. Because of its position the refusal of the Nizam of Hyderabad to accede to the dominion creates an exceedingly difficult situation for Indian officials. They have problems similar to those American leaders would face if several large states in the center of the Mississippi Valley suddenly became independent of the United States. There also are various complicating factors, among them being these: Hyderabad is the only princely state of any consequence on the Indian peninsula that has not become part of India or Pakistan. The Nizam of Hyderabad and his officials are Moslems while most of the people of his state are Hindus. There has been little or no effort under the Nizam's rule to develop modern forms of government. The economy of Hyderabad still is semifeudal.

These facts are among the causes of the extreme irritation shown by officials of India in connection with Hyderabad and behind the vigor of their statements on the subject. Premier Jawaharlal Nehru undoubtedly believed that he had sufficient provocation when he declared, after saying he did not expect war, that "if and when necessary we will commence military operations." Despite the provocation, however, American admirers of the Premier will hope that every effort is made to settle the dispute without further fighting on the Indian peninsula. This should be possible, despite the Nizam's recalcitrance, as the geographical position of Hyderabad gives India a great advantage in its quarrel with the Nizam and his medieval ideas. Because of this advantage Mr. Nehru and his associates should be able to work out a solution satisfactory to the dominion without resort to arms and without creating renewed rioting by Hindus and Moslems in India, Pakistan and Hyderabad.

—*New York Herald Tribune*

The "issues" editorial is common

Undoubtedly editorials that seek to answer the general question, "What's this all about?" are the most common of all informative comments. Readers always want to know "the score," the issues behind news events. These issues are not always clear in straight news stories. Even the interpretive, background feature articles sometimes fall short. This information, however, should be printed on the editorial pages. Readers expect this.

Sometimes a writer will simply identify the forces involved in a situation so that readers may be in a better—more informed, that is—position to make up their own minds. Or he may try to explain why something happened or to predict what he believes will occur in the future. Or he may be developing a whole broad philosophy as suggested by some contemporary event in the news. Always the editorial writer holds back much of his own publication's opinions; at times, he may give the reader a gentle nudge in one direction. He depends primarily upon the weight of the facts rather than the force of his arguments.

In the following editorial, *The New York Times'* writer gives the background, statistically and historically. It is more complex than either the historical or geographical editorials cited earlier and is known in some offices as a "survey" editorial. Sometimes this type of editorial may be among the longer of those published in the paper although the sample is relatively short. Here is *The Times* editorial:

A Crippling Strike

Since July 3 New York's construction industry has been in the grip of a strange and increasingly serious strike that has affected—in whole or in part—$600,-000,000 in public and private projects and brought unemployment to 100,000 building trades workers. But the curious thing about this tie-up is that the construction industry has no quarrel with anyone, and neither does any of the building trades unions.

On the record the adversaries are Local 282 of the International Brotherhood of Teamsters, A.F.L., representing (ostensibly representing, that is) 1,800 truck drivers, and a group of sand, gravel and ready-mixed concrete companies. However, the record does not begin to tell the whole story. Behind the strike is a long history of internal union bickering, largely aimed at removing the local president, John J. O'Rourke, from his precarious post. More accurately, then, the walkout should be called a strike against the union leadership, with the construction industry, thousands of workers and potentially thousands more New Yorkers caught unhappily in the middle.

163

Earlier this week the Mayor's special three-man mediation committee in the dispute told him that its efforts to find a peace formula had been blocked by the frank admission of officers of the striking union that they were "without power or authority to negotiate or to recommend acceptance of any proposals." Under the circumstances it is no wonder that the employers informed the committee that it would be "folly to sit down with a union committee that has no power to bargain and agree." The Mayor thereupon urged the strikers to give their negotiators that power, but up to the moment the request has not been granted.

The strike was precipitated when, contrary to recommendations of union leaders, the local's rank and file rejected a company offer for a wage rise of 30 cents an hour and other benefits that would bring the total increase to $3 a day. But without going into the merits of the dispute—for worthy as they may be, they are clearly of secondary importance at this time—the main concern should to be to convince the strikers that they are doing a vast disservice to others and to themselves by prolonging the stoppage.

Perhaps the Mayor's committee will be able to drive home that point—among others—when it meets at City Hall today with employers and representatives of one group of drivers. We certainly hope so, and so, we are sure, do a lot of other New Yorkers.

—The New York Times

Norman Cousins of the *Saturday Review* used a personal experience to discuss the philosophical question of the importance of headlines and news leads in the following illustration. Use of the first person, as in the following editorial, is not common on newspapers but is found more frequently in magazines.

History Is Made by Headlines

It was during the question period following a lecture on the explosive problems of Southeast Asia. A gentleman in the audience stood up and was recognized.

"Does the speaker believe that war is likely in the near future?" he asked.

The speaker said he had no way of knowing, exactly, but he felt that no one ought to rule out the possibility. He proceeded to summarize two dozen factors that might have a bearing on the question. On the negative side, he reviewed the unraveling fabric of world peace during the past few years and said that, obviously, there was only so much fabric to go around. He also spoke about the danger that incidents could get out of control. On the positive side, he outlined the various factors which offered the basis for legitimate hope, especially the intangibles. Speaking for himself, he said he was hoping for the best but believed that this was a field in which no man could claim expertness. Having said this, he tossed the question back to his audience for their own guesses.

The next morning the local newspaper published a prominent account of the talk under this headline:

SAYS WAR IS
LIKELY SOON

I had been present the previous evening. I suppose there were two or three sentences in the speaker's reply which might have furnished the basis for the particular headline and for the emphasis given in the news account. But it was at least equally true that the basis for a flatly opposite headline could have been found. In either case, the dominant impression that would be created would have been wrong.

In any event, the headline and the news lead were based on some remarks during the question period and not on the main talk itself. That talk, to repeat, was concerned with an analysis of Southeast Asia today. The seven hundred people who heard the lecture probably came away with some idea of the complexities involved in any balanced appraisal of that part of the world. But perhaps fifty times as many people who saw the newspaper account read nothing about Asia but a lot about the imminence of war and had another reason for starting the day with jitters.

The purpose of this editorial is not to complain about one poor headline or news lead in a single newspaper. This incident is used merely as an illustration by way of raising some fairly fundamental questions. Newspapers are basic and important not only as the means of satisfying the popular curiosity about what is happening, but as the means of supplying information essential to the making of decisions. These decisions, whether with respect to our individual lives or the life of the American community depend on our understanding of the facts before us. The climate of public opinion is inevitably shaped in large part by the mechanism of communications—newspaper, radio, television, magazine, book, or whatever. History is made not only by what happens, but by what people think has happened.

Hence our questions. Is there no danger in headlines or news leads that emphasize the startling half-truth? Is there no direct connection between accuracy of information and accuracy of opinion? Does it make absolutely no difference if the controversial or negative aspects of important events blot other major elements involved in those situations? At what point does misplaced emphasis become a real hazard?

These questions are addressed in all good faith to the nation's editors and publishers. There is no intention here to condemn out of hand. Newspapers are a business—and a highly competitive business at that. The front page is the display case. Because of this, many individual editors, no matter how they themselves may deplore the negative emphasis of their headlines and news leads, feel that the matter is largely out of their hands. This makes it all the more necessary and urgent for the American Society of Newspaper Editors or American Newspaper Publishers Association, as groups, to consider these questions from the standpoint of the national interest. It is precisely because their function in the life of the nation is a major one that these questions cannot be viewed as impertinent or marginal.

In the past few years we have made a point of discussing this problem with dozens of people who have figured in the news. Almost without exception, they were disturbed by the news handling of events in which they had a direct part. Invariably, they said they had made a conscientious effort in the preparation of a talk to present a balanced and responsible view. Yet the news angling often gave a turn to the event or speech that defeated the very purpose of the speakers.

Obviously, there is no easy answer. One thing, however, might be helpful, and we offer this for exploration and discussion. The person making the speech or issuing the statement ought to be entitled to have published verbatim his own summary paragraph of perhaps seventy-five or 100 words containing his main ideas. This highlight paragraph might be featured as part of the regular news account of the talk. The newspapers could perform an additional service by indicating how interested readers might obtain the full text. In fact, it is possible that a newspaper might develop good will among its readers by supplying such full texts upon request. Admittedly, there isn't enough space in a daily newspaper to publish full texts. But the newspaper could supplement its regular coverage with such a separate service.

In any event, it might be useful for the newspapers themselves to undertake a scientific survey of the effects on public opinion of headlines and news angling. It might be useful, too, to look into specific cases in which members of Congress or Government officials have spoken or acted on the basis of spot headline news rather than the full story. One such instance comes to mind. Two weeks ago the State Department issued a new statement of policy on its book and library program overseas. That statement was carefully worded and attempted to state the basic principles governing the acquisition and retention of books. It tried to deal with the complexities of the library program. Yet one sentence from the statement was featured in the news lead of one of the wire services to make it appear that the State Department had gone "soft on Red writers." A number of headlines emphasized this erroneous, out-of-context reference. Within minutes Congressmen were publicly denouncing the statement, though admittedly they had not read it in full. Public investigations were ordered and the library program was again in jeopardy.

The newspaper editor will naturally point out that he is not his Congressman's keeper. Even so, the news does not end with the headline. Things happen. The men who operate our communications industries recognize this when they go to considerable effort and expense in calling attention to their influence with the public. The significance of this influence, however, should be measured not only in terms of advertising power but of the national welfare.   —N.C.

—Saturday Review

A somewhat different problem confronts the editorial writer when two opposing viewpoints are competing for public support. He may want simply to make both sides clear to the readers. That is an informative editorial. Or he may want to throw the entire weight his publication has in favor of one side. That is an argumentative editorial, which we will take up later.

In the following discussion of farm programs, the *Christian Science Monitor* attempted to pierce the political fog surrounding various proposals so that the readers might make up their own minds:

Farm Programs—Pared of Politics

It may some day be known as the battle of Des Moines.

Both parties are making this city in the heart of the farm belt a broadcasting center for appeals to the farm vote. And both parties by now are so deeply committed to the idea of supporting agriculture and so visibly marked with records of wielding the idea to get votes that the current duel, before it is over, is likely to look much like shadowboxing.

What is the average citizen to think—the average American who probably doesn't own a farm but has a big stake in the farmer?

We have asked ourselves that question, too. Here, for what it is worth, is our answer:

The economic and physical ("natural") factors which especially affect agriculture being as they are, there probably needs to be some form of insurance, some national sharing of the risks, to protect the farmer. Farming in the United States of 1949, it must be remembered, is no longer the dominant industry in a rural society. It is an age-old, individualistic way of life which survives (because it is utterly indispensable) in a highly organized, mass-production age.

The political factors—the plain fact that the farmer is potent at the polls, although vulnerable in the market place—being as they are, there isn't much doubt that farm stabilization is going to continue.

The issues, then, boil down realistically to these: (1) At what level should all of the nation prop up one sector of the nation economically? (2) At whatever level, how best can the job be done?

To our way of thinking, tax-financed supports should be gauged above the calamity level, but below an altitude that would subsidize inefficient farming and encourage "marginal" farmers to hang on. In this respect, some of Secretary Brannan's recent utterances—although not the essence of his plan—seem more political than sound.

For farmers who wish to and can "insure" themselves at nearer a level of prosperity than of mere survival, might there not be self-financing methods which could be superimposed upon the tax-supported minimum? Here a so-called "Grass Roots Plan," evolved in 1945–46 among dirt-farmer circles in the very center of the corn and wheat country, might reward wider study and discussion.

As to how to do the basic job—that is hard to answer

briefly or conclusively. A plan which would underwrite farm survival but which does not add artificial high prices to high taxes seems better than one which would not. A plan which would clear outlets for surpluses by the old, reliable process of letting prices fall to where demand meets supply looks better than one which would not.

For these reasons and some others we are impelled to keep an open and receptive mind toward the essential approaches (not the political trimmings) of the Brannan plan.

On the side of the Aiken provisions of the Hope-Aiken Act (a Republican-sponsored measure) it should be said that all of its possibilities are not yet understood, nor has any of it had time for a fair trial.

At any rate, if the listener can pare down the current polemics to just these two questions and search for his own answers, he will find more light than if he gets lost in doctrinaire arguments which set city against county and business against agriculture. That's our view, anyway.

—Christian Science Monitor

In still other circumstances, editorial writers attempt to present reactions and explanations. After Dr. Robert M. Hutchins, then chancellor of the University of Chicago, appeared before an early session of the National Conference of Editorial Writers, a Louisville *Courier-Journal* editorial writer tried this light-touch comment, demonstrating that even an informative editorial need not always be dead-pan:

Professor Bites Journalist: Neither Party Poisoned

CHANCELLOR ROBERT M. HUTCHINS of the University of Chicago administered a big dose of medicine to the press last week. The occasion was the meeting of the National Conference of Editorial Writers in Louisville. And his audience swallowed the dose without undue outcry, if they did not exactly lick the spoon. As a group they displayed a highly healthy attitude to criticism. They listened to their attacker with respect, reserving the right to disagree heartily with some of his conclusions, but enjoying such a demonstration of that freedom of expression by which they as American journalists live.

This response was a curious and interesting thing. For Dr. HUTCHINS has charged the press with "exhibiting neurotic symptoms" every time it is criticized. He had built up his accusation with quotations from many newspaper editorials dealing with the Report of the Commission on Freedom of the Press, a document he and a group of eminent non-journalists had issued. Some of these comments were definitely neurotic. They justified the HUTCHINS charge that newspapers like to dish out criticism every day of the year, but can't take it when the slightest adverse comment comes their way.

Why did the Louisville gathering so completely avoid this cry-baby attitude? One answer is that these were editorial writers, not publishers. They had met for mutual and earnest discussion of the problems of their craft, not to drink together and scratch each other's backs. Even the barbed words of Dr. HUTCHINS were no sharper than some of the comments these men had been slinging at each other in their private seminars. There was nobody in this crowd who was prepared to make a noise like a publisher, drape himself in the First Amendment, and proclaim that all criticism of the press is subversive and disgraceful. All publishers do not behave that way, but there are some exceedingly prominent ones who do, with monotonous regularity.

Another answer may lie in the professional admiration which these newspaper men felt for the competence of Dr. HUTCHINS' presentation. His Louisville speech flashed with conspicuous virtues which his Report on the Freedom of the Press lacked. It was sharp and witty, it cited specific instances of newspaper dereliction, it left no doubt at any point about what it meant. The report, on the other hand, was dull and turgid in its expression. That was the main fault this newspaper found with it when it first appeared. We applauded the idea of examination by a lay group, arguing that the press had done a poor job of self-criticism. We praised the "dignity and seriousness" of the report, and the high purpose of the Commission members. But we deplored the fogginess and confusion of the document.

Chancellor HUTCHINS may now accuse editorial writers of schizophrenia. How can some of the same men who maligned and even misquoted his report, he may ask, listen to his acid rebuke with what appeared to be pleasure? On the other hand, the journalists may ask a question about BOB HUTCHINS. How could the man who wrote the plodding and uninspired Report on Freedom of the Press be the same fellow who wrote and delivered so brilliant a speech in Louisville?

Seriously, the editorial writers liked HUTCHINS' high view of their calling. They responded to his challenge that they must be teachers, and good teachers, not merely entertainers or "the hired hands and voices of men who happen to have enough money to own newspapers." Many of them would stand him down on individual points of method, but they share with him a sense of mission in their work. Dr. HUTCHINS, whose family have been missionaries and teachers, found the same sort of fervor in an audience of editorial writers.

—Louisville *Courier-Journal*

Readers, always anxious to learn what may happen next, expect editorial writers to predict what is to come. Some events cast unmistakable shadows before them; others have to be brought into better focus before the future takes on a crystal-ball clarity. In either case, editorial writers should have the time and informational facilities for presenting informed predictions. If they do, their crystal-ball editorials will contribute to the readers' understanding and they will have performed a useful function. This is especially true in the business or trade journal field where the recommendations may have more influence than in other publications. Here is an example from *Power:*

Batten Down the Hatches!

When the barometer fell and the wind rose, sea-wise sailing-ship masters sang out the warning cry, "Batten down the hatches." In the minds of most of us it's come to sum up the many steps taken to make a ship ready for strains and stresses ahead—shortened sail, extra rigging and cargo lashings, manned pumps, a spare hand on the wheel.

It's a good watchword for us today. Like the ship's master, we don't know what kind of blow to expect, what strains we'll have to endure. But we do know our nation and our industry is entering a period of stress. It's time to put our plants and their crews in fighting trim, ready for anything the winds may bring. Here are some points to check:

Bigger Loads. Demand on central stations and industrial power plants is sure to grow as we swing into accelerated production for Korea and after. The first brunt of this must be borne by existing plants. A blueprint doesn't make steam or kilowatt hours. Is your plant ready?

Take a look around now, while you've still got time. Look for weak links that may pull down the output of the entire plant—an inadequate draft system that cuts boiler capacity, poor generator cooling that keeps you from getting full rating, etc. Usually a small change will make the difference, quickly and with modest expenditure of materials and money. Now, when the needed equipment is still readily available, is the time to do something about it.

Manpower. Unemployment is at a relatively low level. There just isn't the manpower reservoir to meet big expansions in war production and absorb losses to the armed forces. You're going to lose some men, have a tough time finding replacements.

Start now to figure how you can swing the job with

fewer men. Plan the training that will fit inexperienced men to step into more responsible jobs when the inevitable losses occur.

Fuels. Right now, and for the immediate future, you should be able to get the fuel you need. It's a sure bet though, if the crisis widens and deepens, that fuel supplies will get tight. As a result of the past war, and unsettled conditions since, many plants are ready to burn more than one type of fuel. In the times ahead, such fuel versatility will pay even bigger dividends. If you're not geared to switch fuels, get going while the job can be done without the headaches of an emergency conversion.

And when it comes to fuels, don't forget that here's one case where "hoarding" is both wise and patriotic. When fuels are readily available, stock them against the future. This irons out seasonal differences in production, relieves the producers' storage problem, cuts the peak load on transportation facilities and gives you mighty good insurance against spot shortages that may develop.

These are just a few general, but practical, suggestions. You know your own situation better than anyone else. If to this knowledge you add a full and sure realization that emergencies will certainly arise as we move farther down the road to a war economy, you'll come up with a concrete program for "battening down the hatches" in your own plant. Remember, there's nothing tougher than shortening sail after the gale's hit.

—Power

The military "well done" upon successful completion of an assignment has its counterpart on the editorial page. Worth-while projects in a community deserve public recognition and editors generally go out of their way to pass out compliments. Many workers in local affairs count as part of their reward a publication's editorial commendations on their work. The same applies to individuals who have done their regular jobs well and are retiring or who have been picked for new and more important responsibilities. We might well christen these "well done" editorials.

Illustrative of this type is the following editorial upon the retirement of the librarian at Atlanta's Carnegie Library:

Thanks for a Job Well Done

Atlanta owes a great debt to Miss Fanny D. Hinton, Librarian of the Carnegie Library, who is retiring from her position after 32 years of service.

Miss Hinton has had much to do with laying the foundations for the Library's expansion program presently under way which will make it possible to provide service in keeping with the needs of the rapidly growing metropolitan area.

Although the full story of Miss Hinton's contribution cannot be told in facts and figures, it is well to note that in the past ten years three branch libraries have been added to the system and a fourth one will be established soon. A bookmobile has been placed in operation to provide service to rural areas of the county.

The Library's 1939 budget was $130,000. This year it is $340,000. As Miss Hinton pointed out, however, this seemingly huge increase is more apparent than real, due to the shrinking purchasing power of the dollar.

Perhaps the most significant indication that the Library, under her capable direction, is keeping pace with the city's progress was Miss Hinton's report that the book collection had increased from 210,000 volumes in 1939 to 330,000 at present.

These advances, representing a few of those that have marked Miss Hinton's tenure, certainly are rooted in the Librarian's own vision and energy. She has had, of course, the cooperation of the Board of Trustees because the Board has complete faith in her ability and foresight.

All Atlantans are deeply appreciative of a job well done. Miss Hinton will retire with their heartfelt thanks.

—Atlanta Constitution

One field where such "well done" editorial recognition has a business value as well as a pat-on-the-back aspect is in those publications directed toward employees and dealers by large business organizations. Frequently it is possible here to present a "message" that will have a dollars and cents application of value to both the readers and the concern. Such an editorial was the following by John Earl Davis, editor of *Shell Progress*, which appeared with an illustration of one of the individuals written about:

People Like You

Once in a while we like to round up a few of the many pleasant things we keep hearing about Shell dealers from here and there, all over the country: how they get themselves liked and respected in their communities—and even by casual transients.

There's Earl Fuller, in Schenectady, N.Y. Earl's Fuller-up Shell station (quoting the story about him in the local paper) "is at the foot of Broadway hill, opposite the former 'Toomey House,' long a landmark at the corner of Broadway and Grand Street."

A Schenectady boy had suffered a back injury while swimming, and had been bed-ridden for a year and a half. He needed help; and civic and school organizations organized benefits to provide it.

Earl Fuller wanted to help, too. He bought newspaper advertising announcing a Danny Czaban Day: all gasoline profits for that day to go to the youngster. Pumped three times his normal day's gallonage—and turned over more than $100 to the fund.

People remember things like that.

People remember little things, too. A man from Massachusetts called us up just to tell us about a small extra service rendered by a dealer in Rhode Island. This man had stopped at Sam's Shell Service in Pawtucket for gasoline. As he got out of the car he noticed a button fall off his coat, picked it up and casually remarked to the dealer that he would have to get a tailor to put it back on.

Not necessary, said the dealer. He went inside to his desk, took a sewing kit out of the drawer, and sewed the button back on. That was all; but the customer remembered, and passed the word along.

Of course you don't have to have a sewing kit to make customers like you. You're doing it every day.

J. E. D.
—*Shell Progress*

Such tributes may be full of color, almost going over into the type of change-of-pace editorial which rests entirely on this. Possibly because of personal involvement and sentiment, the following editorial paid feeling tribute to a New York institution that had more than passing interest for newspapermen generally, and those on the staff of the *New York Herald Tribune*, in particular:

Salute to Jack Bleeck

So Bleeck's has been sold. To some thousands of genuine New Yorkers this is a very personal matter. It has to be understood that the Artists and Writers Restaurant (formerly Club), to use the full and idiosyncratic title, is more than a restaurant, or a bar, or even a club. Of course it happens to be all of these things, but they fail to describe. Our neighbor in W. 40th St. is a hall of intangibles, a place of sentiment and friendship. Those who know it understand; for others there is little use trying to explain. These matters are simply incommunicable.

The facts have been told in the news columns. Jack Bleeck, founder and sole owner for twenty-eight years, has chosen to take life a little easier. Bleeck's will go on as usual; Mr. Bleeck plans to stick around as an elder statesman. There is no need to be sad. One assumes that radio and TV, tablecloths and chrome, will remain forbidden; that Henry, Harold, Leo and Gene will function as always; that the menu continues to abhor ice cream and French-fried potatoes. These may

177

be small things, but they are part of the continuity and personality of Bleeck's.

Over the years a great deal has been written about Jack Bleeck's establishment—about the speakeasy days and the rule against women which went out soon after repeal, the celebrated customers and many more not so celebrated, and all the rich anecdotal ore. It might seem at times that Bleeck's has operated as a pleasure instead of a business. The truth is that it has been both, for host and patrons alike. Mr. Bleeck has enjoyed fun and profit in equally large measure, and this comes because he has at all times conducted exactly the sort of place he wants. He has been true to himself and his friends, a believer in good food and good drink at fair prices, a stickler on principle and performance. The result is Bleeck's, a complete expression of personality if ever there was one. It is good to hear that the new owners, Messrs. Fitzpatrick and Hitz, mean to carry on in the old tradition.

—New York Herald Tribune

Occasionally an editorial writer may want to call attention to a new book, play, radio series, television program, or some other performance in the arts. One way of doing it is to write an informative editorial that condenses the contents so that readers will have such an alluring sample that they will want to see or hear the whole. Or at least that they will know the highlights because they read the editorial. A writer may inject a minimum of opinions or he may do little more than write a review for the editorial page.

This review-editorial type is illustrated by the following comments on a study of literacy in this country:

The Brutal Facts
About Illiteracy

The announcement that 2,500,000 Americans are illiterates comes as a heavy shock to a nation that boasts of its high standard of living and takes great pride in its system of public schools.

The unhappy facts of "The Uneducated" in the United States have been compiled in the first report of Columbia University's "Conservation of Human Resources Project"—a report proposed by General Eisenhower when he was president of Columbia and written by Dr. Eli Ginzberg, professor of economics, and Dr. Douglas Bray, research associate. The report was financed by the Ford Foundation and 13 large corporations.

The effects flowing from such a report are disquieting and even alarming: 2,500,000 men and women who cannot read or write, who are unwanted by industry, rejected by the Armed Forces and neglected by the Government are an obvious drag upon the national economy and upon the national defense. Further, they are an involuntary aid and comfort to the enemy in the continuing Cold War.

For they loom prominently in a new campaign of propaganda being waged by the Soviets to gain sympathy for Communism and arouse antipathy toward the American system; Russians are widely claiming that while Communist countries are eradicating illiteracy within their borders, the boastful American system is fostering millions of illiterates. This argument, hardly disputable from the facts, is of undoubted attraction to millions now struggling to better themselves in Asia, in Africa and in South America.

In noting the excessive cost of illiteracy to national defense, the report recalls that 1,500,000 men of draftage were unable to meet service standards of schooling in World War II. Though the Army accepted about half this group, and gave them special training to fit them for service, the prodigious waste in man power is obvious.

Wherein lies some of the responsibility for this condition is glimpsed in the finding that of 716,000 draftees rejected by the services as "mentally deficient"—a somewhat inaccurate piece of cataloguing—75 per cent lived in the South. Tennessee, Kentucky, Texas and North Carolina had the most illiterate whites per thousand in that order; South Carolina, Louisiana, Alabama and

179

Arkansas had the most illiterate Negroes. (On the side of progress, the report notes that in the last 70 years, the Negroes in America have been transformed from overwhelmingly illiterate to overwhelmingly literate.)

But the problem is not at all isolated in the South. In recent years, some ten million Americans have moved from State to State and there has been a commonly observed migration westward. Migratory farm workers, following the crops at a pace that makes it impossible for their children to attend schools, constitute a large pocket of illiteracy in our population. Migrants from Puerto Rico, the West Indies, Mexico show a high percentage of illiteracy.

But any tendency to shift the blame to conditions beyond our own borders vanishes with a glimpse at a large group of aboriginal Americans—the Navaho Indians of Arizona, New Mexico and Colorado. At the beginning of World War II, they were 90 per cent illiterate. Even now, it is estimated that five out of seven of their children get no schooling. The reasons are to be found in the sketchy roads and antiquated schoolhouses of the Navaho country—and such neglect as lies in the fact that one schoolteacher reported a Government allowance of 21 cents a day for each child who eats three meals a day in school.

On that score, the Columbia report notes as a matter of ironic record: "The Federal Government spends many times as much on assistance to migratory birds as on assistance to the children of migratory families."

The report rightly recommends that the Federal Government launch a head-on attack upon the conditions that breed illiteracy, and do so by giving grants-in-aid to the States for the specific purpose of educating "The Uneducated." The need cries out loudly. "It is no longer possible," says the report, "for our democracy to remain strong unless the citizenry is able and willing to inform itself about many and complex issues far transcending local issues. This can be done only if each individual is able to read, and read critically."

—San Francisco Chronicle

The harassed writer in search of a topic for an editorial needs only to look at his almanac to see what anniversaries are coming up. At least, one might almost draw that conclusion from the large number of poor anniversary editorials that get into print every year. An anniversary is unsatisfactory material for an editorial unless the author makes some contribution in his reaction. One frequently-used way to lift an anniversary editorial out of the rut of mediocrity is to follow the news and give the piece a contemporary peg on which to hang significant comments. That approach certainly gives the reader more to think about than, as two New York metropolitan newspapers did fairly recently, a reprinted Psalm from the Bible for Thanksgiving Day or Abraham Lincoln's opinion of George Washington for February 22.

For instance, this Mother's Day editorial, printed in the *Milwaukee Journal* and widely re-published, tied in a then-current news event with comments on mothers, democracy, and Christianity:

A Thought for Mother's Day

Mrs. Emma Clarissa Clement of Louisville, Ky., the 71 year old mother of seven fine children, has been chosen as American mother of 1946. Congratulations are in order to Mrs. Clement.

Congratulations should also go to the American mothers' committee of the Golden Rule Foundation, which made the selection. For Mrs. Clement is a Negro, the first of her race to be so honored by the committee.

Mrs. Clement has a bright record of achievement in religious, welfare, interracial and civic activities in her state. So impressive was this record of good works that Miss Mary E. Hughes, a member of the selection committee, who is a native of the south and terms herself a "rebel of rebels," said:

"I never dreamed I would ever in my life vote for a Negro. But when I saw her record I couldn't be fair and serve on the committee without recognizing it."

Well said, Miss Hughes. To be judged by what we are

181

and what we do, not by the color of our skins, the language we speak, our race or our religion—that is all we ask in America. That is the essence of democracy. Yes, and of Christianity.

—*Milwaukee Journal*

Most of the editorials reprinted in this chapter have been fairly simple to classify. This is not true of all editorials. Frequently writers combine several possibilities to get greatest effectiveness. But whether he is writing a historical, obituary, geographical, issues, crystal-ball, "well done," review, or anniversary editorial, the writer's chief goal is to present facts that will help his readers better understand an event.

SEVEN

Editorials that try to convert

DESPITE ALL THE COMMENTS AND PRAISE FOR INFORMATIVE EDITO-rials (and, of course, most of such talk is deserved), any news-paper that prizes its influence with readers must print a sizable quota of argumentative editorials. Just as editors of long ago liked to sway their readers, writers today try to guide public opinion along the lines they wish it to go. And one way to persuade readers is to print arguments.

Sometimes we really think

Mental activity may go on at several levels, but only in the highest is there creative thought, which should be the editorial writer's goal. Among the lower levels that sometimes mistakenly pass for thinking are day-dreaming, trial-and-error mental reactions, and rationalization. Let's look at these levels before we investigate what the thinking process and logic can do.

The highest level of mental performance is creative thought, or problem-solving thinking. Here we face a problem or an issue, realize that something must be done, consciously set about to dis-cover what ways are open to us, and then follow the chosen one.

Creative thought or problem-solving thinking follows a fairly consistent pattern, of which the following are the five essential steps:

(1) Recognize the problem.
(2) Define or classify it.
(3) Suggest various solutions.
(4) Test these solutions or premises.
(5) Decide whether other solutions or hypotheses are necessary.

For example, here's a possible reconstruction of how an editorial writer might tackle a problem. A staff member of the *St. Louis Post-Dispatch* actually faced the problem when bills for statehood for Alaska and Hawaii were under consideration:

(1) Newspaper stories and magazine articles showed that Congress was giving serious consideration to bills to admit these two territories. The writer had observed that the public was interested. Certainly there was a problem of whether to admit them as states or not to admit them. The newspaper should discuss this issue, it was apparent.

(2) Hawaii might suggest to the writer a vacationland with leis for visitors, and Alaska, an opportunity to win fame and fortune on an Arctic "last frontier." But day-dreaming of that sort clearly did not affect the problem of statehood. So the editorial writer discarded his day-dreaming and turned to exploring the problem. He came up with several points: that both Alaska and Hawaii were possible defense outposts in a war with the Soviet Union, that they may or may not have enough population to be entitled to Congressional representation as states, and that extending statehood to the two might be an example in applied democracy.

(3) He decided to explore the question of population. How could he determine whether Alaska and Hawaii have enough people to be entitled to statehood? Well, he thought, what about the other states' populations when they were admitted? What was done in the past might be used to gauge the future. He decided to gather comparative information on the populations of Hawaii and Alaska and the population of the other states when they were admitted.

(4) Then he proceeded to test these possibilities. He found that Alaska had 90,000 population and that Nevada when admitted to the Union had less than 90,000 population; thus Alaska had more residents than Nevada when that state was admitted to the Union. Then he could proceed with the argument that if Nevada had enough population to be admitted in 1864, then Alaska had enough. Although the editorial writer considered that other factors might be involved (such as the fact that arguments valid in the Civil War decade might not apply in the middle of the Twentieth Century), he was convinced that the population comparison carried some weight. He then tested the facts about Hawaii's population. Finally he wrote the following paragraph, which actually did appear in an editorial:

> The argument that these territories do not have enough population is not soundly based. Alaska has 90,000 people and that is almost as many as Nevada had in 1930, by which time Nevada had been a state 66 years. Alaska's present population is approximately the combined total of Missouri and Illinois when they were admitted. Hawaii, with about 500,000 people, would outrank Wyoming, Delaware, Vermont and Nevada—and possibly other states—on a basis of population.
>
> —*St. Louis Post-Dispatch*

By applying certain fundamental checks, it may be possible to discover the errors in our thinking. Students of the reasoning process will tell you that creative thinking breaks down into two groups: (1) Induction, and (2) Deduction. We will examine definitions of these terms and then discuss them in brief, simplified style.*

Induction, as defined by Professor Max Black of Cornell Uni-

---

* A reliable text on thinking and logic will present a more complete treatment for those who wish it. Dr. Chilton R. Bush of Stanford University adapted the practices to editorial writing in *Editorial Thinking and Writing* (Appleton, 1932).

versity in his textbook, *Critical Thinking* (Prentice-Hall, Inc., Second Edition, 1952), is "a process of using evidence concerning some members of a class of objects as a basis for an assertion about all or more members of that class," and deduction is "reasoning that aims at *valid* conclusions."

In other words, they are two sides of the same street. Inductive reasoning is a case-history attempt to look at examples and then arrive at some valid generalization; deduction is the application of valid general propositions or premises to establish the truth or falsity of hypotheses and thus to reach a valid conclusion. One goes from the specific to the general; the other reverses the process and goes from the general to a particular. Except for analysis or description, they are not separated—they march side by side in actual thinking.

To illustrate, let us assume that an editorial writer is aware of the current overcrowded conditions for students and wants to discuss whether his community can afford a new public school. He discovers, after research, that six comparable communities throughout the state have built new public school buildings of the same kind recently while keeping their tax rates between $15 and $20 per $1,000 assessed real estate valuation. Applying inductive logic, he reasons that it is financially feasible to build a new school if the tax rate is kept to not more than $20 per $1,000. Now he turns to deductive logic. He knows that his community will be able to build the proposed school and still keep its tax rate below $20. Therefore he concludes that the new school project is financially feasible.

Stated as a syllogism or as a three-part statement of two premises and a conclusion, this deductive proposition would be:

Major premise: A new school is financially feasible when the tax rate does not exceed $20 per $1,000 assessed valuation.

Minor premise: The proposed Washington Street School will not make the tax rate exceed $20 per $1,000 assessed valuation.

Conclusion: The proposed Washington Street School is financially feasible.

A conclusion in a valid deduction follows from the premises, and if the premises are true and the conclusion is derived from the premises by prescribed means, then the conclusion is certain to be true. But formal logic, as will be pointed out later, does not check on the truth of the premises.

Faulty application of logic may be illustrated in the following syllogism in which the major premise is false and therefore the conclusion is false:

Major premise: All cats are wild animals.

Minor premise: Our pet "Beer" is a cat.

Conclusion: Our pet "Beer" is a wild animal.

Any person may fall into error because he is (1) not sufficiently informed to work out premises, (2) too lazy to push his ideas beyond the superficial, (3) dishonest intellectually, or (4) incapable of seeing the truth because he is rationalizing, thinking wishfully, or blinded by prejudices or stereotypes.

How logical is logic?

Logic, according to a dictionary definition, is "the science which investigates the principles governing correct or reliable inference." It is then the process through which we try to find the truth. The difficulty is that too frequently the truth we find through the most logical process somehow is both incorrect and unreliable.

Has this trouble anything to do with formal logic? Yes, replied a number of writers. For instance, Dr. Rudolf Flesch in *The Art of Clear Thinking* (Harper, 1951) called formal logic "an unnatural way of thinking, a contrived technique of going from unwarranted assumptions to foregone conclusions."

Dr. Flesch is correct. Yet, after all is said and done, logic remains a useful tool. But it is nothing more. We should never become slaves to formal logic, but use it—and use our heads. Many of the difficulties arise when it is lifted out of its "yes-or-no parlor game" aspects to a philosophy in its own right.

Students of logic apply the term syllogism to a three-part argument of two premises and a conclusion. The arguments are capable of statement in subject-predicate form and involve only three classes or terms. The middle term or the one that occurs in both premises is not in the conclusion. As was pointed out earlier in this chapter, it is quite possible for a syllogism to be correct by the rules of logic but not true. This arises because the "yes-or-no parlor game" aspect provides no automatic check to insure that premises are geared to factual statements.

H. A. Overstreet appropriately described the syllogism as "a tool only of analysis, not of discovery" but he added that as a tool for analysis it was "surgical in its keenness."

By breaking arguments into their smaller pieces and then having to reassemble them, the editorial writer and others who use logic, together with some horse sense, have a chance to analyze what they could not analyze by other means. Logic is, therefore, a useful "tool."

A Baltimore *Sun* editorial writer used syllogistic reasoning effectively in the following editorial on a state-wide prohibition proposal:

A Drive to Impose
One-Day-A-Week Prohibition

The Prohibitionists are at it again. At Annapolis they have introduced a bill which would forbid the sale of alcoholic beverages on Sunday.

In other words, the bill would impose State-wide prohibition one day out of seven.

And that day would be the day of rest and relaxation. It would be the day on which thousands of families give Mother a rest, too, by going out to dinner. Yet under the provisions of this bill, Mother and Father would be forbidden to have so much as a glass of beer with their Sunday dinner.

That drink is an evil thing for a small minority of the people, no one denies. But it ought to be clear by now that prohibition is no answer to the question of the problem drinker. Seven-days-a-week prohibition was an evil thing. One-day-a-week prohibition partakes of the same evil.

The Legislature should kill this bill.

—Baltimore *Sun*

What undoubtedly will be known for many years as a classic combination of errors, some of them in logic, was the pollsters' predictions of the outcome of the 1948 presidential election. All of the major public opinion surveys predicted that Governor Thomas E. Dewey of New York would be elected, yet when the votes were tabulated, the victor was Harry S. Truman. Much soul-searching took place after the results were known. A number of errors were alleged and most of them were admitted to be true.

This excerpt from an editorial at the time showed how a newspaperman may well have more than a passing interest in logic if he is to comment intelligently:

One thing that stands out most clearly in the post-election analyses is that the pollsters had some of the right clues all along, but went haywire with false assumptions and unjustified conclusions. Fortune magazine, for instance, notes that its own survey developed many clues in terms of underlying public attitudes. The issues about which the public expressed greatest concern, it points out, were those hit hardest by Truman —prices, housing, etc. And every survey in the last four years has shown that more people regarded themselves as Democrats than Republicans; also that the public generally endorsed the New Deal philosophy. Yet no one went farther out on the Dewey limb than Fortune's own Elmo Roper; there's no telling how many experts had their doubts put to sleep by his smug certainty that Dewey would win.

There was no repetition this time of the fatal error of the Literary Digest in 1936, when it based its forecast on a distorted sample. This year's pollsters apparently had a scientific enough cross-section, but failed to ask the right questions, to ask them at the right times, to read the answers correctly, or to make sufficient allowance for the psychological factors that no poll could measure.

Dr. George Gallup, for example, says his organization detected a slight Truman trend at the finish but underrated it and didn't keep polling long enough. He bemoans the many unwarranted assumptions to which the pollsters subscribed—e.g., that last-minute electioneering changes few votes, that "undecided" voters would split in the same ratio as the decided, and that a light vote favors the Republicans.

—*Buffalo Evening News*

And there is always propaganda

If the editorial writer is going to convert, he should know the techniques of the propagandist. First, he may then beware of them himself and detect them. Secondly, he may, when occasion demands, use them to win supporters.

Although the word had been used for hundreds of years, propaganda came to general public attention during World War I. The atrocity stories, frequently false, that were started in an effort to influence public opinion focused attention on the publicists' tools. Propaganda became a bad word. So bad was it, in fact, that many true stories were discredited during the 1930's and 1940's when anyone insinuated, "They're just propaganda; don't believe 'em."

A wit once said with enough truth to make it more than a witticism that if the techniques are used by *our* side it is called "education" but if they are used by our opponents, we call it "propaganda."

Among the many studies of public opinion and propaganda during recent decades, the seven devices formulated by the Institute for Propaganda Analysis during the late 1930's still retain validity in detecting the various techniques used to influence men's minds. These seven devices include:

(1) *Name Calling.* Bad names are applied to whatever the propagandists want the public to reject or condemn without examining the evidence. A labor union executive may be identified as a Communist agitator by one group, while a Wall Street broker may be an economic royalist or a Tory representative of selfish reaction to another.

(2) *Glittering Generalities.* Particular situations are identified with broad, accepted ideals and "virtue words." "The American Way of Life," for example, may mean apple pie and Thanksgiving turkey to a few folk but it probably will bring up almost as many different concepts as there are people reading the phrase. Yet most of them will approve the idea and, the propagandists hope, their special product or cause. The phrase, "Public Interest," is another generalization applied to varying specific situations.

(3) *Transfer.* Certain symbols of authority, sanction, and prestige that are sure to arouse emotions may be attached to things which the press agent wants to promote. On the Fourth of July, for instance, the symbol generally is the United States flag and speakers try to gain support for their pet proposal by wrapping it in red, white, and blue. Freedom of speech is used to cover cases where it has only the vaguest tangent connection—so is the freedom of the press.

(4) *Testimonial.* A favorite with advertisers for many years, this technique may plug a social, political, or economic idea as well as patent medicine or soap. The well-organized campaign for public support usually includes a list of well-known individuals who act as sponsors, and endorsements from others.

(5) *Plain Folks.* The propagandist tries to create the impression that he is just common folk like the rest of us and thus incapable of guile and deceit. The factory owner employs this device with his employees when he goes through his shop slapping the workers on their backs in forced joviality, and the candidate for public office when he speaks of himself as a "neighbor" who can be trusted if elected. One Midwestern candidate for United States

senator is credited with leaving his private railroad car a few miles from rural communities to get into a battered automobile from which he made his pleas for votes.

(6) *Card Stacking.* Facts, illustrations, and statements can be carefully selected to make the maximum impression, either to present the best or the worst possible case for an idea, program, person, or product. This is probably the most difficult technique to detect because many people do not have time to check all the evidence and thus learn what has been left out.

(7) *Band Wagon.* This is built on the idea that if "everybody is doing it," so must the people of the particlular group being appealed to. "Jump aboard the band wagon," "Follow the crowd," and "Don't throw your vote away" are three election clichés that exemplify this appeal. The 1948 presidential election seemed to show that there may be a counter movement in favor of the underdog, the guy that doesn't have a chance. However, the bandwagon appeal is still impressive.

Variations and minor subdivisions exist in the propaganda approach but seven main highways are those listed above.

Editorials should "blow the trumpet"

Talcott Williams, first head of what became the Graduate School of Journalism at Columbia University, quoted the Biblical prophet Ezekiel to drive home to students an editor's obligation to "blow the trumpet, and warn the people." Writers of argumentative editorials should serve the same purpose as the prophets of ancient Israel.

In argumentative editorials, writers demand action of some sort. They may aim at a single official who is considered derelict in his duties. They may appeal to all citizens to go to the polls on election day or to take some other mass action. Or they may refute alluring arguments already in circulation. In any case, editorial writers apply the techniques of problem-solving thinking and, when needed, logic. Here they attempt to marshal their facts and arguments in the most effective fashion. Even the fire and heat of emotion may be used in presentation but these have no place in the cool of impersonal thinking.

Editorial pages should express vigorous opinions because, as publisher John S. Knight expressed it, "it is our duty to cause people to think and very often this can best be accomplished by stating our views so cogently that no reader . . . can possibly be in doubt as to our position." This challenges those who argue in favor of the informative editorial and its "on-the-other-hand" treatment. The obligation "to take a stand" cannot be dodged entirely by the conscientious editor no matter how much he attempts merely to inform.

Argumentative editorials have a value, too, even when the conversion aspect is disregarded. Vermont Royster, senior associate editor of the *Wall Street Journal*, New York City, and a Pulitzer prize winner, told a Sigma Delta Chi convention in 1952:

> People read editorials, first, to get arguments to support their own opinion. Now, that's not as silly or as bad as it sounds because very often people instinctively approve or disapprove of an idea or proposal, but they are not quite sure why. There is a vague feeling there that this proposal is good or this proposal is wrong. A good editorial presentation serves to focus their thinking. It serves to give them a rationale for what they instinctively feel. Occasionally readers will adopt, I think, an editorial point of view when it is on some subject with which they are unfamiliar and where they have general confidence in the editorial writer or the paper's opinion, but very rarely, I think, do we actually change a person's point of view, certainly not with any one editorial.

Although some editors may abdicate the role of guiding public opinion rather than face irate subscribers, angry advertisers, or an annoyed publisher-owner, most of them would agree as a matter of policy with Herbert Brucker, editor of the *Hartford* (Connecticut) *Courant* and former journalism teacher at Columbia University, when he declared:

> Our journalistic Jeremiahs must breathe more hellfire and damnation than ever. Only they need to get all the facts, and not just some of them, first.

An editorial writer, aware that readers can check for themselves on his facts if they desire or may have seen the same performance on television or radio as he did, must insure that his information is correct and that he is not suppressing essential facts that might upset his arguments. This danger is particularly acute during an election campaign when emotions kindle at a low point. If newspapers failed to influence presidential elections during the 1930's and 1940's, the blame may be due, in part, to editorial writers' inability to let only the facts determine their position. Suppression, willful or involuntary, is soon exposed by intelligent readers. Confidence so destroyed is slowly rebuilt.

Editorial writers recognize the dangers of overdoing controversy. For instance, Neil MacNeil, former assistant managing editor on *The New York Times*, in *Without Fear or Favor* (Harcourt, Brace, 1940) evaluated its assets and liabilities this way:

> The argumentative editorial naturally makes the most interesting reading. Editors without convictions and without courage are sad creatures at best. A provocative editorial once in a while lifts the editorial page above mediocrity, but the editorial page that becomes a common scold does not get far either, for it defeats its own purpose. A thunderstorm is a gorgeous spectacle to watch, but one soon tires of it. The influential editorial page is the one that hits hard when the occasion demands it, and only then. When it does strike it shocks the complacency of its readers. It demands attention and action.

Another editor who voiced substantially the same warning was Jenkin Lloyd Jones of the *Tulsa Tribune*. He told the 1948 American Society of Newspaper Editors convention:

Bad as the wishy-washy editorial page is, it is possible to err equally badly in the opposite direction by attempting to bludgeon editorial opinion into the heads of readers. There are still some publishers who think that their subscribers can be mesmerized by red ink, 12-point editorial body type, and endless repetition. This is particularly characteristic of some chains, holding to bullying tactics that went out of style generally about forty years ago. . . .

A good editorial is not a battle-ax. It is a rapier. It doesn't smash. It thrusts, parries, and drives its point home.

The argumentative editorial is an important part of the editor's equipment but the wise writer will not use it for trivial topics but rather to fulfill the function of an editorial page as a keystone in public affairs. Without it, he could contribute little more than glorified background features. With it, he can round out his editorial page and accept his assignment to public responsibility in mass communications.

Argumentative editorials may do the trick

Some argumentative editorials closely resemble informative ones. A distinguishing factor in the argumentative type is that an effort is always made to bring the reader around to the editorial writer's viewpoint, not simply to present the facts and hope that he will be convinced. Always present to some extent is the responsibility to "blow the trumpet, and warn the people." Doing this requires not only the guts to take a stand, to add up the pros and cons of an issue, and then to decide, but also the skill to put across that stand.

Every publication upholds certain worthy causes which it believes that its readers should support, financially or otherwise. Some of these projects have a broad appeal, such as the American Red Cross, the March of Dimes, and the Community Chest campaigns. Others are of specialized interest to a particular reader group, for example, advice to garage men who read an oil company's publication on how to increase service and sales. In any case, the reader-appeal needs to be astutely attuned to the group that it will reach. Otherwise, the appeal may be addressed to a group that will not even see it. Of course, such worthy-cause editorials, as they can well be christened, need not have a direct interest for every individual reader, but the appeal certainly should be aimed at a great portion of them. Such appeal editorials may be handled in a fairly direct and conventional way, that says in expanded form: "This is a worthy cause and we believe you should support it." Or the appeal may be put over with as much originality as the writer is capable of mustering.

A traditional part of *The New York Times'* pre-Christmas activities includes an appeal for "The 100 Neediest Cases." Both news stories and editorials support this campaign for funds. Every year the editorial page staff has the assignment of making a persuasive appeal to *The Times'* readers. Although the assignment had been done annually for years, Edward M. Kingsbury won the 1926 Pulitzer prize for the best editorial during the previous year with "The House of a Hundred Sorrows." It attempted to break away from the conventional and depicted concrete details in an original manner that helped readers visualize the needs of specific cases.

Numerous other editorial writers have extolled the use of concrete particulars and details in worthy-cause editorials. One writer told of contrasting results from two editorials in a campaign for funds to help children. One, written in his best literary style with allusions to the Bible, cited the Virgin Mary and her compassion for children. The other, simply but graphically written, particularized on the cases that would be aided by the readers' contributions. The second was tremendously more effective in stimulating readers to send cash and checks.

In the following editorial, the need for funds to support the Metropolitan Opera House in New York City is outlined and the address to which money or pledges may be sent is included in the conclusion. The writer assumed that it was sufficient to inform

readers that funds were needed and that he did not have to drama-
tize his appeal. Here is the editorial:

In Aid of the Metropolitan

The public delight in opera was never greater, as the
standees at the Metropolitan Opera House daily testify.
New Yorkers have always been enthusiastic supporters
of their beloved Metropolitan with its golden horseshoe
and its magnificent proscenium. Through that magic
arch what treasures of sight and sound have over the
years reached the city's thousands!

In European countries no one expects an opera house
to be self-supporting. A governmental subsidy is a matter of course. Here when a deficit threatens, the directors rightly turn to opera's patrons and friends for help.
They are asking for aid now. The goal fixed is $250,000,
part of which is to be applied to the long-range development of the Metropolitan, most of it to finance new
productions and important revivals next year.

We urge our readers to put this subscription high on
their year's list. Every non-profit organization is in
straits and the calls upon the New Yorker's generosity
are many. But the service of opera runs far and wide,
in sickness and in health, to a vast radio audience, as well
as the packed listeners of the house. It dispenses happiness and inspiration, all the more needed in a period
of worry and confusion. This year the performances
have shown a steadily mounting artistry. This has been
achieved despite rigid economies. Only rising costs make
the present appeal necessary.

Checks or pledges should be sent to the Metropolitan
Opera Fund, 654 Madison Avenue. May the response be
prompt and generous.

—New York Herald Tribune

An intriguing figure of speech attracts attention to this short
editorial in the house organ of the New York office of the Metropolitan Life Insurance Company:

100 Spirited Horses

Imagine 100 frenzied horses—each one deaf, dumb, and blind—stampeding along a highway. When you drive your car, you are operating a machine that is approximately equivalent in power to those 100 horses. Only *you* can make that power obey.

The Health and Welfare has just prepared a new pamphlet for the benefit of the Home Office family. *Good Hints to Good Driving* contains some common-sense rules that make driving safer. During October copies may be obtained at the Information Desk and in the pamphlet racks in the Lounges, Library, Medical Division, and the Gymnasium. Be sure to get a copy and drive safely!

—The Home Office, New York City

The case-history technique in the following editorial appeal for the Boy Scouts was printed as part of the annual national campaign for funds. Its entire appeal to millions of subscribers of a mass-circulation magazine rested upon one specific case. The editors personalized it to the extent of having it written by a person not on their staff.

From Tough Gang To Scout Patrol

By George H. Sibley
VICE-PRESIDENT, E. R. SQUIBB & SONS

I was born in Denver, Colorado, that great Western city sprung out of the toil and good fortune of hardy pioneers. The Denver of my boyhood had a free-and-easy background. At various times, gambling and all forms of vice and juvenile delinquency flourished. As might have been expected at a time when the exploits of Jesse James, Wild Bill Hickok, Billy the Kid and other notorious Western gangsters were fast becoming legends, there were numerous gangs of boys in all neighborhoods who liked to play at emulating them. I belonged to such a gang.

We were not above "swiping" candy hard chews, chewing gum, all-day suckers, and even raiding the dime store for Christmas presents for our friends and families. We learned how to make life miserable for some poor kid from another neighborhood.

One of our gang was the son of a prominent lawyer. We were very fond of him and heartbroken when he developed heart trouble and died. So was his father. He did not let the grief get him down too far, because one day he called our gang together and asked, "How about forming a Boy Scout troop?" We liked the idea and we formed a troop. Our pal's father was our scoutmaster.

It wasn't long after we took the Boy Scout Promise as Tenderfoot Scouts that we agreed of our own accord that we couldn't be real Scouts and continue to deplete the counter stock of the local pharmacy and candy store. That was "kid stuff."

Scouting did a lot for me. I know it does something for a boy which he never loses when a man. It teaches him the value of the Golden Rule. It gives him a genuine affection for his fellows. It makes him appreciate this great, glorious country of ours and the great outdoors. It rubs off the ego, builds up self-reliance, self-respect and respect for others. Lucky the man who has been a Boy Scout.

—*Ladies' Home Journal*

In the arguments-for-action group of editorials rests the core of the argumentative type. It might be called the "do something" variety. It is more directed than the appeal to readers cited above; it requires more than just a contribution of money or time. The editorial writer is appealing for action from a special agency or person. Congressmen or city council members *should* pass such and such an ordinance or law. The park commissioners *should* approve a new playground. Automobile drivers *should* observe the new one-way traffic regulations. The director of mines *should* enforce safety regulations. The mayor *should* appoint a properly qualified man to be police chief. And so on through a long list of things that affect the daily living of the public.

Occasionally, the arguments-for-action editorial may simply cite a particular difficulty and point an accusing finger at several of the possible culprits. This may subtract from the effectiveness of a more direct and unified stand but it generally brings out denials from those not responsible and thus may effectively help to place responsibility. The following "do something" editorial after a traffic death in Denver illustrates this more general approach because it asks what both city and transit company propose to do to correct then-current flaws and it lists four specific points to clinch the arguments for action:

Of Busses, Traffic Lights and Death

A young woman died in Denver Friday, the victim of a tramway bus and careless driving, acording to police.

Mrs. Jeanne Owens was struck down at Fourteenth and Champa streets, while crossing, with the light. The bus driver, who also had a green light, struck her as he made a right turn, then dragged her under the bus before he was halted by the screams of pedestrians.

In the tragic death of Mrs. Owens there are several lessons for Denver.

First, it should teach tramway bus and trackless trolley operators that there are more important things in this world than schedules. Human life is one of them.

Second, it should be a lesson to Denver traffic officers that tramway drivers are to be arrested just as ordinary citizens when they commit traffic offenses. The driver of this bus was within the law except in his "careless driving" as cited by the police. This is not true, however, of tramway drivers in many other cases.

Far too often we see busses, streetcars and trackless trolleys running the traffic lights and committing other violations of law and threatening safety.

If the police gave tickets to tramway drivers as they

do to ordinary citizens, such accidents might be prevented.

Third, it should teach our traffic authorities that we must have some revision of the traffic lighting system in downtown Denver. In this case both parties have the right of way although pedestrian right of way stands over that of vehicles. It might be worthwhile for Traffic Engineer Barnes to consider a system of special lights for right and left turns, while all other traffic, pedestrian and vehicle, remains stopped. That would have prevented this accident.

Fourth, it should teach the city and tramway to examine the system of vehicle tranportation in downtown Denver. The tramway busses have very little field of visibility. Perhaps they have no business operating on streets where they must make turns in heavy traffic. Perhaps, too, we need two-man operation on all tramway vehicles for safe operation.

It may be that these latter things are not needed. Yet we cannot forget that a young woman was killed—while completely in the right. The responsibility for that death lies with the city and the tramway company. We'd like to know what they propose to do about it.

—Denver Post

A more direct, single-track approach is illustrated by the following editorial which contains its own suggestion of what to do: Write a letter when it may have some influence. The editorial said:

Repulsion for Mail Box Ads

Following is a clipping that points to another horible possibility. Billboards have marred much of the countryside's beauty. Now suggested is the plastering of mail boxes with advertising. Are there no esthetic values to be considered?

"Rep. Henry J. Latham, R., N.Y., suggested that the government sell advertising space on the sides of postal trucks and on mail boxes. In a letter to Postmaster General Arthur E. Summerfield, Rep. Latham said he thought the idea would help offset big postal deficits. 'I would be most happy to introduce appropriate legislation if that is necessary,' he wrote."

It would be a good idea to deluge Rep. Latham and Postmaster General Summerfield with protests.

Get busy, Garden Club members, with personal letters—and everyone else with a feeling of repulsion at the suggestion of further desecration.

—*The Register Herald,* Pine Plains, N.Y.

The techniques of formal logic and analysis of causal relationships are applied by writers in the cause-effect editorial category. Although it resembles the prediction type of informative editorial, this classification goes beyond an objective picture of what is causing a present event or what is going to happen. It presents a subjective evaluation. It may, as did one editorial on the situation in Europe, conclude, "That way lies catastrophe." Such a comment fits well into an argumentative editorial of the cause-effect category. Or a cause-effect editorial may start from the effect and seek to ascertain a cause.

How one paper tied a background feature from its state political correspondent with an editorial that sought to explain the cause for delays in investigating murder cases and then argued that the judge, in view of the paper's analysis, should disqualify himself is shown in the following:

Not the Man

The Post-Dispatch's state political correspondent, Curtis A. Betts, has made a thorough analysis of the background of Circuit Judge Ray G. Cowan of Kansas City. It shows that the Judge who impaneled the state grand jury to investigate the Binaggio-Gargotta murders and the tie-up between crime and politics is himself a product of the Pendergast school of boss rule.

No wonder Judge Cowan tossed off the federal grand jury report on violation of state laws. No wonder he asked the state grand jury to "go slow." No wonder he is such a contrast to Federal Judge Reeves, who 12 years ago in the historic vote fraud inquiry, told federal grand jurors to "move on them!"

In view of his own background, Judge Cowan should have disqualified himself. He should step out and permit the investigation to be under a judge who believes in vigorous inquiry.

—*St. Louis Post-Dispatch*

A second class of relationships is arguing from examples that are believed to be related. Here an editorial writer may apply a widely accepted generalization to a particular situation to show an analogy between two groups of incidents or to establish a historical parallel. A telling argument is to apply a generalization to a "horrible example" and thus highlight the faults.

A Baltimore *Sun* editorial writer, after comparing the cost of a proposed state veterans' bonus with a wide variety of existing expenditures, called the proposal "almost exactly similar" to one in the state of Washington that "ruined its credit rating." His arguments, many of which had the familiar ring of a logic exercise, ran as follows:

New Sponsors for the Break-the-Treasury Program

More than 40 members of the Maryland House of Delegates have declared themselves in as sponsors of the giant giveaway program that State Senator Kimble has been promoting for Maryland veterans. Their joint proposal calls upon the State to borrow $100,000,000 (nearly five times as much as the current State debt) and hand it out to veterans in cash rewards for service in World War II.

The handout that the legislators are demanding for veterans is:

Four times as much as Maryland is currently spending per year on public schools.

Four times the current budget for State roads.

Eight times the current budget for University of Maryland and the State Board of Agriculture.

Sixteen times the current budget for State mental institutions.

Sixteen times the current public-welfare budget.

Forty times the current budget for the State Department of Health.

Fifty-nine times the current budget for tuberculosis sanatoria.

Fifty-nine times the current budget for the conservation of natural resources.

Maryland legislators are not the only ones who have made a play for the veterans' vote by supporting schemes to get bonus proposals on election ballots. Legislatures in six other states are now searching for tax revenues to pay for bonus plans that they foolishly allowed to appear on the ballots last November.

In the State of Washington, for example, the voters passed a bonus plan almost exactly similar to that advocated without reason for Maryland: $100,000,000 to be distributed among veterans at the rate of $10 for each month of domestic service and $15 per month of overseas duty up to a $500 maximum. But the State of Washington found out belatedly that borrowing $100,000,000 ruined its credit rating, required stringent cuts in all State services and imposed punitive tax rates for years to come. Fortunately for Washingtonians, the State Supreme Court came to the legislators' rescue by declaring the bonus unconstitutional.

The 42 members of the Maryland House of Delegates should know by now that when they buy into the Kimble jackpot show for veterans they are backing a break-the-treasury program. They should also realize that Maryland already has a welfare program for needy veterans and is under no more obligation to bestow cash on veterans as a whole.

—Baltimore *Sun*

A Bloomington (Illinois) *Daily Pantagraph* editorial writer, H. Clay Tate, who runs a one-man page, used the rules of courtesy as

an effective argument in one of that paper's guest-inspired articles.
It read:

Why Don't You Write an Editorial About . . .?

You get your eardrums split by a horn-happy motorist as you start to cross a street. You call us and ask:
"Why don't you write an editorial about people who sound their car horns full blast on all occasions? Don't they know that a gentle warning is more likely to accomplish the desired purpose?"

Emily Post puts it this way in her Motor Manners:
"A trumpet horn—those penetrating signals for the open road—are as out of place when used in city driving as hobnail shoes in a ballroom."

That's a good thing to keep in mind.
—Bloomington *Daily Pantagraph*

A favorite argument with editorial writers is the historical parallel. Although history repeats itself often enough for the astute observer to find apt comparisons, many persons see parallels that do not, in fact, exist. The writer of such an argument should ask himself, "Are there other essential factors that are not common to the supposed parallel?" If there are such key points, then it is better to discard the argument entirely.

Here is an example of how historical parallels may be effectively used:

History Proves that Travel Broadens

What price congressional travel abroad? Pretty high, as Representative HUGH SCOTT wrily admits in the current issue of *Real*, taking a dim view of the minority of "Good-time Charlies" who get drunk, insult their hostesses, chase blonde secretaries, and lose us friends and influence abroad. But worth it, for the good it does when serious congressmen see at first hand some of the problems abroad which this country, for its own best interests, must help to solve.

We'll go along with Mr. SCOTT on that. Indeed, as we have argued in the past, even congressional missions so pointless as to deserve the label of junket are oft-times worth what they cost if they result in stretching the mind and increasing the vision of a single junketer. And the serious missions, of course, provide the entire Congress with invaluable information and ideas for writing laws that inevitably affect not only the United States but the whole wide world.

What travel has done for some congressmen, as world-shaking events *and* travel did for the late Senator VANDENBERG, is to give them a useful sense of the smallness and interdependence of today's world, a fresh appreciation of VANDENBERG'S belated discovery that no nation can immunize itself against disaster "by reliance upon itself alone."

Kentucky's Representative FRANK CHELF, for instance, was spurred to his highly effective efforts in behalf of displaced persons only after he had seen, for himself, the miseries of post-war Europe. And even Illinois' EVERETT DIRKSEN, a distinguished and extreme isolationist for decades, was moved by his European travels in 1947 to the belief that the United States' frontier against Communist threat was indeed in Germany, that we must "hold the line on the River Elbe."

All of which suggests one of our favorite ifs of history: What strides toward international co-operation, toward a possibly lasting peace, might not have been made from 1918 to 1939 if WILLIAM E. BORAH, the great isolationist of his generation, had ever traveled abroad?

Maybe none, if the Lion of Idaho, like some congressmen today, had chosen to travel with a closed mind. But Senator BORAH had streaks of greatness in him, and it is fair to assume that travel would never have narrowed them. Unfortunately, though, he never left these shores, and his untraveled estimates of the size of the world helped to paralyze American foreign policy for a fateful generation. It made ARTHUR VANDENBERG (with millions of Americans) a long-time Borah disciple, and it led the Old Lion himself to predict in 1939 (from "sources of information better than the State Department's") that World War II would never come, and then, once it had started, that it was a "phony war" and would never amount to much.

Some first-hand acquaintance with the facts of life in Europe would have made Senator BORAH a better guesser, if not a wiser stateman. In any case, it seems highly relevant that the pre-war king of isolationist "ostriches" was a man who scorned to leave these shores, and never did. Travel may not help all of his successors, but it will help some—and it won't hurt any. And even a "Good-time Charlie," if luck is with him, may find himself returning with a soberly wiser head.

—Louisville *Courier-Journal*

And then there is rebuttal

Almost as frequently as they argue in favor of a program or policy or urge some action, editorial writers attempt to answer statements already advanced or arguments already proposed. They seek to tear down their opponents' facts—or his logic. They are in rebuttal. The tone of their opposition may vary from the equivalent of a curt "You're a liar" to a suave "I beg your pardon, sir, but isn't your logic slipping?"

The simplest reply is to quote your opponent, chapter and verse, to show that he contradicted himself and therefore cannot be right. After the 1948 election, the *Buffalo* (N.Y.) *Evening News* caught up George E. Sokolsky when the syndicated columnist smugly claimed that he had never predicted that Thomas E. Dewey would be elected president. The editorial simply quoted from his column on the eve of the election as follows:

'I Never Predicted'

We hate to remind him of it, but George E. Sokolsky is another of those columnists with too short a memory. In last Saturday's News, he dared to boast: "I am in the fortunate position that I do not have to eat crow. I never predicted who would win; I only indicated whom I should like to see win. About that I have not changed my mind."

To refresh Mr. Sokolsky's memory, we herewith quote from his column of the day before election, Nov. 1: "Just as Harry Truman has made cursing the 80th Congress his line, so has Dewey set himself on a high level of philosophic grasp of human problems.... Perhaps that is why Thomas E. Dewey will be president! He mirrored the mood of the people.... Now the campaign is over. The votes will be counted. There will be a change. Then there will be 80 days of interregnum. Then there will be a different president, a new Cabinet, a Congress somewhat altered. . ."

Better come down off the high perch, George—and join the humble company of crow-eaters after all.

—*Buffalo Evening News*

The same effect may also be achieved by two contrasting quotations from different, but reliable, sources, such as those in the editorial quoted below:

None So Blind as He Who Will Not See

"The new relief cuts are not working any hardship on families getting public assistance."—Welfare Commissioner Hilliard in an interview with The Times on the day the reduced allowances took effect.

* * *

Mrs. T threw her arms around her two youngsters and started to cry as a Post reporter talked to her. This family's relief budget was cut $37.10.

"This is the end of my family," she exclaimed. "Now I'll have to put my children in a foster home. We just can't live on this money." Mrs. T's husband, a salesman, has tuberculosis and hasn't been able to find a job.—From a story in The Post, same day.

—*New York Post*

Some editorial writers may take a page from the late Alfred E. Smith and, in effect, say, "Let's look at the record." This is especially effective if there is any suspicion of misquotation. Here's an example of this sort of rebuttal:

Who Misleads Whom?

The current bulletin of the Rhode Island Public Expenditure Council, discussing the unemployment compensation situation in this state, says:

"Rarely has a more misleading statement been made than one which appeared recently in an editorial in the local press to the effect that the Rhode Island unemployment compensation program cannot be made solvent 'unless and until large, continuing new income for the fund is provided from some other source.'"

The editorial statement referred to, which the council has attempted with scant accuracy to summarize, appeared in this newspaper. It was as follows: "The *twin aims* of a solvent unemployment fund *and lower unemployment taxes on employers cannot both be met* unless and until large, continuing new income for the fund is provided from some other source."

We trust the readers of the council's publication will not be misled by the publication's misleading summary of what we said.

—*Providence* (R.I.) *Journal*

Usually, however, the retort to an opponent's arguments is not as simple as finding that he has been inconsistent or as matching two sets of statements. More frequently, the problem is to answer an opponent's arguments or his facts. In the following editorial, the writer tried to answer the arguments, which are first outlined in a quotation from a reliable source, and then he sought to make the special application to the United States. This localizing, as it were, of the arguments is highly effective if it can be done, which is not always the case. The rebuttal editorial:

For the Good of the Nation

In Great Britain both radio and television are the monopoly of the British Broadcasting Corporation, which is a publicly chartered body.

There is a current proposal to permit sponsored television programs to compete with those of B.B.C. The proposal has aroused strong protests—most of them citing the real and supposed derelictions of American television—and action on the proposal has been postponed.

A brief and fair summary of the opposition argument was voiced by the Archbishop of York. He said:

> "Television's influence in the future is incalculable. It may easily become the most powerful of all instruments in the formation of opinion and national character, for it is almost impossible to exaggerate the influence it will have over the young. It is, therefore, of vital importance that it should be under the control of those who will use it for the good of the nation."

That statement presupposes that there is some small group of people who know better than the great mass of people what is good for a nation. One may be permitted to doubt that.

That statement also presupposes that there is some agency capable of finding some people of super-knowledge and super-morality and giving their talents unobstructed scope. One may be permitted to doubt that there is such perfection of impartial and judicial temperament.

From the Archbishop's statement it may be assumed that those who now control B.B.C. and decide its policies are satisfactory to him and those who think like him; indeed, their policies seem generally satisfactory to the bulk of the British people. But suppose the direction gets into different hands?

That is one of the troubles with a monopoly, which is putting something exclusively into certain hands. The hands may be changed and the new hands may have

ideas about the nation's good which are far different
from those who advocated the monopoly in the first
place.

Television is one means of communication. Another
is the printed word. And if it is good for television to be
in the hands of a monopoly, why not the press also?

There are in Great Britain publications of very wide
circulation which outdo the most sensational of American publications. We would certainly shrink from the
task of trying to prove that these publications are for
the good of the British nation.

But should they be forbidden? And if they should be
and the principle of controlling the press thus established, what other publications might be next? The
sensational sheets appeal to a far wider audience than
do the more sedate ones. What would prevent the majority deciding that they should be continued and the
very many excellent British dailies suppressed?

It may seem that all this is something for the British
to settle for themselves and that Americans might do
well to keep out of the argument—particularly when
Americans have sufficient problems of their own, which
are being handled with less than consummate wisdom.

That is essentially so, but the British discussion
nevertheless seems to us something in which Americans
do have a legitimate interest and about which they
should be informed.

The decisions and actions of the British carry weight
in this country. The teaching of economics in our colleges has been considerably influenced by the late Lord
Keynes, whose theories reflected British conditions. The
various economic and social programs sponsored by
American "liberals" were influenced by and in some
cases copied from the British Fabian Socialists.

This country is not without its people who would like
to establish some form of control over the various means
of communication, who would like to make the press and
the wireless "responsible." They would be quick to point
to the British example.

—Wall Street Journal

When the editorial writer believes that his opponent has misrepresented the facts, he may try to set the record straight, as did the author of the following simply by answering the items, point by point:

"Facts vs. Fiction"

The assertions made in Senator McCarran's latest statement on the DP problem, ironically entitled "Displaced Persons: Facts vs. Fiction," are so full of distortion and misrepresentation that they merit some reply merely to keep the record straight. We cite three examples:

(1) *Charge:* The section in the proposed DP law which includes provision for admitting 15,000 present and future DP's from behind the Iron Curtain "would constitute a dangerous threat to the security of the United States," according to an unnamed intelligence official. *Fact:* The bill containing this provision was approved by both the Department of Defense and the Department of State, and the Central Intelligence Agency itself has said it is not opposed to it.

(2) *Charge:* There have been "inadequate screening" of DP applicants for admission to the United States, "innumerable instances of wholesale fraud"; and, furthermore, "not a single displaced person who has thus far been admitted * * * by virtue of such fraud and misrepresentation has been returned to Europe." No specific examples are cited. *Fact:* The security procedure in respect to DP applicants is more severe than for ordinary immigrants, including as it does at least seven special checks, and involving the Displaced Persons Commission, the Army's Counter-Intelligence Corps, the Immigration and Naturalization Service, the FBI and the International Refugee Organization. That this elaborate screening process has been conspicuously successful is indicated by the fact that there have been not more than a dozen exclusion or deportation cases involving DP's after arrival in the United

States, for any cause whatsoever. Of these, perhaps four or five involve possible questions of security.

(3) *Charge:* The number of DP's that the proposed DP bill would admit "is, of course, in addition to the number admissible under our general immigration system." *Fact:* This is untrue. Mr. McCarran should know that both the present and the proposed law provide for charging off admissions against quotas for future years, so that the ultimate total of immigrants will be no larger than allowed under existing immigration legislation. This process is known as "mortgaging quotas."

These are only some of the highlights of Mr. McCarran's statement.

—The New York Times

Then there is the rapier of wit, humor, and satire instead of the massive analysis of the essential points of an argument and their refutation. Although it always is fun to write, satire is tricky. There is often the chance that some readers will misunderstand. A wise editorial writer uses it only rarely. But on occasion this type of reply demolishes an opponent's position most effectively. A good example is the following re-creation of an imaginary conversation:

Civil Liberty Defined

Six German students were brought recently to America to learn the meaning of civil liberty.

What better place than Washington, D.C.? The students were taken to the Capital, where they interviewed the guardians of civil liberty on the Loyalty Review Board.

A member of the Board explained to the students how the Board protected civil liberties by ridding the government of Reds and "pinkos," a new word to the Germans.

"What is a pinko?" the German students asked.

"A pinko," the Loyalty Board official replied, "is a

213

man who is against segregation and who fights for civil liberties."

The German students were puzzled. They asked for more information. The official went on to praise the Board for its educational work in persuading Americans to think twice before joining any organizations.

"After all," the official argued, "why join organizations? The average American never need join more than the Boy Scouts, the Reserves and some lodge or veterans' organization."

"But Mrs. Roosevelt has written that Americans should not be intimidated from freely joining with one another," a student protested.

"To hell with Mrs. Roosevelt," cried the Loyalty official. "I don't give a damn what she says!"

"Thank you," said the Germans and went home with renewed faith in civil liberty in the United States.

—New Republic

Close to the rebuttal, and sometimes the satirical, editorial is that type written in annoyance or anger. It might well be called a mad editorial. This kind also is close to the change of pace type to be discussed in the next chapter. The writer of a mad editorial says, in effect, "This smells; let's do something." Illustrative of this variety is the following on Milwaukee's International Apple Week:

Apples and Love in City Hall

Breathless Milwaukeeans who, if they followed Mayor Bohn's official proclamation, finished celebrating "I've Always Loved You Week" only last Friday, are now given another similar task. We are asked by the mayor to join in observing international apple week from Oct. 26 to Nov. 2.

Is there no limit to the kind of petty endorsement that the city hall is willing to give? Instead of promoting movies and polishing apples let's have the mayor inaugurate an "I'd just love to clean up your ashes and garbage week."

Does the mayor, and do the police, believe that Milwaukee is a completely hick town? They certainly act as though they did. Imagine the city's checking automobile drivers and pedestrians for courtesy on Wisconsin av. and then rewarding the winners with free tickets to a movie as part of a commercial promotion plan!

That's what the mayor and police did. And now international apples—or applesauce—week. Come, come, let's grow up!

—Milwaukee Journal

A similar mad mood is demonstrated in a signed editorial in *The Sohioan*, published monthly by The Standard Oil Company of Ohio for its employees. The author of the following comment was an associate editor:

Arise, Commuters, This Is Too Much!

BY E. A. JACQUET

"Good MOR-ning! You are boarding this bus just in time for a pleasant postprandial interlude of news, music, and witticisms—brought to you through the courtesy of the Flip-Flop Pancake Company in cooperation with the Jerkin-Jolt Transit System, your host for your morning ride downtown."

Dreaming? My God, no. It's real—or soon will be if they go through with this recently announced damfoolidea of putting radios in city and suburban busses.

"Installation of radio receivers on public service busses is going ahead rapidly," says a recent news dispatch. "Only a few passengers object. Of thousands questioned in an extensive poll, nine out of ten liked the idea."

Another poll, eh? And after what happened to Dewey, too. Well, as far as I am concerned that lets the Poll-cat out of the bag right there. In the words of the old gospel hymn, where are the Nine? Moreover, I've been a commuter a long time now, and I'm frank to say nobody ever sleeping-polled *me* to learn *my* attitude on whether I wanted my traditional commuter's "forty winks" disturbed by the blatting of a badly-tuned bus radio on the way to work. They can put me down right now as the "one in ten" who objects—in screaming accents. Maybe I'm not normal. Maybe I'm not up with the times. So be it. I say the whole idea is just too awful to contemplate. I can just picture how it would work.

Grabbing my trolley bus in the murk of the dawn, I fumble for my fare and am greeted by the unctious voice in the first paragraph telling me I'm on board for a joyful jaunt cityward through the courtesy of the aforesaid pancake company. The hell I am! I'm on the bus because I have to work for a living, because I ran my ankles off that last hundred yards, and because some old lady on crutches blocked off the driver from a quick getaway. (The day before, when he slammed the door in my face, I suppose that, too, was through the courtesy of the pancake company.)

Settling myself for my usual snooze, what do I hear? "You'll be simply delighted with Dilldock's Dill Pickles. *Try* a Dilldock Dill today. They're *dillies.*" If I could get hold of one, I'd try it, sure enough, right on that *&-$&!! announcer's bezark. I drowse off again—only to be fetched bolt upright with the startling flash that "Flim Flam Biscuits once more rise to the occasion and offer you the Pied Piper Pie Crust Four in 'Sourdough Days.' " Burp!

Despairing of getting my much needed sleep, I open my morning paper, and with my eyes on the newsprint and my ears on the radio I get a scrambled Tower of Babel bedlam that runs like this:

(Paris)—Addressing a United Nations meeting here today, Abdullah Amir Khan said "to the democracy-loving peoples of the world I say, once and for all, the time has come when we must stop appeasing Russia and tell Stalin to *buy a Bilk Singing Canary for the trill that comes once in a lifetime—if ever.*

Shrinking down behind the paper, I hurriedly plunge into a paragraph under a local dateline:

"Questioned as to how the city proposed to raise the funds needed to beautify its pigeon-feeding stations, Councilman Shortsnorter said a special two-mill levy would be placed on the ballot and he urged every voter to *Visit the Palace Theater this week! See the Belle Arts Brutes chew Munchy Crunchy Dog Pellets while improvising on Bach's Fugue in F sharp major! Take the kids—these famous trained dogs are harmless—in fact, their Bach's worse than their bite."*

Sensing that I am waging a losing struggle, I try once more:

(The White House)—In fine spirits at his weekly news conference here this morning, President Truman said he thought the political Jeremiahs who were predicting a business recession as a result of his election upset were still looking at the world through Polaroid glasses. Personally, quipped the President, he was so unconcerned that he planned to spend the coming week-end holiday catching up on his *Wheee-awp Wheee-awp Wheee-awp Whee-awp.* . . .

"Trolley's off," someone shouted from the rear of the bus. So was mine, by this time. Another block of trying to focus my confused and fading faculties simultaneously on newspaper and blaring radio and I knew I would be a hopelessly split schizophrenic. Haggard and harried, I piled out still ten blocks from the office. As the bus driver closed the doors and pulled away from the curb with a leer, I heard the taunting strains of "Heigh-ho! Heigh-ho! It's Off to Work We Go!"

Awake, America! Especially you commuters. Your snoozing days are over!

—*The Sohioan*, Cleveland, Ohio

The following mad editorial is of interest because it marked one high point in the journalistic career of Hodding Carter, Mississippi editor who was the 1946 Pulitzer prize winner. The editorial appeared on the front page of his paper in 1953 after a Negro had been horribly slain:

Bloodstained Whitewash

When a Bolivar County justice of the peace was exonerated Tuesday by another of his ilk in the slaying of a Negro after a grocery debt wrangle, the Benoit town marshal made a comment which most law officers in this nation would consider strange and savage.

He said: "Tell THAT to your Mr. Carter."

Well, marshal, we got the word. We're repeating it now and later, whether or not any bully boys from Benoit or Bolivar County like it or not. We're stating for the record that the hearing conducted by Justice of the Peace E. V. Reams and County Attorney Frank Wynn was the damnedest job of bloodstained whitewashing that ever sickened us.

We are reporting the whole story to state and federal authorities with the prayer and faint hope that they can find some way to follow through. Meanwhile, Mr. Marshal, Mr. County Attorney, Mr. J. P. the killer and Mr. J. P. the exonerator, here's why we think your actions this week are collectively a stench in the nostrils of decent, fairminded citizens.

A man was shot to death. He happened to be a Negro. It is not for us to say that he was murdered, or that he was killed in self-defense or that his slaying was an unavoidable mishap. But we do say that the hearing Tuesday was a wicked farce. Not a single eyewitness was called, though several were available. The only person to testify who was at the scene of the killing was the killer himself.

In a quarter of a century of reporting and reading about unequal justice in the South, this is the first time to our knowledge that no one was summoned as an eyewitness in a publicly committed slaying except the man who used the gun. It is also the first time in our memory that a so-called officer of the law jibed at a newspaper when a killer came clear.

We charge the county attorney and the justice of the peace with shameful laxity in failing to call upon a single one of the witnesses which the *Democrat-Times* so easily found.

And now for a couple more observations. Recently we spent three not altogether pleasant months in distant lands, trying to defend the South against the kind of nasty accusations for which this slaying and hearing provide bloody material. We know, and all our readers know, that if the victim of the Benoit triple-killer had been a white man, or if the killer had been a Negro, this whitewash would not have been tolerated. When he was an officer of the law in Pike County, Justice of the Peace Thomas was indicted for manslaughter, twice tried and never found innocent by juries which debated a total of 32 hours before successive mistrials. That time the victim was white.

Neither God nor lawful man discriminates between races when the taking of life or the breaking of the lesser laws of mankind are involved. Think on that, you people who profess to be Christian or democratic or fair. Until we in Mississippi look upon law and crime without relation to the color or faith or nationality of the principals, we have no right to lift our heads and ask for equal treatment in the concert of states or the community of nations.

—*Delta Democrat-Times,* Greenville, Mississippi

EIGHT

Editorials that

amuse and amaze

IF EDITORIAL WRITERS DRESSED THE WAY THEY WRITE, MANY OF them would wear blue serge or Oxford gray suits, white shirts, and black shoes. They would be those staff members who repeatedly were assigned the informative and argumentative editorials. Over in a corner telling jokes and enjoying themselves thoroughly would be a smaller group of jolly souls in sports clothes. In our comparison, they would be the successful change of pace editorial writers whose aim is either to amuse or to amaze their readers.

Change of pace editorials can be fun for both writers and readers. Unconventional in writing style and subject matter, they challenge the abilities of their authors. With entertainment as their principal goal, they provoke a chuckle from readers when they are competently done.

Not only the "funny" or humorous editorial will be discussed, but also those dealing with mood and color, the more conventional nature editorials, and the editorial paragraphs.

Change of pace editorials may solve a problem

In his autobiography, William Allen White described the change of pace editorial as "frivolous comment on unimportant events of froth and foam on the daily newspaper's editorial tide." It certainly is all that for writers in this second half of the Twentieth Century but it is more, too. Now editorial writers may use humor to hit a target which in the Emporia editor's day would have merited a full-scale blockbuster of argument. Frequently the short, quick jab of humor is more effective than a long, sober-faced editorial.

During the past decade or two, when editorial page staff members have gotten together to talk over their problems, as they do, for instance, at such meetings as the annual sessions of the National Conference of Editorial Writers and the American Society of Newspaper Editors, their discussions have shifted eventually to the change of pace editorials. All but a slim minority favor more lightness and humor on editorial pages. The heavy weight of information and argument, they believe, has frightened away too many readers who have not yearned for either expansive background or neatly tailored opinions. Impressed by the popularity of comic strips, more sprightly feature articles, and other departments unconcerned with "think stuff," editorial writers saw in the change of pace editorial a chance to bring to the editorial pages some of the appeal of these widely read newspaper sections.

At the American Society of Newspaper Editors' panel discussion of editorial writing in 1948, for example, a prevailing opinion was that there ought to be more light editorials. Since that discussion and others at N.C.E.W. meetings, more change of pace editorials have been printed, proportionately. While serious treatment of world, national, and local issues cannot be ignored, these need not be the only offerings on the editorial page menu. A commentator at a N.C.E.W. critique suggested that, since a little dessert goes well with a meal, editorial writers might also add a dash of humor when planning their pages.

In a change of pace editorial, an author may incorporate comments on many of the wide variety of subjects that by their nature are unsuited for solemn-faced, ponderous treatment, yet which people are talking about. Here is an opportunity to appeal to all readers, not just those interested in politics and foreign affairs.

Expressing an attitude held by a majority of editors, Louis La-Coss of the *St. Louis Globe-Democrat* pointed out that "the light, sometimes whimsical editorials frequently cause much more comment than the profound, two-story stuff."

In addition to increasing readership, such comments may touch a sensitive spot and bring results that no mass of arguments, logically and carefully presented, would achieve.

Sevellon Brown III of the *Providence* (R.I.) *Journal-Bulletin* pointed out the double benefits of a change of pace editorial in *The Masthead* (Summer, 1949) when he wrote:

The beauty of the "funny" editorial is that it serves, when intelligently used, a double purpose. It is reader-bait, sure; but it is also— or should be—something more. Often humor can put across the point as no amount of stuffy fulmination will do, and frequently it will reach readers who just won't plod through three-quarters of a column on the latest from Afghanistan.

But getting the most out of editorial-page humor isn't easy. The really effective "funny" pieces require just as much thought, just as much research and just as much painful polishing as the heavy leaders.

Then to prove that "humor on the editorial page is not simply icing on the cake, not merely a come-on, but an extremely useful and effective tool," Brown cited one single three-inch humorous comment that ended with the single word, "Nuts!" as the appropriate reply to alibis and explanations for the bad Providence bus service. It worked. Improvements in bus service began almost immediately after the editorial was printed.

Bill Vaughan, author of the *Kansas City Star's* "Star Beams" column which provides chuckles for readers of the editorial page, grouped rhymed editorials, nostalgic editorials, sports editorials, humorous comments on current happenings, and editorial paragraphs all together as light editorial types.

At the 1948 National Conference of Editorial Writers, Merlo Pusey of the *Washington Post* pointed out that the light or change of pace editorial is the most difficult thing possible to write. Then he elaborated:

The light editorial is extremely precious and you can't just order a man to sit down and write a light editorial. It can't be done; but when you can get them they add greatly to the editorial page. . . .

Two suggestions to develop this "precious" quality were offered at the same meeting. Harry Boyd of the *Cedar Rapids* (Iowa) *Gazette* asked if an editorial writer might not get the feel of how to write in a light, amusing vein if he spent less time studying topics and tomes to improve his mind and more time reading articles and books with a light touch. William T. Polk of the *Greensboro* (N.C.) *Daily News* suggested writing eight or ten paragraphs each day and then picking one every two or three days to be expanded into a light editorial. "It is a rather laborious method, but it would work," he added.

Although the light touch is always hard to handle, there is no reason why it may not also be used in both informative and argumentative editorials. For example, the editorial from *The Sohioan* in Chapter Seven showed how humor, imagination, and argument could be successfully combined. Readers like to smile and it may be possible to amuse them while informing or arguing. This certainly would step up readership of an editorial page and thus make all ideas expressed there more effective.

It's the way it's written

Frequently part of the editorial's achievement is to offer an unconventional twist. That is the forte of the change of pace specialist.

One sure way to attract attention—and there certainly is nothing wrong with an editorial writer's trying to do that any more than for a headline writer to put a banner on an important news story—is to use an unconventional style. Few limitations exist. As the following examples will show, a fertile mind and ingenuity are among the prerequisites.

Writers have sent Valentines (comic variety and serious ones), proposed appropriate Christmas presents, listed achievement awards, suggested birthday greetings, composed poems, made up Twentieth Century fables, inserted want ads, re-created conversations, written open letters, and offered a wide list of other ideas not commonly associated with editorial page conventionality.

A spoof editorial comment may be extremely effective. The writer obviously has fun; so does the reader. The result is that the community talks and thinks about that subject.

When Robert Ruark, syndicated columnist, defended the use of prepositions at the ends of sentences, Overton Jones of the *Richmond* (Virginia) *Times-Dispatch* wrote an editorial with every sentence ending with a preposition. It follows:

Put Those Prepositions
Where They Belong At

Columnist Robert Ruark made some strong statements Monday concerning the rule against using a preposition to end a sentence with. He said there was no logical reason why you shouldn't put one of those "lousy, skimpy little words" at the tail end of a sentence if you wanted to.

There's really nothing for Columnist Ruark to get excited about. Prepositions always are supposed to govern other words, called their "relatives," and only the laziest writer should find it difficult to arrange the sequence of his words so that the relative is last and the preposition is before.

Sometimes, with all the belittling of the old tried and standard rules, we wonder what modern literature is coming to. Instead of polishing their sentences, as did the old masters of the language, many of today's writers sit down and simply dash something off. Prepositions are left dangling naked at the end of sentences, and you can't tell where they're going to or where they came from. These unclad words, tied onto nothing, appear about to take off.

In the speaking art, too, conformity with standard rules of grammar should be striven after. Here, errors are easier to fall into. A person who wishes to leave a good impression with his listeners should use the very best grammar he is capable of. With anything less, he should refuse to put up.

It is a sad commentary on the literary world today that fundamental rules of grammar are laughed at. This is the age of skepticism when there's little left to cling to. Fortunately, however, there are a few purists in the writing and speaking arts who refuse to cut corners and whose work can be depended on.

Yes, Ruark, end your sentences with prepositions if you want to. But don't try to influence other writers, who to such a flagrant violation of rules of grammar will never give into!

—Richmond Times-Dispatch

The following is self-evident to any reader who has encountered a sinus sufferer in the fall:

Hay Fever Talk?

If you haven't already doticed id, this year's bollen coudt is runnidg somewhat ahead of last year's. Fragly, if id gets buch higher we're headig for the bountains.

—New York World-Telegram and Sun

The following example was accompanied by illustrations of two types of stop signs currently being used in Minneapolis:

Stay, Tarry a While

"STOP : to cease to go on; to halt." (Webster.)

"COMPLETE: Syn. full; absolute; utter and total." (Ibid.)

And therein lies a tale of confusion, absolute, utter, and total.

Have you ever, putting your trust in a "Thru Stop" sign, started confidently across a street—and then had to scramble madly for the safety of the nearest curb? Have you then, silently or aloud, denounced the driver of the offending car, maligning his literacy, his intelligence, perhaps even slandering his ancestry?

Tut. The man is only a student of semantics, an interpreter of traffic signs possessing a keener discrimination than your own.

Observe the two examples pictured here. Obviously the authorities who erected these signs differentiate between a mere "stop" and a "complete stop." And many Minneapolis drivers have caught on.

"Stops," we hear, are currently defined by local motorists as "rolling, faltering or staggering." Plus the "complete" variety, of course, if a squad car is in sight.

Somewhat puzzled ourselves, we explored Webster a bit further and happened upon this semi-synonym of "stop":

"TARRY: To delay . . . linger . . . stay . . . sojourn."

Which suggests the possibility of a legal "lingering" at the octagonal yellow signs, instead of "completely" stopping.

—Minneapolis Star

When a new fountain statue was displayed at the Des Moines Art Center, the *Tribune* printed this editorial together with an illustration of the new art acquisition:

This Horse, Folks, Was Stung by a Hornet

When you go out to the Art Center to see the new Carl Milles fountain statue, don't get caught saying that it "looks crazy."

This is as faithful a telling of an incident of mythological history as we ever saw, and there are probably not a half dozen artists in the world with the imagination and talent to do it as effectively as Milles has done it.

We will concede that, at first glance, a flying horse in the middle of a wing-over has a shock effect. Ditto with the character overhead who is about to execute an Immelman. But that's precisely the idea.

This winged beast, Pegasus (accent the PEG), has

just been stung by a hornet. No lesser deity than Zeus (Zoos) himself sent the insect down to do the villainous deed.

And that was where the rider, Bellerophon (Bel-LAIR-o-fon), and the flying horse parted company—exactly as they are doing in the sculptured representation.

But wait! Let us start at the beginning.

* * *

You see, Perseus (accent the PER) was a son of the great god Zeus, or Jupiter, in ancient Greek mythology. He was sent by a scheming king to get the head of Medusa, one of the three Gorgons with snakes for hair. Though ordinarily this would have been sure death, as the king intended, the gods and goddesses protected Perseus and he whacked Medusa's head off.

Now Poseidon (Po-SIGH-don) the sea god had been visiting Medusa and when her head came off, Pegasus the winged horse sprang from her body.

The next we hear of Pegasus, Bellerophon captured him at a spring, and used the fabulous horse as his mount in many a fierce battle. But Bellerophon made the mistake of trying to soar to heaven on Pegasus' back, and Zeus didn't like this arrogance.

So Zeus sent the hornet, which did its duty, and Bellerophon went tumbling to earth. Fact is, he landed so hard that he was both lame and blind, and thereafter he wandered around grief-stricken and hermit-like, shunning men and hated by the gods.

* * *

Alas, daring young man.

But what of Pegasus, you ask?

Well, the flying horse soared on up to heaven and took his place among the stars, as every student of astronomy knows.

But among the things that Pegasus had done, while flying around the earth, was to click his hoof against Mount Helicon. And there a spring gushed forth—for was not Pegasus the son of the ocean god, Poseidon, and first found at the ocean's source?

In fact, Pegasus clicked off a lot of other springs in

his lifetime of galloping about. But this particular spring on Mount Helicon was important because this was the home of the Muses, and so they paid special honor to Pegasus for giving them the spring.

That is why, later on, Pegasus became the steed on which the poets were supposed to soar away on their flights into the realm of poetic fancy!

* * *

Indeed, the symbolism inherent in this sculpture is much broader than the mere story of Bellerophon, who sought to soar up to the heavens.

It seems obvious to us that Sculptor Milles has embodied in this figure all of Man's aspirations to soar, intellectually and spiritually, through pursuit of the Arts.

So we're depending on you to go out, if you haven't, and get better acquainted with our new friends, Pegasus and Bellerophon, depicted in bronze at the very apex of their respective careers.

You just won't be able to resist soaring a little, at the sight.

—*Des Moines Tribune*

In the lighter, kidding vein, the *Christian Science Monitor* offered the following comments on a ruling of a federal district judge at Trenton, N.J.:

Whodunit: New Angle

The speeder who lays his offense to a fibbing speedometer, the wild rider who says his car refused to stay in control, the overtime parker who pleads that his auto just wouldn't go home when he told it to—these and all other questionable drivers who blame their sins of omission and commission on the old jalopy may say I-told-you-so when reading of the ruling made by a United States District Court judge at Trenton, New Jersey.

He found an automobile guilty of smuggling diamonds. The car, he ruled, was as guilty as its driver, and was subject to confiscation. Its owner contested the ruling and so did a finance company who had made a loan

on the car and who called the car an "innocent by-
stander" in the case. The judge harked back to Biblical
times: "If an ox gores a man, the ox must be put to
death. That's ancient law."

So the next time an officer asks, "Where's the fire?"
the fire-bent motorist may be tempted to retort, "Ask
my automobile." But if he does, he will only be going
into a legal skid, out of which he may be rudely jerked
by a reminder (by a judge) that the driver is as guilty
as the car.

—Christian Science Monitor

Writing memorandums to readers introduces another unconventional approach which may provide added reader interest.
When President Truman's daughter took up a public career in
concert singing, the *Denver Post* saw fit to print a "Memo to
Margaret" with a conversational, somewhat slangy style that
would attract many who might not have read an ordinary editorial.

When a night police reporter on the *Long Island Star-Journal*
left a long memo on "a suggestion for an editorial," the editorial
writer wisely published the notes themselves with a three-line
explanation:

Death on the Parkway

The following was written by a Long Island Star-
Journal night police reporter as a memo to his city
desk:

I have a suggestion for an editorial. It concerns all the
parkways and the lack of signs telling people where
they are, and the few police call boxes in case of emergency.

I have watched this for years and have seen minutes
run into half an hour on a parkway with people bleed-
ing to death because nobody knew where they were on
the parkway. A victim was stretched out on Grand Central parkway at Astoria boulevard less than a year ago
for an hour because of this trouble. He died later.

I have sat in a police station and heard these confusing calls come in to men at the switchboard. This is mostly true after midnight. Every motorist is not a Queens resident. When he comes upon a two-car crash or a car wrapped around a pole, his first thought is to summon aid. He has to find one of the few call boxes which are spread out too far.

When he gets the police on the phone to say there are injured people all over the parkway, the cop will ask him: "Where on the parkway?" Many, many times I have heard the motorist say he does not know where on the parkway.

My suggestion is that if every pole on the parkway and service roads was marked with luminous numbers, the cop could ask, "Did you see the number on the pole at the scene?"

The cop in headquarters should have a chart showing where the pole is located. Even-numbered poles could be on the east-bound lane and odd numbers on the west-bound lane. The numbers on the service roads could have a letter before them.

It may sound a bit complicated but Herbie, the photographer, and I have gone out on these calls and watched ambulances lose a lot of time because they did not know what lane to take.

Where there is a center mall or divider, the ambulance may have to make a long, unnecessary trip to another exit while a man bleeds to death.

When that motorist gives his well-intentioned but inaccurate location, the cop at the switchboard can only give the same location to the hospital ambulance driver and to the prowl-car cops who cover that area.

In that fatal crash at Astoria, the St. John's Ambulance received the location as "Astoria boulevard service road next to the parkway." They found nothing at the scene and made the long trip back to the hospital; the dying man was down on the parkway, a short distance away.

Recently, a motorist called in to say a car crashed into the guard rail and reported it was on the Belt parkway; he thought it was near Jamaica avenue.

We went out on the call and the crash was near Linden boulevard, not far from the Southern State extension. The ambulance wasted the same time we did in getting there.

It is only a suggestion that comes to me after standing at the side of a car at 3 o'clock in the morning and watching some poor guy with blood running out of his ears and an ambulance wasting valuable time up on the service road, headed in the wrong direction, looking for a crash some place on the parkway.

The two-way radios in the Queens General Hospital ambulances have been working fine. As the cops in headquarters receive better addresses, they are able to pass them on to the ambulance drivers.

When the other hospitals' ambulances get radios, it will be better. But there will always be valuable time lost until the parkway situation is cleared up and they stop giving locations as vague as "about half a mile east of this or that bridge."

—Long Island Star-Journal

Typography is another way

Typographical variation simply combined with a light touch may lift a serious subject out of the conventional routine. On occasion, the writer may turn to poetry or direct conversation and again he may depend more on pure typographical design.

The *St. Louis Post-Dispatch* staff, which is particularly apt at giving ideas a distinctive change of pace twist, turned to poetry to discuss a news story. Certainly the following editorial received more attention from readers than any stereotyped comment would have gotten:

Spring Song

Tennyson might have said it:

In the Spring a livelier iris on the dove has made its mark,
And an Elder Statesman's fancy turns to sitting in the park.

231

Shakespeare could have sung it:

When shepherds pipe on oaten straws
More loud than boxes of the juke,
When turtles tread, and rooks, and daws,
There sitteth in the park Baruch.

Swinburne would have had a fling with it:

When the hounds of spring are on winter's traces,
And the plowman treads on the new-cut trench,
And all things take their vernal places,
Bernard Baruch is on the bench.

But all the International News Service had to say was:

Spring was welcomed prematurely to New York yesterday by the return of financier Bernard M. Baruch to his Central Park bench "office."

—St. Louis Post-Dispatch

Or here is a pre-Christmas parody poem for another example:

With Apologies, Etc.

I hope that I will never see,
Another purple Christmas tree.
A tree some goon has sprayed with paint
To make it look like what it ain't;
A tree that God would blush to make—
A garish, ugly nature fake.
Even bad verse by fools like me
Is better than a purple tree.

—Denver Post

Conversation may bring out a viewpoint without any need to use the techniques of argument. Illustrative of how conversation may be used is the editorial reprinted from the *New Republic* (see page 2 1 3), which carried its quota of satire as well as the conversational style.

After the 1948 presidential election proved their predictions wrong, pollsters and correspondents offered to "eat crow" publicly. The following editorial grew out of George Gallup's statement a couple of years later that he felt he could stop eating crow in light of more recent predictions, which, he explained, were successful. The editorial utilized single-word paragraphs which gave additional white space and attracted attention:

A Change in Diet

Because he correctly predicted that Herbert Lehman would defeat John Foster Dulles in the New York senatorial race, George Gallup of the Gallup Poll says, "I feel that I can quit eating crow and try a little pheasant for a change."

But . . .

Gallup predicted that Lehman would get 57 per cent and Dulles 43 per cent. This is an error of 5 per cent—one more than the 4 per cent "permissible error" Gallup gives himself.

And . . .

Gallup predicted that Lehman would have a majority of more than 350,000. Lehman's majority was less than 200,000.

If on the basis of these comparisons Mr. Gallup wants to serve himself pheasant, that is his own affair. But we suggest that he keep a little crow in the ice box to nibble on every once in a while just to keep in practice.

—*St. Louis Star-Times*

Human frailties provide editorial grist

To paraphrase a common saying, "People are so human." Any diligent reader of the news has seen dozens of dispatches on how individuals have gotten themselves into all sorts of embarrassing difficulties. They thought they were behaving as run of the mill human beings would and then suddenly something slipped up and they got themselves into weird predicaments. All of these provided grist for editorial writers in search of material for change of pace editorials.

Even the usually dignified *New York Times* could not resist pointing an editorial finger at a Missouri professor who got himself into an unenviable spot:

The Captive Professor

Every male spouse will feel fraternal sympathy for the Missouri professor whose ineptness as a handyman, while trying to make his little family comfortable, has just made him a laughing stock wherever newspapers are read. The preliminaries of this unfortunate incident will have a familiar ring: as Winter came on members of the family complained that the house was drafty. This was a suprise to the professor, a Mr. Chester Prince, who had noticed nothing of the kind himself. But when the complaints became insistent he, though preoccupied with worthier matters, applied himself to the problem with force and energy. Of a scientific turn of mind, he did not rely on the observations of others; but his own inquiry verified his family's findings, that the breezes came from the attic. He promptly attacked with hammer and nails.

Something, alas, went wrong. It is barely possible that the professor really intended to hole himself in for the Winter, away from the world including his family, and then found he had forgotten to bring along his pemmican. At any rate, after shutting off the drafts with admirable completeness, he discovered that he had also sealed himself in the attic, and had so exhausted himself with his self-forgetful labors that he was unable to pry the boards loose.

His desperate calls for help brought his two daughters and—a further ignominy—one of their boy friends. We may charitably close our ears now to the derisive laughter with which the rescue was made, and the callous speed with which the tale sped over the campus. Best too to avert the eyes as Professor Prince faces his classes and makes the courageous effort to reclaim his dignity. The event will be subject to embellishment and embroidery from year to year, of course, with a garnishment of references to Robinson Crusoe's boat diligently built too far from the water to launch. It is of the stuff that legend is made; so unforgettable, indeed, that the good professor may wish he had stayed in his attic.

—The New York Times

And to borrow again from the *St. Louis Post-Dispatch*, there is this editorial about Missouri's Department of Education:

Duncecap for Educators

We are indebted to John H. Shea, publisher of the Lexington (Mo.) Daily Advertising-News, for an amazing and amusing story concerning the State Department of Education. The department has flunked in eighth grade arithmetic. Of 50 questions and answers it sent to rural schools for the first semester of 1948–49, seven answers were wrong. Here they are:

No. 6. Find the number of board feet in a plank 2 inches in thickness, 10 inches wide, and 18 feet long.

Department of Education answer: 5 board feet.

Correct answer: 30 board feet.

No. 14. Find the area of a round mirror with a radius of 12 inches.

Department of Education answer: $434\frac{2}{7}$ square inches.

Correct answer: $452\frac{4}{7}$ square inches.

No. 21. Find the volume of a cone paper drinking cup whose diameter is 4 inches and whose height is 6 inches (use 3.14).

Department of Education answer: 25.16 cubic inches.

Correct answer: 25.12 cubic inches.

No. 22. What would be the selling price of a car invoiced to the dealer for $1240 if the dealer is allowed a profit of 15 per cent?

Department of Education answer: $1446.

Correct answer: $1426.

No. 26. Find the interest on $1960 at 6 per cent for one year.

Department of Education answer: $98.

Correct answer: $117.60.

No. 41. Copy in columns and add: 8.705, .75, 9.4, 4.86.
Department of Education answer: 23.915.
Correct answer: 23.715.
No. 48. Divide 2 ⅓ by 8.
Department of Education answer: 14.
Correct answer: ⁷⁄₂₄.

Mr. Shea calculates that, if the teachers accepted the department's answers as a guide, a student making 12 mistakes of his own and being charged with the state's seven errors, would fail instead of getting the good passing mark to which he is entitled.

The kids, no doubt, will be gleeful about Jefferson City's mistakes, but the State Department of Education will hardly enjoy the duncecap which it has earned.

—*St. Louis Post-Dispatch*

The whole wide world lies open as material

Subject matter, too, may yield the distinctive touch for a change of pace editorial. Readers are interested in all sorts of things and the astute editorial writer who wants to get attention—and keep it —will discuss what interests them. This is the area where editorial writers may break away from preoccupations with politics and other "think" pieces and discuss topics that Mrs. Smith might talk about with her neighbor over the backyard fence or that Mr. Jones might discuss around a water cooler with his fellow workers.

For instance, everybody talks about the weather yet only a few editorial page writers discuss it. One who did wrote the following diverting comments, with a threat in the last paragraph that undoubtedly there would be more editorials on the subject later:

Unseasonable and Unreasonable

Normally we do not start editorializing about hot weather until August or, in exceptional cases, July. Editorials, like vegetables, are seasonal; they may not follow the sun, but they keep a weather eye on it. But even though this is not yet officially the hot-weather-editorial season, we are constrained to jump the gun by calling immediate attention to conditions.

For the last two days, the temperature has been near 90. This is a fact, an indisputable fact, a cold fact. The Weather Bureau calls this sort of thing unseasonable; a better word might be unreasonable. Signs of the heat already are apparent in various strange forms of behavior: Bus drivers are making off with buses, newborn fawns are hanging around Bronx restaurants, the Giants are winning ball games. People have once again taken to consuming water in large quantities, though it has been carefully explained to us for a year why we should not consume water in large quantities. All these curious happenings indicate we are entering a dangerous period. Right now, all one can do is to think back on the recently departed winter, those pleasant January days when the snow was piled high, the wind howled, and every one was laid up with a cold. In a few weeks even these happy memories will have gone up in fire.

We expect to return to this subject later.

—*New York Herald Tribune*

The controversy over whether Shakespeare was Shakespeare or someone else has intrigued English teachers and a few others for generations but it would hardly seem a subject for almost a column on an editorial page. Yet a writer used this topic as a "seasonable diversion from the daily staples of rape, murder, suicide and presidential politics":

Who Wrote What?

Ever since the Glastonbury (Conn.) Glawakus signed a contract with the circus and the Loch Ness sea monster joined the Alcoholics Anonymous and the flying saucers disappeared into the cosmic dishpans, the public prints have been in sore need of some seasonable diversion from the daily staples of rape, murder, suicide and presidential politics. What was wanting has now been supplied by Mr. Charles Wisner Barrell of New York, and our readers, it seems to us, should be accordingly grateful. Mr. Barrell has entered suit in our District Court against Dr. Giles E. Dawson of the Folger Library, thereby reopening the question of who, if anybody, wrote the plays and poems attributed to Shakespeare.

This controversy is, to be sure, a bit of a chestnut, but we must face the fact that ours is not an imaginative age. Besides, is it not, as the Bard (or whoever it was) said, the destiny of both men and chestnuts "with vilest worms to dwell"? Anyway, the controversy serves a useful and hygienic purpose. It is one of those rare and precious public questions about which it is possible to get excited in hot weather without endangering the peace of the world or the survival of free institutions. It is also the sort of controversy which is eminently suited to democratic methods of discussion, since no particular qualifications of scholarship are required to entitle one to an opinion and each disputant is at liberty to devise his own rules of evidence.

As for the particulars of the suit, it appears that Mr. Barrell took some X-ray and infra-red photographs of a supposed portrait of Shakespeare in the Folger Libary which, he says, prove that it is really a picture of Edward de Vere, the seventeenth Earl of Oxford. Dr. Dawson says that whatever it is Mr. Barrell sees in these photographs, it is something that nobody else can see in them, and also what—not to put too fine a point on it—actually isn't there. This, it seems, constitutes the libel for which Mr. Barrell is asking $50,000 damages and raises an interesting question in epistemology; but perhaps we had better not go into that.

Those who think that it was neither Oxford nor Shakespeare but Lord Bacon who wrote the plays are, we gather, remaining haughtily neutral in this contest between the Messrs. Barrell and Dawson. Probably this also applies to the champions of the Earl of Derby, Sir Edward Dyer, Sir Philip Sidney and other putative authors of Shakespeare. About all these sects have in common anyway is the belief that the Shakespeare myth persists only because of the obscurantism of the English professors who have made it their vested interest. If this is so, it seems to us that the anti-Shake-speareans have pointedly failed to profit by the lessons of the recent Republican National Convention.

Obviously, the only way to depose the Bard from his present preeminence in English letters would be for the Oxfordians, Baconians, Dyerites and the rest to get together in a smoke-filled room somewhere and agree on a single anti-Shakespearean candidate. This, apparently, they are unable or unwilling to do. Another mistake they make is to insist on replacing the barefoot country boy from Stratford with some elegant, court-bred noblemen, on the premise that the Shakespeare plays are just too damn good to have been written by anybody below the rank of a baronet. Naturally, this sort of argument does not go down very well in a demo-cratic country like ours.

Yet it seems to us that a solution of the controversy, satisfactory to all concerned, is quite possible. The compromise we propose is that not only the Shake-speare plays and poems, but the *Novum Organum*, the *Apologie for Poetry* and all the other famous works of the period be declared the products of multiple authorship. In other words, we can assume a sort of general production and editorial board, assisted by an extensive research department, prepared on short no-tice to knock out a masterpiece in almost any field, in-cluding drama and philosophy. Let us assume that Shakespeare's position in this organization was that of chief editor and majority stockholder, and that the sen-ior associate editors included Lord Bacon, Sidney, Dyer, the Earl of Oxford—and just to broaden the democratic base, as they said at Yalta—the first and second grave-diggers, Guy Fawkes, Doll Tearsheet and Queen Elizabeth. This would explain how, by popular con-fusion, Shakespeare got the credit for doing it all by himself. Even today, as you have doubtless observed, there are a lot of people who don't bother to read all the acknowledgments of collaboration which precede a big movie feature.

—Washington Post

How the choice of subject may offer an appropriate opportunity for an editorial writer to vent sarcasm on some topic is illustrated in the following editorial on a Harvard Medical School project:

Incontrovertible Proof
That Men and Women Are Different

In spite of protests, pressure and propaganda we have always held firmly to the old-fashioned notion that there is a difference between the sexes. Our critics might charge that our opinion is biased, our judgment swayed more by emotion than by reason.

So far as the physical aspect is concerned there now is scientific evidence in support of our position. A research group of the Harvard Medical School, after a careful study of both males and females, claims to have found that the male is a weakling in health in all periods of life.

This discovery clears up a mystery that has puzzled many a man. He thinks of himself traditionally as the protector of the home, swinging a club or strangling wild beasts with his bare hands. Because of this traditional function he assumes that he is superior physically to the female. Why is it then, that on a shopping expedition or a visit to a museum of art he tires so much sooner than she does? Why is it that, when he dances, he is ready to stop long before she is? When the hour grows late why is it that he, not she, is the one to suggest going home? The Harvard doctors explain it all. It is because he, not she, is the weakling.

In the light of this discovery it appears that in the distribution of domestic duties the male is mistakenly called upon to perform tasks for which he actually has inferior equipment. If a window is stubborn, it is he who is called upon to see what he can do with it. If a tire gets a puncture, it is he who changes it.

It is he who brings the trunk down from the attic, moves the heavy furniture in the living room, pushes the laden wheelbarrow, holds the child up to see the parade go by, carries the suitcases, operates the garden cultivator and the lawn roller.

Not only is the deficiency of the male true of human beings, say the scientists, but also of the whole animal kingdom. The flowing mane of the male lion, the gaudy tail of the peacock, like man's broad shoulders and quivering muscles, are mere shams to cover inherent weakness.

To achieve a better balance between the sexes, should the women take over the heavy work? There is a question whether even they, with their superior physiques, are equal to the tasks a man is normally called upon to do around the house. In the Harvard survey, one woman was found to have a heart condition. Investigation of the cause revealed that, no man being around, she had herself carried two tons of coal packed in 100-pound sacks from the basement to the street.

—Baltimore *Sun*

Nature takes a bow

The cult of nature lovers among editorial writers has brought into being a whole classification of writing known as the nature editorial. In a paradox that would intrigue psychiatrists, its use generally has been in reverse ratio to the actual contact of readers with nature. Thus *The New York Times* and *New York Herald Tribune* in the nation's most populated area fondly publish this type of editorial at least once a week, while the weeklies in small communities where nature is seen daily in undress may pass the topic by with scant comments during an entire season. This isn't always true. For instance, one well-known exception to the metromania aspect of nature editorials is Marian Ellet of the Concordia (Kansas) *Blade*, whose writings are widely reprinted throughout the Midwest. *Life* (November 20, 1944), discussing "Rural Delights of *The New York Times*" in a nine-page picture spread, claimed these editorials "express the gentle nostalgia of a country boy who, having gone to the city and made good, looks back wistfully to his boyhood on the farm."

Typical of this editorial grouping is this colorful picture of the end of summer:

Confirmation

The sun sinks west, by the compass; dawn rises clear out of the east; there is only a few minutes' difference between the span of a day's light and darkness. Thus ends the summer, with the scarlet feathers of the sumac thrusting from roadside thickets, symbolic of the Indian Summer to come. Thus end all summers, with the bronze of maturity rustling in the gardens, the crispness of autumn in the morning air and the evening starlight.

One needn't be an astronomer to recognize an autumn equinox. The precise time, perhaps, the day and hour and second beyond the minute, is a matter of calculation by rules of celestial mechanics. But the season, the time of change, is written on every bough and punctuated by every blade of grass. The blind can hear it, and the deaf must see it with their eyes half closed. It is there in the touch of a leaf, the texture of a twig, tangible to the most casually inquisitive finger.

The dumb things know it. Woodchucks raid the corn-fields, to add a final ounce of fat for hibernation. Gray squirrels rattle the rusty leaves of the hickories as they take their tithe of the crop. Chipmunks gather grass and thistledown to line their winter nests. Migrant birds start moving south.

The precise time comes at 10:22 P.M. this coming Wednesday. At that moment the sun, though more than four hours set, crosses the celestial equator. That is the mathematics of it, the precise calculation. But the obvious truth is that summer is gone, now, merged into autumn. The winesap reddens on the bough. The cricket chirps in the corner. The equinox is only confirmation.

—The New York Times

Proof that this type of editorial writing is not entirely the monopoly of the city dwellers is the following editorial from one of the country's better known weeklies, *The Vineyard Gazette* of

Edgartown, Massachusetts, which once was called "the last weekly newspaper in the country to preserve its own and authentic flavor":

A Fragrance in August

Just as one might think the most flavorsome time of the summer had ended, along comes the beguiling scent of apples. True, the apple is symbolic of fall, but it helps to have summer blended with a foretaste of what is to come. As a matter of fact, it can be proved that apples belong to summer too. Small boys always have known this and do not seem to have quite forgotten even in the space rocket and atomic age.

The thing about this August smell of apples is that it overtakes the unsuspecting passer on lane or street, and a sudden rush of other things overtakes him too. With this sweet-tart essence is linked a theme of years and adventure that seems to encompass the whole time of man.

To make a fuss about the fragrance of something that is most importantly for the palate may appear to be a disproportion and perhaps it is, but the taste of apples is private and their smell is public and generous, a persuasive ingredient of our Vineyard atmosphere. The apple on the tree or fallen upon the ground distills its presence into the season of the year, and the translation may be made back and forth.

Now August acquires new character, an astringency that runs through the scent of ripening apples to the cool nights, the bright and imaginative Milky Way in the lofty sky, the sunlight and dew in the morning, the whickering of the flickers. All these August things run together, and of them all the apple smell is most immediate and meaningful to the wanderer out of doors.

—*The Vineyard Gazette*

A nature editorial may blend over even more toward the mood piece, as is illustrated in the following, printed during a fall while the Korean War was going on:

Dead Leaves Fall

The sun is hot at midday, but anyone can sense the difference. Autumn is almost here. Already brown leaves go scooting in the wind and the grass looks weary, as if the attempt to grow ahead of the lawnmower were no longer worth the effort.

Autumn can be a gay and dancing sprite with dresses of crimson and gold, filled with the exuberance of youth and possessing undimmed hope for the future. And, conversely, autumn can be the shrouded figure prowling the night, or a tired old man with memories.

* * *

Everything was gray, the North Atlantic, the guns, the men sprawled beside the guns, the hooded figures who kept watch beside the guns, the horizon, the outlines of the masts. The sea was gray and the future was gray and even the voices were gray and muted.

One sat there on the rolling deck, another speck of gray, and wondered how long it would take to whip the Kaiser, for this was World War One.

* * *

Autumn is the L'Allegro of all the months of the year to those who are wise, for the very air is filled with zest and coolness and the pleasant odor of ripening grapes and apples and burning leaves. Even the sounds of autumn are delightful, particularly the thud of a toe against a football; the crack of a shoulderpad against a sturdy pair of legs. And yet autumn can be the Il Penseroso of all the months of the year to one who will let his mood run away with his good sense; to one who is unable to erase things from his brain.

* * *

Everything was gray in the light of early morning; the trees and the hedgerows and the ditch on one side of the hedgerow, and the face of the colonel and the other faces that were there in the ditch beside the hedgerow. Even the voice of the colonel was of a grayish quality as he said: "What the goddam fools will do, of course, is to start hollering about taxes, and then they'll whack off regiments and divisions until we'll be so weak that we couldn't whip a sixth rate power. They've always done it, and they'll do it again, you mark my words."

One listened to the planes droning overhead and wondered how long it would take to get out of Normandy; how long it would take to whip Hitler, for this was World War Two.

* * *

But even a moody man can not fail to be impressed with autumn, even though hay fever wracks him and the state of the world depresses him. He suffers when he reads paragraphs like this:

"Most of the wounded were still, now. They were deep in sleep beneath the merciful peace brought by the drugs, most of them. A few stirred restlessly. One man whose face was swathed in bandages struggled to get out of the litter. The medics pressed back while a young doctor gave him another shot of morphine. Gradually he became quiet."

But still and all, this is not yet, thank God, World War Three. There is always hope that men may hit upon the magic formula that may prevent another worldwide conflict. And until that possibility has been exhausted man would do well to look upon autumn as he once looked; that in admiration of her, he forgot himself and his small problems. Swirl that dress, gal. Faster! Faster!

—*Cleveland Plain Dealer*

Writers try to capture mood and color

Mood and color are elusive at best. For an editorial writer to capture them is an assignment that only a few can do with constant success. Yet the editorial that probably is most widely known of all those millions that have appeared in newspapers—The *New York Sun's* "Is There A Santa Claus?" (see pages 43–44)—was and still is beloved by generations because it succeeded extraordinarily in the difficult job of capturing the real meaning of Christmas.

Ben Hur Lampman of the Portland *Oregonian* turned down a chance to help write speeches for President Herbert Hoover to deliver in the 1932 campaign. He wanted to stay on with his paper to write editorials. Through the decades his editorials have been reprinted widely in the Pacific Northwest and some of them have been published in a book. His special forte is to capture a delicate mood and put it into type so that readers too may feel it. Among his words that have had to be reprinted because of so many requests were "The Wind in the Flag" on Memorial Day and "Where to Bury a Dog," written after a weekly paper's subscriber had asked for a likely spot before his canine companion had died.

Typical of the best of his works, this editorial will ring true for any cat lover:

The Cat Can't Come Back

Sometimes when the east wind leaps the kitchen porch to slat at the screen door, when the dishes are done and it's dark outside, they catch themselves thinking he is there. They think, before they have time to know better, that it is the old yellow cat asking in. For that is the way he used to tell them when he had come home from a cat's nocturnal concerns, with his eyes shining, his tail lifted—and sometimes it would be slightly puffed by recent adventure. How surely he swaggered! Then he told them about it. It is not to be wondered that, after so many years, they sometimes think the east wind is an old yellow cat who has returned, with a purr in his throat and love in his golden and ebony eyes. Instinctively almost they rise to open the door. Then their glances encounter and cling, each with the trace of embarrassment. It sounded like him, didn't it? But it was the east wind, instead.

He used to come out of the east wind, cobwebs in his whiskers, happiness in his heart, with that clean-cat smell of new-laundered linen, the way a healthy cat smells when he comes in from the cold. A leap to the couch, in lithe confidence, and the yellow cat found the crook of her arm. Put your magazine down. Here I am! Here I am! Your cat has come home from the darkness. How closely she held him then—cheek by cheek. So it is when of evenings the screen door slats in the east wind, they find they cannot get over the habit. The place he had in their hearts still is warm. Still is warm. As a cushion where a cat has been sleeping. It would be no manner of use to go call him. He was never the one to answer until he was ready—but now they know he can't come. Yet sometimes they will lift their eyes from book or paper, and quickly, to listen. It couldn't, of course, be the old yellow cat, and it never can be. How empty a house will seem where a cat has been! He used to come in from the east wind, smelling like fresh linen—he used to come in as of right; one of them.

Sometimes when it happens again, and their glances catch and linger, they speak of having another one. But never can they quite agree to, for, you see, there was only one of him, nor ever can there be such another. Don't you see? A cat that is loved isn't just a cat. He is something more than a cat. Why don't they, their friends ask, get another one? That's the easy phrase for it. But not yet. Not quite yet. It isn't so simple as that. Listen! Will they never cease starting when the east wind leaps the kitchen porch to slat at the screen door? O foolish! Go back to your book. The old yellow cat can't come home.

—Portland *Oregonian*

More seasonal is this comment in which an editorial writer pictured the pre-Christmas activities in a large city:

Here We Go Again

Last December 24 most of us inefficient people resolved that it would never happen again. Christmas just slipped up on us. Fate had hurled us into those last hour throngs with still a half dozen gaps in the shopping list.

No, never again, a thousand times no! The next time we would start early before anyone else had seen the calendar. Calm, cool and unhurried we would move through quiet stores—choose from the best and catch the rest of the world flat-footed. At an appropriate time we would sit back with a superior smile for the mobs.

But here we go again. Christmas already slipping up on us. No sooner is the Thanksgiving turkey reduced to hash than feverish humanity is on the march. The Christmas tree vendors say they are already beset by customers. The police department is detailing extra men to the Country Club Plaza to take care of the crowds attracted by Christmas decorations.

Overnight the blood pressure of the downtown district has increased. Out of nowhere crowds have come to the sidewalks. The easy small town amiability of midsummer has disappeared. The men who pause to exchange the street corner stories are jostled into the street and the kicker line is lost. Into the eyes of the women has come a glint of purpose. We have already awakened to that first morning of snow thinly veiling the lawns.

And here we are without a far-fetched hint of a single item for the Christmas shopping list. Trailing again! We don't even know where to start. Where will we be at that next mad hour of late darkness on December 24?

Obviously Chrismas is no problem to the efficient people of this world, the clean desk executives and spic and span housewives. They seem to operate with precision, each hour taking care of its appointed task. Like a perfectly made watch. A watch? Would that start the list? Maybe and maybe not.

It's a shock, that awful suspicion that the history of inefficient shoppers is repeating itself. But somehow the job will be done. And the lights will glow on Christmas morning less than four weeks away.

Perhaps the job of the season will reach the height with those of us who have to struggle to achieve it. And

a fig for those people who always know the right thing
for the right person and buy it at the right time.

—Kansas City Star

Any Irish patriot, by birth or by adoption, would be happy to
read this editorial from the St. Louis Post-Dispatch. It had to be
reprinted the year after it first appeared because subscribers wrote
that it "really captured the true Irish sentiment and feeling." Here
it is:

For the 17th of March

The Irish are the great singers and storytellers of the
Western World, poets all of them. Maybe it's because
they can't resist the lilting names of their land. From
the Mayo Mountains to Bantry Bay, each sign-post is a
song: Ballyvourney and Belashanny, Mallow and
Galway, Maynooth and Athlone, Sligo and Kildare,
Lough Lene and the Ballyhouras, Tara and Killarney.

Or maybe it's the wistful beauty of the land that's in
their blood. The soft, misty mountains of the white surf
rushing out of the gray sea against the Western Isles.
The brown cattle behind the hedges of the lush green
fields. The beech groves and the red-berried rowan
trees. The peat smoke lazing over the cottage roof.

Or maybe it's the fire that smoulders and smoulders
in their hearts, the undying love for their "dark Rosa-
leen." Where else are heroes bred and nurtured as in
Ireland? Who refuses more stubbornly than an Irishman to sheathe the sword? Defeated at home, he carries
on under the banners of a Scottish Queen, a French
King or an American Lincoln.

Out of that comes a melancholy gloom as gray as the
fog-veiled glens over which the eagles bark. But there
is also in the Irish soul an acid of wit sharp enough to
bite through the misery. There is loyalty as well as
fanaticism. There is courage and compassion.

For a Mangan's tragic keening, there is also the sharp
wit of a Gogarty strolling down O'Connell Street. There
is an O'Casey in the Abbey Theater celebrating the

249

1916 Easter Week. There is a Yeats humming an adult lullaby of sweet peace at an old woman's fireside. Nobody knows better than an Irishman how hard life can be, but also nobody knows better what love and laughter can do.

They are a grand people altogether, these Irish. So here's the top of the mornin' to them on this St. Patrick's day.

—St. Louis Post-Dispatch

Editorial paragraphs are short but hard to write

Editorial paragraphs certainly are the shortest of all the pieces in the writer's arsenal but they are far from being the easiest to write. In fact, a well-turned paragraph may be more difficult to compose than an informative editorial with its demands for painstaking research or an argumentative one with its exacting requirements for clear and forceful organization and presentation. Yet, many times, the short type may hit a bullseye while any other would fail.

To hold a person up for the amusement or ridicule of his fellows, especially if he is a public figure such as a politician, actor, author or the like, is an extraordinarily effective technique. That is exactly how the editorial writer may use his paragraph. Numerous times a short pungent jab has brought an anguished "ouch" when dozens of inches of full-length editorials went past without any retort.

This paragraph, for instance, drew the first letter to the editor despite literally hundreds of inches of full-dress editorial attacks:

> The thing that makes Gerald L. K. Smith's doctrine of white supremacy hardest to swallow is that Gerald L. K. Smith is supposed to be some sort of example of it.
>
> *—St. Louis Post-Dispatch*

The editorial paragraph combines two universal appeals. It is short; if it is well done, it amuses, too. A paragrapher may take over the role vacated long ago by the court jester. He may point a finger—and get away with it. Others may fawn and wait for a more judicious or expedient time and place. But not the paragrapher.

Because it must be pointed and sharp, the editorial paragraph should avoid excess verbiage. No free-riders are permitted among its words. This requires polishing and re-polishing, all of which takes time. But if the piece becomes too contrived, is worked over too long, it is not light any more. The paragrapher must sense when to stop polishing.

Most widely reprinted of all the editorial comments is the short paragraph. Let a paragrapher turn out a well-rounded sentence or two and it will be picked up, sometimes without credit to the original source. A few newspapers and magazines never print any of these conventional editorial paragraphs; they make up a minority.

Just what is a paragraph? Rufus Terral of the *St. Louis Post-Dispatch* in *The Masthead* (Autumn, 1949) described it as "a spitball lovingly fired out of a rubber band, a tack placed thoughtfully in a chair." Then he went on: "It should present an idea to the reader in a way in which he would not have thought of it for himself. Perhaps the light you shine on it will be the light that shines on the other side of Alice-in-Wonderland's looking-glass. Or perhaps it will be just a brighter-than-usual light of ordinary day."

Why editorial paragraphs, long recognized as "one of the ornaments of American journalism," are not now more widely used was explained this way by Bill Vaughan of the *Kansas City Star* in *The Masthead* (Winter 1950–51).

The paragraph is a short editorial, chosen for reasons typographical rather than intellectual. The reason why few editorial writers write good paragraphs is, I think, obvious. A good paragraph should contain an idea which could be expanded into a 300-word editorial. Therefore, no editorial writer in his right mind is going to make it tough on himself by taking a day's work and boiling it down into 20 words which certainly aren't going to impress the publisher.

Out of his years of experience, Terral also offered advice on how to write editorial paragraphs. Others have confirmed his approach. Here is what he said in *The Masthead* article cited earlier:

Now if you want to sit down and write a paragraph, I will tell you how I would do it if I were you. I would take hold of the Sunday New York Times and scan it from cover to cover with the constant idea of thinking in terms of paragraphs. The Sunday Times will show you the world through the long end of the telescope and the short end, the focus fluctuating wildly from the supremely important to the utterly dispensable.

That is the kind of world from which paragraphs emerge. Don't think a thing of it if you can't work up a paragraph for hours, or if worse still, you work up lots and they are all superlatively sad apples. I've plugged at my reading for as long as two hours without thinking of a single paragraph, and then a dozen would pop faster than I could write them down. Once you start thinking paragraphs, it's almost as hard to stop as it was to start. Unless you take a firm stand about it, you are likely to spend the rest of the day writing pieces that start out sounding like editorials but wind up sounding like paragraphs.

Like most of the other editorial types, the paragraph may be pigeonholed a number of ways. Possibly the best way includes the boiled-down, abbreviated single-paragraph comment in one classification and then lumping the pointed quips into another group. Thus the first classification would be those streamlined, hard-hitting comments that could, conceivably, be bob-tailed argumentative editorials except for subtle and frequently humorous punch lines. The second puts together the epigram, the pun or play on words, the parody, and the quotation with a single line or so of demolishing comment.

Let's look at the boiled-down, single-paragraph comment first. To compress a publication's comment into a single paragraph is hard work but, if successfully accomplished, it may be more effective than several hundred words of logical arguments.

Here are some examples of these cut-down editorials with punch either in the headlines or toward the end of the comments:

Hot Stove League

Speaking of newspapers and journalists, we note without comment Westbrook Pegler's current charge that Drew Pearson and Walter Winchell slant their copy and assassinate characters.

—New York Post

Never Is a Short Time

The other day we were slightly unsettled by a truck sign. The sign advertised a product called "Neva-Rust." Underneath came the shocker—"Guaranteed Not to Rust for Six Years."

—T. C. Du Mont in Materials & Methods

Million Dollar Thinking

Limited by an authorized $750,000 and balked by the voters' failure a year ago to approve additional bonds, Miami Beach now plans to build its auditorium in several stages. One way or another, the Beach Council keeps thinking of it as a million dollar idea—or more.

—Miami Herald

Not Like Jesse James

No wonder the FBI failed to find Martin Dembin after a 16-year search. He was on the list of 10 most wanted criminals but when he gave himself up in New York it was learned that he had been making a living at the peaceful art of hooking rugs. He was a tired, beaten bank robber and dodging the FBI for so long had given him stomach ulcers.

—Cleveland Press

Artist to the End

Charlie Chaplin is a great actor who has also been a great fool in his personal conduct. Because of these follies, he has found it necessary to give up his residence

253

in America. But there is something about this renunciation worth noticing. It is the first time he has had a chance to act out in his personal life the role for which he made himself famous in the movies—that of the wistful little vagabond who cannot cope with harshness of the real world. So to the very last act of his play, Chaplin, the artist, owes a debt of gratitude to America. It gave him his first professional chance and his last as well.

—*St. Paul Pioneer Press*

Pointed quips should be sharp

If Benjamin Franklin could come back to this second half of the Twentieth Century, one occupation that would suit him admirably would be that of writer of pointed quips for editorial pages. His "Poor Richard" comments set a pace that writers are still trying to match in their editorial paragraphs. Howard Brubaker, who for many years wrote a column of paragraphs for *The New Yorker*, was one of those who could match the Franklin pace.

As pointed out earlier in this chapter, these editorial paragraphs may be grouped as puns, parodies, epigrams, and quotations with comments. Here are some examples:

1. *Puns or Plays on Words.*

To be worth your salt on any job you must have pepper.
—*Morrisons Cove Herald,* Martinsburg, Pennsylvania

The crop of tropical hurricanes this season apparently will be bumper.
—*South Bend* (Indiana) *Tribune*

No matter what other effect it has, American influence on world affairs is leaving its $ mark.
—*Passaic* (N.J.) *Herald News*

Those who insist on government playing the Great White Father shouldn't get so blue when they're asked to shell out the long green.
—*New York World Telegram and Sun*

The former editor of the humor magazine at Pitt turns to a life of thievery, and what a painful path it has been since he stole his first joke.

—Bill Vaughan in *Kansas City Star*

2. *Parodies.*

Some people get up bright and early; some just early.

—*The Hotel Monthly*

The fourth of July isn't and never was what it used to be.

—*Lake County Banner,* Tiptonville, Tennessee

It's a small world, all right, and there are some small people in it.

—*Boston Daily Globe*

It's too late. The 5-cent cigar is back; but this isn't the same country.

—*Denver Post*

There's nothing against a man's tooting his own horn, if he's in tune.

—*Minneapolis Star*

Too many guys and gals are looking at the world through rose-colored cocktail glasses.

—*McLoud* (Oklahoma) *Monitor*

Signs of the times: Polite saying now is "Thanks a *billion!*" A million doesn't mean a thing.

—*Edmonds* (Washington) *Tribune*

3. *Epigrams.*

Bow ties are like dachshunds—you can't be neutral about them.

—*Buffalo Evening News*

A little flattery now and then makes husbands out of single men.

—*Fredericksburg* (Texas) *Standard*

"History teaches us—" says the incurable optimist, thereby differing from the cynic who says, "Here we go again."

—Buffalo Evening News

Life would be a little easier if folks didn't spend so much money for things they don't need to impress people they don't like.

—Nance County Journal, Fullerton, Nebraska

Comes now the trying season in which one must endeavor to remember what Aunt Hepzibah sent for Christmas last year so one will not send it back to her this year.

—Memphis Commercial Appeal

A guy who is always cracking wise told me the other day that he knows what everybody is doing in Craig but he buys an Empire-Courier each week to see if they've been caught at it!

—Craig (Colorado) Empire-Courier

4. *Quotations with Comments.*

"A penny saved is a penny earned"—but what can you do with it?

—Sleepy Eye (Minnesota) Herald-Dispatch

It is said that civilization has failed. We didn't know it had been tried.

—Fillmore (California) Herald

That old expression of something being dirt cheap has no reference to a modern building lot.

—Miami Herald

It's a down east justice who finds that poker playing by women is not a crime. Other judges have gone farther and held it isn't poker.

—Denver Post

A Michigan physicist studying the flight of a golf ball coins the phrase "internal ballistics" to describe those personal quirks which result in a hook or slice.

Alibi seekers should note, however, he did not say "infernal."

—*Christian Science Monitor*

One of those surveys designed to show how stupid everybody is discloses that many American students think W. L. Mackenzie King was a Canadian hockey player. No, No! He was the Canadian who wasn't a hockey player.

—*Hartford* (Connecticut) *Courant*

A corresponding friend, namely John M. Henry of the Des Moines Register-Tribune, is co-author of a good book on "How to Write Columns." But all of the tips aren't applicable to a small town columnist where all one needs do to keep on edge is "drink lots of coffee where several flirtatious waitresses are on duty."

—*Holyrood* (Kansas) *Gazette*

NINE

Formulating

editorial policy

WHAT AND HOW TO COMMENT UPON THE WORLD'S HAPPENINGS IS
a perpetual plague of editorial writers. Is it more important to tell
readers that a proposed traffic ordinance will really fail to clear up
congestion on the city's main streets, what the pinch of announced
new taxes from Washington will be in terms translated for the
typical subscriber, or what the chances are for war as a result of an
overthrow of the administration in, say, Egypt? Is it more important to set the facts out cafeteria-style and hope the readers
will reach valid conclusions or is it essential to crusade in behalf of
the side the newspaper or magazine favors? In other words, just
what should editorial policy be?

Policy building comes hard

The answers never come easily. They are tough to reach on the
metropolitan daily, the small country weekly, the scholarly quarterly, or the monthly business journal. One editorial writer confessed that when it came time to write he felt burdened "as a child
in a candy store forced to make a decision about spending his
nickel." All but a few editorial page staff members feel the same
way.

The best statement yet worked out of the ideals on which an
editorial writer may stand is the code of ethics adopted by the
National Conference of Editorial Writers at the 1949 sessions:

Journalism in general, editorial writing in particular, is more than another way of making money. It is a profession devoted to the public welfare and to public service. The chief duty of its practitioners is to provide the information and guidance toward sound judgments which are essential to the healthy functioning of a democracy. Therefore the editorial writer owes it to his integrity and that of his profession to observe the following injunctions:

1. The editorial writer should present facts honestly and fully. It is dishonest and unworthy of him to base an editorial on half-truth. He should never consciously mislead a reader, distort a situation, or place any person in a false light.

2. The editorial writer should draw objective conclusions from the stated facts, basing them upon the weight of evidence and upon his considered concept of the greatest good.

3. The editorial writer should never be motivated by personal interest, nor use his influence to seek special favors for himself or for others. He should hold himself above any possible taint of corruption, whatever its source.

4. The editorial writer should realize that he is not infallible. Therefore, so far as it is in his power, he should give a voice to those who disagree with him—in a public letters column and by other suitable devices.

5. The editorial writer should regularly review his own conclusions in the light of all obtainable information. He should never hesitate to correct them should he find them to be based on previous misconceptions.

6. The editorial writer should have the courage of well-founded conviction and a democratic philosophy of life. He should never write or publish anything that goes against his conscience. Many editorial pages are the products of more than one mind, however, and sound collective judgment can be achieved only through sound individual judgments. Therefore, thoughtful individual opinions should be respected.

7. The editorial writer should support his colleagues in their adherence to the highest standards of professional integrity. His reputation is their reputation, and theirs is his.

Magazines have the same high standards of ethics as those expressed in the N.C.E.W. code, although they have not been as formally stated. An editorial writer on *The Commonweal* discussed his own frustrating problems as follows in the February 16, 1951, issue of that Roman Catholic weekly publication:

During the course of a week, in an atmosphere like the present, a man comes across a thousand opinions in the newspaper columns, on the radio, in the magazines and in the books he reads. Even with the transoceanic radio, on-the-spot television and multiple daily editions of the same newspaper, events move faster than reports. Things pile up from hour to hour and at the end of a week, or even at the end of a day, whole pictures change. . . .

To piece it all together, to make sense out of the hodge-podge grows more difficult all the time. The temptation to give up trying to grasp the meaning and logic of individual events is ever-increasing.

The alternative is to attempt to create a simplicity that doesn't really exist, to focus one's anger and frustration on a single cause, a single group or even a single man—Communism, perhaps, or the Fair Dealers, the reactionaries, the Jews, F.D.R., Truman, Dean Acheson. It doesn't matter particularly as long as the maddening complexity is removed. This is the temptation that the journalist—and not the journalist alone—is subject to when events pile up and his supposed omniscience, his sureness and authority are challenged. It is a temptation to be resisted as something from the devil.

Under the title of "It Takes Guts To Write Small Town Editorials," the *Stanton* (Nebraska) *Register* commented as could many other contemporaries:

The editor who works in continual fear of the people with whom he lives and works is an editor who does nothing for his community. . . . So now you know why the Register often is criticized, seldom is lauded, but attempts week-to-week to voice an opinion whether it's about the potato shortage or the lack of a parking lot in our community. We are attempting to newspaper.

Inescapably, because of the nature of his work, the editorial writer more than any other staff member leaves an imprint of his personality upon what he writes for publication. Frank W. Taylor, who established himself as one of the great managing editors in American journalism during 27 years with the *St. Louis Star-*

Times, truthfully summed it up: "Men who write editorials put a piece of themselves into type every day."

Yet editorial writing also may be a more cooperative effort than many other sections of a newspaper or magazine. That is due to the fact that it represents not only the viewpoint of the individual but also an institutionalized expression of opinion. The unsigned comments represent the voice of the *News*, the *Times*, the *Quarterly Review*, or whatever the publication may be.

The editorial conference is one way

Part of this institutionalized aspect of the editorial page comes from the practice of holding editorial conferences. So it may be well for us to examine, in some detail, just what this technique includes.

At a typical editorial conference would be found the publisher (or his representative), editor of the editorial page, other editorial writers, cartoonist, news editor (and possibly the city editor and, if the paper had one, the foreign news or cable editor), and on special occasions important visitors. Anyone around the table may suggest a topic; then others join in the general discussion so that a team viewpoint develops. Generally no attempt is made to force a conciliation of varying views. Then the subjects are assigned to writers according to their familiarity with that topic, engagements on other editorials, and, of course, whether they agree with the position to be taken. After the research is finished and the copy written, it goes to the editor-in-chief for approval. On some papers, the publishers also approve the copy before it is printed.

When the *Chicago Sun-Times* used to hold editorial conferences five days a week, frequent visitors expressed their viewpoints on some current issue, answered questions, and then were bid goodbye before the staff got down to the business of deciding positions for tomorrow's editorials.

On the *Providence* (R.I.) *Journal*, celebrated for its rich editorial conference traditions, one member of the editorial page staff regularly has been assigned the job of "devil's advocate." To the best of his abilities, he must be "agin" whatever stand is proposed.

A recent survey of representative daily newspapers across the country found that three out of four editorial page staffs held daily conferences to discuss the news.* Practically all the remaining quarter of papers reported that editorial conferences were held less frequently than each day or "when the occasion demanded."

Typical of this minority's operation was this statement by Forrest W. Seymour, then editor of the editorial pages of the *Des Moines Register* and *Tribune:*

Because our staff is a compact and intimate one, working eight hours every day together, we do not make a fetish of staff meetings. We have them perhaps twice a week for six months, and then we may not have any for six months. It depends wholly on whether the proper integration and intimacy seem to exist, or whether they don't. If they seem at any time not to, then we begin to get together regularly for a while. As a rule, however, we have a half-dozen informal "staff conferences" every day just by gathering around one person's desk or another's. Except for that, we all come to work at our appointed time, and quit when we are done.

The solitary editorial writer has his problems

During recent sessions of the National Conference of Editorial Writers, founded in 1947, small town papers with staffs of one or two men have been praised about as frequently as the better known metropolitan dailies. Yet the editorial writers on papers short-handed in manpower admit readily that they need utmost ingenuity to overcome the obvious handicaps.

Unless he is a rare exception, the one-man editorial staff member will be swamped if he has to fill two or three columns of "think" pieces daily. Few individuals can comment on such differing

---

* Those who wish to read the full report may consult: Hillier Krieghbaum, "American Editorial Writers and Their Backgrounds," *Journalism Quarterly*, Vol. 27, No. 1, Winter, 1950, pages 24–27.

topics as, for example, the latest developments in European recovery, the United States' over-all economic conditions, the
progress of appropriation bills through Congress, the social activities of the governor's wife who is helping his campaign for re-
election, and a humorous exchange of banter during the city
council's discussion of zoning regulation changes. Most one-man
staffs are forced into superficial and banal remarks when they try
to cover every major news event without time to think the topic
through or to gather the necessary background information.
Some, fortunately, rise above this mediocrity, and they deserve
the greatest credit. Others, knowing their limitations, restrict
their comments to a topic or two each issue and therefore have
something of value to say.

H. Clay Tate, editor of the *Daily Pantagraph* at Bloomington,
Illinois, told the 1948 N.C.E.W. how his one-man editorial page
was put together. He bluntly commented:

A one man editorial page that remains a one man page is doomed.
Either it will call upon more brainpower or it will wither. No single
individual can keep himself sufficiently informed to comment intelligently and helpfully on the ever changing local, state, national and
world issues today. So the first thing for the creator of the one man
editorial page to do is to utilize the intelligence of others.

It isn't always possible for the small newspaper to add new personnel for the specialized job of writing editorials, although I am
sure publishers will invest more in this phase of the newspaper enterprise as they become convinced of its worth.

In addition to the syndicated columnists, the one-man editorial page staff may draw on numerous other possibilities. Letters to
the editor, always a popular feature, may be encouraged. Guest
editorials may be contributed by other members of the paper's
staff or by interested civic leaders. The *Daily Pantagraph*, for
instance, carried a standing head, "Why Don't You Write an
Editorial About . . . ?" for some gripe of a local citizen. Tate
reported it was one of the popular features of his paper. A 1954
readership study revealed that *Daily Pantagraph* editorials drew

more readers than nine out of ten comic strips in the paper. A local column is another possibility. Some of the errand work and copyreading jobs may be passed on to another staff member. Some editors realize that they can not "keep up with the Joneses" of the big city papers and so they write only one or two editorials an issue on topics about which they have something pertinent or cogent to say.

One way to generate readership of editorials has been to forge a newspaper into a real force for community leadership through extensive use of local editorials. Admittedly it takes courage to criticize a city council member when you are likely to sit beside him at the next Rotary Club dinner or to differ with the chief of police when you probably will meet him on the street the next morning. Yet it can be done—and an editorial writer can still retain the respect of his fellow townsmen, even those he has criticized.

How this was done in one area was described this way by Robert P. Studer, assistant managing editor and editorial writer of the Alhambra (California) *Post-Advocate*, in *The Quill* (February, 1952):

> About a year ago, we decided to make the *Post-Advocate* a real leader and molder of public opinion in the seven incorporated and unincorporated communities in which we circulate. We tried to think community problems through, and to come up with an analysis and a recommended course of action. We are the daily home newspaper of each of these communities. We have plenty of material with which to work. Today, we average between four and five local editorials a week.
>
> Writing local editorials, if it is to have any appreciable effect upon local thinking, must be handled just a little differently than national and international issues. Psychology is as important as writing ability. You never can forget that the object of your criticism is a human being, subject to the same emotions and the same susceptibility to injured pride (and a stubborn reaction thereto) as the editor himself.
>
> I've been writing the *Post-Advocate's* local editorials for about a

year and a half and in that space of time have had plenty of opportunity to experiment. During that time we have won many an editorial battle until today the editorial page is among the highest rank-
iig in reader interest. . . .

How does one go about writing local editorials that not only succeed in influencing the opinions of local officials but make them like
and respect the newspaper that does it?

The answer goes back to that applied psychology I mentioned
earlier. We do plenty of "differing," but we are just as free with our
praise. If a man does a good job, we say so just as readily as we criticize him if he makes a wrong decision. And, if he changes his mind
as the result of one of our editorial campaigns, we commend him editorially for being "big enough" to change his mind when the public
welfare warrants it. . . .

But every editorial we write is carefully thought through. Some
are published only after weeks of painstaking research. They are all
written to catch the reader's interest immediately, to explain the
problem—and most important of all—to propose a course of action.
We do not believe a newspaper can be a real leader if its editorials
only paint the scene and expect the reader to make up his own mind.

Houston Waring of the *Littleton* (Colorado) *Independent* organized the Colorado Editorial Advisory Board in 1945 so that its
members, selected as "thoughtful citizens" who could supply editorial background and suggestions, could help country editors
"find varying ways of helping readers develop perspective."

Regardless of whether he is a solitary staff member or belongs to
a large metropolitan daily staff, the professional editorial writer
would give very short shrift indeed to the question, "How long
should an editorial be?" Yet the question sometimes is asked by
beginners. Warren H. Pierce, then associate editor, *St. Peters-
burg Times*, gave some advice in *The Masthead* (Spring, 1952)
when he wrote:

The right length of editorials, it seems to me, is about like Abraham
Lincoln's definition of the right length for a man's legs—long enough
to reach the ground. There is an equally simple empiric test for edi-

torials: Do they get action and accomplish useful ends? Alongside that neither arbitrary limits on word-count, nor even literary quality, are very important.

The San Francisco Chronicle does it this way

Seldom indeed does an editorial writer do "an editorial about editorials." For most of the reading public the operations of an editorial page staff are really a far-away land. The *San Francisco Chronicle*, which likes to break conventions upon occasion, printed such an editorial July 7, 1947. It is so revealing on the whole subject of editorial procedures that it is reproduced in full:

The 'How' of Chronicle Editorials

This will be an editorial about editorials, Chronicle editorials, specifically, and how they come into being. In approaching the subject we knowingly risk the accusation of self-indulgence at the expense of leaving world and local events to go shift for themselves, but we have a purpose. It is to afford the reader of this page some understanding of how we reach conclusions, and perhaps some basis for judging the worth of those conclusions. Omniscience is not one of our virtues. But in the preparation of this page we start from the single premise that we've got to be responsible, and the rest of the process is a system calculated to implement that responsibility. It isn't fool-proof; sometimes we're wrong. When that happens, and we discover it, we admit it—that's part of the obligation incurred when one accepts responsibility. At other times, when we come up against one of those imponderables that crop up with increasing and vexing frequency in this twentieth century, we can do no more than give you our best judgment, and when that happens we label it as such.

But most times we deal in convictions, and it is chiefly about those convictions, and how they're hammered out in our shop, that we're going to talk now.

The Chronicle editorials are not the product of one mind in any case, but of a half dozen minds turned loose upon an idea. That idea may come from the mind of the editor, or the editorial page director, or any of the five editorial writers, or any of a hundred, or thousand, different sources. In any case, the process is the same.

The idea is turned loose in a morning editorial conference, during the initial phases of which the editor is absent.

Sometimes the Idea
Just Doesn't Jell

The ball is pitched, and everybody who likes takes a cut at it. It may be batted around for only five minutes before its worth is tested and its form becomes discernible. Sometimes it's kept in the air for a half hour. Sometimes it never comes down at all—it depends upon the nature of the idea itself, the amount of information available upon it and the degree to which it squares with the composite convictions of the group as modified by the fresh information available.

There are, of course, some long-standing, underlying convictions held by the editor and the entire group. These are likely to be pretty basic—more basic, for example, than a political party label or a man's religion or nationality. The desirability of lasting peace, for example, is hardly debatable; neither is the necessity for the advancement of human dignity; neither is the ultimate inevitability of One World; neither is the proposition that the recovery of Europe depends upon resumed production; neither is the necessity for the most foolproof possible system of atomic control. As in any other thoughtful American forum where common sense is held in higher esteem than spite, hate, fear, or any of the blinding passions, these things are accepted as truths.

But the means of achieving them often provides the very meat of editorial conference discussion.

Since we opened with a disavowal of omniscience, we are not going to try to persuade you that the results of the discussions which are in evidence here day after day have any superhuman merit. A half dozen men can be as wrong as one man—but we think they are not so likely to be.

And, too, the systematical lessening of that likelihood is one of the principal jobs of The Chronicle editorial staff.

Apart from the banging together of ideas, there are two chief means by which we go about whittling down that likelihood. We read everything we can get our hands on, and we go out into the field as often and extensively as possible and see for ourselves how things are.

267

Sources Are Numbered
In the Hundreds

The written matter is, we suppose, more or less standard in all editorial offices. The Encyclopedia Britannica is always there—a faithful, stolid pillar of information. Unfortunately a compendium like Britannica cannot be brought out every week, or even every year, so the research must chiefly be in documents of more current vintage. The laws introduced and adopted at Sacramento and Washington are a never-ending source of knowledge; the opinions of the Supreme Court; the utterances and written works of the recognized atomic scientists; informed foreign publications like the Manchester Guardian and the London Economist; and, of course, the daily and ever-growing grist of day-to-day news as recorded by the great wire services and The Chronicle's own staff of reporters. The sifting, weighing, collating and correlation of the information that comes from these and hundreds of other sources provide the bulk of the background against which opinions are examined.

But this is not enough—exclusive resort to the ideas formulated and pre-digested by other people would in itself make for an editorial page that lacked at least individuality and at most a deep personal sense of conviction.

So to supplement the ideas of others the editorial page staff goes out to prospect with its own pick and pan.

A Chronicle editorial writer periodically shows up at the Legislature, probing about for the facts in one or another field of current lawmaking. Prior to writing an extensive piece on conditions at the Preston School for Boys another Chronicle editorial writer spent several days there, getting a mass of evidence and opinion from all quarters, out of which ultimately an editorial crystallized. During the past 12 months still other members of the page staff have been in New Mexico, Wright Field at Dayton, Ohio; Washington, New York, the American occupied zones of Western Europe, and Bikini to gather material which later went into Chronicle editorials. All this in the interests of keeping our antennae up and our incidences of error down.

So (we're back in the conference now) the three or four or half dozen topics in the day's news asserting the most demand for comment are talked out through the morning and tentative decisions reached on the angle of attack and the man who's to write the piece.

The Editor Exercises
Final Authority

Then the editor comes in, lights up a cigarette, tilts back in his chair and receives a summary of each projected editorial from the man who's going to write it. Sometimes the synopsis is approved as offered; sometimes the editor amends it; sometimes he tosses in a new angle that starts the discussion all over again; frequently, in his own mulling over of the day's events, he has been struck with the significance of some piece of news the initial conferees have passed over. In any event, as editor of The Chronicle he holds the responsibility, and exercises the authority, of final judgment regarding what the editorial space of the following day is going to say. When that judgment has been rendered, the writers turn to their typewriters and go to work. In this activity, as in others, the editor is the representative of the publisher, with whom he frequently hammers out basic policy decisions—usually out of normal working hours.

The supervision, of course, doesn't end there. Each editorial as it comes out of the typewriter is read by at least one other editorial writer. Then the original goes to the editor of the page, with duplicates to the editor and the "make-up" man, responsible for the physical composition of the page. The original, if approved, goes to the composing room to be set up in type. Proofs are run from the type when set and read for typographical errors. The editor of the page then determines, under direction of the editor of the whole newspaper, where each piece shall appear in the page—what "play" to give each for maximum effectiveness and best appearance. And when the page has gone into the mold, proofs of the whole page are pulled and studied by the entire editorial page staff for any "bugs" that may have shown up.

Handicaps to Chronicle
Type of Policy

You may by now have a rough idea of how The Chronicle editorial page—and the policy it pursues—comes about.

There are certain handicaps to such a policy, so evolved—handicaps that must afflict any organ of opinion that clings to just a few rudimentary principles and endeavors to give each day's news its due in the modification of its own thinking.

It's a lot easier to make up your mind in advance and watch for events to bolster your opinions. It would be easier, for instance, to be a rock-ribbed Republican paper and read baleful and portentous meaning into every act committed by those addle-brained characters in the Administration. It would also be easier to run a whole-souled left-wing sheet and damn every move of the National Association of Manufacturers, or any member thereof, as calculated to shove the little guy still deeper into the mire. Anyone who has ever written for a living knows the sheer exhilaration of being able to get hopping mad, and stay that way day after day, bedeviling the opposition with endless volleys of short, hard, succulent, colorful invective. It's fun and it's effective—you have your ready-cut audience of like-minded citizens, and even though they know exactly what you're going to say before you say it, you always roll 'em in the aisles.

Newspapers like The Chronicle have to forgo that fun—but there are some deeper satisfactions in our way of doing.

For one thing, we can live with ourselves, not in any spirit of complacency but with the knowledge that we've called the shots to the best of our ability, and if we erred it was honestly and not maliciously.

But There Are Likewise
A Few Compensations

For another thing, we have a feeling of rendering an honest service. Whether you agree with us on any given editorial or not, we've at least taken the time to marshal the facts, to weigh them and hammer them and hold them up to the light, and finally to write down an interpretation that represents the best thinking of the whole group of us. We thus are able to give you not one man's viewpoint but one newspaper's viewpoint, reached on the basis of all the information that comes within the grasp of a modern newspaper.

We're not in all this expecting or asking for your agreement in all our ideas. If in these troubled times we can contribute even a little to the public awareness of the issues we're all facing, and their importance to all of us and the role free Americans can play in their resolution, we shall have done what we set out to do.

270

TEN

Aids for

editorial pages

EDITORIALS, AT BEST, ARE ONLY PART OF THE EDITORIAL PAGE. IF WE can believe the consensus of readership surveys, they are a considerably less popular part than many of the other features that conventionally find a place there. Some of these other editorial page features further the newspaper's or magazine's own march of opinion; others qualify as journalistic tricks to attract the readers' attention and entice them to look at the page with the hope that eventually they may just happen to glance at the editorials.

The well organized editorial page may present a unified effect—or it may be an arena for conflicting opinions to battle for popular acceptance. Cartoons generally reinforce editorial comments; letters to the editor permit readers to have their own outlet for expression; opinion articles allow staff members and other experts to push subjectively beyond the limitations of conventional news reporting and straight interpretation; reprints bring readers the best that others say or write on subjects of interest. The columnists, an increasingly popular editorial page contribution, will be discussed in Chapter Twelve.

Cartoons are editorials in pictures

Like an editorial, an editorial cartoon is somebody's opinion. Only, instead of expressing it through words, the cartoonist presents ideas in picture form. This very elementary fact brings a number of obvious results. For instance, the cartoonist may have to over-simplify because he puts his idea over in one glance. He does not have the editorial writer's chance to add, "But, on the other hand . . ." Again in contrast to the good editorial writer, the successful cartoonist makes repeated use of accepted stereotypes, common expressions, or well known comparisons. Further, a car-toonist is a sort of contemporary king's jester in many cases— although some of the great in the field hesitate to confess this— and thus is allowed considerably more freedom to express his opinions than a writer who uses the more familiar currency of words.

Daniel R. Fitzpatrick, Pulitzer prize-winning cartoonist of the *St. Louis Post-Dispatch*, once illustrated this last difference when he quoted a Missouri attorney general who asked, "I can answer those editorial writers, but what the hell do you do with a fellow who draws pictures?"

When the *Washington Evening Star* collected its cartoons of the 1948 presidential campain as an illuminating sidelight on that upset election of Harry S. Truman, it included this paragraph in an introduction:

A cartoonist is many things to many men. To some he is a clown, tickling the world with the point of his pen. To others he is a wit, drafting cogent comment on the course of events, coming through on deadline with the day's perfectly incisive remark. To still others he is a sort of intellectual gadfly, stinging sinners to repentance with a barb of ridicule. But if he is true to himself he also is a reporter in the finest sense of the word, telling the story day by day with maxi-mum economy, clarity, and truth.

Telling the National Conference of Editorial Writers in 1948 about his work, Herbert L. Block, Pulitzer and Sigma Delta Chi prize winner who signs his cartoons "Herblock," summed up his own feelings this way:

I think a cartoon should have something to say. I think it should represent the sincere opinion of the cartoonist and should be presented with conviction. What's been said today about the editorials being the conscience of the paper, I think goes for cartoons in spades. In the cartoons there is less room to compromise and hedge. In cartoons things are black and white. They deal with right and wrong. I think the cartoonist's job is to be on the right side and to hit hard.

Jacob Burck of the *Chicago Sun-Times,* another Pulitzer award winner, expressed his cartooning philosophy in these words written for *The Masthead* (Winter, 1950):

The editorial cartoonist's job is more than to record a passing event. The cartoonist is essentially a kibitzer at the historical game played by mankind. Like all kibitzers he should have no inhibitions. His humor and wit must have free rein to be telling. His eye for the bizarre, the ironical and the ridiculous must not be clouded by fears and restrictions. He is at best when he holds nothing sacred, even himself. For if he takes himself too seriously, he runs the risk of becoming stodgy and pedantic, his vision distorted. Pictures are best drawn and seen at arm's length.

Although they frequently use humor as a weapon, cartoonists generally have a sense of sober responsibility for their work. Harold M. Talburt, Scripps-Howard cartoonist who won a Pulitzer prize in 1933, incorporated feelings shared by many of his fellow cartoonists when he gave this credo:

I believe a cartoon should be simple.
I believe a cartoonist should work on one thought at a time.
I believe a cartoonist should minimize details.
I believe the ideal cartoon would be drawn with one stroke.
I believe a cartoonist should respect his responsibility.
I believe a cartoonist should believe what his picture says.
I believe a cartoonist is a salesman of policy.
I believe a cartoonist in a small way illustrates history in the making.

Cartoonists, like editorial writers, produce lighter or change of pace cartoons as well as their major efforts. One of the classics in cartooning—John T. McCutcheon's "Injun Summer," which first appeared in the *Chicago Tribune* September 30, 1907—was of this type. A combination of nostalgia and nature editorial, this two-panel cartoon showed a small boy and his grandfather looking at a field with corn shocks as it was in the fall and as the lad imagined it with tepees and dancing Indian ghosts after his grandfather told stories of his boyhood long ago.

Yet almost without exception cartoonists view their best work as that done on attack. The pictorial medium lends itself particularly to those who swing with a wallop.

Because the cartoonist works with a pictorial vocabulary which is much more restricted than that of the editorial writer, he is forced to present his viewpoint in easily recognized stereotypes. When we think back over recent cartoons that we have seen, we will realize the truth of this. Uncle Sam in striped pants, long tailed coat, and top hat, or the Republican elephant, or the Democratic donkey—all of these were pictorial shorthand symbols.

Since he has to make his cartoon understandable at a simple glance, if possible, the cartoonist must use shortcuts. A whole menagerie of animals occupies the cartoonist's stable—the American eagle, the British lion, Russian bear, Chinese dragon, Tammany tiger, rats of corruption, cat with nine lives, dove of peace, and wolf at the door. One nationally syndicated artist estimated he had more than 100 of these symbols that he could draw with an assurance that his typical reader would immediately translate. The cartoonist also turns to common sayings, such as proverbs, Aesop's fables, song titles, and popular current quotations.

Another technique necessarily forced by this one-gulp approach toward a cartoon is oversimplification of the characteristics of people drawn. For most individuals, one or two characteristics stand out. The artist concentrates on these. For example, among the distinguishing "trademarks" of fairly recent figures are Dwight D. Eisenhower's smile and balding head, Harry S. Truman's glasses and bow tie, Franklin D. Roosevelt's cigarette holder, Sir Winston Churchill's cigar and "V" sign, John L. Lewis' eyebrows, and Joseph Stalin's mustache. This particularization may be somewhat unfair but it is imperative if the reader is trying to absorb the entire idea at a glance.

Somewhat related to this is the necessity for a cartoonist to get immediately to the kernel of his topic. He cannot qualify his opinions as a worker in words may do. Unless he gives a single unified impression, the cartoon's value is lost. As Talburt of Scripps-Howard once put it, "A reader gets a cartoon instantly or he doesn't; and if he doesn't, I'm wrong."

Non-metropolitan publications, most of which cannot afford full time cartoonists, have a problem in obtaining vigorous cartoons that fit their individual viewpoints. A workable, but not entirely satisfactory, arrangement is for the publications to purchase supplementary cartoons beyond those supplied by their regular syndicates. Thus they have a wider range from which to select those that come close to their own editorial policies. It is not perfection but such purchases at least permit a certain amount of choice.

How do cartoonists work?

Most cartoonists who have discussed their search for ideas agree that their approach is much the same as the editorial writer's. First, a cartoonist reads the news, generally slowly and carefully, in quest of some point that lends itself to pictorial representation or highlighting. Then he analyzes what he has read, and finally he tries to interpret it for his readers. This interpretation often involves a translating job. Thus the cartoonist is always in quest of some analogy or comparison that will make it possible for him to interpret a situation so that the reader will see it in a new light.

Some of the great cartoonists in this country have achieved the same individual distinction as David Low, whose signed cartoons often varied markedly from the Tory opinions of his publisher, Lord Beaverbrook. The general attitude in the United States, however, is to regard such work as an institutional opinion rather than a completely independent expression. On the more conscientious newspapers and magazines, a cartoonist simply does not draw in those fields in which he objects to the publication's policy. This follows the standard procedure for editorial writers.

One exception to this conformist practice was Dr. John Knott of the *Dallas Morning News*. During the era of Franklin D. Roosevelt, his cartoons occasionally collided with the *News* editorial policy but they were printed just the same. Nobody on the paper vetoed his ideas.

Few cartoonists want more than a fragment of an idea from others—a simple roadside marker on the intellectual road. They do not, as a rule, want to have an editor or publisher tell them what to draw. If they are told, their work frequently deteriorates into ineffective stiltedness.

Some cartoonists sit in on editorial page staff conferences in order to get ideas, to find out the general direction of the paper's policy, or to discover what subjects will be discussed in tomorrow's edition. Fitzpatrick of the *St. Louis Post-Dispatch*, for example, may find out what the lead or second editorial will be about and then draw a cartoon to tie in with that subject so that the paper's page has a pattern and unity. Other artists submit several rough sketches to their editors who then pick the one that will be smoothed up and printed. That, for instance, was the way C. D. Batchelor of the *New York Daily News* operated.

Herbert Block told the 1948 National Conference of Editorial Writers about his approach, which was not unusual:

> I don't happen to like suggestions for cartoons, not because I think nobody else can think of ideas for them, but because I feel you work better when you are not cluttered up with somebody else's thinking. I think it's better to start from scratch, select your own subject and work out what you want to say and how you want to say it.

Time for sketching a cartoon is almost invariably shorter than the time for getting ideas. Some workers spend less than an hour at their drawing boards but the general rule is to take two or three hours.

Techniques vary even more than time requirements. Cartoonists may experiment with various media and then pick the one or several that best suit them. Common methods include pen and ink. brush and ink, crayon, charcoal, soft lead or carbon pencil, and combinations of these to achieve maximum effectiveness. Several artists have made clay models which were then photographed. The cartoon may be reproduced on the printed page from either line engraving or halftone, depending on which will bring out the advantages of the medium the artist picked in creating his work.

The syndicated editorial cartoon presents a problem. Must the syndicated cartoonist, like the syndicated editorial writer, be opposed to sin, juvenile delinquency, and corruption (only mentioned in the most general terms, however)? Certainly these are frequently-chosen subjects. If the syndicate cartoonist attempts to be all things to all editors, then he is doomed to satisfy practically none of them. His drawings have little, if any, bite. Therefore, some of the wiser syndicate executives have given their cartoonists considerably more leeway than they give their correspondents.

Many dailies also reprint drawings by the well known figures in distant and non-competing cities. Thus an editor can find a forceful cartoon to fit his policy. However, these reprints deal in regional, national, and global questions and effective local cartoons are missing. This is Afghanistanism applied at the cartooning level. It is just as bad here as in word editorials; however, all pictorial comments should not be local any more than the editorials themselves.

Increasing standardization of the United States press along with the fact that cartoonists thrive on "the hot issues of the crusader, not on apathy and desperation" were blamed for what he considered the decline in present day political cartooning by Professor Henry Ladd Smith of the University of Wisconsin in the *Saturday Review* (May 29, 1954). He pointed out that in one-newspaper towns few papers woke up mad editorially every morning. Crusading also is difficult when few issues can be pictured as all right or all wrong. But Professor Smith did not feel too badly about the developments, for he concluded:

> Is the decline of the political cartoon any loss to journalism or the public? Not in the opinion of this writer, provided publishers live up to their responsibilities in putting reliability above whimsy. . . If our press is concerned with producing light instead of heat, then the political cartoon doesn't deserve better—excepting, of course, that handful of virtuosos who *can* supply our desperate need for helpful interpretation.

Cartoonists, like their journalistic confreres, have won distinction through prize awards when they were in "that handful of virtuosos." Reflecting possibly the relatively small group of the elite, two cartoonists have won three Pulitzer prizes each and five others have won twice. This concentration of talent is not duplicated among the other Pulitzer awards to journalists.

Rollin Kirby of the late *New York World* garnered three awards, winning in 1922, the first year a cartooning award was made, in 1925, and again in 1929. Kirby's three winners were "On the Road to Moscow," in which a skeleton was leading a group of weary, crippled people; "News of the Outside World," showing Uncle Sam, a Russian with beard, and a Mexican in sombrero in front of a campfire reading, "Forty-eight Nations Agree on League Peace Pact;" and "Tammany" which showed an "Old Guard" Republican, hands up in disapproval, in front of an angel chorus, four figures in prison stripes, and twelve others with wings sprouted.

Edmund Duffy of the Baltimore *Sun* won Pulitzer awards in 1931, 1934, and 1940. His three winners were "An Old Struggle Going On," which pictured a Russian trying to pull down a cross on a church dome; "California Points with Pride—" in which that state's governor was pointing at two bodies of lynched men dangling from a tree limb; and "The Outstretched Hand," showing

Adolf Hitler's hand labelled "Peace Offer" and blood dripping from it with smoking ruins and refugees in the background.

Nelson Harding of the *Brooklyn* (N.Y.) *Daily Eagle* won the consecutive prizes for 1927 and 1928. Jay Norwood Darling who signs his pictures "Ding" got awards for 1924 and 1943. Vaughn Shoemaker of the *Chicago Daily News* won in 1938 and 1947. Herbert L. Block got the award in 1942 for a cartoon distributed by Newspaper Enterprise Association and in 1954 for another drawn for the *Washington Post*. Daniel R. Fitzpatrick of the *St. Louis Post-Dispatch* won in 1926 and 1955. One father-son combination—Clifford K. Berryman and James T. Berryman, both of the *Washington Evening Star*—is among the winners, the father winning in 1944 and his son six years later. Twice in more than 30 years there were no prizes given—1923 and 1936—and both times considerable criticism arose from cartoonists, other newspapermen, and laymen.

All sections of the United States from Brooklyn to Los Angeles and from Chicago to Oklahoma City have gained this journalistic recognition. Newspapers with millions of daily readers and others that measure their readership in tens of thousands have been singled out. Twice syndicated cartoonists—Block of the Newspaper Enterprise Association in 1942 and Bill Mauldin of United Feature Syndicate, Inc., in 1945—won prizes. Mauldin, a sergeant on the *Stars and Stripes* staff, created unshaven Willie and Joe, those irresistible, irreverent G.I. symbols that for most Americans portrayed the "unknown soldier" of World War II.

Since 1942, Sigma Delta Chi, professional journalistic fraternity, has given out medallions for editorial cartooning. Names on its list have frequently also appeared among the Pulitzer prize winners. Herbert L. Block of the *Washington Post and Times Herald* and Bruce Russell of the *Los Angeles Times* have won three and two awards respectively and thus came close to monopolizing the annual competition.

Another recognition for cartoonists comes weekly when *Editor and Publisher*, newspaper trade publication, reprints three of the best cartoons of the previous week. Newspapermen generally and artists in particular follow these selections with considerable interest.

Increasing attention has been paid in recent years to what Dick Spencer III of the School of Journalism, State University of Iowa, called "interpretive illustrations." By this he meant use of pictorial graphs, charts, statistics, diagrams, and illustrated maps.

HERBERT L. BLOCK's defense of freedom won the 1950 Sigma Delta Chi award for cartooning. From The Herblock Book (Beacon Press).

When Texas adopted a uniform traffic code, it comprised 25,-000 words of legalistic language. Ray Osborne in the Austin bureau of the *Dallas Morning News* compressed this into ten readable articles which he called the "Code for Safety" and Herc Fincklen, staff cartoonist, illustrated key points. So popular was the series that 135,000 reprints were requested within a month.

On the *Des Moines Register* and *Tribune*, Bud Sauers, staff artist, has animated maps so effectively that his papers have used them for full page illustrations. Under his craftsmanship, the dullness of a map has given way to an interpretation that is full of spirit and feeling.

Readers, too, write editorials in their letters

Letters to the editor, a practice nearly as old as American journalism itself, have come into a renascence during the years before and following World War II. Many editors and publishers paid increasing attention to what the Commission on Freedom of the Press called newspapers' and magazines' responsibility to serve as "common carriers of information and discussion." One battlefield for all sorts of ideas is the letters-to-the-editor section. Here the press can demonstrate that it is hospitable to ideas and attitudes differing from editorial policy. Here is a potential safety valve which allows opponents to say their pieces and not rankle in frustration nor reach the point of violence. This is particularly needed in one-newspaper communities. In many of these, responsible journalists have accepted the challenge to provide an open forum for their locality. Robert J. Blakely, formerly an editorial writer for the *St. Louis Star-Times*, described these readers' forums as "a substitute for the opportunity to start one's own newspaper, which has now disappeared for all except a few."

Some magazines that abolished their editorial pages have retained a section for letters. Their readers, it apparently was reasoned, had a right to vent their own opinions even if the editors carefully sublimated theirs—except in choice of stories and articles.

Other magazines have built their letters departments into highly readable sections. This has been especially true of *Time*, the news weekly, and some of the trade papers and house organs. Among the conventional weeklies, however, letters usually have been a neglected feature. Several attempts were made to establish all-letters publications but none attained a tremendous success, due no doubt to their one-note melody.

James A. Clendinen of the Tampa (Florida) *Morning Tribune*, writing in *The Masthead* (Fall, 1951), listed these reasons why letters to the editor were worth being made into a widely respected department:

The first is the simple fact that people have a common weakness for reading other people's mail. . . Any letters column which has not shriveled on the vine is bound to arrest the reader skipping by on his way to the sports section or comic page. Once he becomes a letters fan, curiosity may even urge him over to the editorials to see what all the fuss is about. So why neglect your feature with greatest potential reader appeal?

The second reason for pampering letters is the bigness which necessarily afflicts newspapers today. The tremendous costs of investment and operation force an increasing degree of monoply and chain ownership. This is not in itself bad. But the result is to remove ownership farther from Main Street and give an aspect of corporate aloofness to the free press. This situation is exploited by every political demagogue who comes under editorial fire; he retaliates by crying that the big dailies speak only for the stockholders and not for the people. This, I grant, is not a new trend. But I believe it is a growing one. And I believe city newspapers can strengthen their position by demonstrating, day by day, that they value their readers' opinions and provide an impartial forum for their expression.

Readership surveys confirmed Clendinen's contentions on popularity. Whether they were for dailies, weeklies, or magazines, all studies showed the public's fascination with reading other people's mail. When an editor occasionally replied, either seriously or sassily, the interest increased.

But to make the letters-to-the-editor department the final rule for judging public reaction becomes a highly dangerous practice. The people who write letters, by and large, are not a true cross-section of the Great American Public. As Paul Trescott of the Philadelphia *Evening Bulletin* wrote in *The Masthead* (Summer, 1949):

Letters reflect what the public is thinking, but they are no accurate index to a division of opinion. People are far more prone to write against something than for it; to condemn rather than to praise. . . . Minorities are often loud though small, and it would be easy to misjudge their size by taking the letters as a criterion.

He told of one instance when letters to the *Bulletin* ran about three-to-one against a local proposition while a public opinion poll conducted at the same time showed the public favoring it by three to one. This was an error misplacing half of the potential voters, if the *Bulletin* editors had trusted only their mail.

Just what groups and what individuals are most inclined to write a letter to the editor of the newspaper or magazine? One of the few studies on this subject was the topic for an editorial in the *Minneapolis Star*. It follows:

Who Writes Those Letters To Newspaper Editors?

Who writes letters to the editor? A new monthly magazine, Speak Up, devoted largely to reprinting letters appearing in newspapers, reports that more than eight million Americans write letters to editors each year.

Surveying 10,000 letters, Speak Up found that 46 per cent were written by men, 37 per cent by women. The others were anonymous and couldn't be classified. (The Star doesn't print anonymous letters.)

Clergymen accounted for 23 per cent of the letters from men. Lawyers, civic leaders and minor local officials wrote 21 per cent, active politicians 18, secretaries of various organizations 15, disgruntled public servants 12, and publicity seekers 11 per cent.

Of the women's letters, 42 per cent came from spokesmen for various women's organizations, 28 per cent from teachers, 16 per cent from working women, 14 per cent from housewives.

Some persons seem to think that only cranks write letters to the editor. Long handling of the mail leads us to a different conclusion. Sure, cranks are numbered among the correspondents. But much more frequent are ordinary individuals in all walks of life who are so moved by some event that they take the trouble to put their thoughts on paper.

Going through the Star's mail each day is an adventure in human relations.

A small group of correspondents comprise the professional letter writers. Charles Hooper of Coeur d'Alene, Idaho, is reported to have written 78,000 letters during 23 years. His is the climactic record for prolificness among writers of letters to editors. Since many of his proposals eventually were adopted, his activity was far from the crank category. One persistent New York City letter writer was a janitor with an original turn of mind that made most of his letters provocative and stimulating. His correspondence was welcomed in almost every editorial office of Manhattan's numerous dailies. As much cannot be said for an anonomyous writer who sent three unsigned letters to *The New York Times* comprising respectively 632, 300, and 160 pages—a total just under 1,100 pages, or enough to fill most of the news columns of a typical day's edition. Most editorial page staff members who handle letters are familiar with the names of these "repeaters" and hold a figurative stopwatch on them. Some papers limit their contributions to once every two weeks, others cut it down to once every two or three months. Only exceptions are for replies to letter writers who may have attacked the professionals.

Another problem, after the repeat letter writer, is what to do with those who want to express their opinions but do not want to sign their names. Some newspapers, usually those with a smaller inflow of correspondence, permit writers to sign letters with such titles as, "Disgusted," "Puzzled," "A Young Voter," and "Mother of Six." Others insist on initials, which are only slightly more revealing than the generalizations just cited. Some dailies require not only full names but addresses as well. This, of course, makes every contestant in the battle for converts wear his own colors. Herbert Brucker, editor of the *Hartford Courant*, argued with considerable validity that "anyone who asks the right to address the public should not shoot from behind the ambush of anonymity."

Valid exceptions to the rule for signing letters with real names might be comments from (1) a doctor, a lawyer, or other professional man whose ethics might require him to write under the "Name Withheld" category or remain silent; (2) subordinate public employees discussing their own activities, who might be penalized if identified; and (3) cases in which the author might be subject to acute embarrassment. For illustration of this last point, a mother's name might not be printed if she was discussing what she thought was excessive home work assigned her child by a school teacher. In all cases, however, the editor insists on knowing the real name; he then decides whether to suppress the signature. When the *Minneapolis Tribune*, for instance, omits a signature, an editor's note explains the reason for the action. Other papers do likewise.

The *Oklahoma City Times* pointedly used this editor's note once to strike a blow for open discussion:

> Bless your militant, crusading spirit, neighbor, even if it didn't quite reach the courageous level at which one signs his name.

Some newspapers check with interested sources before printing a highly critical but anonymous letter. For example, when five marines in Korea wrote to the *Waterbury* (Connecticut) *Republican* late in 1952, the editor sent the letter to the Department of Defense for comment. Then both letters and the editorial were published in the same issue. This practice in not uncommon and it is unmistakably fair.

Barry Bingham, editor of the Louisville *Courier-Journal*, reported that seven papers he studied for the 1951 National Conference of Editorial Writers printed letters divided up in these proportions: Local and state, 65 per cent; National, 20 per cent; International, 5 per cent; General, 10 per cent. Editorials from the same newspapers showed this distribution of subject matter: Local and state, 20 per cent; National, 40; International, 25; General, 15. He added pithily in *The Masthead* (Fall, 1951):

It is evident that most of us who write editorials choose subjects in inverse ratio to the subjects chosen by writers of letters to the editor. I would never suggest that editors should slavishly follow the pattern of interests displayed by their correspondents. . . . I submit, however, that something is out of balance when writers of editorials dwell most heavily on the subjects least discussed by the writers of letters, and pay least attention to the letter writers' favorite topics.

Discussing somewhat the same problem, Carl R. Kesler, an editorial writer on the *Chicago Daily News*, observed in *The Quill* (April, 1951):

Letters to the editor on the foreign situation are likely to be among the most dispassionate examples of the art. On domestic and local issues, the reader is inclined to be frankly partisan.

Ideal letters to the editor, most newspapermen agree, are timely, interesting both as to content and as to style, and varied. The editorial page staff member who handles the letters can take care of this last point, provided, of course, that enough are received to permit some selection. Whether letters are timely depends in part on the speed of processing—again a matter that can be controlled by the staff. The remaining idea, however, eludes staff control.

On rare occasions letters to the editor may provide exciting clues to front page stories. For instance, a Pittsburgh citizen wrote *The New York Times* before World War II and offered a reward of $1,000,000 for Adolf Hitler "dead or alive." He was serious. The news story broke in papers around the world. Former Secretary Henry L. Stimson was a fairly consistent correspondent when he did not hold cabinet positions. His views expressed in letters to New York editors were widely quoted in news sories of other papers.

Some editorial page staff members stimulate letters by soliciting one by a recognized community leader or expert in a field, either to start an argument or to rebut previous correspondents. An axiom of letter-to-the-editor techniques is "Good letters bring good letters." Some newspapers offer special cash prizes for comments on specific subjects and a few have a daily award for the best letters. The Nashville *Tennessean* featured each day a "Three-Star Letter" and paid the writer $1. At the end of each year, the *Tennessean* held a dinner for all the "Three-Star Letter" authors of the previous twelve months. Any paper that does not give its letters advantageous display is not doing its best to promote this feature.

Some fortunate publications have a plethora of letters and their editors run through to select those topics that bring the most letters and then they screen these to pick the ones that best represent a common viewpoint.

Even experienced newspapermen are occasionally surprised by the outbreak of letter writing. For example, the television industry's advertisement in 1951 playing the theme, "There Are Some Things Your Children Won't Tell You," brought an avalanche to most editors. Political developments, especially during campaigns, are considered fair game for correspondents.

If he does not want to be exploited or to commit a wrong, the staff member who handles letters to the editor has to beware. Here are some cautions that are recognized in the rule book of most newspapers:

1. Look out for propagandists and special pleaders. Many supporters try to exploit a newspaper's letter column. In fact, one technique uncovered by the House Select Committee on Lobbying Activities in 1950 and 1951 was for lobbyists in the grass roots to supply copy for an editorial or, if that failed, to submit it under a local signature as a letter to the editor. This is relatively rare compared with the local "worthy causes" that are promoted.

The New York Times once received approximately 100 letters—all in identical wording—from students in several classes of one Long Island school. Their teachers were trying their hand at organizing a pressure group. The effort failed. During an election, such attempts intensify with supporters of all candidates straining to obtain an advantage.

Not all avalanches of letters, however, result from the skill of a propagandist. Some years ago *The New York Times* referred to St. Joseph, Missouri, as a "village." The error was caught in late editions but the ones sold in St. Joseph contained the mistake. Hundreds of protesting letters, some patient, many angry, flooded in. *The Times* printed some of the more important and apologized in an editorial.

2. Watch out for letters not intended for publication. Infrequently, someone will write a letter "To the Editor" in which he frankly discusses a community problem, compliments the staff on a job well done, or suggests a possible field for editorial activity. Publication is the last thing these individuals seek. This is a friendly communication to the editor or publisher without the "Dear Jim" salutation. This is one reason why it may be wise to check with a letter writer before his message is put into type.

3. Remember that the libel laws and traditions of good taste still apply to letters. In the heat of controversy, a correspondent may be carried away and write libelous, profane, obscene, or violently abusive language. Untrained in newspaper or magazine practices, he does not know that he and the paper may be subject to libel suits. Wisdom requires caution in editing letters to an editor.

4. Correct any known misstatements of facts. The copyreader has two alternatives: (1) he may contact the writer and arrange to rectify the error in the original copy or (2) he may append an editor's note stating what the real facts are. Known statements of incorrect information should be corrected, one way or another. The editor's constant obligation to inform the reader—correctly—encompasses this.

5. Be especially leary of "dare" letters. Some writers, fearful that their letters may not be published, resort to an introduction, "I dare you to print this statement. I believe you are afraid to." Usually such a device is tried only by the more rabid, sensational, or scurrilous. That sort of challenge is no more reason for relaxing the traditional safeguards than a less lurid beginning.

6. Handle all letters with unwavering fairness. Most newspapers and magazines will print honest differences of opinion. While he was editor of the *Louisville Times,* Tom Wallace told his own rule for fairness in an editorial which counselled that "it is necessary to be as fair to writers as a publisher should be to an editor." In some offices, a rule is to publish virtually all attacks on the publication's policies but to file—unprinted—many of the compliments. Regarding the fairness of some daily newspapers, one can only conclude that there are two uncomfortable alternatives: (1) their mail is fantastically unrepresentative of community sentiment or (2) their mail is distorted by editing so that it coincides with the publication's editorial policies on all subjects. A few widely circulated dailies appear to give an illusion of fairness by selecting only the crackpot and irrational criticism, never picking rational statements of opposition.

What to do with poorly written letters that are needed to balance a discussion constantly troubles editors. Some have to solve the difficulty by asking the writer's permission to cut, copyread, and rewrite the original text while retaining the full flavor and viewpoint. Others just trim their correspondence without checking, exercising a prerogative stated at the top of many sections that the staff will condense letters if necessary.

Religious and racial questions present special difficulties. Some papers automatically throw out anonymous letters on these two subjects; others simply refuse to discuss either topic even though writers identify themselves. These reactions can be well argued but a moderate letter might be judged on its contribution, if any, to community or social well-being. Once one of these subjects has been brought up, the staff must exercise the greatest tolerance and fair-mindedness. Fairly recently, the Knights of Columbus purchased advertising space to explain the tenets of the Roman Catholic church. Many newspapers permitted letters to the editor on the grounds that the writers were discussing an advertisement and not engaging in religious controversy.

Whether to publish letters that the editor and his associates believed presented the Communist party line was lustily argued by editorial page staff members in the years following World War II and the outbreak of the "cold war" until the United States Communist party was banned in 1954. One group felt the publications had a responsibility to protect readers from statements considered anti-democratic, especially if subtly packaged. In rebuttal, others reasoned that since no such protection extended to news stories it should not be built up to keep out letters only slightly under suspicion of following the Communist line. Obviously, none argued that an editor should not present his own case in an editorial to counter any ideas in a letter printed in adjoining columns.

Generally, daily newspapers display letters to the editor in one of four ways: (1) a column or special section on the editorial page; (2) a full page or half page feature one or more days each week; (3) section on the page opposite the editorial page or "op edit," or (4) scattered throughout the paper, more or less as filler items. Arguments for the first three practices stack up just about evenly; the last is virtually guaranteed to keep correspondence at a minimum.

The special section or column may be placed anywhere on the editorial page. In fact, some newspapers can be found regularly using one of the quadrants. The *St. Louis Post-Dispatch* surrenders to "Letters From The People" the outside column under the masthead, usually the prize position for editorials. *The New York Times* and *Cleveland Press* use the upper right columns with *The Times* generally running letters at least two full length columns. The Louisville *Courier-Journal* puts "The Point of View" in the lower left hand columns and generally publishes enough letters to have them extend more than half way across the bottom of the page. The *Christian Science Monitor* prints its correspondence in the bottom right while the *Chicago Daily Tribune* fills the same space under its cartoon. The *New York Mirror* centers its single "Today's Letter" at the bottom. Under a cartoon in the middle columns are letters sections in the *Washington Post and Times Herald, Hartford Courant, Atlanta Constitution,* and *San Francisco Chronicle.*

A full page or major part of a page is devoted to letters in the Friday edition of the *Oklahoma City Times,* which has done considerable spade work to stimulate correspondence. It is one of the much discussed papers when editorial page workers get together. Major Sunday edition display is given letters in the *Miami Herald, Des Moines Register* and *Denver Post,* to mention only a few. The "op edit" page is used on occasion by the *Denver Post,* among other papers.

One of the more unusual slogans for a letter column is the *Montgomery* (Alabama) *Advertiser's* "Tell It to Old Grandma." This featured a turn-about of a slur at the daily during the 1890's. Most papers content themselves with such conventional titles as "Voice of the People," "The People's Forum," or the unimaginative but adequate "Letters to the Editor."

Some magazines do a better job of featuring their letters than daily newspapers and weeklies. A few try to stimulate their mail just as newspapers do. The *Sears News Graphic* of Sears, Roebuck and Co., for instance, paid at least $2 for every letter used. Frequently magazine editors put their correspondence toward the very front of their publications, possibly just ahead of the featured article or story. While some readers undoubtedly turn immediately from the table of contents to the item they wish to read, many leaf the pages and stop to glance over the letters section before they start any of the more formal pieces. Despite the popularity of such sections in *Time, Atlantic Monthly, Harper's, Saturday Evening Post, Saturday Review,* and certain trade and employee publications, the daily newspapers remain the chief channel for getting letters to an editor printed.

"What do you think, John?"

After the 1948 presidential election debacle for the pollsters, one publisher got out an impressively bound volume entitled, *What Gallup Knows About Public Opinion.* Every page was blank. That typified many of the bitter and resentful comments aimed at all the pollsters who had picked Governor Thomas E. Dewey as the new President of the United States. It was obviously unfair but it represented the opposition point of view.

As a witness for the affirmative, Eric Hodgins, who edited *Fortune* when that magazine launched its public opinion surveys, pulled no punches when he wrote in the *Saturday Review* (January 3, 1953):

> So long as we hope to continue governing ourselves, however roughly, by majority will, public-opinion analysis will be fully as important as study of the hydrogen-helium cycle, and might have just as much bearing on what happens to our political and social systems during the rest of this century.

Comments upon the value of polling public opinion range between these two viewpoints. Yet despite all the miscalculations and blunders, newspaper readers undoubtedly will continue to be interested in predictions and public opinion polls. The two are not always the same. Fortune tellers generally can draw some crowd and the pollsters, at their worst, should do as well. Then the reading public also desires to know what it is supposed to be thinking just as the spectators at a baseball game read news stories to check their own observations against the writer's. The printed findings of polls may be read by some only to be scoffed at—but read they will be. Since the pollsters' reports frequently are printed on editorial pages, we will discuss them in this section.

They are, in truth, another aid for editors who want to attract attention to their own editorial comments.

Hodgins advocated that the pollsters should give up their business of predicting who will be elected through "a self-denying ordinance whereby they agree never to predict again" and concentrate on analyzing what he called the "decision-making process" and how people alter their opinions and attitudes. Then he added:

The relationship between the pollsters and the press has been ironic for a long time. All the pressure for prediction comes from the press—but it is the press that takes glee in telling the public that the pollsters are "wronger than ever."

Yet it was this business of predicting, in the 1936 presidential election, which launched both Dr. George Gallup and Elmo Roper upon successful careers after the *Literary Digest's* "unscientific" poll backfired. The traditions oppose Hodgins and, at least for the near future, it is a safe bet that his suggestions to omit predicting at election time will not prevail.

On the national level, three polls gather most newspaper attention because they are distributed for publication. These are the American Institute of Public Opinion (AIPO), which is generally referred to as the Gallup poll because it was set up by Dr. Gallup; the *Fortune* surveys, started by Roper; and the Archibald M. Crossley poll. More than a hundred newspapers cooperate to support the Gallup organization; thus in a way it is a creation of a segment of the daily press.

Various papers have conducted their own surveys of public opinion, either consistently or when elections presented special opportunities. The better known ones include the *Des Moines Register* and *Tribune, Minneapolis Star* and *Tribune, New York Daily News,* Philadelphia *Evening Bulletin, Chicago Daily Tribune,* and *Chicago Sun-Times.* Other polling agencies that may appear in the news columns and infrequently on the editorial pages include the Survey Research Center at the University of Michigan, the National Opinion Research Center (NORC) at the University of Chicago, the Office of Public Opinion Research at Princeton University, Bureau of Applied Social Research at Columbia University, and the Psychological Corporation in New York City. Samuel Lubell, onetime Washington, D.C., reporter, attracted considerable attention with his accurate election forecasts and analyses in the *Saturday Evening Post* and more recently in syndicated newspaper articles. Lubell used the long-established journalistic practice of talking to a great many representive people and then writing up the results.

In relation to the press, public opinion polls are primarily the creation of the daily papers. They do not figure largely in magazine journalism except for the *Fortune* and Lubell surveys, summary reports in the weekly news magazines when the polls syndicated to the daily papers become newsworthy, or infrequent adaptations in the business or employee publications.

Error may creep in at many stages of the polling process and, once there, it will be reflected in final results. In picking the sample, the pollsters may select groups or individuals that fail to represent their counterparts in the general public. In drafting questions, unconscious bias or loading may unbalance results. In interviewing, replies may be answers that are considered "right" rather than true ones or, at worst, they may be faked by an unreliable employee. In interpreting raw statistics, evaluators may take a wrong turn in deciding just what the figures mean or, as Hodgins phrased it, may be "imposing their judgment on the facts."

Social scientists have developed at least five separate approaches for testing public opinion. Some are variations of others. During recent years, newspapers and pollsters have utilized all five of these approaches for their investigations:

1. *Quota sampling.* Recognizing that a carefully selected sample may accurately substitute for a larger group, the pollsters have tried to set up in microcosm a duplicate of the larger area they wanted to survey. For the entire United States, for example,

they would make their sample conform with known facts of geography, age, race, religion, income level, educational background, former political affiliation, and other information that might influence people's attitudes or opinions. United States census statistics are the roadmap for this but, unfortunately for the pollsters, the government compiles its general population figures only decennially.

2. *Area sampling.* Depending on the laws of probability, the pollsters here follow the same idea as inspectors who look at every tenth model to see that it is up to standard or those who examine a handful of wheat and then pass judgment on an entire carload. In this approach, the pollsters pick at random several regions (it may be a city block, a small village, or a square mile in farm country) and then poll every person in the area or a select cross-section such as every tenth house or every hundredth.

3. *Pinpoint or barometer method.* With these techniques, the pollsters select a fairly large region as their litmus paper because in the past that area has faithfully represented the whole. Erie county, Ohio, served as a pinpoint or barometer area for many years although it first deviated in the 1940 presidential election. A more common but unreliable generalization about a barometer region is, "As Maine goes, so goes the nation." James A. Farley is credited with rewriting this after the 1936 election to read, "As Maine goes, so goes Vermont."

4. *Special re-interview panels.* A group of persons, picked either on the basis of a quota or completely at random, is interviewed on designated topics; then the individuals are re-interviewed so that a continuity is established for the same people over a period of time. A defect in this approach is that the panel members may become self-conscious and read up, thus losing their value as representatives of the larger group.

5. *"Mass Observation."* Before World War II, a British public opinion evaluating organization set up special observers whose business was to report comments that they overheard. These signs of public opinion were tabulated at a central clearing house. Dur-

ing the 1948 election, Samuel Grafton, then *New York Post* columnist, adopted this approach to conversations he overheard. Harry S. Truman held a slight lead according to a column printed well before the November balloting. Maybe it was luck or coincidence!

None of these approaches for testing public opinions and attitudes is foolproof; none the less all of them undoubtedly will be used for the raw material of newspaper comments for years to come.

Regardless of what technique is used, the relatively few individuals in a sample bothers many laymen. As few as 3,000 people may be interviewed for a national cross section in a Gallup poll. Yet the statistically minded social scientists will tell you that, while this obviously is not perfect, the anticipated deviation approaches a figure so small that it may be all but disregarded. This has been worked out by an involved mathematical formula that we do not need to consider here. What has to be insured is that the sample is truly representative.

Since the type of questioning may not only prejudice the results but is also important for readers' evaluation, let us look at what Dr. Gallup calls the "quintamensional" plan for question design.

Many of the questions asked on public opinion polls have to be answered with the traditional "Yes," "No," or "Don't Know." This may develop some strange perversions of reality. For instance, *Tide* magazine (March 14, 1947) told of a group of advertising men's survey of opinions regarding the Metallic Metals Act. Some 70 per cent of the individuals questioned lined up either for or against. The Metallic Metals Act existed, not on any law books, but only in the imagination of the poll's sponsors. Yet only three out of ten people failed to express an opinion.

To prevent this and to ascertain the "why" of opinions, Dr. Gallup and other pollsters developed a five-pronged battery of questions. These types of questions, with an illustration of each, follow:

1. *Filter or information question.* Example: Did you happen to read that the Soviet had exploded a new hydrogen bomb? Just what did that announcement mean to you?

2. *Open or free answer question.* Example: What do you think the United States should do since the Soviets have tested a new type of hydrogen bomb?

3. *Special issue or dichotomous question.* Example: It has been proposed that Congress appropriate several billions of additional money for improving United States defenses against the Soviets' hydrogen bombs. Do you approve or disapprove of this proposal?

4. *Reasons why question.* Example: Just why do you feel this way?

5. *Intensity question.* Example: How strongly do you feel about this—very strongly, fairly strongly, or not at all strongly?

What may one say about the value of public opinion polls? Here are some of the more common arguments: *

For opinion polls:

1. Polling public opinion helps legislators and government administrators make more intelligent and informed decisions because they know what a typical sample of the people want. This same information may be helpful to newspapermen responsible for determining editorial policy.

2. Polls constitute one of the few checks on pressure groups that misrepresent themselves as reflecting majority opinion.

3. Results of polls expose "areas of ignorance," as Dr. Gallup called them, thus providing opportunities for mass education.

4. Polling the public and publishing the results help to center

---

* For fuller discussion of public opinion polling, see George Gallup, *A Guide to Public Opinion Polls* (Princeton, Revised Edition, 1948) for a favorable presentation, and Lindsay Rogers, *The Pollsters: Public Opinion, Politics and Democratic Leadership* (Alfred A. Knopf, 1949) or Morris L. Ernest and David Loth, *The People Know Best: The Ballots vs. The Polls* (Public Affairs Press, 1949) for critical evaluations.

attention on major contemporary issues, thus stimulating general discussion.

Against opinion polls:

1. Measurements are meaningless because they are, at best, unscientific and, at worst, incorrect or invalid.

2. Even if the figures are correct, the polls fail to measure public opinion. In his critical book, *The Pollsters : Public Opinion, Politics, and Democratic Leadership* (Alfred A. Knopf, 1949), Professor Lindsay Rogers said the pollsters listen not to the pulse of democracy but to "its baby talk."

3. Too many public opinion polls require "Yes" or "No" answers when the more valid measurements of intensity and background information could tell a better story.

4. Like other forms of prediction such as gambling odds, the polls may create a "bandwagon effect" or trend to muffle dissenting opinion and thus upset the democratic process.

In any discussion of public opinion polling, it must be remembered that there are all sorts of polls. Some are conceived to support the editorial policy of a particular publication. And they do. Others utilize all the available knowledge of the social sciences to eliminate potential mistakes.

What may an impartial observer conclude? Robert Bendiner in *The New York Times Magazine* (August 23, 1953) wrote:

Viewed in perspective, then, the responsible polls are seen to play a perfectly admirable role in national affairs as long as their limitations are recognized. What these limitations mean, quite simply, is that we unpredictable humans, unlike refrigerators or ball bearings, happily go on resisting the efforts of science to measure us. When it comes to helping us know what we are and what we think, the polls are no substitute for poets, prophets, psychiatrists, novelists, or even good journalists. . . . Taken along with other revelations of the public temper, as well as an undetermined measure of salt, the polls can be illuminating at best and at worst amusing.

Inquiring reporter columns are a crude sort of public opinion poll although most, if not all, of the professionals who run the more formal surveys would disclaim them. In these features, editors seek to ascertain the attitudes of a strictly limited group of their potential readers. Some may use the popular inquiring reporter column to lure readers to the editorial page or the page opposite the editorial page in the hope that their own comments will also be read. Employee publication editors have used inquiring reporter columns to help build morale through calling attention to individual workers.

Publications may tie their questions strictly to some current news event such as, "Who do you think will be elected in next week's election?" or "Do you favor the proposed installation of parking meters on Main Street?" Or the questions may attempt to find out attitudes and mores of the local community or group. Examples of this second type are the following:

What is your description of an ideal man?
—*The Rouge News* (Ford Motor Company)

How would you answer the Biblical question: "Am I my brother's keeper"?
—*Hello!* (Crowell-Collier)

If offered a good business opportunity elsewhere, would you leave Des Moines?
—*Des Moines Register*

Do you think men should discard coat and tie and wear something more comfortable during hot spells?
—*New York Post*

In some offices, the emphasis is on the provocativeness of the question and the answers. If this is accomplished effectively, substantial readership is assured. One New York City tabloid, for instance, found that readership surveys repeatedly showed its inquiring reporter columns among the first half dozen items in popularity. A readers' survey for *The Diamond* of Calco Chemical

Division of American Cyanamid Company showed that 72 per cent of those interviewed liked the inquiring reporter column.

Except for employee publications, where the reader group is centered around a single core of interest, few other magazines have adopted the inquiring reporter column.

First class stuff may come by second class mail

Many publications borrow from other newspapers and magazines, thus following a pattern that goes back to the beginning of American journalism. Some do this because they want to tap all available sources for stimulating ideas; others just want to cut cost down to minimum budgets. That reprinted articles may be fantastically popular—if carefully selected—has been demonstrated by the rise of *Reader's Digest* to record magazine circulation figures. There is no valid reason why the same approach should not be adapted to editorial pages of newspapers and other magazines.

Writing in *The Masthead* (Spring,1949), Dale Wilson, who had been in charge of editorial page features on the *Milwaukee Journal* for several decades, explained his paper's attitude as follows:

Some newspaper men think that nothing is worth printing that does not come by wire. An old timer on our exchange desk used to call this "telegraphitis," a disease peculiar to telegraph editors.

On The Milwaukee Journal we like to think that some good things may come by freight. We are at least bold enough to say that some of our first-class stuff comes by second-class mail.

Reprints may take practically any form. Editorials, condensations of full length magazine and Sunday newspaper articles, book reviews, background pieces from press services and feature syndicates, or a Sunday anthology of poems—all are included.

Possibly most popular with daily newspapers are the editorial comments of other publications. These reprints may be used to reinforce opinions already stated in the paper's own columns, to advance a viewpoint without committing the paper itself, or to express an opposing stand. These latter two may represent a responsible editor's attempt to permit a true arena for conflicting opinions—or an escape to phony respectability by neatly stacking the cards in favor of what the publication wants.

A variant on reprinting of editorials is a weekly column by an editorial page staff member on what other editors in the region have been writing. When well done, this gives a cross-section of published opinions for general readers and office holders pay special attention. Hal Bjornson of the *Minneapolis Tribune* for years rounded up not only Minnesota press comments but regularly summarized what he considered significant from magazine articles, newspaper columnists not printed in Minneapolis, and radio commentators. The Louisville *Courier-Journal* and *Chattanooga Times* round up state press opinion weekly. The *Kansas City Star* and *Times* cover Missouri and Kansas journals alternately. On the *Oklahoma City Times*, a daily column of "homespun chatter" culled from Oklahoma weeklies sometimes served as bait for readers' letters. For instance, a quotation favoring a prohibition on using white bread, oysters, and chestnuts in turkey dressing brought 50 letters to the *Times* in irate rebuttal.

The *Milwaukee Journal,* which bans syndicated columnists, does a particularly good job on condensing lengthy feature material for editorial page use, usually under a headline of two columns or more. The *St. Louis Post-Dispatch* and *Minneapolis Star* also do this frequently. Of course, such work necessitates a staff that reads, clips, culls, and condenses. It takes man-hours to adapt the *Reader's Digest* approach to the editorial page but, if the popularity of such features with readers is any valid clue, it is worth the effort. One Midwestern newspaper that used reprints widely subscribed to more than 100 daily and weekly newspapers and almost as many magazines. Practically all of them supplied at least one double-column feature during a typical year and the most popular magazine appeared 17 times or an average of once every three weeks.

After decades as a mirror for the personal opinions and whims of its publisher, Colonel Robert R. McCormick, the *Chicago Daily Tribune* in 1954 started a department designated "The Other Side" which reprinted editorials generally reflecting "judgments sharply opposed to our own." An announcement said this was being done so "that its readers may have the benefit of other views in judging issues of national and international policy."

Newspapers that use reprints apply this digest approach for comments on new books. Such editors prefer the review with copious direct quotations that give the book's "meat" to an essay or critique of the volume. A well known, larger town daily may expect to receive at least 200 new books a month and metropolitan papers will get even more. These provide grist for the editorial pages. The *Kansas City Star* and *Times*, for instance, favor this feature treatment and the editorial page staffs keep an eye especially for references to Missouri and Kansas or writings by authors living in the circulation area. When this special material is found, a review of 1,500 to 2,000 words generally appears on the editorial page. On its "op edit" page, the *New York Post* reprints daily a few paragraphs from a current book. The conventional book review that Joseph Henry Jackson wrote for the editorial page of the *San Francisco Chronicle* made him a national reputation.

During recent years, the press associations have supplied more and more round-ups of foreign and Washington news. These often are printed on editorial pages. Interpretive pieces will be discussed in a later chapter, but they should be mentioned here as adjuncts of editorial comments.

A heavy traffic in reprinted poems exists in newspapers, especially on weekends. Possibly this simply reflects the low quality of most home-town production. Only a handful of metropolitan dailies regularly print original poems for which they pay even modest fees.

Most publications' staffs consider a credit line sufficient payment for reprint rights, but a few expect some compensation for a longer condensation. Books sent out for review obviously are exempt; so are the editorials of most newspapers. Most magazines allow reprints although some put a top limit at 400 words. When reprints are a regular editorial page feature, the staff member in charge may telegraph a modest offer for secondary publication rights of articles that he considers especially worthy. Almost always the reply is acceptance.

Opinion articles deserve space

Facts and opinions sometimes blend so strongly that they cannot properly be ripped apart into what might be called an objective news item and opinionated comments. Only an opinion article can adequately supply the reader with the information that he needs and is entitled to have. In recognizing this, many newspapers throw open some columns of their editorial pages for reporters and others who want to express their opinions.

Some stories cry out for subjective treatment. For example, several widely published series by Negroes on the treatment of their fellows in the South needed to have the personal experiences, the human reactions, and the purely emotional impact for readers to get the full force. Raymond Sprigle's report on his trip through the South as a simulated "Negro" won almost as much newspaper attention as his earlier Pulitzer prize stories on Justice Hugo Black's membership in the Ku Klux Klan. William Brower of the *Toledo Blade* and Carl T. Rowan of the *Minneapolis Tribune*, both reporters, wrote articles that would have lost much if the rigid rules of objectivity had been applied. As trained observers, they told what they saw and described their personal reactions. This may happen in various other aspects of news reporting. Correspondents in Washington, the United Nations, foreign countries, state capitols, and city halls may have information that fits an opinion article. Some papers print these reports on their editorial pages;

others treat such copy as interpretation and put it in news columns. The line is narrow; newspapermen frequently differ over where such a story belongs.

Editors and publishers themselves occasionally contribute opinion articles. Erwin D. Canham of the *Christian Science Monitor* broadcasts weekly on the news highlights; these remarks appear the following day on the newspaper's editorial page. John S. Knight comments weekly on the news as he sees it; his writings appear on the editorial pages of all his dailies.

Specialists in a subject much in the news may contribute their opinions explaining what current developments mean. For example, when the United States information program was under attack during the "cold war," the *New York Herald Tribune* printed on its editorial page a lengthy discussion of this program and propaganda in general by Edward L. Bernays, public relations counsel and expert publicist. Such articles generally might almost be considered expansions upon letters to the editor, although some of them were requested. The *Denver Post* utilizes local experts daily by having one guest editorial, written under a byline. A traffic expert may explain the need for better controls or the Community Chest chairman may write why everyone should contribute to the current campaign. University faculty members are tapped in many college towns to supply newspaper readers with meaning of the news that might otherwise be lost.

Smaller dailies use guest editorials, too. How the Bloomington (Illinois) *Daily Pantagraph* published a guest editorial was explained in Chapter Nine.

The *Macon* (Georgia) *News* editorial page often includes a question-and-answer interview with someone in the news or balancing pro and con articles on controversial local and national issues. Joe Parham, editor of the *Macon News*, explained that the question-and-answer interview is "the best way I know of getting over a lot of information in a hurry" and helps "to meet our obligations to tell the people what the leaders of the people are thinking about on certain subjects."

History, whether it repeats itself or not, interests many people and so some editorial pages have anniversary pieces as stand-bys. The *Kansas City Star* and *Times* and the *Milwaukee Journal* have national reputations for this recapturing of the past. The common "In Former Years" or "25 Years Ago" columns of many editorial pages are another effort to capture reader interest in things past. Here the danger may be an Afghanistanism of dead (and therefore safe) issues. This need not always happen. The *Louisville Times'* "Looking Backward" is so brightly written that it carries a byline. Among the magazines, *Time, Newsweek, The New Yorker*, and the women's publications use the profile article to provide background on a personality. Here, however, the bite of opinion seldom is edited out. More newspapers might well borrow some of these magazine techniques to their profit.

In an effort to attract readers to the editorial page, editors may use almost any feature that has followers. Some dailies print health columns, psychological quizzes, crossword puzzles, mood pieces on nature or the passing scene. The idea seems to be that anything that will bring attention is fair game for this page. But the efforts are hardly worth the powder unless the editorials themselves are worth reading. The final decision on whether a certain item belongs on the editorial page should depend on the answer to the question: Will it build up the page and thus help mould public opinion or is it just a miscellaneous feature dumped there because room could not be found for it elsewhere? If the honest reply is the second alternative, then the feature might better be left out.

ELEVEN

Attracting attention to the editorial page

SPREAD FIVE OR SIX WELL KNOWN EDITORIAL PAGES SIDE BY SIDE ON a table and the result too often will be an unbroken mass of neutral gray or, as Louis F. Dey of the Louisville *Courier-Journal* and *Times* described it, "a gray table cloth."

Many critics have pointed out the gray appearance of editorial pages; a few have explained how they might be improved by typographical innovations that have modernized front pages and sports pages. Yet editorial pages too frequently remain the last stronghold of Horace Greeley typography.

Content is seldom sufficient

An editorial page, like a woman, "can be just as wise, just as interesting and influential, if she's good looking and well dressed," argued Professor Roscoe Ellard of the Columbia Graduate School of Journalism. This is entirely true, but too few editors apply it.

Of course, what an editorial writer says is important. Otherwise there would not be much sense in taking space that might be filled with informative news stories or sold to advertisers for a sizable profit. There is no reason why the editorial page has to be the most unattractively made up in the entire paper, yet a sort of psychological block in the minds of some editorial page directors and publishers makes them believe that what was good enough for grandma is good enough today.

Too often those in charge of editorial pages on dailies and weeklies think that their job is done when their comments have come out of the typewriter and the paragraph marks are placed. This is not true; the job is by no means done. Editorial page copy should then begin a series of steps designed to gain readers' eyes so that its ideas eventually will reach their minds. This can be done more effectively with showmanship that seeks deliberately to bring customers into the tent. And it all may be done without loss of so-called "editorial dignity."

Dey, who should know because his redesigned *Courier-Journal* and *Times* editorial pages created admiration and excitement in the newspaper world, put it this way in *The Masthead* (Autumn, 1949):

Those typewritten words are meaningless until they've been read on a printed page. And if they aren't read they are wasted.

But before a person can read he must see. And he sees, first of all, a full page with a lot of type of various sizes, presented in a pretty jumbled sort of way. His eye is looking for some place to light and if his eye doesn't find something to hold his interest he tunes you out and looks somewhere else.

Too many editorial pages look as if they were dressed in styles of long ago. Of course, they look as if they wear rags which makes the picture more uninviting to the eye. These pages may carry the most important message of the day, but it's usually buried so deep in flat, colorless gray that even a "constant reader" has to dig for it.

So a lot of scholarly research and profound opinion are flying out of the reader's sight. Editorial pages simply don't get maximum readership partly because they're not intelligently presented. Oh, sure, editorial writers must have something to say—but you also need somebody to say it to.

Few valid reasons exist for not making editorial pages the brightest and most pleasing in a paper. By their very nature and variety, the contents lend themselves to unusual and attractive treatment. Yet many editors and publishers refuse to take the plunge into experimenting with their editorial pages. The modernists comprise a minority of the daily and weekly publications of the country but this group is growing and already includes most nationally circulated papers.

The traditional grayish and frequently "old-fashioned" make-up of editorial pages cannot be justified on a dollars and cents basis. Professor Albert A. Sutton of Northwestern University's Medill School of Journalism, in his authorative *Design and Make-up of the Newspaper* (Prentice-Hall, Inc., 1948) wrote:

> On most newspapers, little if any additional expenditure would be involved in making desirable changes, and many editors might benefit from re-evaluating the effectiveness of their present practices. In some instances, the [editorial] page might need to be completely re-designed; in others, only a few changes might be required to bring about improvement. . . .
>
> If one or more changes brought about even a small increase in readership, several hundred additional readers would be gained on most newspapers, and on the larger ones, the figure might run into the thousands. In addition, everyone seeing the page would benefit from any improvements made in readability and attractiveness.

Readership studies of editorial pages demonstrate amply that the typographical innovations that bring readers to other sections would be equally effective here. For instance, one Northwestern University study of 30 editorial pages found columns with cuts had 5.3 per cent higher readership than columns without cuts. But editorial writers hate to admit that pictures may have more appeal than words. They feel that, while this may be true for news pages, to concede this for their special section involves a personal humiliation to which they will not consciously submit.

A few editors defend conservative page make-ups on the grounds that they do not want to lure people into reading editorials by use of pictures, diagrams, larger headings, and wider columns. They believe that their publications already are reaching opinion leaders of the communities and feel no need to reach the rest of their readers. With this snobbery, editors certainly are turning their backs on most of the arguments for a well-informed mass opinion and a free, democratic press.

Still others point out that they hesitate to change make-up radically to conform to modern trends because these would shock —and possibly antagonize—their regular readers. Of course, this problem has confronted every editor who ever shifted his editorial page make-up; it has never remained a serious and valid objection for long if intelligence and knowledge were behind the innovation. Few indeed are the readers who change their daily or weekly papers because of such a modification. Within a short time, practically all of them develop an affection for the new style.

One compelling reason for increasing readability is the aging of the United States population. As more and more people live to be 65 years or older, they need typographical assistance for their weakening eyes. More readable type thus becomes imperative.

Yet editorial page directors whose pages are known for their variety and brightness in make-up are disinclined to criticize their fellow editors who are more conservative. For instance, Forrest W. Seymour when with the *Des Moines Register* and *Tribune* gave this summary of attitudes:

Some newspapers are experimental by nature; others are not experimental at all, and I never expect them to be. The *Register* and *Tribune*, the *Milwaukee Journal*, the *Minneapolis Star* and *Tribune*, and a few others have no taboos at all. Yet the *New York Herald Tribune* and *The New York Times* will always be, I suppose, what they are.

And Frank Ahlgren, editor of the *Memphis Commercial Appeal*, explained:

Unquestionably diagrams and pictures lend effectiveness to an editorial, but we are wary of them because they would be regarded as bizarre and distracting in addition to throwing the page out of balance typographically.

We have on occasion used coupon blanks, set in the measure and type family of the page, to be filled out and mailed by the reader in some particularly hot issue where his views could be brought to the interested party's attention.

Unquestionably editorial pages are going to be made easier to read by larger type in line widths calculated to make for easier reading.

We are not unaware of the competition from other media for the public's attention, but there still is no substitute for good, punchy writing.

Obviously writing must stand first in requirements for a good editorial page but that alone does not justify a conventional, eight-column "ocean of gray." Of course, no rational person expects the editorial page to use such flashy make-up that it permanently antagonizes readers. Would any person in his right mind recommend that *The New York Times* adopt whole-hog the least conservative make-up of its metropolitan rivals' editorial pages? Harmony should exist between the front page and the opinion page but that works both ways. Why should the editorial pages be less up-to-date than the front pages?

Barry Bingham, editor of the Louisville *Courier-Journal*, pinpointed this in the *I.P.I. Report* (April, 1954):

Many papers that are as modern as tomorrow keep their editorial pages looking like prim old maids, laced up in the fashion of the Nineties. Stiff column rules hold them together as rigidly as the whalebone corsets of old. The thin columns of type look musty and ill-aired. Too often the ideas they contain have the same flavor.

An editor himself is not always to blame. During the annual critiques of pages at the National Conference of Editorial Writers, a confession may be heard from time to time: "Don't blame me for the make-up; it's the publisher's baby." While this has never been a major problem, these confessions do occur often enough to indicate that publishers' conservatism does block some efforts to streamline the editorial page.

Professor Roscoe Ellard of the Columbia Graduate School of Journalism provided some ammunition for such skirmishes when he wrote in *The Masthead* (Summer, 1951):

310

Where mechanical requirements—and publishers' enlightment—will permit, however, an editorial page designed as a unit—open, dynamic, and inviting—will compete successfully with color movies, radio common-taters, and television.

Here are methods for brightening editorial pages

Innovations that may be adapted to daily and weekly editorial pages vary all the way from changes in the width of columns and the size of body type to a revised make-up that gives harmony to the entire page's appearance. Possibly the best way to study these topics is to take them up one by one:

(1) *Wider columns.* More variety may be possible in column width of editorial pages than on any other part of a newspaper. Readership is promoted because such differentiation marks the editorial page as something special and distinctive. Also, articles set in wider measure require less length and thus appear shorter and more inviting than those set in the conventional eight-column page width. Surveys confirm both these ideas.

Typographers and psychologists agree that approximately 40 characters is an ideal length for a line of type. The range for easy reading, they report, varies from 30 to 50 characters. Editorial pages, more than a daily's news columns, have applied these conclusions—and it is to the enlightened editors' credit.

Like a small boy with a shiny quarter in a toy store, an editor may pick from an almost endless assortment of possibilities. All newspapers formerly used columns of the same width and number for both editorials and news stories. Some still do. For a standard size paper, this means eight columns. Such make-up is used primarily by weeklies and non-metropolitan dailies so under-staffed that no time is left for experimenting. But a cross section of better known dailies shows that by the mid-1950's most larger dailies had shifted to seven- or six-column editorial page make-up. A few had gone to five columns.

Seven columns of equal width is the arrangement of *The New York Times*, Raleigh (N.C.) *News and Observer,* and *Rutland*

(Vermont) *Daily Herald*, to name only three dailies. Others set editorials in the measure equivalent to column and a half, and the rest of the page in five columns the same width as news columns. This is fairly popular. It is used by such papers as the *Boston Daily Globe, Denver Post, Detroit Free Press, Kansas City Star* and *Times*, Los Angeles *Mirror and Daily News, Pittsburgh Post-Gazette*, Philadelphia *Evening Bulletin*, Portland *Oregonian*, Richmond *News Leader, St. Paul Dispatch, Deseret News–Salt Lake Telegram, Salt Lake Tribune*, and *Toledo Blade*. Still others have split the page into two equal parts with editorials set in three columns for the outer half and the other material in four equal columns for the half nearer the fold. The *Chicago Daily Tribune's* seven-column make-up puts two columns of editorials and "A Line O'Type" in the outer half of the page. The *Chicago Daily News* and *Dallas Morning News* have still another variation of the three wide-measure columns; two for editorials are on the outside and one for features is against the fold.

On occasion, the *Des Moines Register* and *Minneapolis Star* use wider measure for a feature put at the right top of the editorial page, and narrower measure (and thus one more column) for bylined syndicate material under the feature. Thus there may be six columns at the top of the editorial page (including the wider measure) but seven at the bottom.

Editorial pages of the *Christian Science Monitor, Louisville Times, Providence* (R.I.) *Journal*, and *Wall Street Journal* are set in six columns of equal width. The *St. Louis Post-Dispatch's* six columns combine varying width for each of the major parts of the editorial page: "Letters from the People" in the outside column under the masthead, two columns of editorials, and three columns of reprints and book reviews under a cartoon.

The *Cleveland Press* and Louisville *Courier-Journal* split their editorial pages into five equal columns, each 18⅔ picas wide. This approaches the widest columns on United States editorial pages, but readers generally agree that they have no trouble following the lines of type. A few dailies set editorials in columns double the width for news. Newspapers in the Hearst group on occasion use even wider measure but when they do they always order large body type.

Magazines long had editorials set in wider measure and thus paced the trend that daily and weekly newspapers have picked up in earnest only since World War II.

In the quest for variety, note one caution. A few editorial page make-up men have come close to going berserk when the conventions were removed. For example, one Midwestern daily with a flair for experimenting used four different column widths in a single issue. Only one column rule ran unbroken for the full length of the editorial page. The chopped-up appearance of this page indicated that the business of variety can be carried too far.

(2) *Column rules versus white space.* A popular song extols the lure of the great open spaces and some editors must have remembered it when they dropped the column rules on their editorial pages. Another description of this attempt to use white space with as much effectiveness as advertisers frequently do is, "Let some air in."

As with selection of column width, possibilities are numerous: from page-length rules between every column to none at all for the entire page. Some papers concede nothing toward modernity here and a column rule separates each column. Typographical experts consider this old-fashioned and have little to say in favor of it. Even on such conventionally styled papers as *The New York Times* and *Kansas City Star*, the editorial pages have column rules cast on wider body that ordinarily used for news columns. This allows more shoulder on either side and lets in more light and air. On other papers, no column rules at all are used. Dailies from coast to coast use this "open spaces" treatment, including, to name only a few from east to west: *Hartford Courant, New York World-Telegram and Sun, Washington Post and Times Herald, Atlanta Constitution, Cleveland Press,* Louisville *Courier-Journal, St. Paul Dispatch, St. Louis Post-Dispatch, Denver Post, San Francisco Chronicle, Los Angeles Times,* and Portland *Oregonian.*

In between are the middle-of-the-road papers that use column rules to separate some sections of the editorial pages but not for every column. The Richmond *News Leader,* for instance, has gulleys for white space between the double columns of editorials but it separates the letters and syndicated columns with rules. The *Des Moines Register* treats its editorials the same way but has a doubly heavy rule to separate editorials from feature articles. The *Boston Daily Globe* puts column rules between its editorial comments but omits them in its syndicated articles and letters department. Cut-off rules square off these sections and column rules would only split them apart again. Modernists would complain that the cut-off rules might well have been eliminated, too, thus achieving an even freer look.

By and large, magazines long ago discarded column rules. And even those publications that still retain them use wide shoulders to let air in beside the body type.

(3) *Size of body type.* Back in the 1890's, immigrants coming to the United States and settling around New York City were supposed to use the large type of William Randolph Hearst's *Journal* editorial pages to spell out words as they learned a new language. Today, however, oversize type appears almost exclusively in grade school readers. While modern newspaper editorial pages seldom serve as beginners' textbooks, few informed editors and publishers will argue that readership cannot be increased by leading editorials. When editors and publishers want to make a splash of an editorial, either by giving it special treatment on the editorial page or by putting it on the front page, they almost invariably order leading beyond that normally used. Consciously or subconsciously, this is an admission that leading insures greater readability. Leading gives a freer, airier page, just as does elimination of column rules or wider shoulders when rules are used.

If the regular body type of the news columns is under eight point, editorial page copy frequently is set in eight point type on nine or ten point slugs. If the regular body type is eight point, then nine or ten or even twelve point type with at least two point leading will invite readers to stop and look around. The *St. Paul Dispatch* has adapted the front page device by setting the first paragraph of its lead editorial in larger than ordinary body type.

If only one part of a page, such as the editorials alone, is leaded, make-up men have to be careful to avoid a streaked effect when leaded type masses are put next to others with minimum spacing. Requirements of attractiveness and high readability may demand generous leading for all columns on editorial pages. Magazines do not often face this problem because those that retain editorial pages give the entire space exclusively to comments.

In experimenting with type to break up the "ocean of gray" effect, some editors and make-up men have tried paragraphs set in boldface, lightface capitals, or even boldface capitals. True, this may relieve the grayness of the page but unless it is done with considerable discretion the result may be a hodgepodge that resembles an over-crowded pawn-shop window.

(4) *Size of editorial and feature headlines.* There is nothing immoral or undignified in using headline type large enough to catch the readers' eyes. As Dey of Louisville has pointed out in discussing editorial page headlines, "It's not bad manners to raise your voice enough to be heard." A single crossline heading in ten point type, boldface capitals, certainly whispers for a reader's attention; it is even worse when an editor puts small type size on his editorials. When this happens, is it any wonder that readers turn toward the syndicated columnists whose articles are topped with headlines two, three, or four times as large as those on editorials?

To get away from purely label headlines, some newspapers use double-column editorial headings. A few even extend them to three columns. Others use two lines. Still others combine both to print double-column, two-line headlines on their editorials and major editorial page features. Usually conservative in typography, the *Kansas City Star* and *Times* put a three-column, two-line head with a three-line, hanging indentation deck or bank on the editorial page feature article. The *Milwaukee Journal* also may use a three-column head on a display feature article.

With only scattered exceptions, dailies put single deck heads on editorials although they may be either single or multi-column and may have one or more lines. The *Louisville Times*, however, places a three-line single-column deck of 14 point type under a single-line, three column top deck of 30 point boldface.

In addition to typographical advantages, larger headlines on editorials, features, and columns also may be justified for another reason. They give readers more insight into the content. More units allow more words and more words tell more facts. After all, the whole thing is to get ideas into readers' minds.

(5) *Re-arrangement of the masthead.* Newspapers used to put the masthead at the top of the left-hand column of the editorial page. It was as natural as having meat and potatoes for the same course at dinner. Then some modernists began to speculate why they should repeat month after month the same dull statements of ownership, required by law, in a position that possibly was the prize place on the whole page. No one read it, they knew. So they experimented, first streamlining it to take less space, then moving it elsewhere on the page.

Among the traditionalists that continue to devote the upper left-hand corner of the editorial page to the masthead, usually lengthy with subscription rates and foreign bureaus' addresses, are *The New York Times*, Baltimore *Sun*, *Buffalo Evening News*, and *Kansas City Star* and *Times*. Somewhat shortened mastheads in the conventional upper left-hand corner are published by the *Chicago Daily Tribune*, *Milwaukee Journal*, *Minneapolis Star*, and *Worcester* (Massachusetts) *Telegram*.

The *St. Louis Post-Dispatch* uses the outside column for an abbreviated masthead but under it is Joseph Pulitzer's 1907 platform for conducting a daily. Below the platform come "Letters from the People" for the remainder of the column. The lead editorial tops column two, thus getting a position where it may still catch major attention.

In the *Washington Post and Times Herald*, *Cleveland Press*, and

Chicago Daily News, the masthead is set double-column over the editorials but in each paper it lists editors and other facts that push it down several inches. The *Daily News* includes the fact it won a Pulitzer prize for "the most disinterested and meritorious public service," along with the monthly circulation figure.

The *Hartford Courant, New York Herald Tribune, Des Moines Register, Denver Post*, and *Deseret News–Salt Lake Telegram* cut the information to little more than the paper's name and a couple of other facts set in double-column measure. The *Post*, for instance, includes only three lines: the label "Editorial Page" and slogan, "So the people may know"; the paper's name; and the date. The *Register* has streamlined its masthead to two lines: its name on one and on the second, "Founded 1849" and the current date. That is all there is before you get into the lead editorial. But the *Herald Tribune, Post*, and *Register* give the missing information of the conventional masthead in the lower right-hand corner.

The *Christian Science Monitor* prints its name, slogan, date, and ownership in two lines that run across the entire top of its editorial page.

The Louisville *Courier-Journal*, frequently an experimentalist, added the names of all its editorial writers to its bob-tailed masthead. Six months after the change, the letters to the editor had increased 25 per cent. Could it be that readers like to write to individuals, not an institution?

To reclaim the prized upper left-hand corner for editorials, some newspapers have boxed the information and put it in any inconspicuous place. The Richmond *News Leader*, for instance, uses the bottom of the outside column.

As with several other topics discussed in this chapter, magazine editors do not face the same problem here as do the men who put out dailies and weeklies. A magazine's masthead generally is neatly fitted into the Table of Contents page or tucked away under an advertisement on the inside cover or some other early page.

(6) *Use of illustrations, charts, diagrams, and maps.* Cartoons have become respectable for editorial page use but that is about as far as many editors and publishers will go. Yet the experimentalists have found extremely effective the use of diagrams to illuminate a discussion of cost of living, unemployment statistics, or the amount of aid to foreign countries, just as the use of maps pinpoints the location of obscure areas that have just broken into the world news.

Case histories could be recited endlessly but here is one that attracted attention not only in its home town but in national journalistic publications. In an attention-getting picture, the *Akron (Ohio) Beacon Journal* of January 5, 1953, showed 91 pairs of "empty shoes" to illustrate how traffic fatalities hit that community during the previous year. Certainly this attracted more attention than a full-page "ocean of gray." And the reason? The editorial itself, after analyzing the figures, pointed out the answer when it said: "These are merely statistics—and Empty Shoes mean far more than that." Graphic, descriptive words might have humanized the "merely statistics," but certainly so did the pictures of 91 pairs of "empty shoes."

Among those who have repeatedly demonstrated the possibilities in using illustrations (taking the word in the broadest sense to include all the things we are talking about), probably none have surpassed the editors of the *Des Moines Register* and *Tribune*, Louisville *Courier-Journal* and *Times, Minneapolis Star* and *Tribune*, and Richmond *News Leader*. Study of these newspapers will give valuable information and background on the techniques.

Papers that have done a commendable job with illustrations stress half-tones keyed to the subject matter of a syndicated column rather than the repeated use of a half-column cut of the author day after day. One critic asked what the "mugs" of syndicated writers added in reader interest after the first day or two. If a writer is discussing rural life in India, why not a picture from that country showing just how a typical village looks? That same concept might be well applied to editorials, too. In explaining and clarifying statistics and geographical locations, digrams, charts, and maps contribute to public understanding in a manner that is hard to beat.

Considerable evidence points to improved use of illustrations (used again in the broadest meaning) as a major innovation in editorial page make-up during the 1950's and 1960's.

Weeklies and tabloids have varied some answers

Weeklies with only six or eight pages and tabloids with smaller pages confront problems differing somewhat from those of their larger metropolitan rivals. Yet typography may be applied to help solve them, too. Suggestions for improving the editorial page, outlined earlier, may be adapted to the full-size page of the weekly or to the three, four, or five columns of the tabloids. Other alternatives also present themselves.

After two years of publishing, William A. Hatcher of *Town Talk*, a weekly published in the St. Louis suburb of Ferguson, felt confident enough to launch a full-size editorial page, "cartoon and all," as he put it. The University of Missouri School of Journalism awarded *Town Talk* a bronze plaque for the best editorial page of any weekly in the state. But that was not the end of the story. Mr. Hatcher told it this way in *The Quill* (April, 1952):

> In thinking it over, I decided that we had been so anxious to look like the big metropolitan dailies that we were wasting a full seven columns of space just to carry one lead editorial. People were reading the editorials and the letters. I knew that, but I discovered that we could have offered a reward of $1,000 for any reader who waded through the book reviews, the fillers on Missouri history and other items used in the page.
>
> The solution was obvious. We simply sold the full page to a grocer for fifty-two weeks and ran the editorials and letters in the lefthand columns of the front page. We like it, the readers like it, and it has done wonders for the bank account.

If anything, I am convinced the editorials have more influence now than in 1949. Last year, in the April municipal election, a front page editorial swept five entrenched aldermen out of office and replaced them with five nice shiny new models.

The editorials in *Town Talk* are set double column, in type larger than the ordinary body type, and leaded for greater readability, thus proving, if it still needs to be repeated, that typography pays off. Also it shows that smaller papers may often contribute most when they give up aping their big brothers in the metropolises.

Probably because the tabloid-sized daily as we know it is relatively new and thus encrusted in fewer layers of tradition, editors and publishers of these smaller papers have been more willing to experiment with editorial page make-up. Most tabloids vary the column width and lighten the display of typography to make their editorial pages stand out as distinct from the news pages.

Typical of one school of tabloid make-up are the New York *Daily News* and the *New York Mirror*. In the *Daily News*, the main editorials are run double-column, usually brightened with at least one small halftone or line drawing, in the left-hand side of the page. In the upper right corner is a cartoon under which is a two-column "Voice of the People." In the middle column is 'The Inquiring Fotographer" column of short interviews with thumbnail halftones of each person asked the question of the day. The *Mirror* puts editorials, double-column and well leaded, under a brief quotation from the late William Randolph Hearst. A syndicated Washington column is run in the left-hand column under a boxed, standing head. Nearly centered is a cartoon that usually ties in with the editorial; a second cartoon appears in the bottom, left hand corner. If there is space at the end of the second or middle column of the syndicated material, a single letter-to-the editor is printed. To emphasize sections of their editorials, both *Daily News* and *Mirror* use regular boldface, italic or lightface capitals.

EDITORIALS

THE SOURCE OF YALTA'S TRAGEDY

The full record of Yalta (see p. 38) which the State Department published last week contains many new sidelights but need not surprise for what it shows about the good faith or the World War III, such as Churchill's (LIFE, Nov. 9 and Nov. 16, 1953) or Chester Wilmot's (LIFE, March 10, 1952). It does furnish the Republicans with more ammunition against the Democrats. Certainly the thinnest Americans who learn how historically impossible it was to make friends with Stalin by means of cheap days at the British School Church. It's clear that Yalta did not initiate a new long argument for greater Anglo-American unity, making Roosevelt's alternative "Grand Design" of Big Three unity seem as anecdotal as ever.

But this is not the whole story. Yalta will call one of history's major tragedies, and its full meaning calls for the full temptation and setback of the West General Marshall envisaging a method from Prussia, the Western allies gave restraint to from this. American casualties to conquer Japan without Russia, etc., etc.; they made war on both Japan and Germany, to make concessions to Stalin. The question is why they made the concessions they did, and how the acceptance of those concessions may be compared to future situations of similar temptation and pressure.

The chief victims of Yalta were free Poland and free China, which went into Communist captivity as a direct or indirect result. Neither country was represented at Yalta. The atmosphere of Big Three arrogance in which their fate was decided is illustrated by a statement of Roosevelt's: "he did not wish arbitrarily to determine the boundaries of a new Polish government, since he thought in some ways there had been in reality no Polish government" administration had all along backed the Polish government in exile and had many signed agreements with it, including the Atlantic Charter. The same treaty note was more bluntly struck by Stalin, who declared at Yalta that, to Russia, "Poland would have an equal voice with the three great powers who had won the war..." "What could not live in such an atmosphere was not only the voice of small nations, but the voice of any general principles of conduct that are the only alternative, in international as in domestic affairs, to the rule of fear and force.

"An increasing disregard of the rights of weaker nations"—that was the source of Yalta's tragedy, wrote Historian G. F. Hudson of Oxford recently last year. "During the last two years of his life Roosevelt fell more and more under the spell of his vision of a world government organized by the Big Three devoutedly, for its implied principles of an authoritarian, and not of a democratic, order. The democracies can never reconcile what interest as democracies lies in a world of enlightened and fresh associated nations large and small." But a world of a more peaceful type—right, easily, become totalitarian. That is what we confront when we turn from recriminations over Yalta to the long task of analyzing the democracies, in which order as a function of consent, and a full Communism and a threat of the right to resist the temptation to oppose Communism with other people's freedom, be then Poles, Chinese or the Albanians for whom the West can well the agenda of liberation. That is what we confront when we turn from recriminations over Yalta to the long task of analyzing the democracies.

THE TRAINING OF SOLDIERS

The argument of a dying man always carries great eloquence. That of Lieut. General Raymond S. McLain on behalf of universal military training (see p. 111), which he wrote in full knowledge of his imminent death, has also the passion of a devoted officer who knew that thousands of younger men had died needlessly because other young men had not been adequately trained in time.

An outstanding example was the U.S. 3rd Division (Eagle) which General McLain led during the landing at Anzio, in North Africa, on Nov. 8, 1942. Before landing at Salerno, then Anzio, then after the capture of Rome, the on-asset of Austria, the redoubtable 3rd, having surrounded the Alps, had outdone Hannibal, who merely crossed them. And from then on were the original strength of the division. In those 30 months of bloody combat in battle-weary survivors, time and again, built its size—the first to reluctant, and yet a relief for the sole reason that there were not enough well-trained new troops to train them.

Such experiences add force to the general argument for UMT. But the fact is that debate on a technical level has found that the bill would not make an adequate Army just as inevitable the other side; not to mention Navy and Air Force are whose services get little or no benefit from UMT. To the many older arguments against UMT they add that the thermonuclear realities have changed combat conditions so much that every soldier of the future will have to be almost as much a specialist as the airman of the past day. UMT would not contribute enough to this needed specialized preparation to justify its considerable cost.

For these, and other reasons, any large-scale form of UMT seems today even less of an offered in an Administration bill now before Congress, which, while continuing to draft, the men needed for 24 months, would provide each year for 100,000 young men who give a good college thing down by volunteering for a six-month training course followed by a 7½-year reserve obligation.

This will not may not be the best possible solution. Some persuasive critics, who point out that a year's training is necessary to ready a soldier for combat, doubt if six months training will rush him for much of anything —and that the little he does gain will be quickly lost. If young men are not needed in the services as draftees, they probably are not needed to man the ranks, even then through a military knowledge when they might be better preparing themselves for specialized war service in electronics, meteorology or other militarily useful branches of technical skill.

Thus the argument stands, one which probably only another war, if it comes, would ever really settle—since nobody can even be sure what the answer of such a war would be. Should it call for rapid expansion of the regular Army, as in all past wars, then the Administration bill ought at least to ease matters, thus providing tactical against the errors of the past which so moved the late General McLain.

BETTER LIVING

Vol. 7   THE DU PONT EMPLOYEE MAGAZINE   No. 1

Lester L. White, editor
Associate editors
Published with the help of Du Pont people everywhere
Copyright 1953 E. I. du Pont de Nemours & Company

THE COVER

NEXT ISSUE

CONTENTS

The Meaning of Anti-Trust

Last month the country's attention focused on a Chicago courtroom where a Federal Judge, in a decision already historic, freed the Du Pont Company innocent of charges filed under the anti-trust laws.

The term applied to these regulations, which are well established features of the Federal statutes, is one that is often misunderstood. If this were an "anti-trust" action, then presumably Du Pont had been sued as a "trust," a term that was popular—or unpopular—in the 1890's.

Judge Leahy's Decision

A "trust," however, was something quite different. (The word was originally defined as meaning "hope, confidence, belief, truth, expectation.") But, in the business sense, a trust was a legal arrangement through which a number of producers would join together by assigning all their assets to a central body of "trustees" which would then operate for all of them as a single, big combine instead of all thoughts of competition between the various units. There was justifiable public dissatisfaction with this and the "trusts" as such were soon outlawed.

Definition Is Broadened

The Sherman Act of 1890 was the first anti-trust law passed by Congress. It not only condemned trusts, but also combinations formed for the purpose of restraining trade, however any legal action alleging monopoly or restraint of trade became known as an anti-trust suit. Even beyond that, many persons erroneously came to associate the word "trust" with any organization which attained large size.

The decision at Chicago will do much to correct this error and clarify the issues surrounding this case. The Du Pont decision and legal verdict is neither a proof of nor an invitation to wrongdoing—that the law is designed to condemn misconduct. In ruling that there had been no violation of the law, the Court reduces the question to its true dimension and clears the air of long-held, hazy illusions.

Artificial Barriers Penalize Progress

It is plain that America cannot afford to penalize progress by constructing artificial barriers. As Du Pont's president has said, "It is hard to plan ahead when ventures are questioned, not because they have failed, but because they have succeeded." The Court, in this instance, cast aside all such considerations—the only question was, "Did someone break the law?"

The Du Pont, like any other citizen, is glad to be judged on the basis. The answer was clear. So, at long last, was the question.

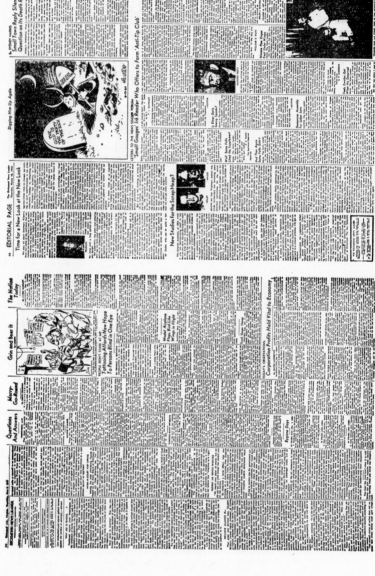

Left: Typical editorial page under Dr. Douglas S. Freeman with only cartoon, three-column feature head, and wide-measure editorials to brighten page.

RICHMOND NEWS LEADER

Right: A recent editorial page showing use of cuts and re-arrangement of masthead in an effort to gain an increase in readership.

Left: Listing the names of traffic fatalities attracts attention to the editorial, centered and boxed on page.

RICHMOND NEWS LEADER

Right: Pictures of slum areas in Richmond drive home an editorial campaign for the improvement of poor housing.

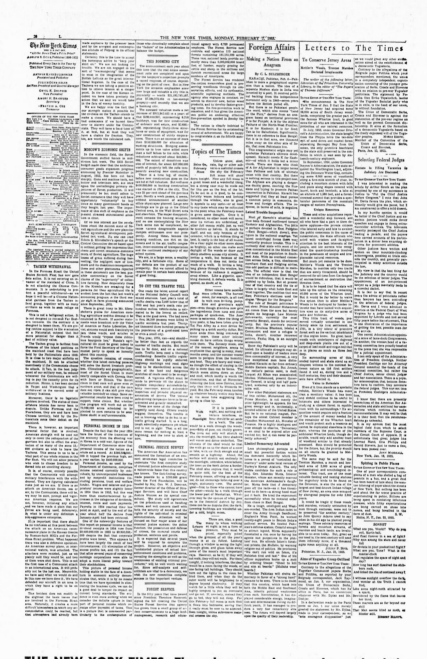

THE NEW YORK TIMES, MONDAY, FEBRUARY 7, 1955.

The New York Times

"All the News That's Fit to Print"
ADOLPH S. OCHS, Publisher 1896-1935
Published Every Day in the Year by
The New York Times Company

ARTHUR HAYS SULZBERGER
President and Publisher

JULIUS OCHS ADLER
1st Vice President and General Manager

ORVIL E. DRYFOOS
Vice President

AMORY H. BRADFORD
Secretary

FRANCIS A. COX
Treasurer

Foreign Affairs

Making a Nation From an Anagram

By C. L. SULZBERGER

Letters to The Times

To Conserve Jersey Areas

Topics of The Times

THE NEW YORK TIMES: The only concessions to the modernistic trend are use of seven columns (instead of eight as on news pages) and wider column rules than those used for news items.

THE MILWAUKEE JOURNAL
L. W. NIEMAN, Founder, 1882

Published by The Journal Company

W. J. GRANT, Chairman of the Board
J. D. FERGUSON .... President and Editor
IRWIN MAIER ...... Vice President and Publisher
DONALD B ABERT, Vice President and Business Mgr.
W. J DAMM ... Vice President and Gen. Mgr. of Radio

PHONE BROADWAY 1-4000. Private telephones connect
225 W. State St. .... MILWAUKEE 1, WIS.
Milwaukee Journal Square, 333 W Michigan St.
Business Office Hours 8:30 to 5 daily, except Sunday

Clarifying Adoption Law

The moderate change in Wisconsin's adoption law that is now proposed by Assemblyman Metzner (Rep., Madison) should meet with little opposition. But there seems no justification for rushing this change through now when it already has been recommended as one of the many changes for the revised children's code.

The measure, stemming from the unfortunate "baby Jeffrey" case, provides for review by county courts of the few cases in which the state welfare department on licensed child welfare agencies refuse to consent to adoption of children whom they have placed in adoptive homes on a trial basis.

It is a substitute for the assemblyman's more drastic and undesirable bill that would have "presumed" the granting of consent if a child were permitted to remain in an adoptive home for at least six months.

The law now requires that the department or agency consent to the adoption of children who are their legal wards. In the Jeffrey case the state supreme court held that the county court had no right to waive that consent.

Under the new bill, when consent is refused, the department or agency would file a summary of reasons with the county court. The judge could agree with those reasons and reject the adoption petition. Or he might hold a hearing. If he then determined that refusal to consent was contrary to the best interests of the child, he could waive the consent requirement and permit the adoption.

A point to be stressed is that such judicial review would be resorted to only in unusual cases. Most adoptions go through happily and routinely. The adoption law is basically excellent; rules and procedures are sound and time tested. Neither the state department nor the agencies act capriciously. Their overruling consent is that the best possible homes and parents be found for the children.

But court review of the few cases in which trial placements are made and consent to adoption then withheld should not prove seriously hampering. The burden of proof that consent was withheld without adequate reason would rest, as it should, on those seeking to adopt the child.

Why, though, the hurry? Why take the legislature a time and clutter up the statute book with a change that, except for rare cases, is already covered by the legislature-council's child welfare committee as one of the many revisions it has proposed in all the laws affecting children and youth? The state board of public welfare has approved the principle of court review.

Assemblyman Metzner is contendtion that the legislature may not get around to approving the entire code this year doesn't justify piecemeal tinkering with the adoption law.

A Leader Who Will Be Missed

Death of Walter White, lifetime crusader for Negro rights, comes at a time when it will be felt most keenly.

This has been his year of triumph. For Walter White, and the National Association for the Advancement of Colored People which he headed, led the unremitting fight on segregation laws aimed at Negroes. And that fight won its greatest victory in the United States supreme court decision of last May, holding that racial segregation in the public schools was unconstitutional.

That decision, however, has created confusion, resentment and defiance which it will take time and tact to overcome. At a time like this Walter White will be missed more than ever. The wisdom that Walter White showed in leading Negroes, and those who sympathize with the Negroes' plight, is greatly needed right now.

Walter White made the nation his everlasting debtor by this type of leadership. And he gave it in the cause of a minority facing what seemed like insurmountable handicaps, a people with whom he had only the slightest—one-sixty-fourth—connection by blood and no connection by color.

Walter White will be remembered as the champion of these Americans who have so much needed a champion of his caliber; also as a man who fought with fervor for freedom in a land which does not yet grant to all the freedom it professes.

Residence Is Unimportant

In providing for the highway needs of Wisconsin, the state highway commission should give thought primarily to building all improving roads where the need is greatest. Considering the sums proven that counties hold over the state and the way local funds are skimmed off the top of highway revenues before the state gets any, the present commission seems to be carrying out its responsibility as best it can.

But the statute relating to the composition of the commission implies that sectional interests should also be given weight. For the law provides that each of the three commissioners shall come from a different section of the state—one each from the north, east and west. Boundaries of the sections are set forth.

With good sense the senate highway committee has introduced a bill to eliminate the regional qualification. Why, for example, should an able candidate from Green Bay be barred from the highway commission simply because, one of the other commissioners might come from Lake Geneva?

Other qualifications and requirements would remain in the law—that at least two commissioners shall have had comprehensive business experience and also practical knowledge of highway planning and construction, that all three devote full time to their duties and have no other remunerative employment.

Those are provisions that mean something. The appearance of residence doesn't.

Fail to Grasp Constitution

It sometimes seems not so cynical, after all, to remark that some people who make such a great show of revering and defending the Constitution would better spend their time reading it.

Some of these people are on the United States senate judiciary committee, no less. Their questioning of John Marshall Harlan, in unfeasible fear that he might ravage the Constitution if confirmed for the supreme court, exposed instead their own failure to grasp constitutional principles.

Basic in the constitutional scheme is the separation of powers—the integrity and independence of each branch, including especially the judiciary. Yet senators like Eastland, Jenner and Welker tried to usurp for the legislative branch the right to test judicial fitness according to their own prejudices.

Harlan answered their objectionable questions as far as he could within the limits of conscience and propriety. He gave ample assurance of his adherence to the Constitution, and beyond that he could not go. He was forced to explain to his inquisitors that it is rudimentary etiquette not to ask a judge or judicial nominee how he would have ruled, or might rule, in a specific or even hypothetical case. It just isn't done—least of all when a threat is implied.

Some other people who rouit justifiably tonidy the Constitution are the extension fee of the American Bar association who favor disbarring any lawyer who invokes the fifth amendment. Of all people, such learned lawyers should know best that the freedom from forced self-condemnation was designed and must stand to protect the possibly innocent against oppression and injustice. To suggest that exercise of a constitutional right should automatically evoke a formal penalty—in this case, no less than loss of livelihood—is most unlawyerlike.

Both these warped viewpoints are symptoms of the disease that still so largely infects the body politic. The senators and the bar committee are both in the race to prove their own patriotism is the purest. The sincerer they do by the principles they profess to be guarding either does not down on them or does not deter them.

Rotary's 50 Years of Service

Each work in communities from Kwethlukan in Alaska to Brussel in Borneo more than 400,000 men of 89 nations meet together in the name of fellowship and service. They are members of Rotary International, which this year is observing its 50th anniversary.

And it is more than lip service that these representatives of business and the professions pay to their motto of service. Particularly in recent years—as the number of members and clubs has expanded and their efforts have become better organized—have resources to improve their communities, vocations and international life have valuable fruits.

Achievements in America and abroad are varied in nature and scope—aid to crippled children, disaster and war relief, college and vocational training promotion, youth exchange, espousal of the United Nations and its programs, adoption of damage communities as recipients of aid.

Proudest accomplishment of all to date is the Rotary Foundation, dedicated to Paul P Harris, the Chicago attorney who founded the club. From contributions of almost 2½ million dollars, more than 1½ million has been spent to date to finance advanced study and research by 600 young men and women of 57 nations.

Under their rugged wheel symbol, Rotarians everywhere demonstrate that their concept of a world neighborhood can be a reality.

Seek City Spawning Another Hitler?

It appears that Roman Reuter has appointed himself "Gauleiter" of Sauk City. It appears that the new publishers [of Leroy Gore's anti-McCarthy weekly) will welcome come to Sauk City if "they behave themselves" and that quieter without flaunting their rights as publishers to speak out if a ward is concerned about the freedom of the people of their town.

What is more amusing is that Reuter's a moderate fair state commander of the American Legion. The legion can do the cause of freedom no good by giving "Gauleiter" Reuter a hickup at the polls when his time comes to elect a commander. The legion, if it means well, could well specify not to endorse any man, with, which constituting the intimidation of the freedom of the people of their town.

Such statements as spouted by Reuter strikes us. Next time we go through Sauk City we shall expect to see the twinkle flying instead of the Stars and Stripes.

Reply to Third Party Talk

If the frustrated unhappy people who rail at Chester's recently want a third party, let them join it. And let them not call it a major parties who have a responsibility to govern this nation and take part in affairs of the world.

That Firebrand Irish Dramatist

For Decades Rebellious Sean O'Casey, Who Once Escaped From Firing Squad, Has Been Pleasing and Enraging Theatergoers

Sean O'Casey, master of racy, musical Irish prose

FOR more than 30 years Sean O'Casey has been pleasing and enraging Irish theatergoers. He incited riots in the theaters and today the old sting is still apparent. A few days ago, his latest play, "The Bishop's Bonfire," had its premiere in Dublin. Prolonged applause accompanied by jeers, catcalls and jeers of one political group are now suspected.

... [additional text] ...

This Creature Lived 250 Million Years Ago

In the middle east it is he can common thing to dig up relics of the past, but even these it is unusual to dig up anything so old as the fossil of a reptile's head believed to be some 250,000,000 years old. But it was found here...

Tom Sawyer Knew His Warts

He Recommended Stump Water at Midnight, Which Is About as Good as Any Cure Yet Discovered by Medical Science

Jerry Klein, in North American Newspaper Alliance dispatch from New York:

TOM SAWYER'S remedy for warts was to go into the woods at night and douse them with water from the stump of a dead tree—just as the clock struck midnight. Not long ago Dr. Herman Vollmer of New York city said that Tom Sawyer's way of removing the skin eruptions is just about as good as any yet discovered by medical science...

Silvery Smears

When warts impart duline, examine, and often other have been found in Dublin—Haslam, South America of Spitzbergen...

Continued on the next page

From the People

Drugs From Grocers

To The Journal: You say that it is a "little silly" when the pharmacists seek to restrict the sale of drugs to drug stores, implying that we are selfishly trying to protect our profits.

Yes, we do want to protect our profits. But—this is the important point—we are also trying to protect the public's health.

The other day a mother asked me in our drug store. Her infant had taken an overdose of aspirin and she could not get in touch with a doctor. I advised her to the symptoms of overdosage and recommended proper counteraction. Could a grocer, untrained in the science of medicine, have done the same?

Recently, a man asked for a bottle of codeine. Ordinarily a nonnarcotic, the heroin of a little man and of a girl who gives her life to save the child...

The famed Abbey theatre gave it a successful production and O'Casey sat diligently in writing what became his best loved and most popular play, "Juno and the Paycock." Here were the jokes and slum dwellers he knew so well as did any man on earth.

Jack Boyle, a self-styled "captain" and the "paycock" (peacock) of the title, is the lazy, drunken husband of the strong, long suffering Juno. Their son has been crippled in the revolution, and their daughter is betrayed...

B. C. TOUSMAN
E. L. Hanson or, Milwaukee 13.

The Protestant Side

To The Journal: In answer to an interview you printed in your Mar. 18 issue I would like to enlighten Mr. Charles O'Neill, executive secretary of the St. Vincent de Paul society, on a few fundamental facts concerning the status of Protestants and Catholics in relationship to the next German government.

"Protestantism and Catholics get along well with the next German government." It is a gross overstatement, hardly a few words only: "During my many months of traveling in almost every section of Germany I found it obvious that the church-state problem is a paramount, hotly debated question confronting every German voter.

It is a sad fact that Chancellor Adenauer, who is a Catholic, favors Catholicism through legislative measures. Consider the education issue. In predominantly Catholic Bavaria, the Rhineland it was not infrequent that the government supported only state funds, whereas equally needy schools of other denominations went without aid.

Since religion is taught in all public schools, it is also very unfair to have the government, which must be free to the universities, cement as 90% of these academies are under the Catholic control. Those issues add bitter criticism in German circles.

Much controversy arose when officials for the Bundestag, one of the largest governmental organizations, is considering the church affiliation rather than ability and preparation of candidates for governmental agencies. In order to obtain better positions is forced to be of the American faith his own party system, but here is where we must face the facts and realize just how much religion is integrated into the German political system.

Mr. O'Neill's unilateral reporting is done in much fairness to the public, if he allows his own interpretation of a problem to the public. Let's remember that there are always two sides to every story and there leave it to the reader to weigh each side so as to forming his opinion.

JACK P CETTEL
GREAT W Mill rd, Milwaukee 16.

Roosevelt at Yalta

To The Journal: Your recent editorial explaining the complete of the Yalta agreement is to be commended...

THOMAS D. CHAMPION.
801 S. M st r.

State FM Radio

To The Journal: I feel that WHA-FM is a grand development of the state radio and I believe that it would be a great loss to the state were it abolished by the present commit. If necessary, it would be willing to pay an annual tax to keep it operating...

WILLIAM J HUGHES.
120 Jonquin st, Fond du Lac, Wis.

"Only one more pay day and he'll have the ring paid for—then we can start on a house!"

CHICAGO DAILY NEWS

AN INDEPENDENT NEWSPAPER FOUNDED JANUARY 1, 1876
JOHN S. KNIGHT, EDITOR and PUBLISHER

Published daily by The Chicago Daily News, Inc., Chicago (3), Ill.
400 West Madison St.

AVERAGE DAILY CIRCULATION FOR JANUARY — 605,482
AVERAGE SATURDAY CIRCULATION FOR JANUARY — 466,780

Entered as second class matter at the Post Office, Chicago, Ill.

12

TUESDAY, FEBRUARY 22, 1955

AS WE SEE IT—

Hail, Rotary!

THE granddaddy of all the service clubs will be 50 years old tomorrow, and Rotarians throughout the world will join in the birthday celebration.

It was on Feb. 23, 1905, that Paul P. Harris, Rotary's founder, and a group of Chicago associates held the first Rotary meeting. Since that day the movement has grown to embrace more than 450,000 business executives and professional men who are members of 8,500 clubs in 89 countries.

Tomorrow they will hold more than 700 birthday parties to launch their Golden Anniversary observance. In its old home town, the party will take the form of a banquet at the Sherman, where the speakers will be the world Rotary president, Herbert J. Taylor of Chicago; Postmaster General Summerfield and Dr. Arthur H. Compton, Nobel prize winner.

Rotary is dedicated to an "ideal of service." From the beginning, it has selected its membership on the basis of one active member from each recognized business and profession in the community. It has stood for high ethical standards in these occupations. In its world-wide program it has been a powerful force for international understanding.

We salute the Rotary Clubs of the world. We wish for them many more years of creative service to humanity.

* * *

Muddled Airline Picture

WHEN the railroads were built, their routes were fixed and the tracks laid, and that was that. It is not so with the air carriers. Competition between the great airline systems for routes and markets is intense. The taxpayers have a considerable stake in this contest, because of the subsidies paid to the airlines in consideration of the fact that they may become overnight an arm of our national defense.

President Eisenhower himself intervened recently in one of these disputes that rattled some special interest to Chicago. After first ruling otherwise, he ordered that Northwest Airlines be permitted to continue flying a Seattle-to-Hawaii route, although Hawaii is served by United and by Pan American World Airways.

In his explanation, Mr. Eisenhower said his intention had been to reduce subsidy payments by assigning the route to the carrier requiring the least aid. He found, however, that it was expected that both Pacific runs would be able to operate without subsidy within two years.

Since Northwest and United enter Chicago, the decision means that the present services to Honolulu from this city will continue. The President said he desired to give both Pan American and Northwest "equal opportunity to demonstrate their capacity to develop adequate traffic to operate without subsidy."

That sounds fair enough. But, curiously, the same reasoning does not seem to be applied to Pan American's request to be allowed to operate the "Great Circle" route between the West Coast and the Orient. This is the "North to the Orient" route that Gen. Lindbergh surveyed in 1931, but which could not be used until after the war because the Japanese were unwilling to permit American craft over their skies.

Pan American is confined to the mid-Pacific route, stopping at Hawaii, Wake and Guam. This adds 1,847 miles to the flight from Chicago to the Orient, which is the direct destination of 80 per cent of Pan Am's passengers. It also costs the government an extra million a year for G.I. mail, allocated to Pan American to take this circuitous route.

Northwest and Canadian Pacific fly the shorter "Great Circle" route; a Japanese and a Scandinavian line are preparing to do the same. It seems strange that the pioneer Pacific carrier should be handicapped in violation of the principle of "equal opportunity" laid down in the Seattle-Hawaii case.

* * *

Senator Soaper:

A sports fan is a man who complains if he has to park four blocks away from the track where he intends to yell "What a bum" at a college boy who fails to run a mile in less than 4 minutes.

Khrushchev makes it plain that in Russian politics he is not a man to be wooed at, but it's a big help in pronouncing his name.

Another advantage of having been a boy in a long-ago winter was that it was a lot easier to find pieces of coal for the snowman's eyes.

Weather experts say our path of hurricanes along the Atlantic Coast has changed in recent years, making them available to thousands of citizens who can't afford to go to Florida for the season.

A Thinning Claim

THE pre-November claim that a Democratic congressman was just manually President Eisenhower's best friend is wearing thin in the rough game of politics. The bill to reduce income taxes by $20 per person, approved Monday by the House ways and means committee, is the newest evidence.

The idea is to tie it to the President's own revenue plan in a way that deprives him of credit for future tax cuts that may be warranted by reduced spending.

Mr. Eisenhower has asked a year's postponement of the drop in corporation taxes from 52 to 47 per cent, now scheduled for April 1. He also wants to keep present excise taxes on liquor, automobiles and cigarets. To this bill, the Democrats plan to add their proposal that in 1956 every taxpayer shall receive a $20 tax credit for himself and $20 for each dependent.

The political appeal of this is that it would take about four million persons off the tax rolls entirely. It would also give identical treatment to taxpayers in every bracket—a formula that is much more popular when taxes are being cut than when they are being raised.

The revenue loss for the calendar year would be some $2 billion, half of which would come in the 1955 fiscal year ending June 30. Inasmuch as the present estimate is for a deficit of $2.4 billion in the fiscal year, action adding another billion to the debt cannot be justified.

In justification of their political motivation, the Democrats can loudly point out that last year's Republican Congress lopped $1 billion off the excise tax rates over the President's opposition. They also have Mr. Eisenhower's statement that the administration hopes that further tax cuts will be possible next year.

The strategy of tying the $20 credit to the extension of other taxes is designed to make it hard for the Senate to block or the President to veto the combined measure. It should not be too difficult, however, to force the extension through at the last minute, when the choice becomes that or no tax bill at all.

With crucial elections coming up, this sort of jockeying for position is to be expected. There is one Democrat, however, who can be counted upon to back the President in this matter. He is Sen. Harry F. Byrd of Virginia, and he holds the key post of finance committee chairman.

No matter how busy the House may get, Sen. Byrd is sure to take the position that tax bills should be determined by revenue needs and not by political advantage. We wish there were more like him.

* * *

New Historians

WHEN the Society of American Historians and the American Association for State and Local History laid their plans for a magazine of popular history, they hardly dared hope for the tremendous success it has achieved after only two issues.

Launched late last year, the bimonthly American Heritage, a magazine in hard covers, sold out a first edition of 80,000 copies quickly. Its second issue carried a print order of $2,500. More than 60,000 readers have bought yearly subscriptions at $12, and the bookstore sale at $2.95 a copy is expected to reach 25,000 an issue.

These remarkable sales are evidence of a phenomenal upsurge of interest in American history.

Behind this interest lie several influences. One is a broad trend to nonfiction in recent years. Another is the dramatization of colorful incidents in our past on such television shows as "You Are There" and "Omnibus." These have inspired listeners to turn to books for further information.

The most important influence, however, has been the rise of a new kind of historian—the nonprofessional who has edged out the traditionally dull historical writer of the past.

Some of the writers who have brought new dimensions of color, excitement and brilliance to history have been newspapermen. Carl Sandburg and the late Lloyd Lewis, at one time managing editor of the Daily News, were in the vanguard with their studies of Lincoln and Sherman. Indeed, most of our great modern historians—Allan Nevins, Douglas Southall Freeman, and Winston Churchill among them—have been newspaper-trained reporters.

Bruce Catton, a newcomer who has "A Stillness at Appomattox" won the National Book Award last year, is the editor of American Heritage.

Special Delivery

COMMISSIONER O'CONNOR
Police Department

Dear Tim:

Are we to believe that the intense police watch over the polls means that among other new developments in Chicago, somebody has just devised a way to steal votes?

DAD DEARBORN

LETTERS TO THE EDITOR

Defends Stevenson and Douglas For Supporting Daley Candidacy

Your intimation in a recent editorial that Adlai Stevenson and Sen. Paul Douglas departed from principle in supporting the Daley candidacy was merely "a wisecrack" which will not stand analysis. While these outstanding Illinoisans have made a record that can well stand harsh from the pens of partisan editorial writers, I feel that as citizens of Chicago I should make my voice heard and protest this attack on their political integrity and ask you these questions.

Is it wrong to support a political leader who was largely responsible for admittedly best titled either party has proposed in Cook County for decades that was overwhelmingly approved by the voters last fall?

Should not a party support a man who has a long record of excellent performance in various responsible positions, as even you have admitted, and who by his sheer industry, ability and strength of character has shown that he has the required leadership so woefully absent at this time in the office of mayor?

Are you justified in condemning party leaders and candidates for rejecting the candidacy of a man, who to high office by that party but who time after time has failed to support them in crucial contests and has shown no interest in the vital problems of that party?

I believe the answers to these questions are obvious and that the action of Stevenson and Douglas in endorsing Daley was consistent with the highest principles of party responsibility and political morality.

BERNICE COMEAUX,
Chicago.

Do Suburbs Admit Crime Problem?

As an exchequer and new suburbanite, I was surprised to note that the "terror" western suburbs are contemplating erecting a curfew less-which is stricter than Chicago's law. Can the suburbs, whose leaders are so quick to criticize Chicago for its crime and juvenile delinquency, actually have a greater problem?

La Grange SUBURBANITE.

Scores Democrats For Budget Hikes

Chicago's budget jumped from $177 million in 1949, 1945, to $472 million in 1953. Board of Education budget flew from $69 million in 1945 to $103 million in 1955. County board budget soared from $48 million in 1949 to $119 million in 1955.

These astronomical figures disclose why over the years our hypocritical politicians get little while our citizens became poorer. Their kite-like annual budget increases represent a totally unnecessary, disgraceful waste of taxpayers' money by our hungry city-wrecking, inflation-breeding Democratic party which has been in charge of these departments for the last 25 years.

JOHN J. MANGAN,
Chicago.

Wants 'Drastic' U.S. Health Plan

In his message on health, President Eisenhower said he is against disease and disability because they provide "a fertile field for the spread of Communism." We can thank all many other good reasons for fighting disease and disability. For one thing, they often bring misery, pain and suffering, which we are against.

Last year the medical bill for America soared to $10 billion. Only 3 per cent of the persons covered by insurance enjoyed full protection. Private health insurance covered less than 15 per cent of the total amount of the medical bill. Sixty million persons have no protection through existing insurance agencies.

It is plain that only a drastic plan can protect and promote the nation's health. Adequate plans have been worked out to do this. Why have these plans gone into the congressional hopper year after year only to die?

The Constitution says one of the purposes of our government is to "promote the general welfare." It is obvious that there can be no true general welfare unless the health of the American people is adequately guarded.

DAVID SPITZNER,
Chicago.

Dulles at Desk Would Be News

"Dulles Off Today for Asia" says a Daily News front page news item.

This, I'm inclined to think, is news in the sense that "Dog Bites Man" is news.

A truly sensational news item (which I hope to see in the future) would read: "Secretary of State Dulles has been at his desk in Washington for 30 consecutive days."

EUGENE MULLANEY,
Chicago.

Commends Daily News On Spelling Contest

On behalf of the Chicago public schools, I should like to express appreciation to the Chicago Daily News and all those who participated in the 1954-55 Spelling Championships.

We are very proud of the new champion, Linda Nelson, 11-year-old seventh-grader at the Hookway Elementary School. You and your associates are to be commended for the excellent arrangement which made possible the outstanding program. I should particularly like to congratulate Mr. Miller Davis, the splendid master of ceremonies, in the finals last Saturday afternoon.

Your continued indication of interest in the program of education of the Chicago public schools is very gratifying.

BENJAMIN C. WILLIS,
General Superintendent of Schools.

Assails Defense Of Chinese Islands

. . . As I understand it, Sen. Knowland wants the United States to provide free burial in China for scores of thousands of American youth to back a geopolitical theory that even Hauxhoffer, the great German authority, would have considered completely ridiculous.

This is the theory that two small islands alone to the Chinese coast are necessary to the defense of California, six thousand miles away. I, for one, am unwilling than a single American soldier be sent to his death in support of any such theory.

READER,
Chicago.

Questions Extreme Penalties for Assault

Illinois has under consideration a bill which would change the penalty from life imprisonment to death for aggravated assaults upon women. Legislators may measure the fact that such crimes are infrequent in other countries.

If enacted, final punishment could be imposed upon young men, who, statistically at least, might not have committed the crime at all had they lived elsewhere.

The question at hand, then, is whether recourse to extreme punishment is not only necessary but sociologically sound.
Chicago   J. H.

LEADERSHIP LACKING

France Losing Out In World Talks

BY WILLIAM H. STONEMAN
Daily News Foreign Service

PARIS—Continued inability of the French to find a new premier to replace Mendes-France has already begun to have important repercussions abroad.

One immediate consequence has been to keep France an effective voice at the Southeast Asia Treaty Organization conference in Bangkok. In the absence of a foreign minister who could speak for an authoritative French government, France will be represented by Henri Bonnet, former ambassador to Washington. He will merely have a watching brief and won't be able to commit his weight felt on such all-important matters as the future defense of non-Communist areas of Southeast Asia.

A SECOND effect of delay in forming a new government may be to damage the chances of Western European Union's ever coming into force.

When Mendes-France fell on Feb. 5, supporters of the Paris agreements—which involve the rearmament of Western Germany under Western European Union—persuaded themselves that the change wouldn't affect the pacts.

They assumed that they would still be ratified by the Council of the Republic (upper house of parliament) after slight delay caused by the government crisis and that the net result would be the same as it would have been if Mendes-France had fallen.

NOW THEY'RE not so sure. It's still believed by most of these people that the Paris agreements will be ratified by the upper house sometime in March. They are not quite so sure as they might be when they don't trust Edgar Faure, likeliest candidate for Mendes-France's job. He would be the premier to come to power in the lower chamber but his real intentions are open to question.

Among other things, his wife is intensely anti-American and warmly sympathetic toward the Russians.

THE ONCE OVER

Gals Act Like Combat GI When Invading Market

BY H. I. PHILLIPS

SUPERMARKET shopping has been a closed book to us as we are strictly a "hit the wife do it" man. But the other day, the missus being ill, we were ordered to the grocery's front and it flabbergasted us.

Here you meet woman in her tensest, more aggressive and woolly creation mood.

She combines the features of Diana the Huntress, Carrie Nation, Mollie Pitcher, Calamity Jane and Olga the Lady Wrestler. Also a hint of Admiral Farragut on his "damn the torpedoes, full speed ahead" day.

She picked up whatever her fancy dictated. At the beginning of a winter has big-sign something unusual, shoved it northwest somewhere, and put it on the bottom of the pile as she selected another which she gave us with the reverence usually associated with an important antiquated portrait.

She held it at varying distances, went over it from all points of the compass, looked at it sideways and headon and seemed about to give it an approval. But suddenly—No, it wasn't to be. Back went it to the bottom of the pile.

IN A CHAIN STORE obviously's radiance fades. Customer gives way to the combat mood. Fingers takes the place of tongue. A friendly disposition gives way to the storm-faced, flat-buying procession. Shoving way to the storm-faced flat, but determined shopper. She shoulders her way like a quarterback.

SHE CONTINUED to examine the stocks for what seemed an eternity, and then, abruptly, dropped the idea of red meat and moved to the fish exhibit. She seemed entranced by a slice of halibut but after examining it with all the care of an inspector from the Bureau of Fisheries she filed it in an older pile and picked up some tentative, about which she seemed moderately perplexed.

Another woman came along and the two of them began lifting, tweaking and interchanging. One smiling oval halibut slice and glanced again with a fresh eye about over the mob of tag others. At last we got the amazed look what we believe to be right.

If we obey only the first part of the paradox, and refuse to judge, then we commit the sin of indifference, softheadedness, and lack of moral fervor; if we obey only the second part, and judge, then we commit the sin of self-righteousness, cruelty, and lack of humanity. We must weld both together, and judge yet withhold judgment, love while we hate, and condemn the sin while we redeem the sinner.

STRICTLY PERSONAL

Paradox Does Describe Humanity

BY SYDNEY J. HARRIS

A READER in Toledo complains that I am "too fond of paradox." The dictionary defines a paradox as "an assertion that seems contradictory, or opposed to common sense, but that yet may be true in fact."

At the very core of human existence, we find a huge paradox. Life is filled with contradictions, compounded by ambiguity; and, at the same time, life is filled with high-est conceptions and noble aspirations.

Which view of life is "true"? It seems plain to me that each, taken alone, is false—a fragile sense of life makes a man ungrateful and a comic sense of life makes a man superficial.

THERE IS ANOTHER deep paradox at the very core of hu-

man existence. All men are equal, and yet all men are unequal. Mankind is one, as the Bible is unanimous on that; and yet must be equally treated as His children. But men are unequal—all differ from each other in countless ways, physical, mental, and spiritual—in their capacities and in their deserts.

Unless we know that all men are equal, we shall treat some like beasts; and unless we know that all men are unequal, we shall impose a false uniformity upon them. It is only by holding both the greater does to the lesser.

There is yet a third profound paradox at the very core of political existence. Each government represents a tension between freedom and order. On the one hand, citizens must have freedom; on the other, they must obey the rules and laws that bind the community together. The state must provide for the right of individuals, and judge the rightwrongness, and judge yet withhold.

Balance is all. A single view of life is necessarily a wrong view. And paradox—not for its own sake, but for the sake of truth—is the only way of describing the human condition.

THE ATLANTA CONSTITUTION

For 87 Years The South's Standard Newspaper

CLARK HOWELL, Publisher   RALPH McGILL, Editor

Established June 16, 1868

Issued daily except New Year's, July 4, Labor Day, Thanksgiving and Christmas and entered as second-class matter at the Post Office in Atlanta under act of Congress of 1879.

The Atlanta Constitution (morning), and The Atlanta Journal (evening) are the Atlanta Constitution and The Atlanta Journal. Published by Atlanta Newspapers, Inc., 10 Forsyth St., Atlanta, Georgia.

Page 4   TUESDAY, JANUARY 11, 1955

Inauguration Day Is Time for Reflection

Gov. Herman Talmadge officially retires from office today. Gov. Marvin Griffin replaces him.

It is a routine exercise, one might say, in the processes of free government . . . the gift of Jefferson, Adams and their associates to the young republic of which Georgia was the youngest of the 13 Colonies which became the new states.

Gov. Talmadge was a fortunate governor in the field of finance. He had approximately $100,000,000 more per year to spend on the state than any other governor had known. He spent it well. He proved to be a skilled administrator, able in the field of politics and management. He retires with the satisfaction of knowing that not only was he able to win over many of his critics but also that he was able virtually to handpick his successor.

The Griffin's administration's income from taxes existing will be about equal to that of the outgoing one. But the new administration inherits a headache which may require aspirin. Costs are up. The population is up. Demands for services are up.

Gov. Griffin's pathway, therefore, will not—unless he is lucky in some turn of the financial cards—be quite as smooth as was his predecessor's. This he knows and is studying.

Today being Inauguration day, with its parades, bands and traditional speechmaking, reminds us that Kipling's "Recessional" is perhaps the most fitting text for the occasion.

"The tumult and the shouting dies— / "The captains and the kings depart— / "Still stands Thine ancient sacrifice, / "An humble and a contrite heart, / "Lord God of Hosts, be with us yet, / "Lest we forget, lest we forget."

All the state level and national, the future of free government for the people lie in the hands of its elected representatives. Above this, with the totalitarian threat of communism increasingly evident in Europe and Asia, we must all do what we can to make free government so nearly what it was and is meant to be as is humanly possible. We cannot afford to abuse it or weaken its principles. Free government is our country is the sum of the whole—local and national. So, today we join with all those who, with an humble and a contrite heart, pray for our and for all free government everywhere and pledge all assistance to the principles of it.

Services to the Blind Should Be Left Alone

A bill to establish yet another state commission, this one devoted to the welfare of the blind, is expected to come before the General Assembly.

As it is now, Georgia's blind receive help from two sources. One is the department of public welfare which administers assistance funds to the needy blind and oversees the operation of the Georgia Factory for the Blind in Bainbridge and its branch in Griffin. The other is the educational and rehabilitation program for the blind under the Division of Vocational Rehabilitation of the Department of Education. This rehabilitation program is the outstanding one of its kind in the nation, and the model for many other states.

The proposed bill would consolidate all these services under a commission with the exception of benefit payments which would remain under the welfare department. The author of the measure is Vaughn Terrell, blind representative from Decatur County and superintendent of the Factory for the Blind in Bainbridge.

Georgia is in the fortunate position of already having one of the finest programs for the blind in the world. It is difficult to see how changing it could improve it. And there always is the possibility that any change would be for the worse.

A commission for the blind logically could lead to commissions for the lame and the halt, and so on ad infinitum. What government needs these days, and this includes Georgia too, is fewer, not more commissions and boards.

Tag Sale at Courthouse Should Be Implemented

Hunting and fishing licenses are available at sporting goods stores and at any courthouse in the state. Marriage-bent couples can get the necessary permit at the county clerk's office.

There is no good reason why automobile licenses should not be obtained from the courthouse. In fact, in the larger, more populous counties it would be well to set up more than one license tag outlet. In at least one of the 40 states, there are

12 official motor vehicle license branches in the capital city alone.

The purpose is the convenience of the customer.

Achievement of that purpose is enough cause for enactment of the Griffin administration's county courthouse license plate proposal.

The only possible deterrent we can think of is the chance of laxity in registration of cars not previously registered. That chance exists now. It will exist until Georgia gets a tight certificate of title law.

Clayton County Urged To Approve Bond Issue

Citizens of neighboring Clayton County will vote on a $700,000 water bond issue today. The first such election in the county's history, it grows out of the growing needs of the community in meeting its problems of growth.

Clayton County is one of the fastest-growing counties in Georgia. Its population has doubled since 1940. School enrollment is up 40 per cent in the past two years.

Despite this growth, Clayton County has no industry. Its Chamber of Commerce points out that only 360 people are employed in the county by firms employing five or more people. This low-mined situation has brought a sound development of its economy and institutions.

The water bond issue will provide funds to construct a filter plant and pumping station to take care of the immediate needs of the hundreds of new residents, as well as for water for industrial. Without this water, the Clayton County Chamber of Commerce expects, there can be no industrial growth.

By all means, voters of the county should approve issuance of the bonds. An affirmative vote today is a vote for the county's future. Without an adequate water supply, continued growth will progress will be impossible.

Fortunately the County Ends Up With a Surplus

It is the job of all good government officials to take a gloomy view of the future and to run a scared race with the budget.

Right now, nations, states, counties and cities are anticipating the new year with fear and trembling. Income never will match the outgo, according to forecasters, and back-breaking taxes may have to be raised if the public is to be served in the manner to which it has become accustomed.

In the midst of the alarums, Fulton County has announced that it collected more than was expected during 1954, and has a tidy cash carryover of more than $1,000,000 with which to begin the year. This is a delightful surprise, for the year looks like a tight one for the county treasury, what with all the new facilities needed to serve the expanding population.

A conservative financial policy is good government, and one usually appreciated by the taxpayer.

If viewing with alarm and living in anticipation of disaster is the mark of good public servants, certainly Georgians, residents of Fulton County and the City of Atlanta are among the best governed people on earth.

Europe's Industry Is Setting New Records

Thanks to American help, industrial production in Europe is now 57 per cent above the pre-war level. In fact, during the past year as the United States economy leveled off, Western Europe's industry countries increased their output by 10 per cent.

Agricultural output is also up 20 per cent from pre-war; exports are continuously high and the buying and the past year Europe added $3,000,000,000 to its reserves of gold and foreign exchange.

The recovery is almost miraculous. A decade ago many people were ready to write off all of Western Europe as a dead civilization, ripe for the Communists to take over. And this might well have happened except for one thing—the Marshall plan moved in to rescue the Old from economic chaos as it had previously rescued it from Hitler's conquests.

We have a right to be proud in America of what we have done. There has never been a nation in history that dealt with its foes more kindly and with its friends with greater generosity. We are reaping some rewards today. Peace, unity and strength are replacing fear, weakness and division.

A strong Europe is now ready to meet the threat of Communist aggression and a prosperous Europe is repaying our investment in trade and an emerging pattern of free-world security.

Parade Route

Pulse of the Public

Power Struggle Among Our Own Military Divides Americans and Hurts U.S. Prestige

Atlanta—The recent launching of the CVA-59 Forrestal again provoked the inevitable outcry that "the Navy is building super-carriers at the expense of national defense." These are examples of excessive development in the field of atomic weapons. There is much to be said for both sides.

Yet, the Forrestal debate touches off a feeling that some of our branches of the armed forces are forgetting themselves in a headlong rush to damage each other's pet project.

Inter - service competition of such a violent nature tends to divide the American people and cost us prestige abroad. If our services cannot try to shed some light on a controversial issue, then it is time that we incorporate and throw into one big force, thereby perhaps eliminating some of the super soul leakage that seems to dominate the scene now.

JOHN J. HUNT III.

* * *

Wonders If Officials Will Get Pay Raise

Atlanta—We note that the city of Atlanta collected $12,776,560 for the year 1954, an increase of $1,027,354 over 1953. What does this mean for 1955 when the anticipated carryover in the treasury, thanks to the tax structure of the city? We are confident the city officials will not want us to forget that there is a shortage of funds somewhere. Yet it is the most important at the state and municipal level an increase of various crimes at a different manner.

We protest the drunk driver to any degree? He is as dangerous to an automobile as a high-wayman with a loaded gun. The trouble but on the streets and highways of the country is terrific and continu-

city employes about 5 per cent over approximately 35 per cent of that carryover instead of paying out on it any other way?

We, as the public citizens, would be interested in seeing this increased currency delve.

* * *

Night of Celebration Inspired Some Verse

Atlanta—Here is a New Year's resolution written at 1:30 a.m. Jan. 1st after quite a bit of celebrating, which I thought you might enjoy:

To all things better than— / ever, / If new, then shall I say I'll / never / Attempt things I should never / endeavor?

M. F. SMITH.

* * *

Pay Raise for Solons Called Well Deserved

St. Louis, Mo.—Members of Congress may term themselves a rise in the near future.

The congressional pay scale was made effective in 1947 when congressmen started receiving $12,500 a year.

There possibly isn't a congressman who feels he is being paid

enough, and where he lives up to his grave responsibilities I think he deserves more.

If members who get that from the increased salary merely will oppose them and their salary as well, it is a just one, on its own as as-I-see-it is reasonable.

FRED WEAVER.

Moultrie Observer

Proposed Press Gag Law Called 'Cloak for Crime'

The people of Georgia should oppose with all their vigor the proposed legislation measure which would withhold from publication the names of persons charged with sex crimes and drunk driving. The intent of the bill's authors may be a noble one, but the effects of such a law would be equivalent to throwing a protective cloak around some of the most dastardly crimes committed against society—sex attacks and drunk driving.

There is a serious danger that the proposed legislation, if adopted, would discriminate against equal rights and opportunities of individuals. The man with influence, money and loose morals might easily escape unfavorable publicity through settlement. The fellow with little influence and no money would be the one exposed to the glare of court proceedings.

The proposed Georgia bill is definitely a step backward in the freedom of the press—a form of censorship backed by jail and fines penalties. When freedom of the press is thus, every citizen will have to door to live citizens is lost, too. But more important at the moment is the cloak of publicity immunity being thrown around two forms of crime which appear to be growing in volume and extent.

Under the present laws of Georgia, the name of a women victim of a sex attack cannot be published if she is living. The name of the accused attacker may be published. Perhaps amendments should be offered to the laws to safeguard innocent men against being falsely accused by a jealous or blackmailing woman. The press of this state has no desire to hold itself innocent up to the glare of false accusations. Yet to postpone legitimate news at law enforcement against all other persons accused of various crimes at a different manner.

St. Louis Post-Dispatch

The Russian protest against firearms by an American Air Force general in England is probably one of those pro forma affairs for the record, not to be regarded as a major diplomatic incident.

But it should provide the occasion for reminding our military officials in Washington and abroad, once more, at an elementary fact.

This fact is that air base commanders in England are there to do a specific military job, and not to make public announcements about arming "an atomic punch" at Russia. They have a critically important and a deadly serious task to perform. Let them carry it out—and let the talking be done by the diplomatic officials who are authorized to do it.

Charles L. Allen

Faith in a Future Uplifts Man's Spirit

An important text for the month of January comes from the Book of Proverbs, written more than 3,000 years ago. The text has become proverbial in our day-to-day speech and I expect that many who quote it are unaware that it is from the Bible. The words are: "Where there is no vision, the people perish" (Proverbs 29:18). I think the translation by Dr. Moffatt offers further enlightenment: "People forsee without a guiding head."

Both the King James and the Moffatt versions have a common thought: vision comes from God and God is the head that guides. Without the guidance of God, as revealed in his law, there is no dependable direction, no worthy goal, no satisfying achievement in life.

If our mental and spiritual lives are to grow, we must have a reason and a purpose which controls and determines our efforts. We can, of course, continue to cling to the tissue of flesh and sustain our physical lives. But the heath of the field have flesh. We never demand for higher thought and more elevated aspirations than they can know.

Human beings are more than flesh and bones. They are bundles and hopes clutched only by the physical. So, if the mind and soul do not grow with the rising tears, then we do not actually live. We exist, but existence is not life according to past and present.

Nothing so gives direction and purpose to life as does the response of man to the requirements of God. For God's love is a transforming love which makes physical men into spiritual sons of God. And the will of God recreates our selfish tempers into instruments of good will and the service. Without that love and that will, the vision of the highest and noblest of which is inborn in us is impossible.

David A. MacLaren of the Yale Divinity School tells of a town in Maine called Flagstaff. The people in that community were told that a new hydroelectric development would result in the construction of a large dam. As the survey increased behind the dam, the town of Flagstaff would in time become flooded and finally lost from sight . . .

The people apparently accepted the inevitable, but they continued to live in their homes, as time drew ahead, drop in their steers during the intervening months. But not much was accomplished. All improvements and repairs to homes and other buildings came to be a dead stop.

What is the sense of painting a house if it is going to be covered with water in six months? Why fix anything? So week by week the town became more and more bedraggled, forlorn and shabby. It had gone to seed long before the deluge came. Nine-tenths before its completion by reason of its people's loss of vision: "Where there is no faith in the future, there is no power in the present."

Roscoe Drummond

'Suspect's' Rights Need a Safeguard

WASHINGTON—One question before the administration's security program will be of concern to conservatives.

The trouble is that while the administration has been consistently active and earnest in the security program of its government and wherever considered and sensitive to the reasonableness of individual false charges.

In the same case arises primarily from comparatively minor 1950 rulers then from differences in theirs own concepts of security. When the same security regulation produces such an opposite application in the same case, based on the same evidence, and their account is suspect as fair, there is something wrong somewhere.

How important? How important it is that the President and Attorney General Brownell is the best method of handling this problem is revealed by the fact that they are now considering a further revision. It would not be the first time since President Eisenhower recognized there was something wrong when he personally intervened, ordered Mr. Peter H. Oppenheimer case reopened and his clearance restored to the regular procedure.

There is President Eisenhower recognized there was something wrong when he personally intervened, ordered Mr. Peter H. Oppenheimer case reopened and his clearance restored to the regular procedure.

Leo Aikman

These Saucers Are Souped Up

The two airmen in the diner were talking about saucers. They weren't in their cups. They were actively earnest.

"I never saw anything," one of them said, "with my own eyes but I know the travel instructions on Saturn within the U.S."

"You mean you actually stood this thing—this saucer thing—this thing you saw from the relationship. They wouldn't be stars. They change course, blink and definite pattern."

"If they're there, they they're ours or theirs or somebody else's," I suggested.

"That's about it," the other airman said. "But they couldn't belong to this planet. They aren't even from this nation we have a 5,500 miles an hour in five seconds. No earthman could take that."

"You've seen 'em?"

"He has," he said, pointing to his partner. "Do the air over Atlanta. I've seen 'em up on the radarscope. They wouldn't be stars. They change course, blink a definite pattern."

"If they're there, they they're ours or theirs or somebody else's," I suggested.

"I'd rather them they're ours," said the other. "It's interstellar travel our weapons would be obsolete."

"I asked, "I mean saucers," he replied.

Thomas L. Stokes

Ike's Hint Raises Educators' Hopes

WASHINGTON—The only "doctor" in President Eisenhower's annual message to Congress was his vague suggestion for federal help of some kind to provide sorely needed new schools. There is a shortage of 370,000 classrooms in this nation.

The fact that the President characteristically posed his suggestion as a "grave" indicated that he, too, felt that increase money of this magnitude of making federal grants for school construction.

Sen. Lister Hill (D-Ala) chairman of the Senate Labor and Public Welfare Committee, has introduced a bill to authorize a billion-dollar grant to the states for school construction.

Many educators and congressmen who would give the poorer states a big-get share per capita than the richer states, such as has been used for hospital construction under the Hill-Burton Act.

Within 35 hours, 27 labor senators, by questioning the bill. Simultaneously, an identical measure will be introduced in the House by another Alabama Democrat, Rep. Carl Elliott, a member of the House committee on education and labor.

Differing with the formula proposed by Sen. Hill is Rep. Carroll Kearns (Pa.). Federal aid should would have funds advanced by the federal government on a matching basis with the states but should give the states freedom to handle their own school construction. This is Republican thinking and probably will have much support, especially in the wealthier states. The inability of many states to carry the

POLICY OF THE MACON NEWS

EDITORIALS

THE MACON NEWS

FEATURES

PEYTON ANDERSON, Publisher

JOE PARHAM

BERT STRUBY   LAMAR PARKER
EXECUTIVE EDITOR   BUSINESS MANAGER

JAY TRAWICK
MANAGING EDITOR

Subscription Rates by Carrier in Macon and Vicinity

Page Four   MACON, GEORGIA, MONDAY, FEBRUARY 21, 1955   ESTABLISHED 1884

"Toys" That Kill

TWO TRAGIC deaths of Macon children from firearm accidents ought to be grim warning to local parents that small guns can kill as surely as .22 gauge shotguns or .45 caliber pistols.

A 13-year-old boy died from a .22 rifle bullet wound in the head on Friday, Feb. 11. Another child, eight years old, died Feb. 15, only four days later, from an air rifle shot in the head.

Parents who put guns and small caliber rifles in the hands of youngsters only a few years removed from babyhood have little regard for the lives of others in their neighborhood community. In such cases, others ought to forget the usual neighborly courtesy and friendliness and be plain-spoken against such a practice before it is too late and another child lies badly wounded or killed by a "toy."

There are dozens of letters in our files from fathers and mothers who are greatly concerned over the fact that some children are allowed to play with deadly weapons as if they were no more dangerous than a stick of bubble gum. For the past several years we have tried through editorials to awaken the parents of these children who possess such guns to the hazards involved.

A city ordinance prohibits the discharge of any firearm or air gun in the municipal limits but there are no such restrictions in the county. We advise worried parents to ask for police action against violators of the city ordinance and to discuss with hesitating representatives the possibility of obtaining a law which would prohibit the practice, without interfering with hunting in non-residential areas, outside the city limits.

Investigate Complaints Against Police Swiftly

OFFICERS of the law have been in the news even more than usual recently.

In Twiggs County, the FBI is investigating the rape of a Negro, who obviously suffered a bad beating and says Georgia State Patrol troopers were present at the time.

In Macon, a bus driver has complained to the police committee of City Council that he was mistreated and threatened over a family matter by a local officer.

Again in Macon, nothing has been settled in the case of two local policemen who were accused by a city councilman and other witnesses of mistreating a prisoner.

Such incidents deserve the swiftest investigation by the proper investigative agency. If officers are conducting themselves in such manner as to indicate a belief that they are greater than and beyond the reach of the law they are sworn to uphold, then the majesty of the law must be reasserted. On the other hand, if these are baseless charges, the officers involved deserve to have the clouds lifted from their names and the accusations labeled false.

Too many such incidents, too much delay, too involved red tape in investigating can cause serious damage to public respect for the law and can greatly weaken the morale of the vast majority of good police officers who have never mistaken their badges for licenses to show brutality or arrogance.

Security and Secrecy

COLUMNISTS Joseph and Stewart Alsop, whose authoritative articles appear on the editorial page of this newspaper, have done a valuable public service in exposing the Washington security curtain which federal officials have used to hide facts from the American people which the Kremlin leaders already knew, under the pretext that the interests of national defense were involved.

The Alsops have long argued that the public be given the awesome facts about the terrible destructive power of the Super H-Bomb as well as the risks involved in the post-explosion radioactive fall-out affect which is a hazard over many thousands of square miles.

Last week, Admiral Lewis L. Strauss, chairman of the Atomic Energy Commission, finally revealed the grim facts. The revelations are frightening but are hardly of such nature as to have justified the secrecy in which they have been cloaked. Indeed, the facts seem to indicate that the AEC was more interested in saving face than in spelling out the A-B-C's of a situation in which the fate of civilization may be involved.

The column-writing brothers were harrassed in their search for information in Washington. They were investigated five times, their friends in government severely penalized for continued association with reporters who sought to find the truth, and they found alarming evidence that the habit of using security classification to screen facts in no way secret, but politically inconvenient to disclose, had become widespread.

Imitation of Soviet-style security in America is wrong and foolish. The system will not work in this country.

We agree with the Alsops that telling the people of the United States the truth is the quickest way to real national security, instead of the false "security" we have today which only breeds insecurity.

And Then There Were Two

★ JOSEPH ALSOP ★

Retreat From the Tachens Doesn't Settle Anything

TAIPEI, Formosa—The essential point to grasp about the retreat from the Tachens is that it does not settle anything. It was a way of putting off the evil day, and perhaps not even a very good way.

★ JOE PARHAM ★

Just How Do Southerners Really Feel on Integration?

"SOUTHERNERS Will Like Integration" contends an article under that title by a white Virginia woman in the current issue of the Saturday Evening Post.

Mrs. Sarah Patton Boyle, a faculty wife at the University of Virginia and a self-described "pretty typical Southerner," has written an interesting article purporting to represent the real, hidden viewpoint of the South on the question of segregation. But her story, like the illusion created by a master magician, it may be interesting but it isn't necessarily so.

★ HAL BOYLE ★

Are Bug, Beetle and Little Causing You Great Worry?

NAMES make news, and right now Mr. Manner is making world news.

So are George Little, Nick Beetle, George Bug and Nicholas Brandshawster.

They've been plotting and feuding over since old Mr. Steel died — a death that made big news in America.

Letters to the editor

★ PETER EDSON ★

Do Congratulations Make Preachers Dull?

Take Your Pick of Theories On Changes Inside Russia

Criticizes Editorials On Dixon-Yates Pact

Dream Train Wreck

RADIO AND TELEVISION SCHEDULES

Our Opinion

Don't Be Too Hard On Today's Prices

[body text columns]

'Creeping' Along

Off-Year Politics

BRISTOL HERALD COURIER

TUESDAY, AUGUST 31, 1954

Business Today

Many Firms Push Efforts To Diversify

By Elmer Roessner

"What I Want Is A New Model City"

Washington Calling

New Agreement Now Sought On U. S. Bases In Morocco

By Marquis Childs

Your Health

Cases Of Lead Poisoning Increase Among Children

By Herman N. Bundesen, M. D.

Othman Observes

Convention And Hearing Pour Down On Washington

By Frederick C. Othman

The President's Boxscore

Ike Finishes '54 Session With .646 Batting Average

By Congressional Quarterly

Barbs

Hambone

EISENHOWER'S 1954 Batting Average .646

BRISTOL HERALD COURIER: The masthead of this Tennessee daily has been moved to the bottom corner; a two-column diagram highlights a syndicated feature article.

LA SALLE DAILY NEWS-TRIBUNE: This non-metropolitan Illinois daily, which won the Ayer Award for typographical excellence for two consecutive years, puts a crossword puzzle and radio-television programs on its editorial page.

THE LAPEER COUNTY PRESS: Calling itself "America's Largest Rural Weekly," this Michigan paper devotes a double-width column to its editorials and a narrower column to "Along the Main Stem."

Mirror
AND *Daily News*

VIRGIL PINKLEY
EDITOR AND PUBLISHER

THURSDAY, FEBRUARY 3, 1955

The Sewer Delay Has Struck Home

Los Angeles is about to pay through the nose for the years of delay and indecision in formulating and putting into effect a long-range sewer program.

The ban on building permits urged by Mayor Poulson in the San Fernando Valley and the western section of the city until adequate sewers are financed and planned is a serious matter for the community.

It's serious because of the health and sanitation menaces presented by our overloaded sewage system and which led to the request.

And it's serious because of the blow the ban would strike at the economy of our community.

At the present writing it's almost impossible to estimate how many jobs the order would affect over the next few months in the construction industry and the materials supply industry. But the total would be high and the payroll loss heavy.

The Mayor's announcement hints that the ban could be relaxed if the voters approve a $60,000,000 sewer bond issue on the April 5 ballot.

But the question arises of the extent to which the ban could be modified at that time. The menace of overloaded sewers will remain until new construction is well under way and such a project takes time.

How did we get into such a mess?

The answer is that for the past eight years we have been financing from one sewer crisis to another without working out through the Council and our engineering experts a firm, long-range program for a city that everyone admitted would continue growing by giant strides.

There was controversy over whether or not to finance our needs by a sewer use charge to householders and industry, the cities or in the building.

It is to Mayor Poulson's credit that he ended the confusion and disagreement. The citizens' committee appointed by him came up with recommendations

on which the warring factions were able to agree.

The sewer delay is history now and can't be undone, even though it has placed the community in a sewage strait jacket.

What can and must be done is to vote approval of the bond issue in April and put Los Angeles back in business as a city.

Plan Curbs for Easter Holiday 'Hell Raising'

With the Easter holiday only a little more than two months away, it's good to note that the authorities and residents of Orange County's beach cities are making plans to curb the teen-age Easter sprees that have become annual scandals over the past few years.

Laguna Beach officials reveal that they will turn the spotlight of publicity on landlords on whose property disturbances occur. They'll also publicize names of owners who for the sake of extra dollars crowd dozens of occupants into quarters meant for a few.

Cramming a lot of high-spirited juveniles into a few rooms is just asking for trouble, they reason.

At Newport Beach and Balboa civic leaders and students have been discussing methods of insuring a good time for the teen-agers during the Easter holiday and at the same time preventing the "hell raising" of the past.

Among the suggestions are registration of juveniles planning the beach vacation, a landlord license limiting the number of renters, official inspection of rented quarters during the holiday and screening of cars and occupants at the Balboa Island bridge.

We've felt all along that the blame for these disgraceful "hell weeks" rests much more on the adults than it does on the teen-agers.

Indifferent parents, greedy landlords and conscienceless liquor sellers can be held largely responsible.

Beach resort civic leaders and authorities can't take the place of careless parents but they can police the activities of the holidaying teen-agers and we're glad to know that plans are jelling for just that.

A-BOMB NOT ONLY DISASTER THREAT

FREEDOM AND THE BETTER LIFE

Soviets Can't Hide the Facts About Their Low Living Standards

BY ROSCOE DRUMMOND

WASHINGTON — From their standpoint the Soviet leaders — obviously have powerful reasons why they do not want outsiders to see behind the Iron Curtain to allow their own people to know what life is like in the free world.

Some of these reasons emerge with new clarity as a result of the painstaking study of the economies of the Soviet bloc and the western world just completed by the Library of Congress under the direction of Howard S. Piquet, an international economics specialist whose preoccupation is to follow the facts wherever they take him.

As they pieced together the economic picture in the Soviet Union and compared it with the west, Dr. Piquet and his associates found so much that was demonstrably false in the free world that they permitted themselves this one personal recommendation.

THE MAILBAG   Should the Press Wear a Gag?

Defense News

It seems to me that some information coming from the newspapers, TV and radio is getting out of hand.

I can never understand why we admit in news-print, radio and TV that we cannot win a general war. Russia can bomb every city in the U.S. right now. We admit also that Russia is ahead of us in hydrogen bombs or at least close to us. We print gloom on how Russia could attack us.

I would like to know why we admit we can be licked. And the Communist block never even hints that this could possibly happen to them.

WILSHIRE III,
Los Angeles.

Spring Dosage

With spring just around the corner, would some reader tell me the correct formula for the dosage of sulphur and molasses that our pioneer ancestors used every spring to "purify the blood."

M. F. L.,
Fontana.

EDITOR'S NOTE: Anyone (ugh) remember?

History's Verdict

In reply to Harry Tullar of Rosemead, who said Stevenson is a cinch to beat Ike in the next election, I would like to correct a draft for a second term: Well, I wouldn't bet I even on Adlai in or near Ike! Outside of Illinois until 1952 Stevenson was unknown.

Ike is and will go down in history as one of our greatest leaders and one of our best Presidents.

BILL WILLIAMS,
Los Angeles.

60 Years Ago

Just 60 years ago tonight, when she was 16 and I was 21, so full of life and love, we were so gay. We are and dow, our faces are wrinkled, our hair has turned white and we have grown old together but that same love is still burning in our hearts.

GEORGE REED,
Los Angeles.

Back to 1600

In answer to Mrs. Garner's letter about family trees I've been tracing mine for about six months. So far I'm back to the 17th century on both sides.

The first thing to do is ask all living relatives. In doing so, find out, if possible, the city and county in which your parents, grandparents, etc., were married; then write to the Hall of Records for a copy of the marriage license and as it you will find their parents' names.

Also, it is wise to check genealogy books at the library if you have two or three of your family names. Sometimes you will find your family tree has already been traced.

MRS. ROY BENNING,
Glendale.

EDITOR'S NOTE: A number of other interesting letters on the subject are being forwarded.

Until Paid For

No more incinerator burning after July, the Supervisors say. For those of us who have purchased new incinerators at the order of the Fire Department controlling us or, I think we should be allowed to use them, at least until they are paid for.

MRS. B. F.,
Los Angeles.

Insurance Refused

I read an editorial that John A. Rose could about "uninsured drivers." On the very day the letter appeared I applied for a full coverage policy with one of the leading writers in the state. To my surprise the salesman wouldn't accept even an application.

He told me his company requires all of its applicants to have had prior insurance including liability before a company will issue a policy.

If they all feel this way about it, how will one ever get liability?

M. B.,
Los Angeles.

Wants to Study

"I am an ex-U.S. Public Health Surgeon from Alaska, 86 years young although failing eyesight makes it difficult for me to read. But I am very much interested in Theosophy and race philosophy. I wonder if anyone interested in the same subject would care to work with me from time to time as a reader.

DR. C.E. JOHNSON,
Los Angeles.

Could Be Cruelty

Terry MacKenzie wrote that she was very sorry for the mother that broke her family's leg. If the law will find her mentally not normal, then of course it is a great pity for both her children. But it could be an act of cruelty, too.

JENNIE BOHL,
Los Angeles.

Inez Robb: TONY DE MARCO HAD TO DANCE

Thirty-nine years ago a disgruntled parent and a stern truant officer broke up a dance act on a Wheeling (W.Va.) stage and hauled one of the performers back to the Fremola (N.Y.) High School where he had fled.

But two years later the father and the truant officer threw up their respective hands and decided for the good of all concerned that Tony De Marco might as well get dancing out of his system.

Tony, long the acknowledged peer and dean of all ballroom dancers, is still going strong and has no intention of hanging up his dancing slippers.

He said as much the other day when he lunched at a midtown New York hotel where he and his delicious Sally, wife and dancing partner, had just completed another sensationally successful engagement.

"I've still got the legs for it," he said. "They haven't deserted me, yet."

If ever there was a typical Alger success story, it is Tony's. The son of an Italian immigrant, Tony danced before he could walk. As a delivery boy for a meat market, he

earned money for his first pair of long pants, a prime necessity for entering the amateur dance contests at the old Academy Theater in Pittsburgh.

Since those days he has danced in every supper clubs all over the world, starred in a dozen Broadway shows and a handful of movies. At some point along the way Tony can remember the time he was the chief entertainer at a fashionable debutante party. A hapless waiter started across the dance floor with a tureen of soup—and the surprised Tony landed in it.

And even, on a Broadway stage, something so terrible happened to him that he has been a devoted Giant fan ever since.

"I was in the Marx brothers' show, 'The Cocoanuts,'" Tony recalled. "I made a heavy bet on the Yankees and it kind of worried me.

"So my partner and I were on stage, doing the most romantic of dances, a tango. At the climax of the dance the orchestra was doing a deep back bend as I supported her with one arm. Oh, it was all very glamorous, and in the middle of this solemn moment, worried about the Yankees, I reached up and scratched my ear!

"At broke up the show. The audience screamed with laughter for 15 minutes. The Marx brothers laid down a flat rule: 'Scratch off stage,' and I have been a Giant rooter ever since."

David Lawrence
SOUTHEAST ASIA TREATY APPROVAL

WASHINGTON—Again the United States Senate has given a stimulating impetus to United States leadership in the world—this time by ratifying by an 82-to-1 vote the new treaty which calls for the establishment of the Southeast Asia Treaty Organization.

Just as the Senate and House by overwhelming vote only a few days ago gave a dramatic demonstration of American unity and firmness in passing the resolution to defend Formosa, so the action which now comes to the United States behind the defense of Southeast Asia as a whole will have an impact far greater overseas than inside this country.

The new treaty commits the United States to an immediate consultation with seven other nations — Australia, New Zealand, Great Britain, France, Thailand, Pakistan and the Philippines — whenever there is an attack on any of the Southeast Asia countries named.

Even when there's no military action by the enemy but a conspiracy to acquire control of the countries in the area by subversion, there is an obligation on the part of the signers of the treaty to get together and determine what is best to do in the circumstances.

The treaty reserves to each government that signs it the right to take action only in conformity with its own "constitutional processes," which means that Congress alone can declare war or ratify steps taken in an emergency amounting to war.

The fact that the United States is among

the first to ratify will have a favorable effect on the other countries, both New Zealand and Australia, are naturally desirous of lining up American potential help, as they recall how powerless they were when the Japanese swooped down on them in 1942.

As for Pakistan and Thailand, they are closer to Communist China geographically and are not so easily defended by anyone as are New Zealand and Australia. But the signing of the treaty and the friendship of America and the other nations with both Pakistan and Thailand.

While the Southeast Asia Treaty Organization, usually called SEATO, is somewhat different from the North Atlantic Treaty Organization, which is said, seems to be the principle of collective security is embodied in each.

Incidentally, there are some academic persons now writing letters to the newspapers declaring that no nation can take a unilateral step while it is a member of the United Nations.

To say that the United States cannot defend itself without asking permission of the United Nations or that it cannot defend its own vital interests in the Far Pacific without the consent of the United Nations or to assume the existence already of a system in which individual nations have yielded their sovereignty.

Thomas L. Stokes
WE'RE LOSING OUR 'WATCHDOGS'

WASHINGTON—A subtle change is coming over your government which can be hurtful to you as a citizen interested in democracy, both as a taxpayer and as a consumer who would like to enjoy the fruits of industrial democracy at a fair price.

This change can be charted in the various regulatory commissions and agencies that are supposed to protect the public interest in the various economic fields which reach your life beyond special and commissions, there is a sort of cabin all the Federal Trade Commission, whose job is to discover and prevent monopoly and the growth of monopolistic practices that cost you money.

What is happening is that the personnel of regulatory commissions has been reshaped through the acquisitive power of the President and purposely. The aim is to produce a "sympathetic" attitude toward business, as it is put.

What is often forgotten is that these commissions are creatures and servants of Congress. They are not creatures at all of the President or the executive branch. They were created to perform for Congress the duty it is assigned under the Constitution to regulate commerce. This duty required such close and detailed attention with the rapid growth of our economy that Congress was unable to give it the time required. So Congress created commissions to keep pace with the developments and economic progress.

In view of the dangerous shift in government, we are lucky to have back in Congress a man who perhaps knows more about this whole problem than anyone in government today, Sen. Joseph C. O'Mahoney (D) Wyo. He got his knowledge from long legislative experience and from specialized study as chairman of a joint Congressional committee

several years ago on the concentration of monopoly in 1938 and came up with a thick study of that subject and a record that is sort of a bible on the subject. The Wyoming Senator, at the annual Roosevelt Day dinner in New York this week, warned about present policies of the administration, which, he said, seems "to be striving with might and main to remove the economic capital from Washington, where it is now being absorbed by the Wall Street."

On the problem with which we are here especially concerned, he said:

"The legislative powers of Congress, outlining the very first article of the Constitution, are the bedrock of popular government, yet they are now being absorbed by the White House.

"Every lobbyist in Washington knows that the time for control, even of the quasi-judicial commissions, are in the hands of the anonymous militants in the White House."

DROODLES
BY ROGER PRICE

"MAN BLOWING SMOKE RINGS WHILE WAITING TO BE SHOT OUT OF A CANNON"

When I was traveling with a carnival I had an act where I shot a man (fellow named McTavish) out of a cannon. But what problems I had! First, I had to drag the 135-mm. cannon around behind my car (I always pointed the barrel to the rear) to the courage wise guys who honk their horns when the lights change) and then before every performance I had to take McTavish and bend him in the barrel. This got too expensive as I got rid of McTavish (it was easy) and worked out a much more novel version of the act. Now it's McTavish-Out-of-a-Cannon Act. I hired a troupe of midgets and shot them out of a machine gun.

WORD GAME

STRAYED

(Strayed: STRADE. Wandered, deviated.)

Average mark 23 words; time limit 25 minutes.

Can you find 20 or more dictionary words in 'Strayed'?

Rules of the game I—Words must be of four or more letters. 2—Words which require four letters by the addition of "s," such as "hats," "rats," etc., or "ed," "used, 2—Only one form of a word at used. 3—Proper names are not allowed. 4—Answers to test on Page 14

The Debate Over Aid to Asia

Under prodding of a whole series of presidents and a whole series of external emergencies, for 15 years the congress of the United States has been setting up and then abolishing one agency after another for shelling out American dollars to build up friendly countries: Lend-lease, UNRRA, ECA (Marshall Plan), MSA and FOA, to name only a few of the major ones.

FOA, the Foreign Operations Administration headed by Harold Stassen, is due to expire under the law by June 30, 1955. But the emergencies are not over. They have simply changed.

The 24 billion dollars in postwar aid poured into Western Europe has built this key area up into a "position of strength" instead of the economic chaos and military vacuum it was at the close of World War II —but the rest of the world (where only 13 billions have been spent by congress) is in more danger than ever, and the danger seems likely to last for many years.

Communist military victories in China and Indochina have swallowed up more than half these 13 billions, and have seriously altered the balance of power in Asia. Unless the United States does a good deal more than it has been doing, disaster looms ahead.

For two months now, President Eisenhower has had Joseph M. Dodge, the former budget director, reviewing the country's long-range economic security policy. Stassen and his staff have been preparing proposals for consideration by the bureau of the budget and the National Security Council.

There is reported to be a lively division of opinion within the cabinet on the subject of foreign aid, with Dodge, Stassen and Secretary of State Dulles recommending greatly increased aid to Asian countries and only a slightly lower total of foreign aid (as aid to Europe tapers off), while Secretary of the Treasury George Humphrey favors trimming aid to Asia somewhat from present levels, though keeping it going for some time.

Dodge, Dulles and Stassen are definitely out of the "tax and tax, spend and spend" school, and in 15 years of foreign aid programs, the United States has learned a great deal about what to do and what not to do. Dodge recognizes, for example, that the amount of outside money you can put into the economy of an industrially-underdeveloped Asian country without wasting most of it in inflation is much smaller than in an industrialized European country.

But technical aid alone is not enough under present conditions; capital investment is needed also of a sort and on a scale impractical for private investors. "Trade not aid," also, is a slogan which applies much more to industrially developed countries. This is disappointing, but it is a fact which must be faced.

Once the differences within the administration are ironed out, the still harder task remains of getting agreement in congress and public. The situation is an odd variant of the boy who cried "Wolf" too often. Successive administrations have cried "Wolf!" The wolf was a real one. Thanks to timely aid, the wolf has been slain by co-operative action. But each time, there has been another wolf just around the corner.

Saving what remains of Asia from Communist conquest or subversion is more important to the security of the United States than balancing the budget, if that stands in the way, desirable as balancing a budget is. The wolf is at the door again. It is a different door and a different wolf. Americans weary of responding to emergencies need to remember that—and to remember how successfully those other wolves were killed.

Legislature Should End Secrecy

This newspaper is in full agreement with State Representative Joe Watson, jr., of Indianola in his belief that committee sessions of the Iowa legislature should be open to the press and public.

Once such a step is taken, we believe, as does Representative Watson, that the change will not "hurt" as much as many of the lawmakers fear it will.

Nebraska legislators broke away from the old practices of committee secrecy quite a few years ago when the unicameral system was adopted. The break was not nearly so painful as it was feared.

The opening of committee sessions in the Nebraska legislature was brought about more or less gradually. It was given a trial during the first unicameral session in 1937. Members of that committee opened all hearings on bills before it to the public. It continued to hold executive sessions at which bills were put into final form. But regular representatives of the press were permitted to attend these executive sessions and to report their results.

Before that first unicameral session closed, most of the other committees voluntarily adopted the same procedure. The practice has continued ever since, despite some attempts to revert to the old system of secret sessions.

Lawmakers are under heavy pressure at times from groups both for and against a specific bill or amendment. They like to take shelter from these pressures as long as they can. For political reasons, many try to avoid facing up to the business of choosing sides so long as there is a possibility that they can escape doing so.

These tactics, more often than not, are based on perfectly honest intentions. Nevertheless, they frequently are interpreted as coverups for suspected illicit practices. And secrecy does make possible shady manipulations by a few individuals.

Representatives Watson's colleagues in the coming session of the legislature could very well give serious sober thought to his proposal.

Uncertainty Ahead For Japan

The resignation of Japanese Premier Yoshida followed a long period in which his own followers have been forcing more and more restive under his leadership.

They have criticized him chiefly for "one-man rule" and for undue subservience toward the United States in the matter of trade and diplomatic relations with nearby Red China.

American observers have criticized him largely for the opposite reasons: failure to rule firmly enough in the face of the harsh economic squeeze confronting Japan, with its mushrooming population and its limited resources. U. S. spending during the hostilities in Korea gave Japan a brief and illusory boom. Yoshida weakly allowed this money to be dissipated in living standards which could not be maintained once the boom stopped instead of plowing it into productivity increasing investments.

Yoshida's probable successor, Ichiro Hatoyama—the man General MacArthur once purged as a militarist—is likely to respond to the Japanese criticisms about trade relations with Red China—while hoping to maintain the same cordial relations with the United States. But it remains to be seen whether he will grapple with the deeper economic problem. Red Chinese trade might help somewhat, but it would not solve this economic problem.

For his statesmanlike calling for the "courage to be patient" that Yoshida has won wide acclaim. But at the same time the Chinese Communists by their provocation and their intransigence are making it more and more difficult for Yoshida to maintain this position. But even this may be too late through the years of tension ahead.

Illinois U. Gets New President

Dr. David D. Henry, who a few days ago denounced the Illinois situation a "deplorable" and asked to be taken out of the running for the job of university president, is now the newly-appointed head of the University of Illinois.

The about-face came as a result of the trustees determination to get their man. They earlier had settled on Dr. Henry, but some brass and dangerous talk intervened. The Illinois state superintendent of public instruction took note of an anonymous letter and started talking in terms of a political investigation. Dr. Henry responded with a condemnation of "public review" in the search for a president and backed away from the job. The board's response was a unanimous vote in favor of Henry and a successful bid to New York to get him to change his mind. The search for an Illinois president thus has a happy ending—at least

Dr. Henry's beginning at Illinois has a happy ending. He spoke up to his prospective employers and let them know exactly where he stood. Dr. Henry served notice he's not the kind of educator to be pushed around.

There is, to his credit, has picked a top flight educator and apparently given him assurance that the job of Illinois president is not going to be a political football.

Two strangers can readily establish a common conversational meeting ground if they find themselves both willing to criticize the same persons or objects.—Violet Lundquist, Anthon Herald.

Checking in its old grade, an Eastern university found that those with the largest waistbands were making the most money.—Paul Wood, Sheldon Mail.

WASHINGTON, D. C.—The direction of American foreign and military policy is in process of a significant reversal in line with President Eisenhower's press conference statement of last week stressing the need for America to have the "courage to be patient."

While it has not yet been written into the language of a National Security Council decision, there is increasing recognition that Communist aggression of a limited nature may arise in the future that will call out, for about atomic warfare but for limited forces to repel and punish that aggression. This represents a decided shift from the policy first in Secretary of State Dulles speech to the Council on Foreign Relations last January when he said that the basic decision was to "depend primarily upon a great capacity to retaliate instantly by means and at places of our own choosing."

Shock And Fear

In the same speech Dulles said that local defenses would be reinforced by "massive retaliatory power". Rightly or wrongly, Western Europe took this to mean that any attempt to meet Communist aggression anywhere would mean the use of atomic and hydrogen bombs.

Coupled with the Hickenlooper in the Pacific last March and the fall-out of radioactive dust that fell on a Japanese fishing boat, this stirred a profound current of shock and fear among America's allies.

The president has been primarily responsible for moving away from the "massive retaliatory concept." He has been influenced by the views of General Matthew Ridgway, chief of staff of the army, who at the president's request adjourned before the National Security Council in the spring to present the case against the use of American sea and air power to save the French position in Indochina. Ridgway insisted their time would be too "thin-stretched too thin without a whole new build-up out of the American ground troops which were not available in any thing like the numbers required.

WOULD FACE DEMAND

You just cannot force 150,000,000 people to consume more than they actually require or feel that they want.

I do not want to be arbitrary or appear critical, but we must face the facts and try to make the best of it.—Fred C. Watts, 1118 First st., E. W. Mason City, Ia.

EDITOR'S NOTE: Egg prices are not being governed by the government at the present time.

It is the president's realization of the solid consequences of thermonuclear warfare that is responsible for the reorientation of policy now taking place. Even the possibility of American forces being heavily engaged in a Chinese border war would come from an isolation of the beleaguered Nationalist position on Tachen islands would be of little interest in realization for Red attacks on the Nationalist-held island of Quemoy. Growing recognition of the need to fight local wars by limited means is further evidence of the influence of the president.

But much stress has been put on the power of the new atomic and hydrogen weapons that the public has seemed to assume in the past that they contained a kind of magic insuring victory for America at little or no cost in blood, sweat and tears. Toward the end of the Korean war the clamor grew to use atomic bombs on Chinese centers. If the public is to share in part at least the president's realization of what these weapons mean, the Atomic Energy Commission is going to have to be a lot less secretive.

For his statesmanlike willingness to face the hard facts the president deserves public support. But at the same time the Chinese Communists by their provocation and their intransigence are making it more and more difficult for the president to maintain this position and to bear to have the economic condemned to a more words—Mrs. Jack Alfred, 109 E. Franklin, Ames.

Caution Urged on Voting at 18

(By James Gonduie, in the Manchester Press.)

Before anyone gets too serious about the "vote at 18" movement there needs to be a lot of study. Governor-elect Hoegh has expressed favor with the movement to allow 18-year-olds of Iowa to vote.

The 18-year-old crowd is of college or just out of high school age. Strange lofe appeal within an impressionable mind that places too great leaders and convicts may be admired, or followed.

Those who have been close to college students (in the larger cities) know through winter at the close of government which some students find. Eighteen is just the age when the most "radical" thing is attractive. Possibly it is a chance to be different or attract attention that prompts the student to become a follower or associate of the "crowd."

The ideas that some adopt in college or after high school—often play out an rest life levels off one's thinking. During this stage, however, it does not seem wise to allow the power of decision to be vested in so untried a group.

You must remember the days of "saving world" and the popular "pamphlets" when you become thoroughly absorbed in the 18-year-old level.

One of the standout arguments in favor is, "if they are old enough to fight, they are old enough to vote." We must not forget that in military service there is close supervision by older, more experienced hands.

There could be nothing more free of supervision than a young person with a ballot in hand! That would be a logical place to show independence, and possibly a dangerous one, too!

To the Editor:

In your column "Letters to the Editor" in the Dec. 3 issue I am a bit perturbed by the remarks of Mrs. Rasmussen. The subject was: "A Question Is Asked About the Price of Eggs."

Here in northern Iowa, I have been getting direct to a farmer producer of eggs 60c to the per dozen almost year around for No. 1, top quality and extra large eggs. We do appreciate the privilege of getting the best quality eggs strictly fresh and therefore are willing to pay a small premium for them plus the expense of driving a few miles out to get them.

BRIGHTER FIELDS

Mrs. Rasmussen also states that she has been picking up the check too long, implying that she apparently is disgusted or getting tired of the situation. Most business people in the city and elsewhere that pick up the check too long, eventually find themselves out of business. If I were unhappy about the situation, I would surely discontinue it and seek brighter fields of endeavor.

She also mentions "oh the day's work of picking up the check" and cannot see where art then're" In my way of thinking, as long as the professional product makes a definite price for production of business. The producer falls off for most any type of business. In most of America's discharge employees and reduce production until such a time as there is a renewed demand for their type of merchandise. No concern can exist by paying for production and not receiving it.

LACK OF DEMAND

Evidently the reason Mrs. Rasmussen is only receiving 25c per dozen for her eggs in June must be that her eggs are not much in demand at that point. It is also important that the cost of transportation on eggs from Iowa to distant points must also enter into the picture.

If Mrs. Rasmussen and 20 million other people that are producing eggs would cut their flock by 20 per cent it is evident that the price of eggs would go up 20 per cent, but as long as we are guaranteed a price for our production, most people are voted are going to continue producing more than the market can consume.

"I suppose this will be grist for Moscow's propaganda mill, but it sure looked like a duck to me."

Why Hickenlooper Opposed Condemnation of McCarthy

Senator Bourke B. Hickenlooper submitted a lengthy statement for publication in the Congressional Record in explanation of his vote against adoption of the McCarthy condemnation resolution. It was published in the Dec. 3 issue of that official publication.

The following excerpts from that statement represent only a small portion of that statement. But they project the core of the senator's reasoning on the question.

My position in this matter is not from a standpoint of agreement or disagreement with the senator from Wisconsin. With many things he has done and said I disagree; my position in this matter is taken because I believe there is a fundamental and very vital principle affecting freedom of the United States and the senate as the real issue in the controversy, and I propose to protect those freedoms as much as I can.

WOULD FACE DEMAND

Throughout the history of this country we have had public figures who have aroused violent feelings, pro and con; they have generated controversies which have affected the course of our nation. It is in the freedom of controversy and in the form of emotional discussion that we have traditionally found greed, strength, and we must take great care, indeed, that the community government power of a majority shall not translate itself into tyranny over the rights of a minority, one or more.

Source of Strength

The very strength of the right of freedom of conduct on the part of the senate is proven by the ability of any system to absorb all manner of discussion and action, sober and serious, and still maintain that attitude which is essential in the interest of exhaustive exploration of the rights of the American people.

I often disagree with positions taken by many of my colleagues and, indeed, with many more of them than I ever have from time to time, and without doing damage to fundamental principles of conduct as enunciated. If the senate that way I shall be helped to think of it.

For all of these reasons and because of the sacred principle of liberty and freedom, I cannot support the vote of censure in either of the two categories set out by the select committee.

Again I point out that this is the first time in the history of the senate, so far as I know, that words spoken by a senator have been the subject of a formalized censure for censure. This seems to me to invite a precedent for the official censorship and suppression of words by any system of men by a predetermined course of action at any time in our future life to silence words which they may not like or disagree with.

Therefore, while I assert the freedom to personally oppose

Doubts Pastors Need To Memorize Texts

To the Editor:

Would most pastors feel they could spend precious hours in memorizing pages of material? Would most congregations want their pastors to spend their time that way? I daresay many clergymen could repeat from memory the lines of funerals, baptisms, marriage, communion, dedication, and so forth. But why should they have to be bothered by the thought of committing to memory seldom used passages to be mixed up in the midst of some service?

Clergymen are also human beings, with the same abilities and inabilities as you and I. One person may be able to memorize many words in a short time, while another may have to spend hours at it. Should this be a qualification of a good pastor?

It is my feeling that most pastors would have so many things to say about and given hours, that they could not have to decide which were the most important points to bring out. I feel this is the way it would be to have the sermon confined to so many more words—Mrs. Jack Alfred, 109 E. Franklin, Ames.

CHICAGO, ILL.—Speaking of misquotations, as I was the other day, let me carry the discussion a step further—from the wrong word to the wrong idea, or from the right word that is misused to give the wrong meaning. Probably like two most popular sayings—among uneducated (or even semi-educated) people today are: "Everything is relative" and "Everything is twisted."

Twisted Meaning

Einstein is supposed to be the authority for the first sweeping statement, and Freud is supposed to be the authority for the second. Actually, neither of these great men said anything of the sort.

Twisted Meaning

Einstein's "relativity" refers to space and time, to the fact that the position of the observer determines the amount of time it requires to go from one place to another. This and nothing more.

Freud's "sexuality" refers to the early historical drives of small children, which must be understood and led in the proper direction if the child is to grow up emotionally mature and able to love with discernment.

But most people, grasping at a word, reject that "everything" is relative, that nothing has absolute value, that what is beliefs or virtues or opinions are as good as any other. This would justify everybody's death.

Eye for Eye

Let us take an older and more traditional example: When people want to exercise revenge, they are fond of quoting the Biblical injunction: "An eye for an eye, and a tooth for a tooth," as justification of their attitude.

But the Bible nowhere tells us we should take an eye for an eye. It tells us that this is the way we have a right to take—but the injunction implies we should take no more punishment than we have received, for an eye, and in truth for a tooth.

The Bible, on the contrary, constantly emphasizes mercy over justice, and love over revenge. If we quote the line meaning of a quotation that is 2,000 years old, we can read into it almost any meaning whatever.

Branded Meat?

(Fool Field Reporter.)

When the meat packers hold their meeting in Chicago recently they heard a proposal that a lot of other producers in the food industry adopt long ago.

One of the speakers is a meat-packing company and executives of big companies said that the recent reverses in business were in part due to deficiencies in meat retailing, suggested that individual cuts of meat might be branded by each packing company as a means of advertising its products.

The man the packer was advertising was the adoption of brands so that when buying a piece of meat, the customer would have some assurance that he could rely on it.

If this was suggested that a good place to begin is with the now abandoned approach was when the customer is presented with a nicely wrapped package of dinner.

What the packer was advertising was the adoption of brands so that when buying a piece of meat, the customer would have some assurance that he could rely on it.

It was agreed that a good place to begin is with the now abandoned approach, and when the cuts of meat is covered into a cut that has been processed too perfectly.

Question: Could you make directions more intelligently if expectations which asked to be wanted to wake (all financial statements each print?

Mrs. Jane Patterson, 41, of 4011 Fifteenth st., production worker: "Yes, I do think so. I'd like to see these prices from such a company as they're asking for money."

Ann Reiten, 22, Newitadall, Germany, clerk-typist: "Oh, I just arrived from Germany four days ago and I haven't made up my mind."

H. C. Berry, 30, of 5219 Ovid ave., assistant manager, insurance firm: "I definitely do. I'd like to see any group from such a statement as they're asking for money."

John Whelan, 60, West Des Moines, assistant comptroller, insurance company: "I would be in favor of these doing it, so we know what's going on."

Mrs. George Haines, 45, of 2513 Fifty-fourth st., housewife: "I doubt it because I have full confidence in my bank and organization."

Des Moines Register

[masthead and subscription information, rates]

Daily $30,603
Sunday $70,055

Are Increased Bus Fares The Only Solution?

A Return Visit To Louisville

New Jersey's Booming Toll-Road Traffic

Bit of Advice To The Young About Depressions

Chicago Has Its Bitterest Primary In Many Years

By CHARLES B. CLEVELAND
Chicago Daily News Service

Mayor Kennelly
Angered Chicago Democratic Machine

CHIPS ON BOTH SHOULDERS

LETTERS TO THE EDITOR

Renaming Streets Decided

Homes on Incinerator Site

Stands By Cherokee Parkway

Praises Greyhound Drivers

LOOKING BACKWARD
By MARTIN MOORE

10 YEARS AGO TODAY—1945

25 YEARS AGO TODAY—1930

50 YEARS AGO TODAY—1905

Admiral Turner
Directed the Jima Invasion 10 Years Ago

A.E.C. Is Subverted By Dixon-Yates

From the Milwaukee Journal

It So Often Happens

Our Chromatic Corn

THE LOUISVILLE TIMES: Use of illustrations and second decks for features (and occasionally, for editorials) plus elimination of column rules have made this paper representative of the modernistic trend in typography.

CHICAGO SUN-TIMES: Wide columns for editorials plus illustrations attract readers to this tabloid page.

NEW YORK DAILY NEWS: Use of a wide-measure editorial column, cuts, and cartoon make this a lively tabloid page make-up.

CHICAGO DAILY SUN-TIMES
WEDNESDAY FEB. 16, 1955

'Who Threw The Overalls?'

Choices In Wards 2, 12, 33 And 40

OPINION OF THE PEOPLE

Loyola's Fine Example

There'll Always Be An England—Or Will There?

DAILY NEWS

The Inquiring Fotographer

THE PRICE OF AN ORANGE

JACKPOTS FOR JERSEY

WEIRD AND TERRIFYING

Her Husband's Still in Jail

VOICE OF THE PEOPLE

GANGWAY FOR FIRE WAGONS

ONE MORE FOR HOOVER

Ask Frances Story

Can Marriage Last Out Another Storm?

By Davis Fleason

Washington Calling

Behind the Formosa Decision

Shocking Swapping on Increase

Gen. Ridgway's Testimony

Change of Pace

By Hal Burton

The Men on Horseback

'Just a Ripple'

· · · · Newsday · · · ·

"Where there is no vision, the people perish."
Proverbs XXIX, 18

MacArthur's Noble Dream

Maybe Dulles Should Take In a Few Movies

Strictly Personal

—SIDNEY J. HARRIS.

Mr. Malaprop In Washington

Industry Means Tax Relief for Homeowners

County Federation

Grateful for GG

Backyard Dust Bowl

Friday, January 28, 1955

Newsday

NEWSDAY: Facing pages of editorials, cartoons, comments, and columnists as used in this Long Island, N.Y., tabloid illustrate some good ways to achieve typographical harmony.

A few tabloids make up their editorial pages and "op edit" pages so that they resemble a single standard-size page. One tabloid that does this is the York (Pennsylvania) *Gazette and Daily*. On a typical day, each of these pages is divided into four columns with no cartoon or other illustrations on either editorial or "op edit" page to break up a fairly grayish appearance. Use of white space instead of column rules gives the pages airiness but fairly light headlines on long features and columns provide too little contrasting blackness in the lower parts of the pages.

The *New York Post* treats its editorial and "op edit" pages as a modified unit but wider columns for the editorials and two syndicated columnists on the facing page, use of halftones and a thumbnail sketch, and boldface type for some paragraphs, as well as a cartoon, break up the two pages into considerable contrast.

Newsday, Alicia Patterson's tabloid in suburban New York, uses three columns on both its editorial and "op edit" pages and gets away from a gray appearance with a cartoon on each page and thumbnail cuts with the columns.

The *Washington Daily News* uses boxed editorial paragraphs and a Talburt cartoon to break up the grayness of its editorial page and on the "op edit" page it employs a two-column cartoon, halftone cuts of columnists, bold headings with white space to headline its syndicated material.

After splitting its tabloid editorial page down the middle so as to have two wide-measure columns for editorials, the *Chicago Sun-Times* puts a cartoon in the upper right hand corner below which is an "Opinion of the People" section with letters set in three "narrow gauge" columns. The *Los Angeles Mirror* used to have narrow columns for some of its non-editorial material. These narrow-measure columns are exclusive with the tabloids and tend to keep the readers' eyes jumping from line to line. Most typographical specialists favor wider, rather than narrower, columns.

In conclusion, we should realize that editorial page makeup is, after all, mainly another matter of taste. Yet it is well to remember that there is nothing undignified and unethical about wanting readers to glance at an editor's comments. If innovations in such things as type size, column width, heavier headlines, and so forth will help increase the number of readers, then a responsible editor or publisher should be willing to say, "More power to it!" And what's more, he might even experiment with his own page make-up and find that it reinforced the effectiveness of what editorial writers said.

TWELVE

The columnists

PRESENT-DAY EDITORS AND PUBLISHERS DO NOT KNOW WHAT TO DO about columnists, particularly the syndicated variety. Certainly, the columnist has become a part of the contemporary daily press. Only a hundred or so newspapers fail to print at least one or more columnists and several metropolitan dailies use more than a score. But some editors and publishers have had qualms about surrendering part of the opinion-forming function.

Within a generation, the columnists who came on the newspaper scene during the depression and early New Deal years have found for themselves enthusiastic followers and partisans. After the 1929 stock market crash, readers of the spot news were baffled, bewildered, and confused by falling prices, mounting unemployment, lengthening bread-lines, and increasing foreclosures on mortgages. Then as President Franklin D. Roosevelt and his associates sought to solve the problems of the depression, the federal government vastly extended its activities at the local level. Citizens everywhere wanted to understand what was happening; newspaper stories that recited only the surface facts of the day-to-day developments were not much help. Washington correspondents saw this need and acted. The columnists, as we use the term today, came into existence. In many cases, they were down-to-earth news men who had the facts of what was happening—but they put these facts together to make them understandable instead of presenting them baldly. These columnists became popular, in part, because they filled a real demand on the part of many puzzled readers and many local editors recognized that these writers could supply information that the newspapers could get from no other source. Another group of columnists vented their opinions, prejudices, and biases and the frustrated readers found it satisfying thus to have their own ideas reinforced.

Despite the several decades of the columnists' existence, newspapermen have not evolved a criteria for impartially assaying them. Columnists admittedly build circulation. Selected judiciously, they should provide a "battle page" of opposing ideas. Yet a paper's staff never can be quite positive about where a columnist will lead readers. One contracted for as a rabid Republican may suddenly lurch over into the Democratic camp. One with a long record of unbroken conservatism may dash off an enthusiastic, but unexpected, defense of civil liberties. One who is highly regarded for his light, humorous comments may start crusading against an Army general overseas. Editors who want consistent opinions may find a syndicated columnist in violent disagreement with an editorial in an adjoining column. And those who want the widest variety of ideas may discover a monotonous uniformity.

But let the editor leave out a popular columnist and irate letters and protesting telephone calls from loyal followers will threaten the most dire consequences.

What do they say about columnists?

What newspapermen think about the rise of column writing varies from extravagant praise to vitriolic denunciation. Some of it is said in the privacy of a conference in a publisher's office and some is voiced before audiences of hundreds.

Most newspapermen would agree, at least reluctantly, with this appraisal by Charles Fisher, then himself a columnist on the late *Philadelphia Record*, in his book *The Columnists* (Howell, Soskin, 1944):

The successful columnist of our time engages the instant daily attention of a greater number of clients than any author who ever set quill pen to paper or explored the keyboard of an Underwood with burning forefingers. The broadcasting of his notions is without parallel in the history of print.

The more popular columnists' opinions, speculations, and gossip are printed in daily newspapers with a total circulation surpassing 20,000,000. That is a potential readership considerably better than one tenth of the total United States population. Even those columns that are tailored for the elite "opinion leaders" reach out for potential audiences of millions.

Far fewer journalists would agree with President Franklin D. Roosevelt's annoyed comment at his December 22, 1944, press conference:

All that we can say is that columnists are with us, an unnecessary excrescence on our civilization.

Dwight E. Sargent of the *Portland* (Maine) *Press Herald* lamented "a spreading tendency to kneel before the columnist's altar" and what he called "evidence that too many editors and publishers are taking the lazy way out, hiring syndicated Washington writers instead of developing home talent, thus becoming parties to the usurpation of their own editorial responsibilities." Writing in *The Masthead* (Summer, 1950), he continued:

Syndicated columns should be used as auxiliary motors on the editorial page, not as main sources of power; they should be readable, instructive, accurate, fair. By these norms they shall be judged . . .

The syndicated columnist, in my opinion, should be to the editorial page what the visiting lecturer is to the university. He's a fit person to round out a curriculum, but whoever heard of letting him run the faculty? . . .

A newspaper's soul is a precious thing, by its very nature a local thing; it should not be compromised by syndicated thinking.

J. G. Ferguson of the *Milwaukee Journal* said this at a 1951 panel discussion of the American Society of Newspaper Editors:

Frankly, I think the syndicated opinion is one of the biggest rackets ever put over on worried editors and publishers . . . Even though it may sound sacrilegious to say it—we wouldn't trade one experienced reporter for all the syndicated columns we could crowd into the editorial page of the Milwaukee Journal.

The *Milwaukee Journal*, it is proper to point out, is able to join *The New York Times, Christian Science Monitor,* and a few other elite daily papers that have no traffic with syndicated columnists because they all are strong enough financially to bid for writers who otherwise might be hired for syndication.

Some newspapermen, especially those on the smaller dailies with one- and two-man editorial page staffs, would go along with what columnist Ernest Lindley said in defending himself and his colleagues before the same A.S.N.E. panel:

The only practical way in which most newspapers in this country can get a variety of competent analytical and interpretive journalism is by buying syndicated columns. They can't afford anything more.

Talk with a dozen or more harried (and undoubtedly hurried) editorial writers on dailies with circulations under 50,000 or with their fellows on most of the weeklies, and you will find out the truth of Lindley's argument. They may pine to spend their time leisurely gathering background information and developing it for their readers, but who would do the rest of their assigned jobs? Even those who might be inclined to "blow their tops" in private confess that limited budgets compel them to split the costs of opinion columns and interpretive pieces with hundreds of other publications whose finances are equally tight. Yet some papers have money available and refuse to spend it for a locally written column. Their sense of a responsible press seems sadly blunted.

Part of the diverse reaction to columnists arises because of unresolved questions about the function of the editorial page itself. Should the primary emphasis be to educate or should it be to indoctrinate? Should an editor view himself as impartial and non-partisan as, say, Western Union or the Bell Telephone System? How fair must he be to a crackpot, for instance? Or should he survey the facts and then take an intelligent stand with courage enough to exclude those who would subvert his readers to what he thinks is error? If he does not believe what he advocates, why write it in the first place?

The "common carrier" concept was strongly advanced by the Commission on Freedom of the Press. This distinguished, non-journalistic group held that newspapers had a responsibility to present all points of view, to provide "a forum for the exchange of comment and criticism." Their arguments were both impressive and attractive. Yet dissenters protested loudly. Should an editor or publisher, these critics asked, ever forfeit his right to select the items for his paper? Jenkin Lloyd Jones of the *Tulsa Tribune* decried the idea: "Under the strict 'common carrier' interpretation it would be impossible to conduct an anti-rodent campaign without carrying, in a parallel column, statements from the leading local rats."

While few newspapermen make a point of it, use of columnists allows considerable editorial page passion without any painful responsibility of possible consequences. An editor and publisher can hit and run, as it were. When a reader or advertiser protests, he is told reassuringly, "Of course, you know HE doesn't reflect our point of view."

Henry R. Luce of Time, Inc., touched on this in the 1953 Eric W. Allen Memorial Lecture at the University of Oregon when he said:

If an owner-publisher is seriously responsible for every word in his newspaper, he ought not to publish any columnist whose basic integrity he doubts or with whose *basic* philosophy he disagrees. That is not the fashionable doctrine. The fashionable and convenient and profitable doctrine is that, in order to amuse the reader or in order "to give the readers various viewpoints," the owner-publisher has the right, even the duty, to print what personally he deplores or detests. In my view that is a childish evasion of a man's responsibility. It is worse than that: It is cynicism at the heart of American life.

The rise of one-newspaper towns and monopoly publishers has forced revision of some newspapermen's thinking. They felt that it was permissible to shut an editorial door upon an individual or group when a rival daily stood ready to listen; but when no other way exists to reach the newspaper-reading public, editorial attitudes must be less arrogant. Here too, however, the surrender of editorial judgment has to know some bounds. The location of these bounds has created another headache for those in charge of editorial pages.

While the successful columnist offers a newspaper a ready-made readership, purchasing such writings adds further to the problems facing a responsible editor or publisher. Some of those on smaller papers have given up the struggle to compete head-on with a syndicated Washington columnist who may have a staff of five legmen, but they still retain their editorial prerogatives by commenting in their own editorials on what the columnist may say.

A syndicated column exists almost exclusively for the daily or weekly newspapers. Mass distribution of the same material implies little or no overlapping in potential readers. Magazines, business journals, and trade papers circulate over wide areas of the country, if not the entire United States. Because of this, these publications create their own columns of signed opinion, trends, and predictions. The only exception is an occasional humor column that may appear in several members of a group of publications under common editorial direction.

Columnists do all sorts of jobs

Like others who write for a newspaper, columnists aim to inform, to persuade, or to amuse. Beyond that, we must be wary of generalizations. Some columns tell a president just how the country should be run. Some explain intricacies of the quest for a cure for cancer. Others expound on the wonders of color television. Still others take you, by a sort of legerdemain not known to all reporters, into the private conference rooms of the great.

Columns, like news stories, may fit into several pigeonholes at the same time. For what it may be worth, let us try to set up some classifications for column writing. Here are some definitions for such a breakdown:

1. *Reporting-in-depth columns.* Here the writer pushes only slightly beyond what a byline reporter does in a news story. He writes what he would answer to an intelligent person who asked, "Tell me the whole story. You know more about it than I do." In its purest form, this is a rarity among the columnists. The urge to pontificate apparently is hard to stifle. No one covering the political scene has consistently followed these techniques since the death of Raymond Clapper, who carried over into column-writing practically all of the practices he had learned during a brilliant career as a United Press correspondent. On occasion, the Alsop brothers and Thomas L. Stokes, to mention a few, turn out columns close to this pristine state. Such syndicated columnists as David Dietz and Thomas Henry show how perspective, background, and interpretation may be used effectively in the non-political field. Others, however, relate the current news chapter to those that went before and those that may come in the future with varying blends of their own biases.

2. *"I think" or opinionated columns.* These writings may come close to being signed editorials although not infrequently the "I" becomes most important. The columnists, either because of extensive training, long-time observations, or sheer lack of modesty, set themselves up as experts and then expound their opinions for the general public. Syndicated book and art criticism also fits in here. At their best, such opinion columns may contribute much enlightenment; at their worst, they simply reinforce existing reader bias. The self-appointed experts try to compensate in heat

for what they can not provide in light. Frederick Lewis Allen once described the analyses of Walter Lippmann, a pioneer in syndicated opinion columns, as "able to reduce a senseless sequence of events to sense," which "brought first aid to men and women groping in the dark for opinions." The description still applies to the better columns. Columnists who write frequently in the "I think" category include John Crosby, David Lawrence, Max Lerner, Walter Lippmann, Westbrook Pegler, and George Sokolsky.

3. *Gossip or chitchat columns.* Practically everybody likes to learn a juicy bit of gossip or chitchat; one whole field of column-writing is built on this characteristic. While some of the "keyhole" gossip that gets into print in such columns contains little except its titillating value, this need not be the writer's exclusive domain. The uncovering of a government scandal may have profound (and beneficial) ramifications, for instance. Among the more widely syndicated of such columnists are Leonard Lyons, Louella Parsons, Drew Pearson, and Walter Winchell.

4. *Humorous or "funny man" columns.* Even the most serious things in life usually have a lighter side. This type of columnist tries to find that humorous aspect and write an article that will amuse readers. Frederick C. Othman, to mention one, writes on the news from Washington so that it has a different dimension than in the serious "think" pieces. Sometimes these humorous columns spotlight an event more clearly than 1,000 words of expounding and explaining. A variation of the humorous column is the collection of shorter items—poems, wisecracks, bits of dialogue, puns, and so forth. Illustrative of how this is done are the occasional columns of this sort by H. I. Phillips. Other humor columns may also be entirely contributed by readers, although these usually are locally compiled rather than syndicated.

5. *Essay columns.* Just as nature and color editorials have appeal for many a metropolitan daily editor, so the columnist who arouses a similar nostalgia and mood in his writings attracts attention. This requires a perceptiveness or possibly just an overpowering interest

in people that all authors do not possess. John Gould of the *Lisbon Enterprise* of Lisbon Falls, Maine, writes such a column for the *Christian Science Monitor*, and William Chapman White told of life in Adirondack country in the *New York Herald Tribune* and other papers. Although not syndicated, E. B. White's "Talk of the Town" comments in *The New Yorker* exemplify essay column writing at its best. Some columnists travel around the globe to combine the lure of "the elsewhere" with mood. Dean of these was Ernie Pyle in his "*Home Country*" pieces written before World War II.

6. *Personal diary columns.* Closely related to the previous group, diary columns come from the typewriters of public figures. Mrs. Eleanor Roosevelt began such a public diary while she was in the White House as First Lady and readers continued to demand her story years after the death of her husband. Such columns also may emanate from those who fancy they belong in the public spotlight, and most columnists occasionally attempt this kind of writing.

7. *How-to-do or advice columns.* These cover a wide range of subjects from how to introduce your fiancé to your aunt to what to do when you have a stomach ache, or from how to plant a rose garden to what you should do to improve your child's personality. More often than not these appear elsewhere than on editorial pages. However, these columns do contribute to the mores of readers and thus should not be omitted from consideration here.

Some examples may help clarify

How does such a spate of columnists operate? Again each may have his own eccentricities and unusual approach to a topic, but here are some illustrations of some of the more widely circulated varieties of column writing.

Digging up missing background may be done either by a columnist or by a reporter not too shackled by news writing traditions. More and more responsible publications are permitting these attempts to compensate for what has been called "dead-pan reporting." This involves leg work and when a columnist is willing, he can contribute much that readers need to know. He has the time, resources, and background to probe into the little known. He is a reporter de luxe.

Senator Joseph McCarthy had been much in the news when Martin S. Hayden, Washington columnist of the North American Newspaper Alliance, sought to resolve some of the conflicting stories with his own investigating at the Pentagon. The following syndicated column shows how one writer dug out the background on a controversial person in the current news and then passed it on to readers:

BY MARTIN S. HAYDEN

WASHINGTON.—A check of the official record of "Tail Gunner Joe"—now Senator Joseph McCarthy (Rep.) of Wisconsin—indicates some confusion in the story of the Wisconsin solon as a World War II marine.

McCarthy's marine career was made an issue in a goading letter in which former Senator Millard Tydings (Dem.) of Maryland accused him of boasting that he carried "ten pounds of shrapnel in my leg" when, in fact, he never was wounded.

Pentagon records confirm Tydings' assertion that McCarthy never was wounded. They fail to confirm both the repeated McCarthy claim that he entered the marines as a "buck private," and the claim in his behalf that he quit the corps in 1945, at the peak of the war, because of a leg injury that would not heal.

In biographies that he prepared, for the congressional directory, when he became a senator in January, 1946, and for the 1950-'51 "Who's Who in America," McCarthy stated respectively that he entered the marines as "a buck private" and as "a private."

His Pentagon file shows that McCarthy started his service career as a first lieutenant.

The record shows that McCarthy applied in writing

for a marine corps commission on June 2, 1942—two days before a Milwaukee Journal interview in which the then "Judge" McCarthy announced that he was seeking service as "a private, or anything else, in the marines," On July 10, McCarthy wrote Capt. Kenneth L. Moses, at marine headquarters, Washington, canceling a previous request for a two-week delay between acceptance of him as an officer, and his induction. On Aug. 4, the record showed, he was a civilian and a judge, in Appleton, Wis., when he was sworn in as a marine corps officer.

* * *

Tydings' gibe at McCarthy, the "wounded" veteran, was based on a speech the senator made at Badger village, a veterans' housing project at the University of Wisconsin. According to reports of the meeting, a student listener asked McCarthy: "Why do you wear built-up shoes?"

"I'll tell you why I wear this shoe," McCarthy cracked back. "I wear it because I carry ten pounds of shrapnel in my leg."

McCarthy's official file shows no record of his having been either wounded, or injured, while on duty. He did not receive the Purple Heart, which is given to all American fighting men wounded in combat.

The file does contain a letter, written in July, 1943, by one Walter Melchior of P.O. Box 192, Appleton, Wis., who enclosed a newspaper clipping reporting that "Judge" McCarthy had been wounded and asked the marine corps if it was true. M. G. Craig, a marine corps second lieutenant, answered Melchior on July 22.

"A check of the records of this office (i. e. the marine corps headquarters), as well as the records of the bureau of medicine and surgery, navy department," he wrote, "fails to show that a report has been received that Captain McCarthy was injured."

McCarthy's own narration of his military exploits has undergone changes in the last six years, the congressional directory showed.

When he became a senator, McCarthy submitted to the official directory a 226-word biographical sketch which included the statements that he enlisted as a marine private, was later commissioned, was assigned to marine aviation as "a ground officer," was "later qualified" as a tail gunner, and had seventeen "official missions" in the south Pacific, including "strikes over Rabaul, Kahili, Buka, Munda, Balalae and other Japanese airfields."

By February, 1949, the McCarthy biography in the directory was down to 106 words, and, of his war record, said only: "In June of 1942 enlisted in the marine corps and was assigned to marine aviation—served thirty months active duty." This session McCarthy cut the biography to thirty-one words, and made no mention of war service.

*   *   *

McCarthy gave himself the nickname "Tail Gunner Joe" in his campaign literature in the summer of 1944, when he got leave from the marines to make an unsuccessful run against Senator Alexander Wiley (Rep.) of Wisconsin.

His Pentagon record of marine corps service carries no notation of his having qualified for an aerial gunner's wings, or being credited with combat missions. It shows that, starting in 1943, he saw overseas duty as a "squadron intelligence officer" with the First marine aircraft wing in the New Hebrides, Guadalcanal, Munda, New Georgia the British Solomon islands, Efate and Bougainville.

The file contains, however, the record of a citation, issued by Admiral Nimitz's headquarters, after McCarthy had returned from the Pacific, in which the senator was praised "for meritorious and efficient performance of duty" on flights as a marine observer and rear gunner.

The matter of how McCarthy got home in July, 1945, and out of active service the following February, was last explained by a friendly colleague, Senator Harry P. Cain (Rep.) of Washington. On July 13 Cain told the senate that McCarthy got out after he told the marine corps that "it would either be necessary to place him in a naval hospital, or permit him to return home so that his leg (which had been injured) could benefit from medical attention."

The Pentagon file shows that, on Oct. 19, 1944, McCarthy, who had been back in the United States several months, and in Wisconsin to campaign for office, applied in writing for further leave to return home again to straighten out his personal affairs. This was turned down, and he was told that he either could stay on active duty, or resign. The record shows that he was finally "relieved of active duty" on Feb. 20, 1945, and "resigned under honorable conditions" on March 29, 1945.

Presumably submitted in connection with one of McCarthy's applications to get off active duty to show he was "needed" back home was a letter in the file originally written by Arnold F. Murphy, chairman of the circuit judges of Wisconsin. It showed that McCarthy's fellow judges took a dim view of his departing for military service while still holding onto his elective judgeship.

"It may be," Judge Murphy wrote, 'that time will prove the wisdom of your decision and that Judges Hughes and Boileau will not lose their enthusiasm as time goes on in taking over your work, but I am confident that even though they (give their) best and I help them, that your absence from the bench will be a serious hindrance to orderly procedure in the courts in the three counties of your circuit."

North American Newspaper Alliance
—Denver Post

For most newspaper readers, tomorrow holds more interest than yesterday. So it is not unusual that predicting is a big business for syndicated columnists. It does involve dangers, however, because all crystal balls, including those of columnists, become clouded on occasion.

Two famous predictions that backfired with a vengeance involved two respected newspaper commentators: Walter Lippmann and Dorothy Thompson.

While Governor Franklin D. Roosevelt was being considered as a Democratic presidential possibility, Mr. Lippmann wrote this estimate, on January 8, 1932:

> Franklin D. Roosevelt is no crusader. He is no tribune of the people. He is no enemy of entrenched privilege. He is a pleasant man who, without any important qualifications for the office, would very much like to be President.

And Miss Thompson, after an interview with Adolf Hitler, wrote for the March, 1932, *Cosmopolitan Magazine:*

> When I walked in Adolf Hitler's salon in the Kaiserhoff Hotel I was convinced that I was meeting the future dictator of Germany. In something less than fifty seconds I was quite sure that I was not. It took just about that time to measure the startling insignificance of this man who has set the world agog. He is inconsequent and voluble, ill-poised, insecure—the very prototype of the Little Man.

History proved both spectacularly wrong. But as Mr. Lippman himself explained long ago, he changes his opinions "sometimes because they appeared later to be wrong, sometimes because I have lived and learned, and sometimes . . . because events themselves had changed."

To be fair, however, it should be pointed out that many columnists have built themselves into outstanding students of their field and know as much about a situation as any but those in the innermost circle. For instance, any veteran Washington political columnist has served longer on Capitol Hill than most of the committee chairmen. But that still does not mean he knows all the answers.

Batting averages for columnists' predictions are not of themselves reliable clues of their competence because, as Drew Pearson once said, "We can always boost it by predicting things like tomorrow will be Monday."

Just how a syndicated columnist may play it safe is shown by this tongue-in-cheek piece written by Peter Edson for publication the day after the 1952 presidential election:

BY PETER EDSON,

NEA Washington Writer

WASHINGTON, Nov. 5.—An editor called up this week to say he wanted two pieces from this writer for the early editions of Wednesday, the day after election. One was to be good in case Gov. Stevenson won. The other was to be good in case Gen. Eisenhower won. It just shows you how forehanded we get in this business sometimes. Never overlook a bet.

Since both of these pieces were to be written before the election was over and before the votes were counted, it obviously put something of a strain on the writer's interpretive powers as well as on the credulity of the reader.

Then the thought occurred, that instead of doing two pieces on this subject, it could all be wrapped up in one. That way it would avoid the horrible possibility of the wrong piece getting in the paper.

What follows, therefore, is a split personality sample of what you are going to have to read from now till 'Nauguration day, explaining what happened. With tongue in cheek, a wink in the eye and all 20 fingers and toes crossed, here are a couple of forecasts on the type of double-domed analytical, political slush you will have to wade through all fall:

I. If Stevenson Wins

The voters of America have rendered their verdict. They showed unmistakably that they prefer a professional politician to a professional soldier as their commander-in-chief in the White House for the next four years.

The election results were as much an expression of distrust in the Republican party as they were a vote of confidence for the Democratic party. The difficulty in having to carry Sen. Taft, Gov. Dewey and Sen. McCarthy was too much of a load for Ike.

A majority of the voters said unmistakably in this election they did not believe the Republican promises to run the government better, to conduct foreign affairs better, to continue full employment, to promote the best interests of farmers and factory workers, to safeguard the social security and welfare of the common man.

The election results must be set down as a great personal triumph for Gov. Stevenson, in any fair appraisal of the situation. At the beginning of the campaign he was far less known than Gen. Eisenhower, an heroic war leader whose fame reached into every village and farm. Overcoming

II. If Eisenhower Wins

Mr. and Mrs. America have rendered their verdict. They showed unmistakably that they want a brand new administration in Washington, with a complete clean-out of the Truman White House gang for the next four years.

The election results were an expression of repudiation for the Democratic party and all its works. The double handicap of Harry Truman and Dean Acheson, of corruption and communism, were too much for Gov. Stevenson to overcome.

A majority of the voters said unmistakably in this election that they were fed up on Democratic inflation, the disastrous foreign policy in Europe and Asia, the extravagance and waste in Washington and the unmistakable trends toward socialism and labor union domination of the past 20 years.

The election results must be set down as a great personal triumph for Gen. Eisenhower, in any fair appraisal of the situation. He started the campaign with an unfamiliarity of political ways. But he learned rapidly for a political amateur, and he carried his great crusade to every village and farm.

this handicap, overcoming the handicaps of the Truman record, Gov. Stevenson kept plugging away at his campaign "to talk sense to the American people."

And now that he has won, it is the duty of every citizen, Democrat and Republican, to get behind him and give him the fullest possible support for the hard tasks that lie ahead.

The general kept playing his most effective note on "The Need for a Change." And so he won.

And now that he has won, it is the duty of every citizen, Democrats and Republicans of all beliefs, to get behind him and give him the fullest possible support for the hard tasks that lie ahead.

—Newspaper Enterprise Association

A columnist, like an editorial writer, may try to fit known facts into a new and somewhat different arrangement so that his readers will be able to see events more clearly. Obviously, to do this the writer has to know the facts himself, but he also has to possess an almost intuitive perceptiveness. This kind of column grows less from the hurly-burly of spot news reporting than from contemplation in an Ivory Tower. At its best, a column on new relationships, such as we are now discussing, would be written by a newspaperman who had been on the scene but who then retired to think things over quietly before he sat down to type his comments.

After the Atomic Energy Commissioners ruled in the case of Dr. J. Robert Oppenheimer in 1954, Roscoe Drummond wrote a column which combined their findings with those of the Special Security Board and the A.E.C. general manager and likened them to a Supreme Court decision. These "integrated findings" provided a somewhat novel approach. Here is the column in full:

BY ROSCOE DRUMMOND

Nine responsible, respected, trustworthy, Federal officials—three not regularly connected with the government—have now ruled in the case of Dr. J. Robert

Oppenheimer. They are the three members of the Special Security Board headed by Dr. Gordon Gray, Maj. Gen. Kenneth D. Nichols, general manager of the Atomic Energy Commission, and the five A.E.C. commissioners. When you put together all their pertinent decisions, their verdict emerges as follows:

On security—they stand 7 to 2 that Dr. Oppenheimer is a security risk and should be denied further access to restricted data.

On character and associations as the basis for denying security—they stand 7 to 2 that Dr. Oppenheimer's conduct and testimony raise disabling doubts.

On loyalty—they stand 4 registering positive affirmation of Dr. Oppenheimer's loyalty, 3 withholding by silence either affirmation or denial of loyalty, 1 (Commissioner Murray) finding against Dr. Oppenheimer's "loyalty," and 1 (Gen. Nichols) entering no visible opinion.

On safeguarding secrets—they stand 8 to 0 in affirming Dr. Oppenheimer's good record, with Gen. Nichols' view unpublished.

On the H-bomb controversy—they stand 6 to 2 that Dr. Oppenheimer did or said nothing which bears upon or transgresses security. The two majority members of the Gray board found his role in the H-bomb "sufficiently disturbing as to raise doubts." Gen. Nichols' view is not recorded although he approved the Gray board's recommendations.

* * *

These are the essential, integrated findings of the three security reviews which have been given to Dr. Oppenheimer in the last two months—one by the Gray board, another by the chief operating officer of the Atomic Energy Commission and the third and final examination of the evidence by the five commissioners themselves.

On the central finding that Dr. Oppenheimer is a security risk, the verdict is decisive and cumulative.

There is no evidence whatsoever that political or partisan considerations entered into the decision. The nine participants comprise five Democrats or Truman appointees, three Republicans or Eisenhower appointees, and one retired military officer. Of the four A.E.C. commissioners who ruled Dr. Oppenheimer a security risk, two were Truman nominees, two Eisenhower. The one A.E.C. commissioner (Dr. Smyth) who ruled for the scientist was a Truman appointee, and the one Gray board member (Dr. Evans) who also ruled for him was a Republican. The two majority members of the Gray board who found against Dr. Oppenheimer were Democrats.

There is no political nor partisan motivation here.

The reason I have integrated the rulings of the nine officials bearing upon the principal aspects of the case and have cited its non-partisan—or at least its bi-partisan—basis is that it seems to me the verdict is comparable to a court decision, and therefore deserving comparable respect and response.

*   *   *

Courts have been known to send innocent men to jail. It is our right and the proper exercise of free speech and assembly to argue that a jury has made a mistake or that the Supreme Court has rendered a bad decision. But their verdicts and their decisions require our respect and our acceptance if we are to maintain the orderly processes of government.

Some deeply disagree with the 7–to–2 decision on Dr. Oppenheimer.

Some deeply disagree with the 9–to–0 decision on anti-segregation.

Neither decision is above criticism, above dissent or entirely beyond the possibility of being reversed by history; at least the Supreme Court's decision is a reversal of previous verdicts.

*   *   *

Obviously the analogy between the nine participants in the security review of Dr. Oppenheimer and the Supreme Court can be overdrawn. I do not argue that dissent should be muted or that disagreement is "disloyal." I do not argue that respect and acceptance of such verdicts require silence. I argue only that respect for an acceptance of the judicial and quasi-judicial judgments of the government are part of the social contract of orderly democracy.

The verdict is an exceedingly strong "reproof" to Dr. Oppenheimer. If new evidence should ever reverse the dominant judgment, we will owe this man unmeasured atonement.

But the verdict has been honestly rendered by good men after faithfully hearing the evidence in procedures transparently fair. There is reason, therefore, to honor the verdict.

—New York Herald Tribune

The literary essay has almost vanished from contemporary dailies. Infrequently, you may find it condensed into a change of pace editorial. A column is about the only other place in which it appears. When a syndicated writer wants to reminisce or grow nostalgic, an essay is the solution.

Years ago, when Heywood Broun was asked why he wrote so much about himself, he replied that on the subject of Broun he was certain he was the world's greatest authority. Some contemporary columnists have followed his example and written personal essays, although possibly not in the same quest for authenticity.

Following is an example of the essay column. Max Lerner describes in it his personal efforts to meet deadlines and reveals why columnists mark pieces "AOT":

BY MAX LERNER

When I first started writing for daily newspapers, almost a decade ago, I was told that a four- or five-a-week column set a stiff pace. You never know (my mentors said wisely) when you will have a stomach ache or lose a leg or get into a crash or stop for one drink too many or just forget. So have a few "barrel" pieces ready, they said: the kind the editor marks AOT—Any Old Time—and files away with a sigh of security.

I did it a few times, but it never really worked. Whenever I was one ahead, it would be only a few days before
I would get lazy and consume my substance. The rainy-
day column would be hauled out and used on the sun-
niest of days, when I was able-bodied and sound of mind
and wind, and could have written something. Then I'd
be back where I started.

* * *

As a result, I have been a day-to-day, hand-to-mouth
wastrel. This has meant some close calls. Often I have
found myself in some small Southern or Midwestern
town, after a lecture at the college or local forum, followed by the routine entertainment. Say it's midnight,
and the local telegraph office has been closed since sun-
down, and the only open one is 50 miles away, and you
have two hours before deadline for filing and you have
left your notes at home, and you haven't an idea in
your head. That's when you review your wasted life, and
wish you had put an AOT away in the editor's safe.

It's even worse abroad. Say you have been to a Paris
cellar-cafe, and have found a ravishing girl who insists
on talking about Sartre to you in a language that requires your concentration, and you take her to an all-
night joint that has good scrambled eggs, and you are
about to surrender yourself to Existentialism—and
then you recall the home office, and you leave her to
write something for the mail plane. It doesn't contribute
to Franco-American friendship.

* * *

Some years ago I got a scare. The boys on the desk had
a copy of my page printed up, with a big blank space
where my column was supposed to be, and in the center
of it a tiny notice that the space was reserved for me
but my copy had not shown up. For a moment it shook
me. But when I discovered the hoax, I grew cynical
about all threats.

Yet I should like to say, with modest boastfulness,
that in almost ten years—during which I calculate the
dismaying total of at least 2,000 columns—I can't re-

member missing a deadline. Maybe it's because I'm such a healthy ox, or maybe there is some Puritan in the marrow of my conscience.

* * *

The question remains: why the compulsion to wait for the last moment? I think the world is divided into two categories of people: those who arrive at the railroad station an hour and a half ahead of time and wave the train in, and those who dash up the platform and board it on the run, as in spy movies. Nature or nurture put me somehow into the second class.

No doubt this is something neurotic—the fag-end of the romantic tradition about living dangerously on margins. Maybe the psychiatrists have a name for the disease—some kind of "deadline compulsion." I'm afraid to ask one of them, lest I be turned over to the American Psychoanalytic Assn. as Exhibit A. I should then have to admit to them that I'm this way about everything—catching planes, coming upstairs to dinner, walking into a class room or lecture hall, applying for passports or visas, showing up for radio shows. No doubt, if I ever reach the Heavenly gates, I'll just manage to get under the ropes before they close.

* * *

Let me say, in my defense, that too much leeway is degenerating to any craftsman. Alas, no one put a deadline on the book I am trying to finish now, and as a result I have already taken seven years. If I start a column with hours to spare, it sprawls over the terrain. Maybe I need a deadline to give me moorings—at one end, anyway. Like the sonnet form, or the rondel, it sets a frame for your work. If you never had to think about a budget you would enjoy spending less than you do. The deadline is my budget; it gives a finality to my waywardness.

* * *

P.S. I had hoped to consign this column for reserve stock, as an AOT. But it never worked out that way until the deadline—which is now.

—*New York Post*

Frederick C. Othman blended annoyance, humor, and a personal touch in the following illustration of how a skilled writer combines a variety of reactions into a single column:

BY FREDERICK C. OTHMAN

WASHINGTON, Nov. 25.—This is National Cage Bird Week and a good time to buy a canary. It also is National Accordion Week and on that I have no comment.

National Cat Week as sponsored by the regional National Cat Week, Inc., of Pittsburgh, which is not to be confused with any other national cat week, has just passed. So has National Tuna Week and I suppose I'll have to wait another year before I can feed the cat a can of tuna fish.

What I'm driving at is a really serious national crisis: the shortage of weeks. Next year, as usual, will have only 52 weeks, but the forces for good in this nation so far have designated more than 200 special weeks for 1954. To celebrate them properly is going to take a good deal of doubling up and I doubt if I'll even survive the second week in May.

It is National Frozen Food Week, National Cotton Week, Armed Forces Week, and National Pickle Week. The following week, among numerous things, is National Foot Health Week and not a moment too soon.

* * *

The good old Commerce Department always comes up in the spring of the year with a list of special weeks, but a far better list of weeks I have received from Henry William Marks, assistant publisher of Printers' Ink, the advertising men's trade paper. It missed nothing, including the week of Jan. 15, during which will be celebrated the anniversary of the tea bag.

On Jan. 20 comes Large Size Week No. 1. On April 25 arrives Large Size Week No. 2. I thought maybe these weeks were dedicated to stylish stouts, but it turns out that two different outfits are sponsoring separate weeks to push the sale of economy-size packages of toothpaste and shampoo.

Almost simultaneously in January will arrive National Potato Chip Week and then comes February, which is Large Size Month, devoted to sale of whisky in large-sized bottles.

February also includes National Kraut and Frankfurter Week and National Peanut Week. It is in addition National Butter Frostings Month, which, I understand has to do with the icing on cakes.

* * *

March brings Pancake Day, National Smile Week, and Dried Fruit Week. April has weeks devoted to hobbies, babies, gardening, photography, strawberries and cream, laughs, honey for breakfast, and daughters. The week for daughters is in charge of the National Cedar Chest Assn. of Chicago.

May is the month for National Sun Glass Week, the Milk Festival, hearth-baked Bread Week and National Secretaries (be nice to same) Week, while June produces Comfort Week.

June also includes National Bow Tie Week and National Iced Tea Time. July is the month of ice cream and vegetables. August is National Sandwich Month as sponsored by the Wheat Flour Institute, but September is Butter Sandwich Month, as promoted by the National Dairy Assn.

—United Feature Syndicate

To edit or not to edit?

After a publisher or editor has signed a contract for a syndicated column, what then? Does he process it like a Rotary luncheon talk in which he spots a couple of misquotations by his reporter and edits them? Or does he only put paragraph marks on the copy because the paper has an obligation to print Mr. Syndicated's opinions uncut and unchanged? Responsible newspapermen line up on each side of this argument.

The problem is not a new one. More than a quarter of a century ago, the *New York World* printed two of Heywood Broun's passionate columns on the Sacco-Vanzetti case and then directed that he "select other subjects for his next articles." But Broun refused and left the paper after its publisher, Ralph Pulitzer, insisted that "it is the function of a writer to write and the function of an editor to edit."

When Harold L. Ickes' first syndicated column was distributed in 1946, editors were told it was to be neither "expurgated nor amended." Paul C. Smith, then editor of the *San Francisco Chronicle*, cancelled his contract with the syndicate, insisting his paper would not compromise "the principle of unhampered exercise of free editorial judgment."

Applauding this action, *Editor and Publisher* (April 6, 1946) commented editorially:

Any editor who agrees to print anything and everything a columnist may choose to write is abdicating his editor's chair. . . How many editors would agree to print verbatim an article by a free lance writer, or even an important local official, that the editor had not read? Not many. Is there any difference between that and the offerings of a "name" columnist?

But a week later *Editor and Publisher* clarified its viewpoint:

We endorsed only the time-honored editor's right to edit copy, which never has, and we hope never will, be interpreted to give an editor the right to change the written opinion of a contributor.

Dwight E. Sargent of the *Portland* (Maine) *Press Herald* and a former N.C.E.W. chairman, put it this bluntly in *The Masthead* (Summer, 1950):

Editors using columns owe it to their readers to be selective, not to be afraid to use pencil or wastebasket. I am not suggesting the editing of syndicated columns to conform to the opinion of newspapers in which they appear. This, I think, is done too often. My point is simply that if editors are responsible to their readers for the honesty and decency of editorial page content, they should not make exceptions of syndicated columnists. Naturally, we verge here on matters of personal opinion, but there are some fundamental principles of factual and fair news interpretation, and of clear writing, on which I think a majority of editors would agree.

Mr. Sargent raised the question of motivation, which can plague anyone who edits or kills a syndicated column. Was it really misinformation and bad taste? Or was it an opinion that outraged the editor's sensibilities? Partly because of the complexity and sometimes the impossibility of separating motives, some newspapers print uncut what they get from syndicated columnists.

Answering a reader's query why the paper published Westbrook Pegler's "singularly offensive descent into goulishness," the *Louisville Times* explained editorially:

Once or twice some years ago we killed a Pegler column that seemed peculiarly scurrilous to us. But we got to thinking about it and came to the conclusion that the problem for us is not whether to publish Pegler on any particular day, depending on our opinion of his content, but whether to publish him at all. If we were going to publish him at all for the sake of presenting opinions generally different from ours, then we thought that we ought, to be strictly honest, to publish him in entirety, instead of attempting to edit him through the eyes of such long-time Roosevelt supporters as ourselves.

Up to now that has been our policy. It is a policy, of course, subject to change. But the change, if it were made, would be to drop Pegler altogether, rather than intermittently on a basis of how violently we happened to object to him one day or the next. After all, our dropping him would not be the end of him, except for a relatively few of his readers.

Shortly after President Eisenhower's inauguration, the Louisville editors did decide to drop Pegler's column. Mark Ethridge explained, "We felt obligated to carry him as long as there was a Democratic administration, but we didn't feel that obligation when the Republicans not only had a spokesman, but the primary spokesman in the country."

Most responsible editors and publishers agree that to kill syndicated columns solely because they disagree with a paper's policy is, as *Editor and Publisher* once described it, "a short-sighted editorial policy." Yet columnists can cite dozens, if not hundreds, of cases where their opinions have been cut, edited, or killed. One Washington writer had more than a quarter of all his columns killed by one metropolitan daily during a ten-week period, yet its publisher declined to release the syndicate from its contract, as it requested, so the pieces could appear in a rival paper. To determine in all cases whether editing and killing a syndicated column reflected the "unhampered exercise of free editorial judgment" or whether it was intellectual dictatorship would require the wisdom of a Solomon. Certainly any editing of syndicated material should not be done frivolously.

Local columns have tremendous popularity

Locally written columns, whether they are comments or gossip, are tremendously popular. And why not? Just as local news outpulls comparable national or world news, so local columns can outdraw the syndicated variety. Difficulties, however, include finding a staff member who can competently perform such duties and then getting the money to detach him from the other assignments. Where it has been done, results for the paper have been most rewarding. For the columnist, it frequently meant that he was soon drafted by a syndicate for wider audiences and more money.

Ralph McGill of the *Atlanta Constitution*, Bruce Gustin of the *Denver Post*, and Royce Brier of the *San Francisco Chronicle* exemplify the successful home-grown opinion columnist. All three are featured writers of their papers. Years ago Gustin replaced the entire editorial page. Both McGill's and Brier's columns have been printed on the first pages and, at other times, on the editorial pages. These writers do not need to concentrate exclusively on either local or regional topics because their keener understanding of what their own readers think and what they want to know about national and world affairs provides a built-in local angle. Syndicated columnists have to write for the man on Broadway, Michigan Boulevard or Hollywood Boulevard, not simply for the man in his own Main Street.

The "Uncle Dudley" column in the *Boston Daily Globe* attempts to bring personality to editorial page opinion. Louis B. Seltzer, editor of the *Cleveland Press*, contributes for his editorial page infrequent columns which range from philosophical comments to sentimental reminiscences of his own family life. These colorful, human articles are simply signed "L. B. S." and consistently they rank near the top in readership surveys.

May Craig, often a sharp-tonged questioner at presidential press conferences in Washington, concentrates not on a single paper but on a group in the fairly homogeneous state of Maine. One editor credited her with giving "more zip, regional flavor, and provocative thinking" than any syndicated columnist ever could. That "regional flavor" is one thing that her syndicated colleagues could never match.

The breezy, gossipy local column appeals to readers, too. In Minneapolis, for instance, Cedric Adams' items are read with interest, then collected for a wider audience that saw them in advertisements in *The New Yorker* or published in book form. Herb Caen, who has been on both the *San Francisco Chronicle* and *Examiner*, has a large following in the Golden Gate area.

For the small country weekly, a syndicated column boiled down from those that have been printed earlier in larger form in dailies becomes little more than an embarrassed bow to newspaper conventions. At worst, it simply fills space that otherwise might have been better used for news stories or advertisements. But a locally written column may by-pass the objective thinking of a calm, deliberative mind concerned with editorials; it may be a free-wheeling extension of an editor's personality without becoming too time-consuming.

Charles A. Sprague, former Oregon governor and editor of the Salem *Oregon Statesman*, started a successful personal column during World War II and spotted it in column one, page one, with an usual break-over to the editorial page. He said a column "permits more informal style in the treatment of material," while the front page position "helps to snare the eye of the reader when he opens up the paper, and the carry-over exposes him to the editorial page." The regular editorial columns were maintained.

Talking at the College of Journalism, University of Colorado, in 1951, George Ver Steeg, editor of the *Pella* (Iowa) *Chronicle*, said a personal column had become a widely adopted "fine companion" to the conventional editorial page and, on some weeklies, a substitute. He described the personal column on the weekly paper as "a proper place for observations not of editorial stature, a fine place for humorous quips, a place for compliments to deserving people, a POT-POURRI if you please, an outlet particularly for wit, and occasionally, a vehicle for community service."

After World War II, columnists turned up from an unexpected source when some senators and representatives in Washington began writing news letters to the folks in the home district. These appeared usually in weeklies, with the pay-off in publicity, not cash. The congressional columnists obviously made no attempt to be non-partisan; however, they provided a local angle to Washington news that won wide readership. Some told of their own hopes and frustrations; others included sidelights on the capital's social life after the fashion of a gossip writer.

"Who is the best columnist?"

Some people ask, "Who is the best columnist?" The truthful reply to that should be, "Best for what?" The column that may be "best" for an Eastern metropolitan newspaper may not be "best" for a medium-sized town in Texas or a small community in Colorado. Who then is to determine the standards for measuring bestness?

Several attempts have been made to rate syndicated columnists. When Leo C. Rosten asked Washington correspondents in 1936 what daily column was "most significant, fair and reliable," 25 of the 77 who answered selected Raymond Clapper. Paul Mallon received 13 votes; Walter Lippmann, 9; and Arthur Krock, 7. Henry F. Pringle reported on a comparable poll eight years later in the *Saturday Review of Literature* (October 14, 1944). Of a total of 160 polled, 51 picked Arthur Krock as the Washington correspondent "who exerts through his writings the greatest influence on Washington;" 32, Drew Pearson; and 19, Walter Lippmann. Asked for the correspondent "who exerts through his writings the greatest influence on the nation," 56 selected Drew Pearson; 28, Walter Lippmann; and 13, Arthur Krock. In reply to a question to name the Washington correspondent "who, in my opinion, does the best all-around job as measured in terms of reliability, fairness, and ability to analyze the news," Thomas L. Stokes was first with 25 votes, followed by Marquis Childs with 23. Bert Andrews and Roscoe Drummond tied with eight each. Krock, who rated first in Washington influence, received seven votes while Pearson, who was first in national influence ratings, got only two supporters here. Professor A. Gayle Waldrop of the College of Journalism, University of Colorado, reported in *Editor and Publisher* (September 19, 1953) on answers from 111 editorial chiefs or writers whom he had asked what columnists they considered "the best all-around, in terms of reliability, fairness and ability to analyze the news." Walter Lippmann nosed out David Lawrence, 54 to 53. Following were Marquis Childs, 33; the Alsop brothers, 32; George Sokolsky, 20; Peter Edson, 14; Thomas L. Stokes, 12; and Doris Fleeson, 11.

In the battle to climb the popularity ladder, columnists have been under extreme pressure to outdistance their rivals, to make their writings more dramatic, and, in short, to sensationalize to the limit. Most of them have been guilty of this sometimes and a few of them make it almost a daily performance. Those who indulge in predictions are most prone to this practice. The 1948 presidential election pricked practically all of the columnists and commentators—but that lesson was soon forgotten. The lusty battle to get more attention—and more contracts—goes on.

In picking a columnist for his paper, an editor or publisher has to consider such an invited guest's record for truth and reliable reporting. Then he would do well to visualize a typical reader and ask himself, "Is this columnist best for him?" After all, the thinking should include the question, "Best for what?" A syndicated columnist who reinforces the publication's own editorial policy may stimulate neither thinking nor circulation; chitchat from Hollywood or Broadway may provide interesting reading but do little to mould public opinion.

THIRTEEN

Explanatory writing within news stories

THE ASSOCIATED PRESS REFERENCE BOOK, DISTRIBUTED IN APRIL 1947, said this under the heading, "Explain the Unusual":

One recurring flaw in our news writing lies in our failure to provide adequate explanatory background for the benefit of the average reader. Frequently we fail to define unusual terms or phrases; to explain historical or other allusions; or to tell the background of political, economic or other groups. These all are well-known to the writer but almost never to the average reader.

Since the end of World War II, increasing attention by newspapermen has centered on problems of supplying readers with as full and complete a story as possible. Yet this trend is not a new one. As many publishers, editors, and reporters have pointed out repeatedly, journalistic ethics always stressed giving readers the whole story. Most newspapermen approve *The New York Times'* slogan of "All The News That's Fit to Print" although some have lamented that few, if any, publications can really do it.

In the great devotion to the unattainable goal of pure objectivity, as was pointed out in the first chapter, "dead-pan" reporting came into vogue several decades ago. The first paragraph of a United Press memorandum to bureau managers demonstrates that some newsmen were dissatisfied with objectivity even while it was in high favor generally: "More background, more interpretation, more explanation, more 'lowdown'—in our handling of the news—that's the latest appeal of editors." What was the date on that memo? October 17, 1933.

Editors felt the same way 20 years later. Those replying to a United Press questionnaire in 1953 voted two to one in favor of more explanatory and interpretive material from the press association on such subjects as United States economic developments, science, and foreign news. The editors were almost equally divided on whether interpretation should be written into the main story or carried separately.

The name frequently varies but the concept persists

When newspaper and magazine writers and editors get together to discuss the use of explanation, interpretation, or background in news writing, the first thing that advantageously can be done is to agree on terminology. Probably few areas in journalism are as beclouded by semantic troubles or word-fog as this one. Lester Markel of *The New York Times* gave a valuable definition before the 1953 General Assembly of the International Press Institute:

As I see it, interpretation—or background (I make no difference)—is the deeper sense of the news. It gives meaning to the bare facts; it places an event in the larger flow of events. It is in short, setting, sequence and, above all, significance.

There is a tremendous difference between interpretation and opinion; the first is objective, or as objective as human beings can make it; the second is subjective. Let me illustrate:

To report that the Kremlin is launching a peace offensive is news;

To explain why the Kremlin is setting the doves cooing at this time is interpretation;

To state that any Kremlin peace offer should be rejected out of hand is opinion.

Interpretation is an essential part of the news columns; opinion should be confined, almost religiously, to the editorial columns. This is a prime point and it cannot have too much emphasis.

Now I realize that many editors believe that the moment you depart from what they call the "facts" and attempt explanation, you move inevitably into the minestrewn field of opinion.

371

This argument falls down, I hold, because it is based on a false assumption: namely that the attainment of pure objectivity is possible in journalism.

At the same I.P.I. gathering, George H. Pipal, general European manager for the United Press, backed Markel by saying, "I do not think the story has ever been written which did not contain interpretation in one sense or another."

Yet, as critics of the interpretive approach to news writing explain, it is exceedingly hard to set up boundaries for what has been called "this whole tricky field."

Lloyd M. Felmly of the *Newark News* rightly warned, "The reporter's impressions must not be used to make up a reader's mind." But Carl E. Lindstrom of the *Hartford Times*, with equal correctness, listed "letting mere accuracy substitute for truth" as one of the seven deadly sins of news writing.

Interpretation, explanation, or background should not be used to make the reader come to a certain conclusion. It should not even, if it is humanly possible to avoid it, give him a shove in any direction. The human factor is what bothers most of those who eye jaundicedly these insertions into news stories. What is wanted are explanatory facts and interpretive details, not opinions and not points of view.

The business of a "third dimension of basic truth in news coverage" admittedly is complicated and dangerous. It is more than a balancing act between two sides of a dispute. This was pointed out aptly by an unidentified editor quoted in a 1952 Associated Press Managing Editors' report:

> Too often we get both sides of a controversial issue and shout our objectivity to high heaven. But the story we carried was far from the *truth*. This business of getting at a basic, fundamental truth in a news situation can be most difficult. And can lead to a loss of objectivity. There is work yet to be done in this field.

James F. O'Neil, past national commander of the American Legion and publisher of its magazine, warned that interpretive news handling made it possible for "the wrong kind of people" to exert terrific propaganda pressures. True, but as Barry Bingham, president of the *Courier-Journal* and *Louisville Times* Company, pointed out in the 1954 Kenneth C. Hogate Journalism Lecture at DePauw University:

> We need to be extremely careful not to take advantage of our readers in such reporting. A poor or unprincipled reporter could blot his story all over with the inkstains of his own prejudice. A good reporter can keep a story honest and yet double its usefulness to the reader who must read as he runs.

What is needed seems to be more competent, trained, honest reporters rather than rededication to an old sterile objectivity.

When journalists talk about "a good story," most of them unconsciously mean the full recital, not just some pigmy fragment without attention to what went before. They point with pride to news items that provide the complete picture and the real meaning. Usually it is only when they get down to the hair-splitting of philosophical discussions at professional conventions or during talks before college students or women's clubs that they resort to this departmentalized thinking. Why should the quest for truth take second place to an ideal of so-called objectivity? Why, indeed, if it really is a search for truth?

Two purely mechanical difficulties do arise, but they need not be unsurmountable. Interpretation, explanation, or backgrounding usually requires more words. That means more space in news columns and more time on press association or leased wires. It also implies that repetitions will take place. A Frankenstein monster of mounting details is conceivable; this might increase operating costs, already near record high figures. So common sense must be added to the already exacting qualifications of the successful interpretive news reporter.

Dr. Edwin E. Slosson, who helped pioneer in newspaper coverage of science, once illustrated how translating terminology might be carried too far and thus might waste precious space. He said that almost all readers would understand a correspondent who wrote:

> At zero hour the barrage was raised and the poilu and doughboy sprang over the top sticking their bayonets into the boche.

But, Dr. Slosson pointed out, this might have been explained and expanded as follows by an over-conscientious writer:

> At zero hour—to use the military term for the time set for the beginning of an offensive—the barrage—that is to say the line on which the artillery fire is directed—was rased and the poilu—this is a French slang term for soldier, meaning "hairy" and corresponding to our "rough-neck"—and the doughboy, this is an American slang term for infantryman derived from the round buttons worn in the Civil war or the "dobe" huts inhabited in the Mexican war or the pipe-clayed belts of the Revolutionary war or because the secretary of war was named Baker—sprang over the top—that is to say surmounted the parapet of the entrenchments—sticking their bayonets—a weapon invented at Bayonne, France, in 1650—into the boche—a contemptuous term referring to the Germans, probably an abbreviation of *caboche* or *blockhead* originally applied to Alsatians.

Explanatory writing aims at making the news story clear to the typical newspaper or magazine readers. If most of them know the term, then why waste space explaining it? If the background is generally known, then do not write it into the story. If the significance is obvious, then leave it out. But if these things are obscure or little known, then put them in. Above all, however, explanations should not be clumsy and unreadable.

Far more than radio broadcasting, television revealed a traditional weakness in United States newspapering. Now it is possible for a reader to sit at national political conventions, to witness United Nations debates, to take a ringside seat at championship boxing bouts, to hear and see for himself official announcements settling a nation-wide labor dispute. The reader can join the

reporter at the event. What does that mean? Interest in a correspondent's play-by-play has dropped off because the reader, too,
was there, thanks to electronics. He may check his own impressions against those of the reporter but what he wants more is background, interpretation, explanation, or the facts that a good
journalist knows but does not learn at the scene of the story.

Reporters in the past too frequently concentrated on the
"what" of the news and neglected the rest of the conventional
five W's and H of news writing. To meet the challenge from
competing media, the press needs to tell the "why" and "how" of
the news and, less often, concentrate on the "who," "what,"
"where," and "when." News weekly magazines have done this
from the beginning. More and more newspaper editors and publishers are using the new techniques. The 1952 report of the
APME Creative Newspapering Committee, for instance, lamented that too many editors had been "almost primitive in the
slavish worship of the terse 50-word bulletin" and thus had helped
to choke off any chance for imaginative, creative work.

Some journalists hesitate to venture into the field of interpretation and explanation because there are few ground rules. The
chances of making mistakes are tremendous, as nearly everyone
will admit. But to stand by the conventions also involves dangers,
as was pointed out in Chapter One. News has become more complex. Whole new areas are now reported for the first time. The
artful presentation of half-truths has seldom been more expertly
done.

The press, to keep its place as a major channel for communications, cannot stand still in a changing era. Raymond H. Mc-
Connell, Jr., of the *Lincoln* (Nebraska) *State Journal* told the
1951 APME meeting that newspapers should face their responsibility "to make the affairs that affect his destiny, fortune and
pursuit of happiness meaningful to the man and woman in
Trampled Terraces, our little residential neighborhood." This
can be done through interpretive reporting, which he called
"just a 75 cent word for damned good reporting." Then he added:

The challenge to the American press is to devise ways of making the average individual want to be fully informed as to the swirling tides of events which threaten to engulf him because he neither comprehends nor tries very hard to comprehend—since they are, as he says, "beyond" him.

Unless the newspapers meet this challenge, their readers undoubtedly will turn to other media for enlightenment and understanding of events. The press thus would be abdicating because it could not present the news so as to make it meaningful.

The primary function of the press is to supply the news, all the news the readers need and want to have, or, as James Reston of *The New York Times* put it, the "essential truth" of the story, not just the literal or surface truth. This function of the press can only be carried out if reporters and editors explain, interpret, background, or put into perspective what has happened. Call it what you wish—but the job should be done. Otherwise, one of the key foundations on which a sound, informed public opinion rests will collapse. Is it too far-fetched to wonder whether democracy itself could survive such a disaster?

And now some case histories

Probably the best way to illustrate what may happen when explanation, background, or interpretation is omitted is to cite some concrete examples that members of the press have discussed when they got together in recent years:

CASE ONE. In July, 1951, William N. Oatis, Associated Press correspondent, was convicted for "spying" in Prague and sentenced to ten years in jail. Suppose that the United States press had insisted in printing the following strictly factual and accurate beginning on the story:

> PRAGUE—Associated Press Correspondent William
> N. Oatis confessed today that he had acted as a spy. He
> told the Communist court in Pankrak Prison at the

opening of his trial that he used a number of Czechs as informers.

"Did you carry out espionage?" the president of the court asked.

"Yes," Oatis replied.

Sounds like a bit from *Pravda*, does it not? Without the background, the story is grossly misleading. What is missing is shown by this sentence which *The New York Times* correspondent Drew Middleton included well up in his story:

> Its [the trial's] object seems to be to prove that Mr. Oatis and all American or British correspondents working behind the Iron Curtain, save those of The Daily Worker, are spies and should be treated as such.

CASE TWO. When Congress in 1949 considered a bill to raise pay in the armed services, news stories reported that privates first class would receive a three per cent increase and brigadier generals a 50 per cent increase. What were newspaper readers' reactions to that information? That the proposal favored the "brass" at the expense of the G.I.

What was the missing background? Pay of enlisted men had been increased numerous times during recent years; general and flag officers had not had an increase since 1908.

The bill died for that session. Why? Possibly because it was bad legislation. But who can discount entirely the reactions of readers who protested because they believed the proposal discriminated against enlisted men?

CASE THREE. Competing media occasionally rush in to fill a vacuum in daily newspaper coverage and thus expose defects. A rash of prison riots broke out across the nation in 1952 and 1953. News services generally covered in good fashion the spot news of the rioting. Yet here was a social problem: the causes of these mass rebellions and what could be done, if anything, to prevent a recurrence. Little attempt was made by most daily newspapers to explore this aspect of the story.

377

A television network, a mass circulation magazine, and a book author found fruitful material in what the newspapers neglected. The National Broadcasting Company television built a carefully documented performance upon scores of interviews from twelve prisons where there had been riots. The *Saturday Evening Post* printed a four-part series giving the background on the Jackson, Michigan, riots. John Bartlow Martin's book, *Break Down the Walls* (Ballantine, 1954) focused attention on the whole question of prisons as social correctives.

CASE FOUR. After Joseph Stalin died, the free world awaited clues to the probable conduct of the new regime under Georgi Malenkov. When Premier Malenkov made his initial public addresses, there was great interest. Yet the biggest news (and this time the United States press did display it) was not what he said but what he did not say. Omitted was the usual abuse of the Western powers. Reporters pointed this out and highlighted a temporary modification in Kremlin policies. Without this perspective, this background, the story would have had considerably less meaning for the general public.

CASE FIVE. Reporting of the activities of Senator Joseph McCarthy, Wisconsin Republican, possibly caused more discussion among members of the press than any other single news source during the early 1950's. Admittedly there have been numerous self-contradictions in what Senator McCarthy has told the press. Many people remember that he said at different times the State Department had 205, or 57, or 81 Communists. His other inconsistencies were less well known. Should the responsible reporter covering a new statement by the Wisconsin senator mention his earlier statements on the same subject, pointing out any discrepancies? He should, even if it means he has to become what Elmer Davis called "a McCarthy specialist."

Of course, there is no reason to confine this kind of news coverage to the senator from Wisconsin. Every news source in Washington or elsewhere should get it so that readers of the press may have the truth, the whole truth, which can help them to be informed and to remain free.

These case histories could be increased endlessly but these five give an idea of what background, explanation, or interpretation may do and what may happen when it is missing.

It is done in a variety of ways

How does a writer know when to put explanatory material into his own copy?

One test that might be most helpful is for him to visualize that mythical "milkman in Omaha" that newspapermen cite as a typical reader and ask himself, "Will that 'milkman in Omaha' understand what I mean?"

Here is an example that may explain the point. In a farewell statement, the retiring state budget director mentioned the size of the state's tax stabilization reserve funds. The reporter, of course, knew about these funds and could explain them to anyone who asked him. When he wrote his story, however, he might forget that the typical reader of his publication did not have the same background that he had. He thus would do well to ask himself: "Will the 'milkman in Omaha' know what the state's tax stabilization reserve funds are?" The truthful answer would have to be "No." So the reporter would have to explain it.

Recalling that these funds have been called the "rainy day funds," he might write:

> The retiring official reported that the tax stabilization reserves, sometimes called the "rainy day funds," amounted to $142,000,000.

While this sentence does give a catchy explanation of the reserves, it still does not make it entirely clear to those readers who want to bring the news into sharp focus. So the reporter decided that he had to explain it in even more detail. This time he took a full paragraph to do it. One newspaper actually did handle it this way:

> These reserves can be drawn upon to meet current operating expenses in any year that budget revenues fail to reach estimates because of a change in economic conditions. Withdrawals from the fund to make up deficits must be replaced within five years.

And that gave the reader a fairly adequate explanation of what the retiring budget director meant by the phrase "tax stabilization reserve funds."

Most frequently a writer will draw on his own background to supply the explanatory material. If he is a competent reporter and if he has been assigned to the story or beat for any length of time, he probably will have the information well in mind. But suppose that it is an initial break or a new development on which the writer lacks the needed details. What then?

The writer may obtain the missing information through interviewing the news source. It is self-evident that the reporter should have the facts—all the facts, not just the surface ones—in hand before he attempts to explain them to readers of his publication.

Sometimes a news source is unavailable. In that case, the writer should consult reference books in the morgue and clippings that provide background. For what these references may be, check back to Chapter Four, especially pages 120 to 123.

Another possibility is for the writer to get in touch, probably by telephone, with some specialist or expert in the field who is a friend of the paper and would be willing to explain the whole situation as he saw it.

If the writer wanted to interpret what a news development meant, he should make every effort to insure that his article is grounded on honest facts and is not just a reflection of his own biases and prejudices. One way of doing this is to talk to as many experts as possible. If they disagree, then the speculation should reflect some of these doubts, too.

Explanatory writing may vary from a single word or phrase to a whole series of background articles. This section will show how it may be incorporated into news stories; the following chapter will discuss background and interpretation when they take a whole story rather than just an insert into the conventional news item.

Sometimes the explanatory writing is riveted right into the lead paragraph as in the following:

> WASHINGTON—(AP)—The government today estimated this year's corn crop at 3,525,741,000 (B) bushels—a figure which virtually assures federal controls next year to hold down production.

As an Associated Press memo said in citing this lead paragraph, "No chance of 'what it means' being edited out of that one."

Other times, the explanatory writing may be several paragraphs inserted well up in the news story so that the reader will better understand the current chapter in a continuing story—and there are few news items that are not continuing stories. In an article on new methods for the early detection of cancer of the digestive tract as demonstrated before an American Medical Association convention, William L. Laurence of *The New York Times* wrote the following as his second and third paragraphs:

> As cancer in its early stages is most amenable to treatment and possible eradication, the development of improved methods for the detection of one of the most deadly forms of the disease may serve in time as an effective new weapon in the fight against the second major natural killer of mankind. The new method, it was asserted, has led to the diagnosis of cancer of the digestive tract with an accuracy of 90 per cent.
>
> This opens the possibility that the lives of about 74,000 of the 82,000 who die annually from cancer of the

stomach, colon and the esophagus may be saved as a result of the perfection and widespread application of the new diagnostic methods.

The veteran science writer drew on his general knowledge of cancer and wrote in the necessary perspective for *The Times'* readers to appreciate the significance of the medical advances reported.

Now, let us look at the use of a word or phrase to explain.

Most readers know their neighboring communities well but they are foggy on far-away places of which they have heard. When the printed name jumps up at them, they think, "Just where is that, anyway?"

In a story from Hong Kong, the Associated Press once put in the phrase, "this British colony" to assist the readers in placing it. After mention of St. Cyr, a *Washington Post and Times Herald* writer added, "the French West Point." A *Chicago Daily News* reporter added after mention of the Gatineau, "north of Ottawa," and after the Laurentians, "above Montreal." *Time* explained after a reference to Esso's refinery at Fawley in Hampshire, "aproximately 83 miles southwest of London."

On the other hand, some places are so well known that identifications are seldom included. For instance, Hollywood need not be described as "a part of Los Angeles, California, and center of the United States motion picture industry." Or the Statue of Liberty as "a giant statue, on Bedloe Island, of a woman with a torch in one upraised hand and a tablet in the other." Nor do to, add a few more, Westminster Abbey, the Eiffel Tower, and Pearl Harbor require further pinpointing.

People may be identified by their positions or some distinction—either good or bad—in their careers. Public office holders, officers in the armed services, doctors, ministers, and professors almost always are identified by their positions. Nobel and Pulitzer prize winners have news tags that follow them the rest of their lives. While even a cub reporter would think of using these handles for identification, they actually comprise explanatory writing in a simple form.

Relationship may be another tag used. Sons and daughters of Presidents of the United States often have cursed this journalistic practice, but for the hurried reader who has no time to check on family trees, it is good. Religion and race, too, may be news handles.

Identification tags, some newsmen believe, may be overdone. When Dr. Edward U. Condon was called "one of the weakest links" in our atomic security set-up by a House Sub-Committee on Un-American Activities in 1948, that identifying phrase stayed with him so constantly that *Scientific American* used him for a study of "trial by newspaper." Editors have questioned whether it was fair to Thomas E. Dewey to mention that he was twice defeated for the presidency in stories in which this fact had only tangent relevancy.

Keeping straight millions and billions in United States dollars causes newspapermen their share of headaches. So it is not surprising when readers give up on foreign currency. It is usual to convert British pounds, French francs, Japanese yen, or Soviet rubles into their dollars and cents equivalent. When black market prices vary from the legal exchange rate, it is customary to add the phrase, "at the official rate of exchange."

All sorts of terms, some technical, some newly-created allusions, often need explanation.

When former President Harry S. Truman referred to "a political debt to the Shivercrats and Dixiecrats," one paper inserted in the sentence, within parenthesis, "a reference to Allan Shivers, Governor of Texas and leading figure in the struggle over the offshore lands." That was an exercise in translating.

Here are other examples:

Biological warfare—"the stealthy implanting of germs in people, animals or crops."

Glaucoma— "hardening of the eyeballs."

Cloture— "the parliamentary term for a time-limit muzzle on nonstop debate."

Cholesterol— "a fat-like substance produced by many tissues of the body and sometimes deposited on the walls of the arteries."

Fair trade— "a principle that permits a manufacturer to set minimum prices in 45 states."

Deficit financing— "borrowing cash to meet current bills because outgo is larger than income."

Sometimes a phrase is insufficient to permit adequate backgrounding. A whole sentence may be needed. For instance, when a man wanted as a suspect in a slaying had registered at a hotel with a New York City address, that became a key fact in the news story. Readers wanted to know the address and the story told them. But most of them also wanted to know, "There is no such street number." Those who lived in that section of New York City might know, but most of the metropolitan readers needed that additional sentence for reminder.

Other examples from stories with more lenghty explanatory writing are:

When Bureau of Labor Statistics figures were released—"The B.L.S., which is part of the Labor Department, hands out information on such things as prices, earnings and jobs."

When an uncommon word was used in debate in the House of Lords— "Megalomania is a type of insanity in which the subject thinks of himself as great or exalted, and is inclined to brag."

When a national figure was ill from acute gastro-enteritis— "The lining of the stomach and intestinal tract is inflamed in such an illness."

When a senator called a proposal "a baby Townsend plan"— "Francis Townsend for years has proposed a wide program of aid to the elderly."

When Chinese Communists bombed an island off the mainland of China— "Quemoy is an important outpost of the Chinese Nationalist stronghold on the island of Formosa, 100 miles to the east across the Formosa Strait."

Whole paragraphs may be needed to tell the story's background, such as in these illustrations:

Foreign political explanation. When Canadians went to the polls to choose a government:

> They don't do it in the same way as Americans in the United States. Their system of parliamentary democracy is modeled on that of Britain, and the Prime Minister is elected, not as a United States President is by a nation-wide vote, but is chosen by the party that wins a majority in the House of Commons.

Scientific information. When a patent was issued for procaine penicillin:

> Pencillin, a "wonder drug" that came into wide use in World War II, is highly effective against disease bacteria. In application, it is now generally combined with procaine, a local anesthetic. The procaine not only lightens the pain of injection but also prolongs the action of the penicillin.

Historical background. When the Navy built a super-carrier, U.S.S. Ranger, eighth ship to bear the name:

> The first Ranger was a Continental frigate built at Portsmouth, N.H., in 1777. It sailed under the command of John Paul Janes. The seventh Ranger, launched in 1933, was the first American ship specifically designed and built as an aircraft carrier. It took part in landings in North Africa in 1942 and in the raid on Norway in 1943, later sailing to the Pacific to qualify carrier pilots for the remainder of World War II.

Geographical perspective. When the Columbia Valley Authority proposal was debated:

The Columbia river discharges into the Pacific and is the borderline between Oregon and Washington. Its basin reaches into Montana, Idaho and Canada.

Biographical background. When Lord Beaverbrook turned over a large block of shares in his newspaper enterprises to the Beaverbrook Foundation:

> Lord Beaverbrook, Prime Minister Churchill's Minister of Aviation Production during World War II, bought "The Daily Express" as a bankrupt news sheet in 1915. He built it up over the years to its present positon as Great Britain's second largest selling daily, with a circulation of 4,140,667.

Allusion explanation. When a British House of Commons debate involved a reference to the "unconditional surrender" policy toward Germany in World War II:

> The unconditional surrender policy for Germany, Japan and Italy was announced Jan. 26, 1943, at Casablanca after a conference between President Roosevelt and Churchill. Newsmen reported that Churchill nodded assent when the President reported "complete agreement" on unconditional surrender demands.

The foregoing illustrations were inserted within news stories by the original writers or their immediate superiors. Another type of insert commonly used is that which a copydesk puts into dispatches that come from the publication's own correspondents in far-away places or over press association wires. The copyreader or press association editor may want to highlight some point in the story, yet he wants to make it absolutely clear to the reader that the material did not originate with the correspondent. Thus the readers will know that this information is just what it is—something added in the newspaper office or at the press association headquarters.

This inserted material may be indicated by several techniques. An entire paragraph or two may be put within parentheses. Or it may be set in italic or boldface type. It may be indented on both sides. This shows that it is not part of the original wire story itself but rather background or additional information that the paper has inserted to make the news more intelligible to readers.

Here are some illustrations of how such inserts have been used:

Reaction from another place. When a dispatch from London discussed the British government's attitude toward a proposal of Soviet Premier Georgi Malenkov:

> (At Washington, the State Department declined to comment on Mr. Malenkov's offer, but officials dismissed it as a high-level restatement of past Soviet proposals which the West has turned down.)

Information from another source. This is frequently used when a publication subscribes to several wire services and selects one agency for its main story but wants to include some additional facts from another's copy. When one paper used an Associated Press story from Cairo on an election:

> (The latest official returns gave the Wafdists 161 seats—one more than an absolute majority necessary to put them into power—and it appeared that they would get many more, The United Press reported.)

Localization of a national round-up dispatch. When a Washington wire story reported the latest cost of living index from the Bureau of Labor Statistics:

> *Atlanta's living costs have receded 1.4 percent from their peak to a level of 173.7 for the quarter ending Nov. 1, according to B. A. Bagdon, Regional Director of the Bureau of Labor Statistics in the South. A 4.5 percent drop in food prices pulled down the total cost, although all other major items advanced slightly, Bagdon said.*

387

General perspective or background. When a Formosa dispatch reported that Nationalist Chinese naval sources claimed Chinese Communists and the Soviets were massing ships for a possible invasion of Formosa:

> (Arrival of Russian warships at Dairen is not unusual. Dairen is ice-free, which makes it a good harbor in winter. Russian warships have been reported berthed there in winter in the past. Apparently it is the timing which has the Nationalist Navy nervous.)

Instead of inserting interpretation into the body of the news story, some editors prefer to use either underdash or precede material. Illustrative of this technique is the following paragraph under a dash at the end of a London item telling about salary increases for members of the British Parliament:

> Senators and members of the House of Representatives in the United States receive $15,000 annual compensation—$12,500 in straight salary and a $2,500 personal expense fund for which no accounting is required.

Precedes may simply plug a story or they may tell the reader some fact he might overlook. For instance, *The New York Times* warned its readers in an editor's note ahead of its correspondent's stories on living conditions in Russia that the dispatches had passed through Soviet censorship. Before World War II, the *Washington Evening Star* experimented with paragraphs giving the background on current events as precedes on major news stories. Early in World War II, many United States newspapers tried to evaluate the news for propaganda content by classifying dispatches as "probable propaganda," "official statement," and "truthfulness unestablished."

On the basis of the illustrations just cited, we can probably agree with Walton Cole of Reuters who suggested that the oft-repeated definition of news being "when a man bites a dog" needs amending. Contemporary readers, he said, also want to know why the man bit that dog and what happened to both dog and man.

Then blend it all together into a meaningful story

Some stories cry out for a generous addition of explanatory writing to put spot news developments into perspective. One news item that combined background—both historical and technical—and significance and foreign reaction with the spot news of a presidential action is the following:

BY EDWIN L. DALE, JR.

WASHINGTON, July 27.—President Eisenhower put up the tariff on Swiss watches today. His decision had been awaited eagerly by all foreign governments. They hoped he would leave the tariff as it is.

The increase was the full amount allowed by law— back to the tariff level that existed in 1930. Today's action increases the present tariff by half.

The increase actually comes on watch movements. Swiss movements are in 70 per cent of all the jeweled watches sold in this country. The tariff increase will almost certainly raise the price of watches, by up to $7.

The President took the action because the Tariff Commission had found that imports of Swiss watches were injuring the domestic watch industry, which he considered an essential defense industry. The watch tariff was reduced under the reciprocal trade law in 1936, and the domestic industry has been fighting to get it restored almost continually since.

The decision has major significance as a symbol of American tariff policy, particularly policy under the "escape clause" of American trade agreements. This is the clause that allows a tariff, once reduced, to be increased again if resulting imports injure or threaten to injure a domestic industry.

In seven other "escape clause" decisions the President has rejected Tariff Commission recommendations for increases three times, put off a decision three times (including one major case), and imposed a higher tariff only once, on an extremely minor item. The watch ruling, because of the import volume and other factors, was regarded as a test.

The Swiss Embassy promptly launched a protest with the State Department, saying the President's decision "deals a serious blow not only to existing good relations between Switzerland and the United States but also to the very principle of freedom of trade." Watches make up half the Swiss exports to the United States, running a little over $50,000,000 worth a year.

The Swiss protest said: "The restrictions imposed by the United States could tend to discourage international efforts toward a freer world trade."

The domestic industry was able to build up formidable political pressure on the President to raise the tariff. Aside from impressive statistics on their loss of sales and employment because of import competition, they argued—with some government backing—that the loss of watch-making skills would be an important blow to the "mobilization base." The White House agreed.

Concern abroad over the decision was based on belief that world economic problems can be solved only by a gradual increase in American imports. This "escape clause" case was regarded as the major test of whether foreign nations can gain access to American markets without the fear of having the tariff raised if they are successful.

Although the White House announcement said some watch imports would have no duty increase and that only watches of seventeen jewels and less would be affected, today's proclamation by the President raises the existing tariffs on well over 95 per cent of the jeweled watches that are imported. Some estimates placed the affected watches at more than 99 per cent on actual watch imports.

The President's decision was based in part on a finding by a special "interdepartmental committee on the jeweled watch industry" which reported to the Office of Defense Mobilization that preservation of the special labor skills associated with watchmaking is essential to national security. A Senate Armed Services subcommittee recently made the same finding. The subcommittee was appointed by the chairman, Sen. Leverett Saltonstall, R., Mass., whose state contains one of the four domestic watch factories.

The case for and against a tariff increase was fought out in public by an avalanche of press releases and statistics furnished by both sides. There is no doubt sales of domestic watches are off—but so are sales of Swiss watches this year. There is also no doubt that imports from Switzerland have increased tremendously since the tariff concession was made in 1936, while domestic sales have fluctuated up and down. Last year the domestic companies made money, but they said most of all of the profit was on their non-watch lines.

Generally speaking, only watch movements are imported from Switzerland. They are put in cases here, in factories employing an unspecified number of thousands of workers.

As a result of today's decision, Switzerland will have the right to cancel concessions given to the United States in the 1936 agreement. These concessions included not only tariff reductions on goods which the United States exports but commitments to buy specified quantities of some products.

The watch was one of the "big three" in this difficult field facing the President. He has already rejected a higher tariff on one of the three—fish fillets—and postponed a decision on the second—lead and zinc.

—*New York Herald Tribune*

FOURTEEN

Interpretive and background news articles

PUTTING THE NEWS INTO PROPER PERSPECTIVE FOR THE TYPICAL reader, in some ways, is like working on a jigsaw puzzle. The important thing in both cases is to get the pieces together so that they make sense. Having bits of a puzzle scattered all over a room is not very helpful. Having scattered bits of spot news provides only part of the answer. To put either the puzzle or the news picture together requires both time and space.

That is why interpretation, background, explanation, or whatever one wishes to call it, almost always requires more column inches and more writing time than the spot news reporting of a 50-word bulletin with adds. But it is worth both because it may make the difference between a momentary vicarious thrill and a basis for an informed public opinion. This chapter will discuss how experts for newspapers and magazines have supplied perspective through "with" stories or sidebars, interpretation or reaction, historical background, speculation, a "situationer," or personality articles.

Interpretation often takes different forms

When an event breaks into the news, an editor or a reporter frequently is confronted with the problem of making the current spot development meaningful to the readers who know little about the incident. How does he do this? He may use a wide variety of approaches. Here are some of the more common ones:

(1) *"With" or sidebar shorts*. Here the writer wants to supplement the information in the main story. It may be a box that gives some background or definitions. It may be a comment from someone who knows about the news situation, possibly some local resident who has special knowledge of the development. It may be a bit of explanation that the individuals concerned with the news would not stand behind for quotation but which the readers need to have in properly assessing the events.

(2) *Interpretive or reaction stories*. This type of article tries to answer the question "What does it mean?" It may be a lengthy explanation of a complicated development. It may provide the thinking of experts on a topic that shoots up into headlines. Few events have impact only at their site of origin; there may be dispatches on the reaction from other localities. To illustrate, a decision on foreign policy in London may touch off resulting reactions in Washington. For United States readers, the story from their capital may be more significant than the original and motivating news items.

(3) *Historical background*. What went before always plays some role in understanding the news. This type of story supplies the previous chapters in the continuing developments of the news. It tries to answer, "Why did this happen? What's back of it all?" A story breaks in the news and there have been only isolated reports leading up to the current spot news item. The reader has the problem of relating what happened last week, last month, or last year with what has just taken place. There is need to pull together somewhat unrelated incidents to help the readers understand how they lead into what took place today.

(4) *Predictions or speculative articles*. Here the writer deals with the question "What will happen next?" As are all predictions of the news, this can be dangerously unreliable. But, if a reporter is honest, he will put in at least as much time gathering facts and information and as much thought as he would for the story on the

393

initial news break. Here he should attempt to provide honest speculation as to the future.

(5) *The "situationer" or survey piece.* In this type, a writer tries to pull together the whole pattern of news developments and to give the reader perspective. He may also write about a social problem that develops in a community but of which most readers are only vaguely aware until it breaks into the news with tragic and sensational developments. For example of this last, fires in Chicago's slum tenements with heavy loss of lives led the Chicago newspapers to expose the whole slum situation and the appalling conditions under which people lived.

(6) *The personality piece or "profile."* This is an attempt to illuminate some individual who has skyrocketed into the headlines. Readers want to know what makes him tick, what kind of person he is. This type of story tries to supply the information.

A crusading newspaper may go beyond these categories in some of its reporting; it may grind an axe or presume to play God. To assume a sense of omniscience while writing interpretation or background is to go far beyond the assignment of reporting what one Washington correspondent called "the fact of opinion," the reprinting of which may be as important as telling "the fact of an event."

John M. Hightower, Associated Press correspondent at the State Department in Washington, emphasized this need for utmost integrity in the writing of interpretive or background articles. Back in 1945, long before he had won the Sigma Delta Chi award for Washington Correspondence and the Pulitzer Prize for International Reporting, Hightower wrote the following credo as a reporter:

My main objective is to strive for understanding. The more I see of the complexities of government the more I am convinced that is my first obligation. To me, it is not enough to report the bare facts of a news incident. They must be related to the other facts that have gone before, and they must be given meaning for the future.

I work on the premise that people want to know two things about every important development. First, "why did it happen?" The answer to that one is background. Second, "what does it mean?" The answer to that is not guesswork. It is work—to interview the experts, constantly, endlessly, and report their views of what it means.

It is work—to talk daily with officials who are shaping their actions according to those views. It is work—to listen to the critics who dislike the official views and assail the official actions, so that my stories will be in balance and as free of slanting as is humanly possible. For especially in interpretive writing, I conceive that I have an awesome responsibility to be absolutely fair and accurate.

To sum up my personal standards of news writing: understanding, fairness, accuracy.

Obviously, the amount of background required in news reporting varies. A huge fire, a spectacular bank robbery, an exciting murder trial, or a hotly contested political campaign may seem to be self-contained news topics. The installments follow each other so rapidly that most readers do not forget the earlier ones. Yet even here the spot news may be related to an over-all social problem. For instance, why is it still possible to rob banks despite electronic burglar-proofing devices? Or what might be done to revise criminal trial procedures so that attractive defendants have no better chance of "getting away with murder" than ugly ones?

Slower paced stories frequently make explanatory writing and backgrounding mandatory. Science discoveries, financial developments, economic trends, and foreign politics may land on the first page of newspapers after many readers have forgotten the earlier news breaks. Then it is essential, as Hightower pointed out, to answer the questions "Why did it happen?" and "What does it mean?"

In newspapers, interpretive and background news articles

may vary from short "with" stories or sidebars no longer than boxes to full-length series running every day for a week or more. Near the maximum length was Victor Cohn's "Never Too Old" series of 15 articles in the *Minneapolis Tribune* concerning problems of America's aged; this ran 70-odd pages of double-spaced copy. Its comprehensiveness helped it win the 1951 American Association for the Advancement of Science–George Westinghouse writing award.

"With" stories may comprise first-person, eyewitness accounts of some events or they may be the full text of an official pronouncement or a talk by a prominent person.

In longer interpretive articles, editors may choose between a "blockbuster" or a single piece that runs to many thousands of words for a definitive reporting job and a series that splits the information into pieces of more conventional size, usually less than 1,000 words each. Both treatments have their ardent supporters among newspapermen; the deciding factor seems to be the general policy of the publication itself. Another debate centers on whether such articles should be used daily or the longer ones saved for the Sunday or week-end edition. Here again the paper's policy seems to be the determining factor.

Specialized papers of the business and trade press frequently utilize interpretive and background articles. The *Wall Street Journal's* round-ups are nationally known for factual accuracy and bright writing style. Typical of how business publications use interpretation, a single issue of *Retailing Daily*, Fairchild Publications' home furnishing paper, contained a two-and-a-half column weekly sales survey, a two-page roundup of new products at a housewares show, and a full page text of proposed trade practice rules drafted by the Society of Plastics Industry. All told, interpretations took up approximately one-tenth of all the 36 pages. That excluded columnists and explanatory paragraphs in spot news stories.

Writers on magazines, with deadlines less frequent than those of daily publications, may take more time to think things through. Articles of criticism and appraisal in magazines appeal to a large audience. Writing in the centennial issue of *Harper's Magazine* (October, 1950), Bernard DeVoto evaluated the role of a magazine of appraisal among the various competing communications media as follows:

But if journalism stops with reporting, then a necessary part of its job is left undone. There must be something that says, Wait a minute! and asks, But just what is this, just what does it mean, and how can you be sure? What is reported must also be examined, interpreted, criticized, and reconsidered. If large-scale publishing cannot perform this function, it cannot therefore be allowed to atrophy; someone else must take care of it. . . .

The forces that have produced the modern newspaper have incidentally enervated the editorial page. Even if they had not, it would not now be possible for a paper to exert such a national influence as several did seventy-five year ago. To compensate for what it has lost, daily journalism has invented the syndicated column to interpret the news, but it has rather opened a new field than plugged the gap. A columnist cannot qualify himself to cover all the news, though some try to. He is a specialist, usually a specialist in politics, and he has to work under the same pressure of haste that drives the city desk. His frequently expert competitor, the radio analyst, is under a double exigency, for his space is measured in time. What the news weekly offers, a compound in which reporting and editorial interpretation are pressed together in register, is not a substitute for critical inquiry. But there has to be comment on the news that escaped from the tyranny of haste and the limitation of space. *Harper's* has become a vehicle for comment by experts.

How a story gets told

How interpretation, explanation, and background may be supplied to a spot news story of world importance is illustrated by press accounts of the killing of the European Defense Community (EDC) by the French National Assembly on August 30, 1954.

Here are the first two paragraphs of the main news story as printed in the *Miami Herald* the morning following the vote:

> PARIS—(AP)—France scuttled the European army plan Monday night, refusing to allow Germany to rearm within the program backed by the Eisenhower administration and Germany herself.
>
> The action lowering the guillotine on the European Defense Community—launched three years ago at France's own suggestion—came on a procedural vote in Parliament. After bitter debate the National Assembly voted 319–264 to postpone debate indefinitely. The action was as clear-cut as if the EDC itself had been up for decision.

The rest of the dispatch provided additional facts and some more information. The news development certainly required more backgrounding, interpreting, or explaining if the daily papers were to do their job of making the action of the French National Assembly understandable and meaningful to their readers.

Among the things that readers wanted to know, for instance, and which they expected their newspapers to answer were the following questions:

(1) What does the defeat of EDC mean to United States foreign policy? How serious a defeat for this country was it?

(2) What is EDC anyway? How did it start? What does it do?

(3) Can't someone explain the "crazy" French political system? How do the parties operate over there?

How did reporters and correspondents do the job?

James Marlow, Associated Press news analysist, provided full length historical background—how EDC was born and how it grew—along with an explanation of EDC—who belonged and what its goals were—in the following dispatch for afternoon newspapers the next day:

BY JAMES MARLOW

WASHINGTON, Aug. 31 (AP). This is an ABC on what President Eisenhower has just called a "major set-back" in the fight against Communism: the French refusal last night to join a single European army.

The Western allies decided on a military alliance when, after the war, it became apparent the Communists were determined to take by force what they could not get otherwise. The big example was seizure of power in Czechoslovakia.

The allies created NATO—North Atlantic Treaty Organization—under which they pledged to help one another in case of attack. Each member would keep its own army but there would be a general staff for planning.

NATO now has 14 members. Twelve signed the NATO agreement April 4, 1949: The United States, Britain, France Italy, Canada, Belgium, Luxembourg, The Netherlands, Denmark, Iceland, Norway and Portugal. Greece and Turkey joined in February 1952.

U.S. Pays One-Third

The United States contributes one-third of NATO's cost. The other members put up four-fifths of the forces. This country has six American divisions with NATO in Europe.

West Germany was not included in NATO. There were obvious reasons. This country, Britain and France —still keeping occupation troops in Germany—have not restored its independence or what diplomats call sovereignty.

Lacking sovereignty, Germany cannot rearm. So long as Germany is defenseless, the Russians have a soft spot for attack. The Russians have opposed not only NATO but also rearming of Germany. The Allies faced a question:

How to let Germany rearm but in a way to prevent its becoming a menace to its neighbors some day. In June

399

1950 the Communists showed how far they were willing to go in aggression with their attack on South Korea.

Four months later, on Oct. 26, 1950, Rene Pleven, then French Premier, proposed a plan which in that early stage won approval of the French Parliament. It was the single European army idea, called EDC—the European Defense Community.

Six European countries—France, West Germany, Italy, Belgium, Luxembourg, The Netherlands—would pool their armies in a single European army under a unified command of their own choosing.

No National Armies

Except for West Germany, all these EDC countries were already members of NATO. But whereas the other NATO allies would keep their individual armies, the EDC countries no longer would have national armies of their own.

This single European army—made up of troops from the six EDC countries—would be part of NATO's defense planning.

On May 27, 1952, the six EDC countries' foreign ministers signed an agreement to set it up. This did not by itself create EDC. It could not come into existence until the parliaments of all six countries approved.

Four of them—West Germany, Belgium, Luxembourg, The Netherlands—gave approval. The Italian parliament did not approve but was expected to when the French did. The French parliament, rent with factions, balked.

Russia tried every trick to keep EDC from being born. Communists in the French parliament, following the Russian line, fought EDC approval. French nationalists, who wanted France to keep its national army and not merge it in EDC, fought it, too.

In addition, there was French fear of Germany rearmed under any circumstances and fear, no matter how EDC was unified, that Germany would control it. Russia played on these French worries.

The United States and Britain looked on EDC as essential for defense of Europe, making use of German manpower, and at the same time keeping Germany from becoming a menace as it might with its own national army.

Hostile Mood

Although France had proposed EDC four years ago and France agreed to set up EDC two years ago, no French premier chanced asking parliament, with its hostile mood, to vote on it. The French would have felt safer tied into EDC with Germany if Britain would join EDC also. Britain would not.

At last the present French Premier and Foreign Minister, Pierre Mendes-France, decided to put EDC to a vote in parliament. First he tried to get the other five EDC countries to agree to changes in the 1952 agreement which would have made EDC more a fiction than a reality.

He suggested, for instance, that EDC be on trial for eight years and that anyone of the six members could veto what the other five wanted to do. The other five turned him down.

No lover of EDC, Mendes-France asked parliament to vote. It did, last night, against EDC. That wrecked it.

—*St. Louis Post-Dispatch*

James Reston of *The New York Times* sought to interpret what the EDC defeat would mean in terms of United States foreign policy. He told how officials in Washington appraised the news from Paris. As frequently happens in such dispatches, names of the officials were conspiciously absent yet the story unquestionably helped to guide public thinking in numerous communities because it was printed by subscribers to *The Times* news service as well as the New York paper's editions. The somewhat edited version from the *San Francisco Chronicle* follows:

401

BY JAMES RESTON

Exclusive to The Chronicle

From The New York Times

WASHINGTON, Aug. 30—Official Washington did not trust itself tonight to comment on the French National Assembly's rejection of the European Defense Community. It was "counting ten" this evening and promising to say something sensible tomorrow.

Those few U.S. officials who did agree to discuss privately the vote, seemed to agree on the following points:

1—This is not the end of the road; it merely seems so because we over-sold the EDC. "We must merely find another vehicle and go on."

2—There must be a re-appraisal of United States European policy, but "let's do our 'agonizing', and our 're-appraising' with the allies and not in isolation."

3—The ideal of an international army has been rejected, but the practical problem of rearming Germany as part of the Western allied coalition remains.

4—The best hope of this is in trying to bring Germany into the North Atlantic Treaty, or some variation thereof, where United States and British troops will minimize French fears of joining a coalition dominated by Germany.

The defeat of the EDC automatically reduces United States military and legal commitments promised to Western Europe. The legislation passed by the 83rd Congress stipulates, in general, that no United States military supplies put into the pipeline after Jan. 1, 1954, can be delivered to countries that refused to ratify the EDC.

The United States will also be released from certain important commitments it took about keeping its troops in Europe to help co-operate with the EDC.

—*San Francisco Chronicle*

J. Emlyn Williams, Central European correspondent of the *Christian Science Monitor*, writing from Bonn, Germany, told of the disappointment of West German officials over the Paris National Assembly's action and then concluded with the following paragraphs of outright speculation on what might grow out of the inevitable new negotiations to solve the persistent problem of German rearmament:

It is probable that since new negotiations on military matters will be reopened, there also will be a demand for a general stocktaking on the political side which will examine changes in West German conditions from the time the treaties were negotiated.

New Form Sought

All agree that since EDC is lost, a new framework for German rearming must be found which provides safeguards as to size and organization of German forces and of any future German armaments industry. This, it is realized, will not be easy, for not only will French reservations have to be considered, but also, it is stressed here, those of the Federal Republic, which now is far more conscious of its own strength in potential and position than it was a few years ago.

In some ways this looks very much like an attempt to square the circle. Theoretically, four possibilities for new military agreements exist. It remains to be seen, however, whether they are practically realizable—that is whether they can satisfy both France and German objections of one sort or another.

One is a German national army directly linked with the North Atlantic Treaty Organization. This is spoken of as the United States plan, but France could still veto it.

The other is a great coalition army of most European states which would include Britain, Scandinavia, and Greece. This idea appeared to be favored by Premier Pierre Mendes-France. But it remains to be seen whether all the states mentioned would agree to join it .

The third is a strengthening of the existing West German frontier force to about four or five times its present size, namely, to 80,000 to 100,000 men. This could serve as a counterweight to the East German People's Police. This idea has been propaganda, but finds no favor here or in France.

The fourth possibility is a European coalition army of the six European Coal and Steel Community countries. If Britain joined it then probably France would agree to it. This idea is probably most acceptable at the moment to Bonn, especially if it could later be developed into some kind of supranational EDC.

—*Christian Science Monitor*

Henry Giniger of *The New York Times'* Paris bureau analyzed the voting in the National Assembly and the splits within the various political parties. Thus he was able to highlight in understandable fashion for American readers the oversimplified statement that the vote was 319 to 264. His story follows:

BY HENRY GINIGER

Special to The New York Times

PARIS, Aug. 30—A breakdown of the voting by which the National Assembly in effect rejected the European Defense Community treaty shows the deep split the issue caused in all political groups except three. They are the Communists and Gaullists on the opposition side and the Popular Republicans, the great majority of whom favored the defense community.

The ninety-five Communists from the extreme left of the Chamber joined with sixty-seven of the seventy-three followers of Gen. Charles de Gaulle, now known as Social Republicans, who sit on the extreme right, to form more than half of the 319 Deputies who voted to put off consideration of the defense treaty indefinitely.

On the other side, the Popular Republican party

maintained most of its cohesion, with eighty of its eighty-six members voting against halting the debate. Two Popular Republicans, Jean Aubin and Henri Bouret, voted with the treaty opponents, while four abstained.

From then on, party unity was tossed away, with Deputies voting according to their own dictates or interests.

Fifty Socialists opposed the end of the debate, while fifty-five others voted for it. This was a particularly grave split, in view of the fact that a party congress, which officially sets Socialist policy, went on record in favor of the treaty and enjoined its parliamentary representatives to support it or suffer disciplinary action.

Radicals Are Divided

The Radicals were as divided as the Socialists. Voting to end debate and in effect kill the treaty were thirty-four, while thirty-three opposed this move. Two abstained and one was absent. Six Radical members of the Government, including Premier Mendes-France, remained faithful to the Cabinet's neutrality stand and did not take part in the vote.

In the Democratic and Social Union of Resistance, a Center group allied with the Radicals and once headed by former Premier René Pleven, one of the architects of the treaty, ten voted to end the debate, eight voted against and one abstained. Five did not take part in the voting, including four Cabinet members.

In the Peasant party, a conservative farm group, ten were for ending the debate and nine against.

Among the group known as Gaullist dissidents, who broke away from the general, sixteen favored ending the debate and fourteen were against it.

Among the conservative Independent Republicans, twelve were for ending the debate and thirty-six opposed it, including former Premiers Antoine Pinay, Joseph Laniel and Paul Reynaud.

Tabulation of Vote

A complete tabulation follows:
Number voting: 583.
Absolute majority: 292.
For adoption of motion to end debate: 319.
Against motion: 264.

Party	For	Ag'st.	Ab-st'n.	No Vote
Socialists	53	50	1	1
Communists	95	—	–	–
Popular Republicans	2	80	4	–
Radicals	34	33	2	6
Gaullists	67	2	–	4
Independent Republicans ...	12	36	1	5
Dissident Gaullists	16	14	2	1
Independent Peasants	6	20	–	1
Democratic and Social Union of Resistance	10	8	1	5
Peasants	10	9	–	3
Overseas Independents	3	11	–	1
Progressives	4	—	–	–
Unaffiliated	7	1	1	3
Total	319	264	12	30

One Radical Deputy was absent.
Abstaining is considered as taking part in the vote, since it involves putting a ballot marked "abstention" in the box. No vote means the deputy did not take part.

—*The New York Times*

Illustrative of "with" stories or sidebars on the EDC voting are the following two dispatches. The first, an Associated Press dispatch from Vienna, gave the quoted reactions of Senators Alexander Wiley and Estes Kefauver. The second was boxed within the main Paris story in the *Bristol* (Tennessee) *Herald Courier*. Some larger papers devoted up to a full column to President Eisenhower's speech but the *Herald Courier* cut it down to a single nugget side bar. Space limitations force many papers to do this.

VIENNA, Aug. 30 (AP)—"I wonder what Lafayette would say." That was the comment by Senator Alexander Wiley (R-Wis.) tonight on France's parliamentary rejection of the European Defense Community treaty.

"The French assembly has spoken," said Wiley, who is attending the Vienna Congress of the Interparliamentary union. "EDC, a great idea which came from the soul of France, has been denied fruition."

Senator Wiley is chairman of the Senate foreign relations committee.

Senator Estes Kefauver (D-Tenn.) also here for the lawmakers convention, declared: "This is very disappointing. It will set back the idea of North Atlantic security for many years."

—*Kansas City Times*

DES MOINES, Aug. 30. (AP)—President Eisenhower tonight described the rejection of the European Defense Community (EDC) as a "major setback" in the fight against international communism.

—*Bristol Herald Courier*

"With" stories are interpretive

Now let us see how these interpretive or background pieces are handled, starting with the shorter ones and working up to the longer.

Late in 1950, the Associated Press Foreign News Desk decided that some of the terms that its writers had been bandying about needed explaining to a generation that was not reading newspapers and magazines when these words came into use. So the following undated sidebar was sent out:

BY THE ASSOCIATED PRESS

Here, for the benefit of the younger generation, is an explanation of two words—Dunkerque and Munich—which have been used repeatedly in the last few days in connection with the Korean crisis:

Dunkerque—This seaport is the northernmost town of France, near the Belgian border. In 1940 the Germans swept through Belgium and on into France. It looked as if the British force in that area would be wiped out. But an armada of 900 vessels, ranging from yachts to warships, moved in and rescued 337,000 men from the beaches, and they lived to fight another day. It was one of the epics of the early days of World War II. Since that time "Dunkerque" has come to mean a seaborne evacuation or rescue of armed forces from a position they cannot hold.

Munich—This is the capital of Bavaria in Germany. An agreement was reached here in September, 1938, among Britain, France, Germany and Italy. It broke up Czechoslovakia, in response to German demands, and was designed to pacify Adolf Hitler. The Munich agreement became known as a symbol of attempted appeasement.

Such a background piece also may be used to keep the essential elements of a story in focus for readers. An example is the following box which *The New York Times* printed each day along with the text of testimony during the Senate sub-committee investigation of the Army-McCarthy controversy in the spring of 1954:

The main charges in the Army-McCarthy controversy now before a Senate investigating subcommittee are:

BY THE ARMY—That Senator Joseph R. McCarthy and two aides—Roy M. Cohn, his chief counsel, and Francis P. Carr, subcommittee staff director—sought, separately and collectively by improper means to obtain special and preferential treatment for Pvt. G. David Schine, former subcommittee consultant.

BY SENATOR McCARTHY AND HIS ASSOCIATES—That Robert T. Stevens, Secretary of the Army, and John G. Adams, the department counselor, tried in vain to stop the subcommittee's exposure of alleged Communists at Fort Monmouth, N.J., and that they used Private Schine as a "hostage" to this end. It also is asserted that the Army officials sought to black-mail Senator McCarthy and his associates out of the Monmouth hearings by threatening publication of the report on Mr. Cohn's activities in behalf of Private Schine.

A subsequent charge was that H. Struve Hensel, Assistant Secretary of Defense, aided in the preparation of the Cohn-Schine report in order to stop a threatened investigation of an allegation that he, as a wartime official in the Navy Department, had improperly aided in the organization of a concern supplying private shipping companies.

The charges against Mr. Carr and Mr. Hensel later were dismissed by the subcommittee.

Summaries of highlights of the news attempt to provide readers with simplifying short-cuts on complicated events. These include, to mention only a few, a presidential press conference where a wide range of subjects is discussed, a series of developments in Congress or at the United Nations, legislation covering a number of points, or quotations of key paragraphs from the leading newspapers' editorials on a major development in the news. What might have been the lead paragraphs of a range of stories are stacked up under an introductory statement such as, "The President at his news conference today made the following points" or, "Following is a summary of the major provisions of the compromise tax bill, completed today by a Senate-House conference."

When the Atomic Energy Commission in 1954 released testimony before its Personnel Security Board hearing on Dr. J. Robert Oppenheimer, one metropolitan newspaper took more than a column to give thumbnail identifications of 37 witnesses along with several pages of excerpts from the 991-page printed transcript. These identifications served much the same purpose as a cast of characters for a play or motion picture.

Whenever there is an election—national, state, or local—newspapers print statistical tables of election results because that is the easiest way to give readers that mass of information. Frequently the comparable vote of a previous election is included. Much the same techniques may be used to report national census figures, United States income tax collections, and other information of a statistical nature.

Closely allied with these are the graphs and diagrams used to tell in pictorial form how, for instance, the national income is earned, how persons over 50 years die, or how many school children there will be for the next ten years.

For those who want documentation, the entire text is necessary. Texts provide the raw material of the news so that the reader may draw his own conclusions without coloring by a reporter or the publication's editorial policy. *The New York Times* has built an international reputation over the decades and won Pulitzer prizes for reprinting official papers and speeches. Most papers print as many as their editors believe they can—with limitations of space and of reader interest.

Political leaders have capitalized on this predilection of the press to print the text when possible. In 1944, President Franklin D. Roosevelt wanted to keep the Democratic party platform down to 500 words so that the text could be used as a box on front pages instead of a longer version that would be printed on an inside page. The final platform, however, totaled 1,500 words. At other times, President Roosevelt was more successful, as when he sent a two-paragraph message to Congress advocating the legalization of light wines and beer. It was printed on the front pages of almost all the nation's newspapers.

Readers want to know the answers

Probably the commonest interpretations fill in the historical background, behind-the-scenes information, or explanations of a complicated news situation. These articles include not only those that give background but also those that pull together various parts of a news situation, the mood and color of a development that may be missed in conventional spot reporting, or a survey to uncover little known aspects of a situation. In short, writers try to answer the recurring questions of "How did this come about?" and "What does it mean?"

How geography, history, economics, and religion may all be combined into a background story to inform readers is illustrated in the following article which appeared when tensions developed between two Central American countries:

> Costa Rica, called "Central America's Switzerland" for its high mountains and fertile valleys, lies between Nicaragua on the north and Panama on the south, with an area about equal to the combined states of New Hampshire and Vermont. Most of its 825,000 population is concentrated in the central plateau, which includes San Jose, the capital city. The second smallest Central American republic, it has no standing army except a 1,500-man National Police.
>
> Its rich soil of volcanic ash chiefly produces coffee, bananas and cacao. The United States is Costa Rica's best customer, both for imports and exports. The country has fine schools and claims the highest literary rate of any Central American nation.
>
> ### Uprisings in 1948
>
> Pirate raids, internal revolutions and a nineteenth-century adventurer, William Walker, preyed on Costa Rica, which declared its independence from Spain in 1821. Revolutions ripped the country in the last century and an uprising in 1948 brought a new constitution. Under it, the country is governed by a President and a single-house Congress, with voting compulsory and non-voters subject to fines.
>
> Roman Catholicism is the state religion, but religious freedom is maintained. Ninety per cent of the inhabitants are of Spanish descent, with a much smaller admixture of Negro and Indian blood.

* * *

Nicaragua Bigger

Nicaragua, largest and least densely populated of the Central American republics, lies between Honduras and Costa Rica on the Central American isthmus. Its 1,200,000 population is concentrated in a triangular area between Lakes Managua and Nicaragua on the Pacific Coast. Small towns are scattered through the central highlands, but the steamy jungles of the Caribbean coast have few settlers.

Nicaragua's long history of revolution and unrest have made it one of the poorest and most backward of Central American countries, with 60 per cent of its people illiterate.

A Nicaraguan canal has often been discussed, but never begun. Civil disorders brought the United States Marines into the country in 1912 in an attempt to stabilize conditions with a two-year hiatus, the Marines remained until 1933, when peace was made with Agustino Sandino, Nicaraguan guerrilla leader.

—*New York Herald Tribune*

Reporting the mood or color of an event sometimes eludes the reporter concerned with spot news. He is so busy watching the minute-by-minute that he fails to perceive the less obvious aspects. To many news writers, a science convention involves only a multitude of progress reports. Accordingly they picture their jobs as presenting these developments as interestingly as possible so that their stories will intrigue general readers who have forgotten most of their high school and college science. But one science writer saw something else in an American Chemical Society convention and wrote the following piece for his Sunday edition:

BY EARL UBELL

CHICAGO.

It is a "slave block," where scientists—important and not so important—find jobs. It is an informal forum for the exchange of information. It is a meeting of old friends. It is a report of technical and fundamental advances.

All these things and many others make up a scientific convention such as that of the American Chemical Society, which ended here Friday.

That is why this meeting attracted 10,000 scientists, who traveled great distances, ostensibly to hear dry, technical papers that many scientists themselves find insufferably dull.

Yet in the corridors of the hotels where the technical sessions are held, scientists can be heard telling one one another, politely:

"I heard your paper, Bill. It was very good."

Getting Down to Facts

After the amenities are over, however, the conversations get down to business. Details of chemistry and techniques, omitted from the short formal talks, are exchanged. Notes are taken. Criticisms, withheld in the lecture rooms, are offered freely. Suggestions are made. The basic scientific meeting really goes on in the corridors.

At such a meeting, scientific gossip flows easily from mouth to mouth. Knots of men crowd about a chemist who has something "big." The "big shots" on company expense accounts move briskly through the crowd, basking in the glances of recognition. The government men —their travel allowances cut—are absent.

Then there are the thin-faced youths—still studying for or having just received their PhD.s—looking for that good job. They have spent some important money to come to Chicago. They move through the crowds, looking for a familiar face.

Then, after lecture hours, the meetings move down into the bars, to the restaurants, the dinner parties and into social hours. The talk goes on. The business of the meeting continues with scientific information continuously exchanged.

Late at night the scientists go back to their hotel

413

rooms to check the next day's program, put the finishing touches on their technical paper, or just rest.

Some Things Learned

But the work gets done. Except where chemical and pharmaceutical companies hold back trade secrets (and there are many of these), the science and technique get reported, and the scientists learn.

They learn, for example, that sucrose—common table sugar—has been made in a test tube, cracking a problem that has resisted solution for fifty years by the world's greatest chemists. The two Canadian chemists—Raymond U. Lemieux and George Huber—who did the work, don't think that the next step is to build sugar factories. Sugar, the purest organical chemical sold in bulk, is too easily grown.

The achievement, likened to the climbing of Mt. Everest, may mean that special sugars, with radioactive elements incorporated in the molecule, may soon be prepared. These sugars could be used to find out what the human body does with sugar, but sugar from the air and water tomorrow? No!

Dazzling Report

The scientists also heard that the big pharmaceutical companies are working very hard to find chemicals to cure virus diseases like mumps, measles, polio and rabies. Hope was seen in the findings that there are some chemicals that cure or slow some of these diseases in animals, in test tubes, or in hatching eggs.

It seemed apparent that the drug company representatives were not telling the full story. Although they said that none of their chemicals were being tried on human beings, the scientists indicated that maybe one or two compounds would be tried on humans soon. But they said it would be at least five years before the problem was fully solved.

Dr. Britton Chance, a combination chemist, biologist, physicist and yachtsman, dazzled his fellow scientists with a description of a machine that examined the inner workings of a cell while the cell was still alive. Before Dr. Chance perfected his device, chemists could only surmise what went on inside these living, basic units of life, by killing them, staining them, tearing them apart, or just guessing.

Now Dr. Chance looks toward the day when he can check the chemical reaction of life itself in the raw in a nerve cell, a muscle cell, a cancer cell or a cell attacked by a virus.

New uses for antibiotics were also described at the meeting. Drugs like streptomycin and terramycin were reported effective in the control of fireblight—a germ disease of apple and pear trees that blackens the young blossoms in fruits. Halo blight in beans was also controlled. This was reported to be the first time that these plant ailments were effectively put down with the mold drugs, which were used in very small concentrations.

Also there were the "sleepers": drugs reported by organic chemists as having some effect on this or that disease. Many of these drugs worked in the test tube or animals; few had been tried on humans.
—*New York Herald Tribune*

Much the same sort of interpretive reporting is done in the magazines, too. With less frequent deadlines than their colleagues on daily papers, magazine writers may have more time to probe for illuminating details.

A classic example of great magazine journalism is the report on the Centralia mine disaster by John Bartlow Martin in the March, 1948, *Harper's Magazine*. It was reprinted in *Harper's Magazine Reader* (Bantam, 1953). "The Blast in Centralia No. 5: A Mine Disaster No One Stopped" took 28 magazine pages; the editors said it was the longest piece *Harper's* had ever printed. Few stories are worth such reporting-in-depth, but when they merit it Martin's pattern may well be followed. Marc Rose, senior editor of *Reader's Digest*, called it, "One of the most magnificent examples of magazine journalism I've ever seen." Along with the *St. Louis Post-Dispatch*'s coverage of the Centralia disaster which will be discussed in the final chapter, the *Harper's* article not only forced revision of Illinois mining regulations but also helped elect Adlai Stevenson governor of Illinois.

Martin's article is too long to reproduce in full here but the beginning of the story will give some idea of the wealth of detail he gathered during the three months he spent researching the piece:

> One afternoon a few years ago William E. Rowekamp and a few other coal miners, their day's work done, were sitting around underground at the bottom of the shaft of the Centralia No. 5 mine, waiting for time to go "on top" and home, when all at once a foul cloud of coal smoke and powder smoke billowed from the mouth of the Main South Entry, the main tunnel leading southward into the mine workings. An ex-GI asked, "What is it, Uncle Bill?" Rowekamp, an old coal miner and an official of the local union, knew the lad was nervous so he said only, "It could be several things." But Rowekamp knew what it was—an explosion. Somewhere far back in the catacomb of entries and crosscuts and rooms, somewhere among the fifteen-odd miles of active tunnels or the hundred-odd miles of abandoned workings, an explosion had occurred, and this cloud of smoke was the backwash of the tornado of flame and blast. Rowekamp had no way of knowing it then but one hundred and eleven men were dead or dying.
>
> Quickly Rowekamp and the others went up in the cage. On the surface all was calm. The sky was gray, the day was bleak and raw with a strong wind blowing. They grew chilled. Uncertain what they ought to do, Rowekamp and another man did what they did at this hour each day: went to the washhouse to bathe and change into their street clothes. Word came that they were wanted back at the tipple.
>
> The Superintendent, H. C. Niermann, the top company official on hand, had put in phone calls for the State

Mine Inspector and for state mine rescue teams at other Illinois towns. Nobody knew how bad the explosion was. A sick miner who had just come from underground said he had been walking toward the shaft bottom along the First West Entry when a roaring, smoky wind hit him from behind, and to keep from falling he had begun to run, and he had run all the way to the shaft bottom. Others working near the shaft bottom also had escaped. But more than a hundred men were still below, nearly all of them far back in the mine, and, ominously, nothing had been heard from them.

Superintendent Niermann and several others descended the 540 feet to the bottom. They got aboard a motor, a small electric locomotive used to pull cars of coal, and rode about 1,200 feet south to the intersection of the First West Entry, where the airshaft and fan were located. Here the chunky underground boss, Mine Manager William H. Brown, told them the explosion's great force had knocked out the electric power and reversed the fan; in remedying this Brown had collapsed. Cliff Copple and John Lorenzini, having hauled him to safety, now had gone on down the Main South Entry to look for Cliff Copple's brother. They had not returned. To rescue them Superintendent Niermann sent Rowekamp and two others. Rowekamp, a man of fifty-eight with high cheek bones and thinning hair, headed their motor slowly down Main South through dust and smoke. After a half mile Rowekamp said he saw a light. One of the others said, "Uncle Bill, you are just seeing things," but Rowekamp recalled later, "We got closer and we saw it was a man—Brother Lorenzini." Lorenzini, a wiry, agile little man, now was staggering around in the tunnel, flailing his arms, crazed with gas and smoke. Where was his buddy, Cliff Copple? They went a little farther. One of them was getting sick from the fumes. They found water and washed their faces. They reached a place where the roof comes down low. The smoke was billowing through thick. Copple must be beyond. But they would have to crawl; they needed more men and equipment. So they took Lorenzini to the shaft bottom. (Copple died.)

417

Superintendent Niermann, Mine Manager Brown, and some other men, exploring the First West Entry, had found the pumper, a man of seventy-one. They thought fresh air might revive him but it didn't. They went on. More than a mile back along the First West they found 20 men, 16 dead and four living. The dead were lying on the fireclay floor of the entry as though asleep; gas, not violence, had killed them. The four living were like wild men. One of the rescuers knew that his own father was somewhere back in the mine but they dared go no farther: the corridors were full of gas, the doors and stoppings were scarred by violence —beyond lay the actual area of explosion.

This ended impromptu rescue work. The State Mine Inspector, Driscoll O. Scanlon, took over. It was now 9.00 P.M. on March 25, 1947, five and a half hours after the blast. Thirty-one had come out alive, 17 were known dead. What of the 94 others? This was the question that lay on the minds of those in the crowd all that night and during the succeeding days and nights. . .

—Harper's Magazine
Copyright 1948, by John Bartlow Martin

In contrast to the interpretive or background article, a question and answer style is used by some publications to put across complicated aspects of a story. This resembles a prosecuting attorney-witness presentation. While space-consuming, it does break down a news development into many smaller segments that may be explained in detail.

An extension of interpretive reporting is the survey that most larger newspapers use because they have the manpower available for extensive research. These articles may involve a local problem such as traffic or juvenile delinquency. Or they may be national or world reactions to some news development. These latter surveys can only be undertaken by the press associations, larger syndicates, or metropolitan newspapers with correspondents abroad and in numerous parts of the United States.

Representative of what a metropolitan newspaper may do, *The*

New York Times survey of New York City's physical plant before the 1953 mayoralty election comprised six stories, totaling 28 columns. Before the survey was finally turned in by Peter Kihss, who wrote the articles, 18 other reporters had helped gather facts. *The Times* considered this a record mass assignment for its local staff. Kihss spent one day less than two months from the time he drew the assignment until he finished typing his copy.

For a "This Is Greater Philadelphia" series of 18 articles on what had happened to the nation's third city since World War II, staff members of the Philadelphia *Evening Bulletin* spent several months gathering material.

Non-metropolitan newspapers usually assign a single reporter to handle such a series or campaign and give him enough advance notice so that he can familiarize himself with background before the first of his articles is printed. This in no way means that the smaller papers do not do an effective job. The material to be uncovered is less expansive and possibly more familiar, thus it requires less time to gather.

An example of how large-scale, national roundups may be done is the survey by Benjamin Fine, reprinted in Chapter One, on United States attitudes toward the United Nations Educational, Scientific, and Cultural Organization. (See pages 23 to 28.)

Perception of trends may mark the difference between the profit or loss of a retail store, the assuming of industrial leadership by a manufacturing concern, or the contribution of a professional man to his field. Thus it is understandable that editors of specialized publications spend considerable space on such topics. For example, *Women's Wear Daily*, retailers' daily paper of the Fairchild group, prints many roundups of what is happening in the fields in which their readers have special interests. One such series dealt with the spectacular increase in sales of sportswear over recent decades and was worked out jointly by the Fairchild Publications' Research Department and the National Retail Dry Goods

Association. In a broader field, *Fortune* magazine has discussed the future of whole segments of the national economy.

Since people interest people, it is natural that biographical features comprise part of the traditional fare for readers of both newspapers and magazines. Let an unknown name skyrocket into headline prominence and reporters soon will be digging up the individual's life history and writing it up for a curious audience. When Dr. Alfred C. Kinsey's report on male sex habits broke upon an unprepared public, dozens of writers went to Bloomington, Indiana, to learn what they could about him, his family, his research, and other bits of biography. When a president or governor is chosen, a sports hero breaks a world record, or great good fortune or bad haunts a person, some publication inevitably will tell the story of his life.

This is grist material for weekend editions of newspapers. In the magazines, the profiles of *The New Yorker* and the biographies of the women's publications illustrate how extensively this type of material is used.

Predicting the future is a favorite field, too

As any crystal ball gazer, horoscope reader, palmist, or writer of speculative news predictions will tell you, the business of trying to foretell the future involves a frightfully ticklish assignment. It may backfire with a vengeance. Yet the news writer, if he bases his predictions on a sound background and knowledge of what already has taken place, knows that he has more than a gambler's chance of being correct.

Picking the 1948 presidential election winner will remain for years a classic of how wrong the forecasters can get. Morris L. Ernst and David Loth preserved many of these miscalculations in their book, *The People Know Best: The Ballots vs The Polls* (Public Affairs Press, 1949).

Kiplinger's Magazine was so positive that the New York governor would be elected that it devoted a whole section of its issue for release the week of the balloting to "What Dewey Will Do." As a wit remarked at the time, "What will Dewey do? Go back to Albany." But that was not what the magazine discussed.

When dealing with the future, a news correspondent, as James B. Reston of *The New York Times* pointed out just after the 1948 election, should not be carried away "by facts he did not verify, by theories he did not fully examine, and by assumptions he did not or could not check."

Yet an "Iron Curtain," either abroad or at home, may prevent United States news writers from obtaining the vital verifications. In such cases, predictions may be well watered down toward insipidness. But readers still expect such guidance as is available.

A. J. Liebling, an avid advocate of the objectivity theory that news is news and opinion is opinion and never the twain should meet, explained the dangers in an article in *The New Yorker* (March 28, 1953) on the New York City papers' coverage of Joseph Stalin's stroke and death:

> According to newspaper canon, however, a big story calls for a lot of copy. The New York papers rose to the occasion by resorting to a procedure known, variously, as constructive journalism, interpretive reporting, and the crystal ball, but for which I now prefer a term I owe to James Reston of the New York *Times*, one of its recent, and probably reluctant, practitioners. Mr. Reston, in the *Times* of March 5th, a day when Stalin lay moribund and so did the real news, recounted a conversation he had had with a Democratic senator who had lunched at the White House on the previous day. He asked the senator what the President seemed to think about the situation. The senator told him that the President had discussed the Stalin illness "about the way everybody else discussed it all day, saying 'on the one hand this and on the other hand that.' " This is a perfect description of what the newspapers filled up with, and they ended by completely submerging the news story, which was simple enough: A formidable old man had died and nobody knew what to expect as a consequence.

At times, a reporter tries to find out what is ahead for some project of general community interest. It may be relatively uncomplicated and obtained by interviewing several news sources, as in the following forecast about the future of Salt Lake City's temporary housing:

BY LOUISE JUDD

Although definitely on the skids, the temporary war homes in the Salt Lake area still have a vague sort of future here. It has been estimated at from five to eight years.

Officials from both projects have indicated that the housing will remain in operation until it is completely worn out. As long as the units can be kept in reasonable repair they will be rented.

'When there is no further need for low-cost housing in Salt Lake City, we will discontinue operations at Airbase Village," Commissioner L. C. Romney, Salt Lake City Parks Department, said recently.

Waiting List

At Stadium Village there is a waiting list a year long. "We are leaving the housing where it is because we need it," officials said, noting at the same time, that it would replace the 300 units in the village.

Occupancy at Airbase Village varies from 91 to 98 per cent each month during the year. Some 40 units have been divided among larger units there during the past few years. Others gradually are being dropped from use.

"It is an expensive operation," Mr. Romney said. The village receipts last year were over $98,000. Operations and maintenance (including repairs, water, garbage disposal, power and light and fire department and recreation facilities) totalled about $71,000. The profit was $27,307.

"This year, the village will show a profit of better than $30,000," he said. The property on which the village is built is a portion of the Municipal Airport, and the annual "profit" reverts to the airport for maintenance and capital improvements. "It is a vital source of income to the airport."

Public Decision

Whether or not the housing projects continue operations seems to rest with the public concerned. Students regard the low-cost housing with relief; working people with hope for balanced budgets or savings.

But while the residents are saving for a home of their own some day, the war housing projects are "home" now. No expense is spared in their efforts to make their houses and yards more homelike. Many man hours are put in each month in landscaping and painting, independently of repair work done by the owners of the projects.

—Deseret News-Salt Lake Telegram

Again a writer may give meaning to elaborate statistical projectons through a careful job of translating them into meaningful ideas, as in the following article from a trade publication with a highly specialized audience:

BY MED SERIF

Managing Editor

The farm—one of the LP-Gas industry's best customers, present and potential—is to play a major role in the America of the future. An America that's to be a vastly bigger place with more people, more workers, and bigger markets.

All these things and more, too, are projected for the year 1975 by the closest thing we yet have to a time traveling machine—the Resources for Freedom Report. Predictions contained in this report are those of a group of experts brought together to study U.S. resources in the light of future demands.

The massive five-volume report which marks the efforts of the President's Policy Commission contains material gathered from government and private industry's sources. Heading the commission was William S. Paley, Columbia Broadcasting System's chairman of the board.

In a nutshell, here is the United States of 1975. This country will have about 193,400,000 people; cities will have about 50 per cent more dwellings; employment will be close to 80,000,000: passenger vehicles will number 65,000,000; trucks about 20,000,000; and the standard of living is to be at a peak hard to visualize.

A big job in the growing years ahead is to fall to the farmer. Land is the essential base for the production of most of the needed resources—both food and nonfood. Increasing population and better standards of living in the next quarter of a century coupled with greater industrial requirements for agricultural raw materials will impose a heavy burden on the farmer and his land.

The farms of the United States must supply many raw materials important to industry—cotton, wool and other fibres, hides and skins, fats and oils for paints and soaps, tobacco, industrial alcohol and countless others. In addition, a number of crops grown primarily for food or feed have secondary uses as sources of industrial materials as plastics and starch.

The Materials Policy Commission found itself confronted by two great questions in analyzing the agricultural questions: (1) Can the farmland of the United States provide the food and industrial materials needed in 1975? and, (2) Is any change to take place in the relation of agriculture to the nation's economy?

In answer to the first, the commission predicts that agriculture can meet the needs of the U.S. of the future. To the second, the commission says no. It feels basically, meeting estimated requirements will be a domestic responsibility just as it is today.

Now, let's delve deeper into the problem facing the farmer. The U.S. of 1975 will be a highly urbanized nation. This means that the present trend of increasing demand for farm products and a declining farm labor force will continue. Between 1939 and 1949 the number of persons employed in agriculture dropped nearly 10 per cent to 10,756,000. In 1950 alone, 400,000 left the farms. In 1975, only an estimated 7,000,000 will remain part of the farm labor team.

That means less workers will have to fill the needs of 28 per cent more people. The 1975 population of 193,-400,000 will require 41 per cent more food and will consume 25 per cent more farm nonfoods—a boost of 38 per cent for all farm products. New industrial uses for farm products, not counted in all the estimates, might raise this to 40 per cent.

To handle the enormous task set before them with the smaller labor force available, farmers must continue the trend to complete mechanization. The commission estimates that needed production will require more than a 40 per cent production increase from each farm worker. This can only be accomplished by a highly mechanized force using the latest technological methods.

The needs of agriculture for machinery and equipment over the next 25 years are to be in the main for replacements, the commission feels. New types of machines will be used for replacements. In addition, agriculture will continue to substitute machines for hand labor. This means an increasing use of mechanical cotton pickers, field hay bailers and field hay choppers and other harvesting machines, and also new types of tillage equipment to replace hoeing, chopping, and the like. Perhaps the biggest demand will be for fertilizer distribution equipment, the commission feels.

The scope of the report did not go futher into the subject of mechanization, but you, as an LP-Gas operator should. The sales possibilities on the farm in your areas are limitless for the jobs LP-Gas can handle are legion.

There are few markets that can mean as much in terms of winter-summer ratio improvement and profitable operation as the farm. Most farm utilization of LP-Gas is at its peak in the summer when gas consumption is traditionally low.

Let's take a look at the farm as your market. We'll start at the house first. Farm women, required to do a larger share of the chores because of tighter labor conditions, will be an even better market for labor-saving equipment in the kitchen as well as other parts of the house. The convenience of the modern, automatic clock controlled gas range will permit her to put her meal in the oven, do her chores, and return to find a meal for a hungry family completed. Hot water from a gas water heater, heat from central house heating or space heating equipment, food fresh and appetizing from a gas refrigerator, clothes fluffy and wholesome from a gas clothes drier will be here as gas helps the farm women keep pace with the greater demands of the nation.

In addition to its domestic uses, LP-Gas is playing an increasingly important role in farm production. In this role, LP-Gas is lightening the burden of work, increasing production, improving quality and in most cases doing these things cheaper than any other fuel could . . .

[Then followed a discussion of present applications which LP-Gas offers the farmer.]

—*LP-Gas*

Some stories deserve saturation coverage

During World War II, the United States Army Air Force used saturation bombing when it wanted to guarantee blasting all objectives within an area. Some news developments are so large that they need saturation coverage to reach all the various aspects.

The New York Times considered the Supreme Court decision outlawing segregation in public schools an event meriting saturation coverage in 1954. Not only did the paper print a two-and-a-half column main news story, headlined over the full width of page one, and the complete text of the decision, but also such additional stories as how the Voice of America handled the court's decision for world broadcast; reaction of educators, Negro leaders, and historians; nearly half a page of excerpts of national editorial comment; historical background of related earlier court decisions; a state-by-state analysis of pre-decision conditions together with an extensive table of statistics for 17 states and the District of Columbia. All in all, it added up to seven of the edition's 60 pages and *The Times* could truthfully call it "journalistic achievement rarely equaled."

The story behind the coverage was told as follows by *The Times* staff:

The story starts several months ago. Arguments in the case had been completed. Informed sources agreed that a decision was likely to be handed down on a Monday morning in May, before the court's summer recess.

New York Times editors lost no time in mapping their coverage of what might be a momentous decision, affecting the lives of millions. The coverage they planned involved using reporters and correspondents in Washington, in New York, throughout the U.S. and even abroad.

Focal point in the coverage was The Times Washington Bureau. Luther A. Huston, Bureau member regularly assigned to the court, got busy on extensive research. He would write the big story when it came, but interpretive stories would have to accompany it. Assisted by other Bureau staffers, Huston dug deep to get the background, turned to previous court decisions on segregation, reviewed arguments in the present case. The facts turned up provided material for several background articles that ran Tuesday in The Times.

Meanwhile messages went out to Times regional Bureaus throughout the U.S., particularly in the affected areas. John N. Popham, regional correspondent for The Times in the South, with headquarters in Chattanooga, was alerted. The home office asked him for an appraisal of what a ruling against segregation would mean to the South, another on the status of Negro education in states practicing segregation. Supplementing Popham's stories were reports from Times correspondents in each affected state.

In the New York home office, reporters got to work. They interviewed educational leaders, did extensive research on the whole broad problem of segregation for background and interpretive pieces. Times picture editors combed sources for photographs. Map makers provided charts and a map.

In all, nearly 50 Times staff members were involved in the operation. And by the time the decision was actually handed down, much of what they wrote was already in type.

Monday, when the story broke, this vast newsgathering organization moved into high gear again. The Washington bureau filed thousands of words on the ruling. Reporters and correspondents in affected areas interviewed government and education officials for reaction. From New York, law professors, historians, sociologists, other experts were interviewed by phone. Editors tied the whole thing together.

The result, in Tuesday's Times, was a complete, clear report on every phase of the story . . . a report *in depth*, for it gave Times readers not only the facts, but the explanation and interpretation that give a news story its full dimension.

Every newspaper and magazine does not have the resources to do what *The New York Times* did. But this statement of the story behind the story provides a pattern for giving news "its full dimension."

FIFTEEN

News magazines
and weekly
news summaries

THE WEEKLY NEWS MAGAZINES, SUCH AS *Time, Newsweek,* AND *U.S. News & World Report,* and the counterpart weekly summaries in newspapers' weekend editions represent the application of packaging techniques to journalism. Here a fragment of world history is wrapped in cellophane, as it were, tied up in ribbons, and presented to readers in as attractive form as possible.

Some of the appeal of these publications is due to inviting processing and presenting of the week's events, but a considerable part is due to the almost passionate urge on the part of writers and editors to put that news into perspective. Both news magazine and newspaper review staffs realize that their typical readers already have gotten the surface facts plus, in some cases, a dash of interpretation from their daily papers or radio and television announcers. Their job is more than just slick rewriting of the week's front page stories; they see their assignment as providing the background, significance, explanation, or prediction that makes the news meaningful. This does not mean that they work frivolously or carelessly. As a matter of fact, their job generally is harder to do than day-to-day reporting. Nor does this mean that the daily papers always do a poor job. By the ruthless rule of the clock, a week provides more hours than a day and each of those hours allows more time for adding up a news event. And by the same relentless rule, news reported in the weekly versions is becoming older and staler.

Let us look carefully at weekly news summaries

Some facts in the news stand out just as clearly a second after the event as they ever will—for instance, the name of the winner of the third race at Belmont. If that is all the reader wants, he does not need interpretation. For many other news events, as earlier chapters in this book have attempted to demonstrate over and over again, readers need to learn the associated information. Even for the third race at Belmont, interpretive reporting might explain that the winner paid so much because the horse consistently had lost earlier races in the season.

Those who write these weekly summaries, as the editors of *Time* once pointed out, seek "to tell the man who came late to the ball game what the score is, who made the runs, and how the prospect looks. Nobody is on time for all the ball games." And since they cover a seven-day period, they can relate the daily installments to the whole week's story, thus, in effect, covering the whole ball game to date and not reciting just today's inning. The daily paper's reporter depends primarily upon the happenings of the preceding 24 hours.

With this in mind, let us take a careful look at the daily papers, weekly news magazines, and news summaries in weekend editions.

Daily papers and radio and television announcers almost always get there "firstest." Little can be done to stop the clock. Obviously the weekly versions have to overcome the disadvantage of being late and this their staffs try to do by bringing the readers the "mostest." How do they do that? More and better interpretation. Writers on the weeklies (including the newspapers' review staff members, too) hope to make the details a little sharper, the insight a little keener, the perspective a little clearer, and the style a little easier to read and understand. If they do not do this, then the value of these weekly news summaries and reviews is nil.

But as the news magazine and newspaper weekly review writers swing away from the traditional reporting of obvious facts into interpretations they run into potential hazards. All three major news weeklies as well as most of the newspaper reviews have been accused of sometimes grinding an ax. Weeklies' staffs have the problems of those who write for daily papers, only they cannot lapse back into the protection of quoting directly and letting the reader beware. They are committed to giving the news perspective.

Editors and writers are well aware of these difficulties. For instance, *Newsweek* cautioned its correspondents:

Don't dream up your analysis from a background of personal prejudice or wishful thinking.

And *Time*, in one office memo, said:

Let us take no risk whatever except when conscience compels us. We should not expend any "risk" for the sake of having a scoop, for the sake of being the "wise guy," for the sake of attracting attention or being entertaining. . . . We must be scrupulously careful not to confuse what is happening with what we devoutly wish may happen.

Yet despite instructions and cautions, opinions do sometimes creep in and editors fail to cut them out. In some stories, conjecture and opinion are presented as interpretation. Those that agree will argue that the publication is a strong force for what they call "right thinking;" those who disagree will protest that it hinders the democratic process by poisoning public opinion. But most readers concede that, regardless of whether they agree or disagree, the over-all effect of the news magazines and weekly news reviews has more plusses than minuses.

All those who have studied news magazines, however, are not enthusiastic. For example, Max Ascoli, editor and publisher of *The Reporter*, wrote in the February 14, 1950, issue:

The seven-day span between issues is most frequently used to chop up, retouch, and slant the news to a point where resemblance with the facts is purely coincidental. Distortion, which to a large extent is unavoidable under the daily pressure of the news, has become the standard product of assembly-line processing. By selecting news on no other criterion than sheer "newsiness," the news magazines . . . offer their readers a weekly assortment of glamorous, luscious, and smart tidbits about everything and nothing.

Of the group of news weeklies we are talking about here, *Time* probably makes the least effort to be impartial. Its editors explained some years ago that they cared about what was going on in the world and they certainly hoped that their readers cared, too. What the editors said they wanted to do was "to try to communicate the sense of the news." And they admitted that sometimes they might be wrong. *Time's* goal, they said, was fairness, not impartiality. Then they explained:

The responsible journalist is "partial" to that interpretation of the facts which seems to him to fit things as they are. He is fair in not twisting the facts to support his view, in not suppressing the facts that support a different view.

What is the formula, if there is one, for the news magazines and weekly news summaries and reviews of newspapers?

We should remember that although much common ground exists for all these publications, many people believe the differences are more pronounced than the similarities. Admitting some truth to this belief, we still may point to the following generalizations:

1. All have more interest in putting the news into perspective than most daily papers. That point is mentioned again and again in the promotion material. They differ from day-to-day, spot reporting. As John H. Sweet, publishing director of *U.S. News & World Report*, explained it, "Each week we try to keep abreast of the news and tell its meaning as it happens."

2. All pay attention to what Lester Markel of *The New York Times* described as "spread news" in contrast to "spot news." He

said that "spread news" dealt with the continuing current of events or, as he phrased it, with "matters that never quite focus into news dispatches but are in their way our most important and pressuring issues." As illustrations, he cited the psychology of the teen agers and modern educational concepts.

3. Events are told, whenever possible, in terms of people and illuminating detail. Thus the news is personalized. This makes it possible, as *Newsweek's* editors said, "to set the stage with colorful details, and literally take the reader by the hand and make him feel he has witnessed the event."

4. Related to the previous point, the narrative or dramatic technique is commonly used. This promotes reader interest and suspense but it demands that the entire article be read if the essence of the news is to be reached.

5. Editors of news magazines and newspaper weekly news reviews pride themselves on their good style. With more time, writers may rework their original copy to bring it to high polish.

News magazines go back to the 1920's

Contemporary news weekly magazines represent a Twentieth Century journalistic innovation, yet their antecedents go back logically to the newspapers and earlier opinion weeklies. Henry R. Luce and Briton Hadden, as related in Chapter Two, started *Time* in 1923 and get the credit for launching a new form of United States journalism. They announced a publication that had "adapted itself to the time which busy men are able to spend on simply keeping informed."

But the *Time* they started had no army of reporters around the world, no spacious morgue full of information, no multitude of researchers, and no innovations in writing style. All these came later.

In 1929, David Hulburd went to Chicago as the magazine's first correspondent and *Time* editors discovered what on-the-spot reporting could add to the narrative quality. But through the 1930's, the change came reluctantly because the staff feared the publication might lose its quality of perspective and become a polyglot grab-bag of unrelated reports. World War II finally settled that problem. Now *Time* staff members reside in the world's chief news centers.

The research and checking system developed slowly from a file labeled by a foreign news researcher as "material which ought to be kept." It has grown into "a vast fact silo," which took professional movers in 1946 a full week, working every night, to shift to new offices. This morgue is a hunting ground for *Time* researchers.

"*Time* style" of inverted sentences and coined words such as "cinemactress" was embraced enthusiastically as a showman's device to impress readers; then, that job done, its excesses were curtailed—reluctantly.

Newsweek originated with an English journalist working in the editorial offices of *The New York Times*—Thomas John Cardel Martyn. His idea was a news magazine whose cover would include seven photographs, each picturing the outstanding event for one day of the week. In February, 1933, on the eve of the ill-omened bank holiday, he launched a 32-page publication that sold for ten cents. By June, 1934, Martyn concluded that the seven simultaneous cover ideas confused newsstand customers. With the issue of June 30, he adopted a single-picture cover.

In October, 1937, Malcomb Muir, for ten years president of the McGraw-Hill Publishing Company, reorganized *Newsweek*, with Astor and Harriman family funds. Under a remodeled editorial formula, the publication became *Newsweek, The Magazine of News Significance*. When he announced his plans, Muir said, "The tumult of communications, bewildering to the average man and woman, has created a need for a magazine which will report events in their proper perspective and also interpret this changing world."

Newsweek interpretation was put under a heading of "Significance," a section that followed the important news reports and attempted to explain them in terms of their likely effects. The editors added predictions of forthcoming news and trends in a division called "Periscope."

U.S. News & World Report traces its ancestry back to the *United States Daily*, which David Lawrence began in 1926. This newspaper reporting the day-to-day story of what was happening in the nation's capital little resembled the news magazines of today. It contained a minimum of interpretation, after the fashion of daily newspapers of that period. Under the pressure of the depression, the daily shifted to a weekly in 1933 and changed its name to *United States News*. It continued to present full, unbiased reports on government affairs. In 1940, it became a magazine and gave more space to translating government actions into reports more meaningful for business man, student, and historian. After the close of World War II, Lawrence launched *World Report* as a companion journal on foreign affairs. In 1948, the two publications were merged and became *U.S. News & World Report*.

Long a weekly journal summarizing front-page news of the week for small-town Americans, *Pathfinder* magazine in the late 1940's reorganized to join the news magazines that provided not only the unembellished facts in the news but also their meaning. With the April, 1953, issue, *Pathfinder* shifted to monthly, thus leaving the weekly news magazine field again to the "Big Three."

Here is how the wheels go around

If you were on *Time's* editorial staff, your work week would start on Thursday, the day the previous issue of the magazine appears on newsstands so that its readers can catch up on world events during weekends. You would have had Tuesday and Wednesday off as your own "weekend."

In the Time and Life Building in Rockefeller Center, New York City, the senior editors each call a story conference Thursday morning. Attending are the writers and researchers of each department under that senior editor as well as representatives of the picture department, news bureau, and clip desk. Story ideas from staff and string correspondents are discussed. News events and anticipated developments are evaluated and weighed. A tentative story list is drawn up at these conferences. A writer and researcher are assigned to each accepted idea. So that the departments, such as National Affairs, Business, Science, Radio, or Education, may know what the others are doing, the story lists of all the senior editors are assembled, mimeographed, and distributed.

Writer and researcher plan their assignment in detail. The researcher consults the morgue, wires or cables correspondents for illuminating details and interpretation, and interviews experts in person or by telephone. The quest for details may be most exacting, as witness this not unusual telegram that a *Time* stringer in Texas received giving him the green light on a query about a blind sheriff killed by a motorist while walking to work with a "seeing eye" dog:

NA [National Affairs] scheduling Sheriff Hodges. Need brief bioperse, including age and few lines of physical description. Need more detail on fight in which he was blinded. How long had he been sheriff at that point? How did he run sheriff's department after losing his sight? How big an organization is it, how many deputies, how good are they? Did he have any particular gimmicks for running it though blind? What was his routine on the average day? On what basis did he campaign and what did people running against him use as campaign arguments? Any of them use his blindness as a campaign issue? Did he get his dog from the Morristown New Jersey Seeing Eye Center? What kind of a dog was it and what did it look like? How much training with the dog did he receive and what happened in the accident which caused his death? Need Saturday.

When the researcher has all the material that she (*Time* researchers are always women) thinks the writer will need, she turns it over to him. Using this, plus his own background and his ability to evaluate the material, the writer organizes the facts, relates them to background and perspective, and types out the story to fit the space it rates in the week's news. This draft goes to the copy desk, senior editor, and finally managing editor. Processed into nearly final form, the story is retyped and a "checking copy" sent to the researcher for authentication of each fact with red dots to indicate an authoritative printed reference and black dots to show some other source. Not only must the researcher satisfy herself that the facts are stated accurately but that they add up to a true news picture. Then the article goes back to the copy desk, senior editor, and managing editor. Generally the copy is sent to the printing plant by the Monday night deadline but infrequently a sudden spurt of news may crowd out the story. Then the edited copy is simply filed in the *Time* morgue.

Time editors regard the National Affairs section, up in the front of the magazine, as equivalent of the newspaper's front page. Here, they tell the story of the general American scene—"its big political stories, public controversy, national policy, crime, heroism, corruption, news and notes on federal, state and local governments." As a handbook for correspondents explained in commenting on this section, "Here we report what is happening to the people, their habits, customs, prejudices and opinions."

Because they frequently regard mood and manner of as much importance as surface facts and spot reporting, *Time* editors may focus attention on such events as this lead of the first article of the October 1, 1951, issue:

> Autumn came to the U.S. last week with a souse of wet snow on Denver, a spatter of cold rain on South Dakota's Black Hills, a chill wind in Chicago that moved on to New York. Autumn found the nation prosperous as never before, its people uneasy as seldom before.
>
> It was a time of transition and suspension. Along New England's shores, the squeak of a fisherman's oars against thole pins sounded lonely and clear in the

> fog of early morning, lately shrill with the cries of the vacationist and his young. The town greens had subsided into their dreaming quiet and the beaches were left to surf-casters. Vermont's fields were gilded with goldenrod, shadowed with purple asters, and the swamp maples glowing red.

A far cry, indeed, from the 5-W newspaper lead. But then it never was intended for the read-and-run customers.

Again, it may be colorful comparison or wealth of detail that lifts a *Time* paragraph into the class of memorable writing, as in the following:

> The old man puffed into sight like a venerable battle-wagon steaming up over the horizon. First a smudge of smoke, then the long cigar, then the familiar, stoop-shouldered hulk that a generation has come to know as the silhouette of greatness. Prime Minister Winston Churchill scowled as he emerged from the *Queen Mary*, took a firm grip on the rope handrail and eased himself across a gangplank to the U.S. Coast Guard Cutter *Navesink* in New York Harbor. Once safely on board the cutter, he politely doffed his hat to official U.S. meeters & greeters.

Since *Time* editors favor telling the news in flesh-and-blood terms, their weekly "cover story" or article concerning the person pictured on the cover is a biography built around the individual brought into the foreground by the news. That person is, in effect, presented as "The Man (or Woman) of the Week," just as each year *Time* picks "The Man of the Year." Unlike newspaper obituaries, these cover pieces present the person so intimately and in such detail that readers feel they actually have known him. Anecdotal stories and direct quotations are bread-and-butter techniques.

Infrequently, the magazine prints a cover piece geared to a trend or a phenomenon in contemporary life that can best be told without being built around a single individual. One of the most widely reprinted articles in the first 35 years of *Time's* history belonged to this group: William Miller's piece on human relations (*Time*, April 14, 1952). Among other outstanding reports of this kind have been those on the younger generation, boat sailing, and the do-it-yourself hobbies, an excerpt from which is reprinted below:

> *He was a Yankee, the very character of whom is, that he can "turn his hand," as he says, "to any thing."*
> —John Neal, *Brother Jonathan*, 1825.

In New England modern-day Yankees are indeed turning their hands to anything. But so, too, are the Hoosiers of Indiana, the Sooners of Oklahoma and the Cornhuskers of Nebraska—along with Texans, Californians, New Yorkers and Iowans. North, South, East and West, Americans have joyfully taken up a new hobby: "Do-It Yourself."

In the postwar decade the do-it-yourself craze has become a national phenomenon. The once indispensable handyman who could fix a chair, hang a door or patch a concrete walk has been replaced by millions of amateur hobbyists who do all his work—and much more—in their spare time and find it wonderful fun. In the process they have turned do-it-yourself into the biggest of all U.S. hobbies and a booming $6 billion-a-year business. The hobbyists, who trudge out of the stores with boards balanced on their shoulders, have also added a new phase to retail jargon: "The shoulder trade."

Cabins & Comics. In Los Angeles last week, the Pan-Pacific Auditorium held its second annual show for the shoulder trade. There were 300 exhibitors displaying everything from a build-it-yourself log cabin ($600) to assemble-it-yourself swimming pools, garage doors, gymnasiums, and gas stoves. In five days 100,000 West Coast fans paid $1.10 apiece to browse through the show and buy $1,000,000 worth of paints, power tools, plywood and plastics for their new hobby.

That was only a drop in the flood of products that goes to the shoulder trade. Last year 11 million amateur carpenters worked on 500 million sq. ft. of plywood with 25 million power tools, burned enough electricity to light a city the size of Jacksonville, Fla., for a year. Amateur decorators slapped on 75% (400 million gal.) of all the paint used in the U.S., pasted up 60% (150 million rolls) of all the wallpaper, laid 50% (500 million sq. ft.) of all the asphalt tile, enough to cover the entire state of Oregon. And while the menfolk labored mightily, 35 million U.S. women made their own clothes (using 750 million yds. of cloth), gave themselves 32 million home permanents, leafed through millions of copies of do-it-yourself magazines and books, looking for still more projects for their husbands and themselves.

In the do-it-yourself cult are such bigwigs as U.S. Steel Vice President David Austin, who has a two-room, $5,000 woodworking workshop packed into his Pittsburgh apartment; former Secretary of State Dean Acheson, who makes his own furniture; TV and Radio Luminaries Desi Arnaz, Edgar Bergen and Fibber McGee, who spend their spare time puttering around with shelves and kitchen cabinets; Movie and Recording Stars George Montgomery, Perry Como, Dan Duryea and Jane Russell, who do their own handiwork, build boats and furniture; the Strategic Air Command's General Curtis LeMay, who is currently helping fellow airmen rebuild a private airplane, and has set up do-it-yourself workshops at SAC bases for everyone from airmen to SAC's vice-commander, Major General Francis H. Griswold, who is reconditioning a sports car. Recently, the hobbyists found themselves in a comic panel called *Do It Yourself*, now syndicated in 83 newspapers.

Cooks & Cats. In addition, there are 100 "How To" magazines, and in New York City's public library there are 3,500 how-to books, 250 on cooking alone, both for the gourmet (*Escoffier Cook Book*) and the not-so-rich and not-so-particular (*The Can-Opener Cookbook*). Gardeners can pore over *Perennials Preferred, Rockeries, Principles of Weed Control,* animal lovers over such volumes as *How to Tempt a Fish, How to Live with a Cat*. There are dozens of books on *How to Buy a House* and how to make it better. There is even one on *How to Make Sense*.

To do-it-yourself buffs, there are few projects too difficult to try. Examples:

¶ In Pleasantville, N.Y., the Easi-Bilt Patterns Co. puts out nine different blueprints for do-it-yourself home builders. Since the war it has sold 250,000 plans, estimates that 70,000 of its do-it-yourself customers have managed to build their own homes.

¶ In Milwaukee, a Korean war flyer named Paul Poberezny formed the Experimental Aircraft Association for do-it-yourself flyers to make their own airplanes. So far, the group has 600 members spread around the U.S. who have flown 500 of their creations. One man is working on a combination plane and car with a pusher propeller and folding wings; another hopes to sell a do-it-yourself small plane kit for $1,000.

¶ In Los Angeles, dozens of hot-rod clubs built their own sports cars out of junk-heap jalopies fitted with souped-up, modern engines. Some of the youngsters take surplus airplane-wing fuel tanks and turn them into 170 m.p.h. racers for speed trials on Utah's Bonneville salt flats; others build elaborate racing cars with Fiberglas bodies and 300-h.p. power plants (often with two engines hooked together) that can do up to 240 m.p.h.

¶ In Northfield, N.J. (pop. 3,500), Mayor G. L. Infield thought bids to paint the City Hall were too high. So His Honor and 23 councilman and citizens rolled up their sleeves, wangled free paint, and did the job themselves. Cost: $30 (for beer), a saving of $1,470.

How It Began. The great postwar hobby got much of its start from the war itself. During their service years, millions of Americans learned for the first time how to repair radios, engines and dozens of other machines. Housewives who had been punch-press operators, welders and electronics technicians found that it was no trick to fix a leaky faucet or paper a room, especially as it was hard to hire anyone to do it. Doing it herself

441

was also less expensive, since the wages of carpenters and plumbers had jumped far higher than those of many other workers. Says one do-it-yourselfer: "A $1.25-an-hour bookkeeper is not going to pay a $3.50-an-hour carpenter very long."

For many Americans, do-it-yourself makes possible luxuries that once existed only in their dreams. In Santa Fe, N. Mex., Joseph Wertz, a retired architect, lives handsomely on $3,000 a year by making what he wants, with the help of his wife Jean. Like many others, they have found a new source of happy companionship in doing tasks together. Working as a team, the Wertzes have built their own ultra-modern fieldstone house with a small swimming pool. They also turn out household dishes, vases and ornamental ceramics, belts, jewelry and furniture. In Hingham, Mass., Jozef Piekarski came home from World War II dreaming about a house far beyond his bankroll—a 17th century Cape Cod Colonial of shingle and red brick. Joe Piekarski has been working on his house for six years; it is still not completely finished, but it is snug, neat, and beginning to look luxurious. Its appraisal value already is $25,000. Cost to Do-It-Yourselfer Piekarski: $11,000. The difference, he says, "came out of my hide."

Sense of Accomplishment. Economic necessity was not the only cause for the boom. Housebuilders had more time, thanks to the five-day week, longer vacations and more holidays, and they had a new interest. In the mass migration to the trees and lawns of suburbia, some 7,000,000 people got houses of their own for the first time—and immediately set to work improving them.

Furthermore, the whole character of U.S. life has been undergoing a complex change. As mass-production techniques have broken jobs into smaller and smaller parts, the average American worker has often lost sight of the end product he is helping to build; his feeling of accomplishment has been whittled away as his job has become only a tiny part of the whole production process. In the same way, the meaning of the tasks performed by white-collar employees and executives often becomes lost in the complexities of giant corporations; it is hard for them to see what they are really accomplishing. But in his home workshop, anyone from president down to file clerk can take satisfaction from the fine table, chair or cabinet taking shape under his own hands—and bulge with pride again as he shows them off to friends.

Good Medicine. The therapeutic value of do-it-yourself is hard to overestimate. One Dallas doctor, a do-it-yourself addict himself, often advises patients to "go home and start doing things themselves." A harried executive who took up woodworking in his spare hours to ease the tension swears that it kept him from suicide. In Minneapolis an elderly dowager recently walked into a hardware store to look at power tools. "For your husband, Madam?" asked the clerk. "Good heavens, no," said she. "I want them myself." Her doctor had told her to take up knitting, but she thought woodworking sounded more interesting.

One sucessful Zion, Ill. jewelry-store owner, Wesley Ashland, cured himself of a nervous breakdown by building his own home. He got out in the woods, found a plot with a small ravine and creek, oaks, elm, hard maple and hawthorn. He drew his own design for an L-shaped ranch house, planned it so that he could save all but two of the trees. He built a bridge over the ravine with 340 bolted railroad ties, and laid a 350-ft. winding lane, bought saws, an electric drill, a jeep, and an old concrete mixer. He built a concrete and limestone house, worked through the winter in 10°-below-zero weather. Inside the four-room house all closets were cedar-lined, all screens and storm windows handmade of aluminum. He did all the plumbing, wiring and paneling himself. To him, the backbreaking work "is a relaxation." Now, at 60, he is healthier than he has been in years.

Lilacs on the Roof. But for the beginners, do-it-yourself is often a painful succession of bashed thumbs and bruised egos. In their haste to build, they often take on complicated projects for which they have to learn a dozen skills, often find themselves in tragicomic jams. One enthusiast, who decided to build two bedrooms and a bath in his attic, put his wife to work tacking insulating paper between the room partitions and outside walls of the house. An hour later, when she tried to crawl out, she found herself nailed in between inner and outer walls. In Boston a do-it-yourselfer soaked his roof shingles in a preservative mixture of kerosene and 20 gallons of scented brilliantine, which he got from an aunt who was once in the cosmetic business. It worked fine, but for days the entire neighborhood reeked of lilacs. Another do-it-yourselfer indignantly returned a can of blue paint, complaining that she could not make it bluer. "What did you use?" asked the dealer. "Why bluing, of course," she replied.

After running into such trouble, some beginners give up and call in a professional. But most do-it-yourselfers are a hardy, bulldog breed, and constantly astound friends by their ability to overcome obstacles.

[Then followed a detailed case history and numerous other illuminating examples.]

What Next? Has the do-it-yourself boom reached its peak? No one thinks so—least of all the do-it-yourselfers. As their skills increase, they see themselves tackling bigger and bigger projects. The man who has put together an 8-ft. pram begins to leaf through plans for an 18-ft. outboard cruiser. The woman who has restuffed and recovered an old chair begins to wonder if she could not make a set of furniture for the dining room. Sales to the shoulder trade are climbing so fast that by 1960 the estimates are that they will be well over $10 billion.

Conceivably, then, millions of Americans will live in the happy, independent state of James W. Lowry, 45, of Cleveland, purchasing agent for Republic Steel Corp. Over the years, he built his daughter a wood-paneled game room, installed a new furnace in his home, made Venetian blinds for all the windows, laid a concrete drive, screened in the front porch, made a suite of bedroom furniture and slipcovers for chairs, built a snowplow, and rigged a darkroom for his other hobby, photography. Says Lowry, in the independent voice of all his breed: "I don't believe I'd know a plumber, elec-

trician or carpenter if I saw one. I haven't hired one
for years."

—Time

Unlike *Time*, which entwines its information and interpretation in a single report, *Newsweek* tends to separate out the news
significance and put it under a special label so that readers may
identify it easily. Its editors have explained, "*Newsweek*, rather
than taking what interested parties say, wants to tell its readers
what train of events led them to say it."

Since the "significance" formula was developed chiefly by
Newsweek editors, it might be informative to quote what they
tell their correspondents about it:

Significance, of course, is what the news means. It should be:
1. A clear statement of outlook in broad strokes.
2. An informed analysis of trends and purpose which do not
readily meet the eye in the factual report.
3. Wherever possible, a personalization from the reader's viewpoint: How does the news affect him?

These elements can readily be brought together though naturally
all three cannot be employed invariably in every Significance. The
main thing to keep in mind is outlook. In other words, Significance
must be forward-looking, not backward-looking. Background is
naturally important, but should be used as an explanation of what lies
ahead. This, of course, is not a green light to prediction of events. It
is, however, an urgent recommendation to obtain reasoned forecasts
of situations.

An example of how this is done is the following quotation
from the *Newsweek* report when the Department of Defense announced in 1954 that four of the six United States divisions in
Korea soon would be pulled out:

Significance

The pullback of the four U.S. divisions is intended
to strengthen, not weaken, the American military pos-
ture in the Far East as well as in the whole world. It
releases a major segment of the U.S. Army which had

been tied down, at great expense, in a tiny theater that is strategically almost meaningless. It also increases sharply America's truly ready and mobile reserves, both in the continental United States and at strategic Pacific bases.

This action confirms that the U.S. has no intention of being forced into renewing the sort of confined war that was waged for three years on the Korean peninsula. Not that the U.S. is abandoning its Korean ally. Rather, if the Reds start the war there all over again, the U.S. will strike back on its own terms and in an arena of its own choice—not in the trenches of Korea.

—*Newsweek*

Other *Newsweek* features include the "Periscope" pages, which add prediction to the news dimensions of background and significance, and also signed opinion columns by such writers as Raymond Moley, Ernest K. Lindley, John Lardner, and Henry Hazlett.

Newsweek uses somewhat the same operational pattern as *Time* in that its chief editors hold weekly story conferences to plan the next issue, teams of writers and researchers are assigned, and stories are checked and rechecked for accuracy. Occasionally a *Newsweek* writer will be sent to cover an important news development in person. For example, one editor flew 30,000 miles to gather first hand information on Southeast Asia. Incidentally, he lost 15 pounds on the journey—but he got his stories.

Centering more on detailed reporting of economic and legislative happenings, especially in the nation's capital, *U.S. News & World Report* has revived the exclusive interview with an important news figure of the week. These are printed in full transcript form with questions and answers. So revealing have some of these been that daily newspapers have printed news stories on the highlights brought out during the interviews. This is journalistic praise from Caesar, indeed.

Success depends on the selection of the individual to be interviewed and on the probing quality of the questions. Both have been done consistently well by *U.S. News & World Report* editors. The person is invited for an interview which, if possible, is held at the magazine's offices in Washington, D.C. A few have been held over the telephone, usually with foreign news figures. A battery of top editors sit around a table asking questions. The conversation is recorded. The person being interviewed is permitted to correct the transcript, which then may be reorganized to give it to readers in more understandable form. Thus the reader gets the full flavor of the interview, studies the man's own words, and makes up his own mind. The magazine makes little effort to personalize further than full quotations, and human interest angles generally are played down.

Reprinting of the week's more important documents also provides readers with additional background on which to build their opinions. *U.S. News & World Report* devotes more pages to reprinting speeches, official documents, and court decisions than the other news magazines, and probably is surpassed in the daily newspaper field only by *The New York Times*.

Opinion and predictions are provided in publisher David Lawrence's one-page signed article, a two-page "Tomorrow: A Look Ahead," and "Washington Whispers," which includes what is heard in other news centers as well as the District of Columbia. The "Tomorrow" newsgram, printed on yellow telegram-colored paper, may include such introductory paragraphs as "You can set these things down as quite well settled" or "What business is assured of in the period ahead is this." After each follows highpoints of what the staff believes is coming, written after the fashion of Washington news letters.

U.S. News & World Report, possibly because its news focuses on Washington and foreign capitals where it has staff members, utilizes group journalism less than *Time* and *Newsweek*. Most writers do their own research and dig up their own information from Washington or foreign sources. Of course, some reaction roundups represent exceptions but most articles apply the newspaper practice of one reporter's going out to gather the facts and then coming back to write the story.

Closely related to the weekly news magazines, although by their very nature different, are the pictorial reviews such as *Life* and *Look*. Their principal aim is to give readers a visualization of the world's news, but they also present interpretation. In *Life* and *The New York Times*, for instance, Sir Winston Churchill first told his autobiographical story of World War II. *Look's* series on religious beliefs provided a background for more tolerance between creeds. The widely-acclaimed "The World We Live In" series in *Life* performed an educational function that most other publications would have forgone because their editors would have viewed it as too off-beat.

Newspapers review the week's events

Each weekend a smattering of the nation's daily newspapers review the week's events and, like the news weeklies, round off the news in an attempt to have it make more sense for their readers. If helping the public to understand what is going on is a primary function of the press, then these papers are performing on a high level. Yet an overwhelming majority of daily papers and almost all the weeklies by-pass this assignment in favor of the conventional, routine job of telling who struck John, not why.

Shying at this task is not perversity on the part of publishers and editors. All the arguments against interpretation of the news may be marshalled here. It is hard and dangerous business to select the right background, focus on the correct perspective, and grab on to the accurate prediction. Competent writers trained in interpretive reporting are hard to find. Some newspapermen pause because they believe it is the duty of editorial writers—not news writers—to help the reader make up his mind. And all the rebuttal reasoning applies here, too.

448

Best known of the papers with news reviews is *The New York Times*, which distributes Sunday editions of more than a million copies around the globe. However, reviews of the week's news appear in such papers as the *New York Herald Tribune, Newsday, Newark* (N.J.) *Evening News, Washington Evening Star* and *San Francisco Chronicle*. The AP Newsfeatures distributes a single-page weekly news review in mat form ready for casting by smaller dailies. It is called "The World This Week." Picture strips of the week's news events at the top and bottom allow make-up men to reduce page depth to fit variations for most eight column papers. Started in 1934, the Associated Press' page is the only major news review available nationally for non-metropolitan newspapers.

Most editors connected with the contemporary news summaries predict that the number of newspapers using these weekly reviews will increase, not decline, during the 1950's and 1960's as more weekend papers meet, through better interpretation, the challenge of spot news coverage by television.

Lester Markel, Sunday editor of *The New York Times*, described the operations of his paper's Sunday news summary staff as follows in *The Newspaper, Its Making and Its Meaning* (Scribner's, 1945):

The summary is designed to pull together the threads of events; to link up disconnected dispatches; in short, to provide a sort of "Outline of History" of the week. But it is much more than a rewrite of the daily news. A great deal of research work goes into it, in an effort to enrich it, both in the way of fact and of color.

That research work is a sort of treasure hunt. Each day, out of the leads we find in the daily paper, we seek out additional facts and atmosphere to provide a rounded and graphic picture.

Some of that material we find in our own files and morgue and through sources available in the city [New York]. Some of it is the result of queries sent abroad or to our men in Washington or throughout the country, who supply to us, by wireless or telegraph, memorandums which are incorporated into the summary.

The New York Times summary staff includes six writers who do their own research, are their own leg-men. Those in charge feel that this achieves greater unity than the team approach of *Time* and *Newsweek*. The work week begins on Tuesday and continues right up into Saturday afternoon, if there are late news breaks of consequence. Each writer contributes, roughly, 1,500 words a week toward the two-page "Review" section total of 8,500. This production may seem low compared to that of the re-write man who thinks he has a normal day if he handles that wordage during a single eight hours. But each of the writers must allow for "thinking time" or the hours when he is trying to add up news developments so that he can pass his conclusions on to the readers. In recognition for bringing "enlightenment and intelligent commentary to its readers," *The New York Times* "News of the Week in Review" section won a Pulitzer prize in 1953.

Although the regular news staff of *The New York Times* filled seven pages with news stories the Tuesday after the United States Supreme Court banned school segregation (see pages 426 to 428), "The News of the Week in Review" section the following Sunday devoted approximately 2,000 words to summarizing the story and included some information not printed earlier. The article consisted of four parts: Introduction, "The Background," "The Decision," and "The Future." The first part is reprinted below:

> Now, therefore, I, Abraham Lincoln, President of the United States, by virtue of the power in me vested * * * do order and declare that all persons held as slaves * * * are, and henceforward shall be, free * * *

> In the ninety-one years since Lincoln's Emancipation Proclamation, there have been many efforts to reconcile the reality of the bi-racial system in the South with the American ideal of equality for all men. The Negro has scored many gains and segregation has often

been decried as a blot on the nation's conscience. But the bi-racial system has continued as an accommodation to habit, tradition and political necessity.

Last week the Supreme Court cut through to the heart of the problem and issued a historic judgment for racial equality. Unanimously the nine high court Justices ruled that enforced segregation of Negro children in public schools violated the Constitution.

Before the decision was issued there had been dire threats of violence in the South if the Court ruled against segregation. Yet it was received with general calm. Last week attention turned to the vast task of translating the decision into educational fact.

—The New York Times

Most other summary or review staffs consist of one or two men. To them, *The New York Times* set-up appears to be a dream arrangement. Yet these other papers generally present highly readable copy because they center attention on local news interests. The New York City Sunday papers and the news weeklies cannot hope to compete with local papers in local news coverage; that applies to weekend news summaries just as in the other fields. For example, "This World" magazine of the *San Francisco Chronicle* leads off "The News in Review" with a section entitled "The West" and then covers the United States and foreign affairs. In New York's suburbia, *Newsday's* four-page "Weekly Report" on Saturdays plays up Long Island news along with national and world happenings.

More widely used than news summaries are weekend interpretations of current events. *The New York Times* does this in signed articles in the inside pages of its review section and in its Sunday Magazine. So do most other dailies with news summaries. Others with weekend sections containing a large measure of news interpretation include the Louisville *Courier-Journal, Washington Post and Times Herald, Atlanta Constitution, Minneapolis Sunday Tribune,* and *St. Louis Post-Dispatch.*

SIXTEEN

This thing
called style

IN WRITING, THE PRIMARY THING IS TO HAVE SOMETHING TO SAY.
That applies equally for editorials, columns, explanatory writing,
or news interpretation. But when you have something to say, then
it is vital to say it so readers will understand.

If this chapter happens to offer advice on style that is not applied in writing about it, the final advice is, "Do as I say and not
as I do." Anyone faces that hazard when he writes about writing.

Style has its critics

William T. Polk of the *Greensboro* (N.C.) *Daily News* wrote
the following in the lead article of the initial issue of *The Masthead* (Spring, 1949):

> The necessary equipment of a writer is a seeing eye, a hearing ear
> and a lot of nerve; a good mind can be a help but it is not a prerequi-
> site. Literature from Homer to Hemingway is evidence of the neces-
> sity of the sensitive eye, ear, nose, throat and epidermis; modern fic-
> tion is proof of the essentiality of nerve and the dispensability of in-
> telligence.
> Probably the editorial writer *per se* is a cut above the novelist. His
> thinking process is similar to that of the lawyer; his business is to
> analyze a complicated set of facts and arrive at a conclusion that can
> stand up and take it. But his writing process is that of the artist. The
> lawyer uses words like bricks—habeas corpus, estate by entirety—

452

which can be counted on to stay the same shape, size and consistency yesterday, today and tomorrow.

Writers who aspire to write "the literature of power" use words like flames; it is their business to make them leap, crackle and shine by giving them, as Bacon phrased it, some sparkle of "liberty, spirit and edge." Editorials built of bricklike words cause readers to shy off —they look too much like deadfalls. Editorials are on live topics and their words should have life in them. When you cut them, they should bleed, instead of going "Pop!" or "Whoosh!"

But too often, as any honest editorial or interpretive news writer will confess, their style is dull and their words do go down with "Pop!" or "Whoosh!"

Jack Kilpatrick, editor of the Richmond *News Leader*, evaluated his fellow craftsmen with a cynical eye during a 1953 lecture at Columbia University:

We are, by every rule of classification and description, *writers*. That is how we earn our living, buy our children's shoes, pay the weekly milk bill. Yet we write, all too often, like butchers' apprentices, or Congressmen.

What it is that comes over the editorial writer, when he puts his belly against the Underwood, I cannot say. I feel it often enough myself, God knows. It is a sort of pomposity trying not to be pompous, a straining after dignity—high school principals addressing the parents and teachers. If there is a hard way to say something and an easy way, nine times out of ten we pick the hard way. We say "nocturnal" when we mean "at night," and "distaff side" when we ought to say "woman." This is *editorialese*, the gingerbread trim on a newspaper's portico, as stylized as the minuet and as full of phony elegance. Oh, there are many exceptions, and if I seem severe, it is not that I do not recognize and applaud the many superb editorial writers who do go at their task with a sure touch . . .

When I said that I could not explain this artificial style, this elephant's gavotte that the editors dance, I was perhaps a little sweeping. One honest explanation for the trouble is that we simply haven't enough time, most of us, to do any better. *Good writing takes time.* There may be geniuses here and there who can produce superb paragraphs, full of pithy thought and subtle epigram, as popcorn flows from the nickel machine. But you will find few of them in the editorial offices of daily newspapers. For most of us, good writing comes like good cabinet-making—slowly, and with infinite writing and re-writing, with a rubbing and sandpapering and polishing of rough phrases.

Lack of time for "rubbing and sandpapering and polishing" may be forced upon writers by publishers unwilling to spend more money for better writing. But writers may do something about their occupational preoccupation with pontificating. Editorial writers and news interpreters tend to climb up on a pinnacle and there harangue the multitudes, like the prophets of old. It almost seems part of their job; they spend so much time becoming better informed that an expansive arrogance comes naturally. Too many writers for newspapers and magazines forget a sense of humility when they express opinions. Those who write news interpretations or explanations face the hazard less often but they, too, should keep this caution in mind, especially when speculating about the future.

Newspaper and magazine writers, to be truly effective, need to visualize their publication's typical reader and then pick words that he will understand. For example, a news analyst for the Associated Press needs to be more down-to-earth in vocabulary than an editorial writer of *The New York Times*. Is the goal to reach the classes or the masses? Some writers deliberately set out, like intellectual snobs, to reach only what sociologists call "opinion moulders" and pick language that most of their readers will not comprehend. This is particularly true of editorial writers on medium-sized dailies. Such limited appeals are short sighted for all but a few publications that admittedly have a class approach, as, say, *Scientific American* or some engineering and electronics journals.

These snobbish American editorial writers are like their con-freres in Greece who print their editorials in "High Greek," least known of the three Greek languages in contemporary use and read only by the better educated. When an American journalism teacher questioned these editors, they replied, "Oh, the people are impressed by it even though they may not be able to understand it fully."

How two New York City newspapers commented editorially on the reports after the Army-McCarthy hearings in 1954 illustrates how language is tailored to a publication's typical reader:

> Army Secretary Robert T. Stevens was saluted as a very upright fellow, and no doubt good to his family, but then was ticked off in polite language as a guy who, in blunt language, doesn't know beans about the important government job he still surprisingly holds.
>
> *—Daily News*

> All agree that Secretary Stevens followed an unwarranted course of appeasement and that he and his counsel, John Adams, did try to terminate the McCarthy investigation of Fort Monmouth. All agree that neither Stevens nor Adams is "soft" on communism.
>
> *—The New York Times*

Writers must know how to use ingredients of style

Words, phrases, sentences, and paragraphs form the ingredients of style. How they are used will determine whether the author plods along like a tired pedestrian homeward-bound after an exhausting day or soars like a jet plane pilot scrambling for a maneuver in refresher training.

Strong verbs add greatly to style and they can provide illuminating details that intrigue the reader. For instance, to write "He was in his office when the visitor came in" simply conveys his presence when something happened. To say "He got up from behind his desk and extended his hand as the visitor entered the office" describes action. But it is unnecessary to make all planes soar, all engines puff, or all motorists speed away. Descriptive verbs should not be overdone.

Nouns, too, may be strengthened by being made specific and

descriptive. Why say "the man" when it is "the traffic policeman on the corner." And if the writer explains that he wore white gloves, that improves it still more.

The concrete and familiar word or phrase insures greater reader understanding than the abstract, the Latinized, the academic, the *editorialese*, or, as Maury Maverick christened the governmental version, the gobbledygook. Writers were so intrigued with governmental gobbledygook that a tongue-in-cheek textbook is available in *Federal Prose: How to Write in and/or for Washington* (University of North Carolina Press, 1948).

Probably the most widely quoted illustration is a proposed World War II instruction for air-raid defense:

> Such preparation shall be made as will completely obscure all Federal buildings and non-Federal buildings occupied by the Federal Government during an air raid for any period of time from visibility by reason of internal or external illumination. Such obscuration may be obtained either by blackout construction or by termination of the illumination. This will, of course, require that in building areas in which production must continue during the blackout, construction must be provided that internal illumination may continue.

When President Franklin D. Roosevelt saw the draft, he ordered: "Tell them that in buildings where they have to keep the work going to put something across the window. In buildings where they can afford to let the work stop for a while, turn out the lights."

Another example, if one is needed, is this winner in a Columbia University Press contest "to translate English into federal prose:"

> A detached fragment of the terrestrial lithosphere, whether of igneous, sedimentary or metamorphic origin, and whether acquiring its approximation to sphericity through hydraulic action or other attrition, when continuously maintained in motion by reason of the instrumentality of gravitational forces constantly acting

to lower its center of gravity, thus resulting in a rotational movement around its temporary axis and with its velocity accelerated by any increase in the angle of declivity, is, because of abrasive action produced by the incessant but irregular contact between its periphery and the contiguous terrain, effectively prevented from accumulating on its external surface any appreciable modicum of the cryptogamous vegetation normally propagated in umbrageous situations under optimum conditions of undeviating atmospheric humidity, solar radiation, quiescence, and comparative sequestration from erosive agencies.

—*The Pleasures of Publishing*,
Columbia University Press

And what is the original version?
"A rolling stone gathers no moss."

Newspapermen and magazine writers better look again at their own copy before they laugh too loudly. The 1949–50 Nieman Fellows did not have to exert themselves to cull the following "from editorials in random issues of half a dozen top-drawer American dailies:"

circumambient	magisterial admonitions
de gustibus	
moiling	nexus
cachet	winching
satrapies	apocryphal
antithetical	piling Pelion on Ossa
fustian	theocratic feudalism
exacerbation	intransigence

Professor David Manning White of Boston University found that 65 college graduates missed almost half of the words when asked to pick the exact synonyms for 25 words taken from five United States newspapers. But in editorial dissent from Professor White's alarm over his findings, the *New York Herald Tribune* argued, "We think that a tendency toward colloquialism and the language of the man in the street is more present today in a great deal of newspaper writing than ever before." Yet news analysts, explanatory writers, and interpreters, as well as editorial writers on occasions, commit sins that have been called "evasive verbosity."

Many words and phrases carry emotional cargoes. When does a party leader become a "statesman" and when a "political hack"? When opinion helps to pick the words. In 1953 and 1954, a decline in business was variously dubbed as "rolling adjustment," "disinflation," "readjustment," "deflation," "dip," "recession," and "depression." The selected word depended mainly upon what the person was trying to establish. A writer can show his emotions by his language but he should be sure he knows what he wants to do. If he wants to be neutral, then he should shun the emotion-freighted word or phrase.

Clichés once were good, fresh words and phrases but they now are worn out and broken down from overuse. Best advice: Avoid them when possible. After reading a batch of editorial pages at one sitting, one writer listed these "stock phrases which we use to cover our doubts": "apparently," "it may well be," "it remains to be seen," "may have a point," "it seems evident," "at any rate," and "it is difficult to see." And he forgot to include "on the other hand," "by and large," and "but we must remember."

Infrequently, a publication may print an unfortunate exhibition of falling over its own clichés, like this sentence from a New York City paper:

> It is not only that the Democrats, when it comes to throwing stones, live in a glass house, they live in a house that is putrid with the odor of venality and scandal; and the beam in their eye festers with rottenness.

Sentence length relates directly to readability. With scant exceptions, the shorter the sentence, the more readable it is. The

458

first grade primer with its simple, short sentences is highly readable. Sometimes writers for more sophisticated audiences deliberately choose the longer sentences. But a short sentence may
pound down an idea with sledge hammer force. For evidence,
re-read the editorial by Frank Cobb on pages 47 to 49.

Figures of speech aid readers to picture and understand. A
simile may tie an abstraction into everyday living and so make
it clearer. The descriptive comparison may bring the topic into
focus for a reader. An alliteration may please the eye and rivet
itself into memory for easy recall. Concrete details may back up
an argument more effectively than a wealth of logic.

Here are some phrases, sentences, and paragraphs that this author liked and maybe you will too:

> . . . the fine art of being wrong in a loud voice.
> —*Minneapolis Tribune*

> . . . yearns for privacy like a mid-Victorian maiden
> with a busted garter.
> —*New York Post*

> . . . the familiar Communist process of grinding the
> masses to mincemeat in order to mold a new nation.
> —Joseph Alsop, syndicated column

> . . . that corporation lawyer-agrarian whose busi-
> ness address is in lower Manhattan, a stone's throw
> from Wall Street.
> —Louisville *Courier-Journal*

> With this opinion anybody is entitled to disagree. We
> do.
> —*St. Louis Post-Dispatch*

> Liberty pays off in pork chops as well as in free minds
> producing undictated thoughts.
> —New York *Daily News*

> He was a wretched, sick and snarling little man. But
> he had the voice of a brass trumpet blaring venom and
> racism.
> —*Time*

After all these lessons, the world could wonder if what the Communists mean by peaceful co-existence is this: You do as I say and I'll do as I please.

—William L. Ryan, Associated Press

The pituitary gland, which lies in the middle of the head, is like the conductor of a symphony orchestra. It directs all the other hormone-secreting glands of the body.

—Waldemar Kaempffert, *The New York Times*

Despite a Nobel Award to our William Faulkner, the foreign reader must be warned that life in the U.S. is not exactly as the great novelist says—all magnolias and mildew.

—*Buffalo Evening News*

At the start of the year, even a couple of months ago, the President approached this weekly ordeal [press conference] like a rookie pitcher with the bases loaded, but he looked like a veteran today.

—James Reston, *The New York Times*

All the old familiar signs were present in the first genuine snowfall. The suburbs lay under what is technically known as a mantle of white. Traffic, to use another technical expression, was snarled. Bridges were slippery. Subways were delayed. Railroads were behind schedule. And the outlook was bleak.

—*New York Herald Tribune*

For us, one of the excitements of New York in these racy times is living near enough to the United Nations headquarters so that we can wander in now and again and sit in the new chairs and listen to the old debates. For about eight years, we have followed the U.N. around the country, have sat with it in sadness in the queer dwellings where, for lack of any better place to go, it has parked its briefcase. Opera houses, hotel rooms, college gyms, skating rinks, gyroscope factories. And now the little green shebang on the East River. All its homes have been queer; all have had one quality in common—a kind of dreaminess compounded of modern interiors, ancient animosities, and the aching hopes of invisible millions.

—E. B. White, *The New Yorker*

(Copyright 1953, by E. B. White)

A month ago, the oil industry discovered it had a bad case of indigestion—too much supply, too little demand. It promptly reached for the bicarb—imports and domestic production of crude were cut, gasoline price wars flared widely to ease the glut.

The trouble is, after a month of treatment the patient seems to be making no progress to speak of. Wall Street has been able to detect no improvement at all, and it is swinging to the belief that the period needed for a cure is going to be a lot longer than either its own experts or the general public believed.

—*Business Week*

Flesch and Gunning offer some formulas

Dr. Rudolf Flesch, whom *Time* called the "Mr. Fix-it of writing," discovered readability during graduate work at Columbia University. He has shared his discovery with all who would listen. Among the more interested have been newspaper and magazine writers and editors. The Associated Press hired him as a consultant. Dr. Flesch wrote a shelf of books explaining his formula, including *The Art of Plain Talk* (Harper, 1946) and *The Art of Readable Writing* (Harper, 1949).

Just what is the Flesch readability formula? In *The AP Writing Handbook*, issued in 1951, he boiled it down to the following two key paragraphs:

There's no need to give you here my formula in detail. Briefly, it stresses short sentences (an average of not more than 19 words each), short words (an average of not more than 150 syllables per hundred words), and liberal use of words and sentences that have human interest. . . .

The Flesch formula is keyed to averages, but don't forget one

461

point: Readability means variety, not monotony. By all means don't let it cramp your style.

Robert Gunning, director of Readable News Reports, devised a similar three-fold set of standards. He tested (1) sentence pattern, (2) fog index, and (3) the human interest factor. He said that sentences averaging more than 20 words in length begin to be hard reading. *Time*, he found, averaged 16 to 18 words to the sentence. Fog index measured the abstract and complex words such as "prodigious expenditure" for "big expense" or "rendezvous" for "meeting." The human interest factor rested on the well-known fact that stories told in terms of people attract greater readership than those that are not. But Gunning admitted that it is extremely difficult to report some facts in terms of people.

Both Dr. Flesch and Gunning have been denounced by some journalists as trying to ram writing into a rigid formula that would kill any vestige of creative work. But both have disclaimed the excesses of their over-zealous partisans. They explained that they were attempting to provide some mechanical standards for measuring readability or reading ease, not to develop formulas that would guarantee great and brilliant prose if only the rules were rigidly followed.

While Dr. Flesch and Gunning formalized the measuring rods of readability, interest in the subject by newspaper and magazine editors and publishers runs back into journalism of other centuries. For instance, Alleyne Ireland wrote in *An Adventure with A Genius* (Dutton, 1920) that Joseph Pulitzer "watched the style of each man with closest attention, examining the length of the paragraphs, of the sentences, of the words, the variety of vocabulary, the choice of adjectives and adverbs, the employment of superlatives, the selection of a heading, the nicety of adjustment between the thought to be expressed and the language employed for its expression."

Gordon M. Connelly, director of research for the *Denver*

Post, picked four random editorials from five newspapers and applied the Flesch formula to determine reading ease. He reported his findings in *The Masthead* (Winter, 1952–53) as follows:

Paper	Words per Sentence	Syllables per 100 Words	Score
Richmond News Leader	19	162	50
Denver Post	21	160	50
Newsday, Garden City, N.Y.	21	164	47
Christian Science Monitor	19	168	45
Daily Sentinel, Grand Junction, Colorado	31	166	35

According to Dr. Flesch's table of readability, a score between 60 and 70 is standard and can be understood with ease by readers who completed eighth grade; between 50 and 60, fairly difficult, for those who attended high school; and between 30 and 50, difficult, for those who completed high school or went to college.

Applying this table shows that none of the editors were on target for that majority of United States citizens who never got beyond the sophomore year in high school. If they want to win friends and influence people, their writing style lacks something: mass appeal.

Somewhat the same lack of appeal applies to the editorial "we," so widely denounced yet so frequently used by editorial page writers. The "we" scores as a personal pronoun in the readability formulas so its sins do not show up there, but its use does hinder forceful writing. One midwestern writer tried to perk up his lead editorial by starting, "We did a double-take the other day." His shocked associates asked, "How can 'we' do a double-take— 'we' means the newspaper?" Impersonal editorials represent the paper as an institution. But the editorial "we" raises problems.

Carl R. Kesler, editorial writer on the *Chicago Daily News*, confessed his own doubts about the editorial "we" in *The Quill* (December, 1950):

It is easy to dismiss the editorial "we" as a convention that offers no real handicap to the thinker behind it. But it can be a handicap, not to thought itself, but to communication of thought. It can rule out use of the personal experience, of the hopes and fears and tastes of the individual human being that do so much to translate his thought into words and phrases that will reach the minds and hearts of other men.

And that is where the objections to the editorial "we" would show up in applying the Flesch and Gunning formulas.

Now let us add it all up

Just as the proof of a pudding is in the eating, so the test of a style is in the reading. Here are some examples of how effective style can provide good reading.

First, look back to pages 43 and 44 and re-read the original editorial on Santa Claus from the *New York Sun*. Now you are ready for the following parody that appeared in *The New Yorker* (December 24, 1949; copyright 1949 The New Yorker Magazine, Inc.; reprinted by permission of the author):

To a Little Girl at Christmas

(How a Famous Question Might Be Answered If It
Were Asked Today and Mr. Westbrook Pegler
Happened to Be Writing Editorials for the "Sun")

You're damn right there is a Santa Claus, Virginia. He lives down the road a piece from me, and my name for him is Comrade Jelly Belly, after a poem composed about him once by an admiring fellow-traveller now happily under the sod.

In a manner of speaking, this Jelly Belly is in the distributing end of the toy business, and I guess the story of how that came about has its points for the social historian. Mr. Claus is understandably a reticent man but the facts would seem to be that he was born quite a while back in the Red Hook section under the appetizing monicker of Sammy Klein. His mother was employed in a celebrated bucket of blood known as the Haymarket, also in what you might call the distributing end, and his father was any one of a number of slick operators, though the weight of evidence would seem to point to Police Lieutenant Becker of fragrant memory. How his mother happened to name him Sammy Klein is not known to this deponent, but there is a suspicion that she got it off the front of a clothing store she was in the habit of looting. It is not my way to speak ill of the dead, Virginia, but you'd have to go a long way to find a scurvier pair than the two who spawned the tot we're discussing.

In his youth, Jelly Belly did a short stretch of military service with the Hudson Dusters and the Dead Rabbits, two pinko front organizations of the period, and then passed on to the less perilous profession of rolling lushes in the subway. According to surviving court records, an operative in this classification, variously known as Sid Kline, Saul ("Fingers") Klem, and K. Stein, was arrested no less than thirty-seven times between 1908 and 1916, and stored in the poky for periods ranging from ninety days up. This was presumably Santa Claus.

So much, Virginia, for our hero's boyhood. In 1917, as you probably remember, a sick college professor in the White House ranted us into what he called a war to make the world safe for democracy, and Jelly Belly had one of the first numbers they pulled out of the bowl. This, however, was one rap he knew how to beat, and young Klein sat out World War I in a hospital for the criminally insane, having prudently assaulted a six-year-old girl on the very day his draft board invited him to call. He was pardoned in 1919 at the special request of the Assistant Secretary of the Navy, whose name happened to be Franklin Delano Roosevelt, and even then displayed a strong affinity for the unbalanced.

It was at this time that Jelly Belly changed his name to Santa Claus, partly to escape from his too vivacious past and partly because he had just become a full member of the Communist Party and needed an alias with a sanctimonious flavor. His affiliation with the toy business began soon after that. When F.D.R. sprung Jelly Belly, or Santa Claus, from the loonybin, he went to work for the New York *Times* as a bushwhacker in the circulation department, his job being to mess up delivery boys from the rival *Herald*. This was naturally an employment highly to his taste, but when one boy died as the result of his attentions, it seemed sagacious to move on. It was in this manner that he came to F. A. O. Schwarz, where they made him first a shipping clerk and then the driver of a truck. The rest of the story—the prearranged hijackings that proved profitable enough to set Santa Claus up in the toy business for himself, the deals with Henry Agard Wallace, Felix Frankfurter, and his old friend Roosevelt that permitted him to pick the taxpayer's pocket to the tune of about eighty million dollars a year—is too complicated and dirty for a lady of your tender years. The important fact is that there *is* a Santa Claus, Virginia—a fat old party, with nasty habits and a dirty white beard, who, for reasons best known to himself, likes to go around either wholly undressed or else in an ill-fitting red suit.

Today, Jelly Belly enjoys what is sometimes called the odor of sanctity, being generally regarded as a hell of a fellow by little children, soft-headed women, and the kind of deep thinkers who openly profess their opposition to the sterilization of all Communists. My own information is somewhat different. Jelly Belly gets around even more than Eleanor the Great, and I can't speak for his activities in other parts of the country. In my neighborhood, however, it is a matter of common knowledge that the burglary rate never fails to hit its peak at Christmas. No one has ever been caught for any of these misdemeanors, but the evidence in each case is always the same—a few shoddy toys in a stocking on the mantelpiece and a mink coat or a pearl necklace missing from the hostess's effects. One victim I know said she wouldn't mind so much if the toys were any good, but they are just the cheap, tasteless junk that crooked labor unions have been turning out ever since the Great Brain decided to sell out his country to the lazy and incompetent.

I could go on for a long time telling you about Jelly Belly, Virginia. I could tell you, for instance, how the

THIS THING CALLED STYLE

gross old slattern who passes herself off as his house-
keeper would be described in less respectable pages than
these by quite another word. Or I could tell you how he is
a member of the Westchester Commuters Association,
the National Association of Dahlia Growers, the Society
for Improving the Condition of the Poor, and any number of other thinly disguised Communist organizations.
Or I could even tell you with what drooling pleasure he
beats his eight undersized reindeer, whose cruel whip
sores I have seen with my own eyes. But these are probably not good things for a little girl to know. Youth is
a time for innocent dreams and illusions, Virginia, and
I don't believe I could live comfortably with myself if I
destroyed yours. Yes, Virginia, there is a Santa Claus.
There is old Jelly Belly.

—Wolcott Gibbs, *The New Yorker*

And there is this spoof editorial which shows what an effective
style can do for reader enjoyment:

Hurrah for the Stanley Steamer!

We could have told you days ago that the Stanley
Steamer was going to win the big auto race to New
York. It simply stands to reason that a vehicle that runs
by steam can beat one that runs by gasoline. We were
surprised when the driver of the gas contraption, a fellow named Rube De Launty, even said he was going to
make the race in the first place. You could just look at
this thing, a Stoddard-Dayton they called it, and tell
that it didn't have a chance to beat the raw power of a
steamer. Rube should have got a horse.

These gas things are just too complicated to be any
good. Besides, where are you going to get all the fuel
from? You can't expect people to put up filling stations
or something all up and down the roads just to take
care of gas machines. And even if you could, anybody
with any sense would know that a Stanley Steamer can
beat anything on wheels. But there you are, some smart
alecks are never satisfied and have to go tinkering
around with newfangled ideas that just can't work.

467

Well, old Rube ended up eating the dust of Jack Brause and his mighty steamer. We hope this will be a lesson to the gasoline fellows, but we doubt it. They'll keep fooling around with the gas buggies until the cows come home. Some people never learn.

—*New York Herald Tribune*

SEVENTEEN

Qualifications and background for commenting on the news

IF A NEWSPAPER OR MAGAZINE HAS ITS QUOTA OF WISE MEN (AND most of them do), a high percentage of them should be writing editorials, interpretive articles, columns, and opinion pieces. The men and women who explain what is going on need to be mature and talented if their conclusions are to be worth reading.

This chapter outlines some of the contributions the press' commentators on the news have made besides their editorials, columns, and interpretations. Then it surveys the background of these writers—what schooling and what newspaper and magazine jobs they have held.

Interpreters of the news are important people

Indicative of the intellectual caliber of editorial writers, columnists, and news interpreters has been the individual recognition that many have won outside their own publications.

Representative of a generation of editors and writers no longer on the stage, William Allen White of the *Emporia* (Kansas) *Gazette* and Ed Howe of the *Atchison* (Kansas) *Globe* won international fame from their books and articles as well as their contributions to small town Midwestern dailies.

Dr. Douglas S. Freeman, distinguished historian of the Confederacy and biographer of George Washington and long-time editor of the Richmond (Virginia) *News Leader*, Herbert Agar, who

469

wrote for the Louisville (Kentucky) *Courier Journal*, Merlo J. Pusey, associate editor of the *Washington Post and Times Herald*, and Bruce Catton, former Washington writer for Newspaper Enterprise Association, won Pulitzer prizes for historical volumes not intimately associated with journalism. Mark Sullivan, syndicated columnist, Ernest K. Lindley of *Newsweek*, Walter Millis, long with the *New York Herald Tribune*, and Frederick Lewis Allen, late editor of *Harper's Magazine*, all wrote books on our times which critics widely praised as among the best. Millis also edited the popular *Forrestal Diaries* (Viking, 1951). Irving Dilliard of the *St. Louis Post-Dispatch* edited a collection of papers of Judge Learned Hand that reached the best seller lists.

Jonathan Daniels, who followed his father as editor of the Raleigh (N.C.) *News and Observer*, travelled 3,000 miles to gather material for the widely hailed *A Southerner Looks at the South* (Macmillan, 1940) and the following decade William T. Polk of the *Greensboro* (N.C.) *Daily News* wrote *Southern Accent: From Uncle Remus to Oak Ridge* (Morrow, 1953). Irving Brant, former chief editorial writer on the *St. Louis Star-Times*, wrote on such varied subjects as the federal constitution, economics, and the life of James Madison; all his books have been highly praised. Alan Barth, editorial writer for the *Washington Post and Times Herald*, wrote the challenging and widely-circulated *The Loyalty of Free Men* (Viking, 1951). Henry Beetle Hough of the weekly *Vineyard Gazette* on Martha's Vineyard demonstrated in several books that the William Allen White traditions of a generation ago still held reader appeal.

Foreign correspondents who interpret events abroad for the daily papers and magazines frequently turn to books, as witness William L. Shirer, Vincent Sheean, Eddy Gilmore, Marguerite Higgins, E. J. Kahn, Edmund Stevens, and Herbert L. Matthews, to mention just a few.

Among the syndicated columnists, Walter Lippmann has a well-filled shelf of books to his credit. Marquis Childs' *Sweden:*

470

The Middle Way (Yale University Press, 1936) was frequently cited in the post-depression years. Collected columns of Raymond Clapper, Max Lerner, Dorothy Thompson, Samuel Grafton, and Westbrook Pegler all appeared in individual books. Thomas L. Stokes and Mark Sullivan have written autobiographies. George Gallup has explained public opinion polling not only in newspaper columns but in magazine articles and several books.

Presidents have called successful editors to their aid, sometimes to repay campaign support. Woodrow Wilson turned to Walter Hines Page, editor of the magazine *World's Work*, to represent the United States at the Court of St. James, and to Josephus Daniels of the Raleigh (N.C.) *News and Observer* to be Secretary of the Navy. Half a generation later, President Franklin D. Roosevelt called upon not only Josephus Daniels but his son, Jonathan, who held a key White House staff position.

George Harvey, one-time editor of *Harper's Weekly* and founder of *Harvey's Weekly*, was President Warren G. Harding's envoy to Great Britain. Mark Sullivan, reporter turned columnist, was a welcome member of President Herbert Hoover's "medicine ball cabinet."

Among the early New Dealers, a heavier weight was assigned college teachers but many newspapermen were recruited to fill the expanding number of public information positions. Two of President Roosevelt's cabinet had journalistic backgrounds— Henry A. Wallace, an agricultural periodical publisher who became Secretary of Agriculture and later Vice-President, and Frank Knox, who was drafted from publishing the *Chicago Daily News* to be Secretary of the Navy. Two other administration leaders became columnists after they left the government—Hugh S. Johnson, National Recovery Administrator, and Secretary of the Interior Harold L. Ickes. President Roosevelt named Ernest H. Gruening, one-time managing editor of *The Nation*, to be governor of Alaska, and one of his ambassadors to the Court of

St. James was Robert W. Bingham, publisher of the Louisville *Courier-Journal*. During World War II, many prominent editors and interpretive writers went to Washington from their civilian jobs. Elmer Davis, former *New York Times* feature writer and outstanding radio commentator, was selected to head the Office of War Information. One of his short-time associates was Paul Smith of the *San Francisco Chronicle;* later ones included Gardner Cowles, Jr., of *Look* and Palmer Hoyt, then with the Portland *Oregonian*.

President Harry S. Truman chose his boyhood friend, Charles Ross, chief of the *St. Louis Post-Dispatch* bureau in Washington, for his press secretary and listened to his advice on many matters. W. W. Waymack, Pulitzer prize winning editor of the *Des Moines Register* and *Tribune*, was one of the five original members of the Atomic Energy Commission.

President Dwight D. Eisenhower picked Mrs. Oveta Culp Hobby of the *Houston Post* as first secretary of the new Department of Health, Education, and Welfare.

Particularly during presidential campaigns and when political programs were being offered for public approval, officials of federal, state, and local government have turned to newspaper and magazine people for aid and assistance. Those who interpret the news have attained the V.I.P. plush carpet.

Writers themselves have backgrounds

Neil MacNeil, former assistant managing editor of *The New York Times*, paid a newsman's respects to editorial writers in the following resume of their qualifications in *Without Fear or Favor* (Harcourt, Brace, 1940):

Great ability, a power of expression, and specialized knowledge are requisites for the editorial writer. He should be a sound journalist of wide experience.

472

If MacNeil had been writing during the 1950's after the de-pression-fostered columnists had made a more substantial record and after news interpreters had invaded even his own paper, he could have set much the same requirements for columnists and news interpreters.

First, let us consider those who write editorials.

Editorial writers themselves set impressively high goals. For instance, Philip Wagner, editorial writer on the Baltimore *Sun*, detailed the requirements as he saw them during a talk before the 1947 National Conference of Editorial Writers in Washington. He said:

> Let's consider what it takes to make a top-notch editorial writer.
>
> A good editorial writer has to have a first-rate intelligence; I should say an "I.Q." of 140.
>
> That has to be strengthened by wide reading, habitual reading. Formal education helps, but, as we all know, it is no necessity.
>
> He has to have the habit of intellectual discipline; which is to say that he must respect reason and stick by it.
>
> He must have a sense of responsibility; which is to say that he has to be a man of good faith when he goes into print.
>
> He has to have a real urge to communicate. He must have some-thing to communicate, something to say.
>
> He must have a feeling for the language and a pronounced talent for using it.
>
> In short, he must be able to command the interest and the respect of intelligent people. No matter how eagerly he may be read by the unintelligent, he is not in my view a top-notch editorial writer unless he has the attention of the intelligent as well. Call him anything you want to—a copywriter, a publicity man, a propagandist—but don't call him an editorial writer.

Strict as these standards are, they are attained by an exception-ally high number of professional editorial writers. Most educators in journalism would claim the I.Q. figure was needlessly high. In practice, all would agree that these men are mature individuals, ex-perienced writers, and capable newspapermen. Intellectual curiosity, an interest in people, qualities of leadership, and writing skill all aid an editorial writer as much as they do others on a newspaper or magazine staff.

A recent survey of editorial writers' backgrounds showed that approximately seven out of every eight on which data were submitted were college graduates and about the same ratio were graduates of the local news room.* Out of 118 writers, 102 were college graduates. This is an impressive record, considering that many of these men were in their 50's and 60's and that college training was not as common when they were young as it is today. A comparable percentage had worked on reporting assignments. Out of 132 on whom information was obtained, only 18 had not had previous newspaper experience before joining the editorial page staff.

Assigning experienced reporters to editorial writing follows the advice that Frank I. Cobb, editor of the *New York World*, gave several decades ago before the American Association of Teachers of Journalism:

You cannot make a good editorial writer out of a man who hasn't a sense of news. That is why the best editorial writers are men who have had experience in gathering and presenting the news of the day. I never knew a good editorial writer who was not a good reporter.

Rufus Terral of the *St. Louis Post-Dispatch* voiced the same idea even more strongly in *The Masthead* (Fall, 1951) when he wrote:

Every capable editorial writer of my acquaintance has had a thorough background in reporting.

Herbert Lewis, editor of the *St. Paul Dispatch* and *Pioneer Press*, said this about the background of those papers' editorial page staff members:

---

* See Hillier Krieghbaum, "American Editorial Writers and Their Backgrounds," *Journalism Quarterly*, Vol. 27, No. 1 (Winter, 1950), pp. 24–27.

We have a staff of three full-time editorial writers. They have usually been college graduates; the exceptions have been few. At one time all of our men had masters degrees. We have had outstanding success with young political science and history graduates though ordinarily our staff men have had some news room experience.

Most editors agree with Forrest W. Seymour, who when editor of the editorial pages of the *Des Moines Register* and *Tribune*, once said that he would not insist on a member of his staff having a college degree "if a man had obvious comparable qualifications." Apparently men with "comparable qualifications" are hard to find; at least few of the non-graduates get to be editorial writers and when they do, they are almost always graduates of the news room.

Quite a number of today's editorial writers have held major positions as news executives before they began to write editorials. Malcolm W. Bingay, late editorial director of the *Detroit Free Press*, described his staff—all former reporters and editors before becoming editorial writers—as representing "a generation of experience in every line of newspaper activity." On the *Chicago Daily News*, all five editorial page staff members had extensive background as reporters and three were news executives. On the *St. Louis Globe-Democrat*, one editorial writer was formerly city editor; another was city hall reporter for many years; a third was feature writer for ten years before going to the editorial page section. All four of the *Fort Worth* (Texas) *Star-Telegram* editorial page staff were reporters and three were rewrite and copydesk men before starting to write editorials. This illustrates that the copydesk on some papers is a pathway to editorial writing.

Against the impressive educational and professional background of editorial page staffs on the metropolitan papers and the widely-quoted smaller dailies and weeklies, we must balance those writers on hundreds of small journals who have little training for writing worth while comments and scant time in which to do their

475

thinking. True, a large staff does not guarantee editorial excellence, but it can help by distributing a heavy workload.

Some small dailies and weeklies hold their own easily against the best editorial offerings of any metropolitan paper. To cite only two examples in each field, Hodding Carter of the *Delta Democrat-Times* of Greenville, Mississippi, and Robert White of the *Mexico* (Missouri) *Ledger* for dailies, and Houston Waring of the *Littleton* (Colorado) *Independent* and John Gould of the *Lisbon Enterprise* of Lisbon Falls, Maine, are editorial voices heard far beyond their own circulation areas.

Editors of country weeklies and specialized publications, such as trade journals and house magazines, have one undisputed advantage over their colleagues on the editorial page staffs of the larger city papers. If they do a competent job, far greater attention is paid to what they write because their readers know them personally or have a professional interest in what they discuss.

Professor Roland E. Wolseley of the Syracuse University School of Journalism in *The Magazine World* (Prentice-Hall, Inc. 1951) described the present day magazine editor as "a combination editorial executive, businessman, and graphic artist." To meet these qualifications, any person certainly would need a wealth of knowledge, both general and journalistic, although he might have scant opportunity to apply it all while writing editorials.

Of the fast expanding field of business and trade publications, Julien Elfenbein's *Business Journalism* (Harper, Revised Edition, 1947) said:

There is no short cut to being a businesspaper editor or to writing editorials on a businesspaper. Years of maturing, wide and deep knowledge of his field and related fields, and of the background of the news, these things fortify the businesspaper editor. He is the mouthpiece. On his editorial page he lays bare the soul, one might say, of the businesspaper.

476

Beyond education and journalistic experience lie a wide variety of other characteristics of the outstanding editorial writer. For instance, integrity is one. A few editorial writers believe that as experts in words and paragraphs they may peddle their talents where they will bring the highest salary. Most of them, however, are evangelistic individuals who see things wrong and want to put them right. These people try to find a publisher whose views parallel their own as much as possible so that there will be a minimum of compromise. Most publishers, too, select editorial page contributors who view the world from about the same vantage point that they do. Fearlessness is another characteristic. The crusading editor is not as common today as he once was, but most editors still possess a quiet courage which, if need be, would drive them down the same road that brought death to Don R. Mellett in a battle against corrupt politicians and gangsters in Canton, Ohio, on July 16, 1926. Other characteristics include intellectual curiosity and an interest in people.

And now, what about the syndicated columnists?

A survey of 26 nationally syndicated columnists who comment seriously on the world's affairs showed that 24 had gone to college and that all but two of these 24 were graduated with a bachelor's degree. Two received a second bachelor's degree, one as a Rhodes scholar and the other in law. Five earned master's degrees and an additional three did graduate work but received no formal academic recognition. Two earned doctor of philosophy degrees and several received honorary degrees. Thus 10 of the 26, or well over one in three, studied in college beyond a single bachelor's degree. If college training provides clues to understanding the world, then these syndicated columnists entered their work with a tremendous asset.

Of 19 such columnists, only two lacked some journalistic experience before they started writing a syndicated column. The indoctrination period extended up to 23 years for one writer and three in the group had more than 20 years of experience before

477

they began column writing. The average was just under 13 years for all 19. Rare exceptions indeed are those "bright young men" who start out at the pinnacle of syndication without training in the city room.

What is the score among the news interpreters?

A study of ten nationally known newspaper interpretive writers showed that every one of them had gone to college although only four stayed on to be graduated and that they spent an average of 15 years in more conventional reporting before they started interpreting the news. The college figures do not vary significantly from the findings of Leo C. Rosten's 1936 survey of 127 representative newspapermen in the national capital. In *The Washington Correspondents* (Harcourt, Brace, 1937), Rosten reported that 51.1 per cent were college graduates, 28.3 per cent went to college but did not graduate, and the rest did not attend colleges.

Whether they are editorial writers, columnists, or news interpreters, and whether they work on metropolitan dailies, country weeklies, or business trade journals, the men and women who help make the world's happenings meaningful have attained their jobs with a wealth of college knowledge and journalistic competence. Students who hope eventually to obtain jobs in these fields should be introduced to the backgrounds that they will need. Numerous courses in English, both composition and literature, are not enough. Students need also at least an introduction to economics, some knowledge of labor problems and public finance, a background in political science beyond an initial course in American government, a thorough grounding in American history as well as European, and a broad understanding of general sociological problems upon which they may have to comment. That is why qualified schools and departments of journalism around the country pay attention to these non-journalistic requirements. Most of them do not pretend to turn out candidates who can immediately take over the jobs of matured and experienced writers and editors, but they do attempt to give philosophy and background that will be invaluable when an opportunity does come.

Sizes of editorial page staffs defy the rules

Writing editorials, columns, and news interpretations is a strictly limited vocation. Possibly less than 50,000 individuals contribute such writings to the nearly 12,000 newspapers, daily and weekly, and to the approximately 12,000 other periodicals printed in the United States. The number on different publications varies widely. *The New York Times*, for example, used nearly 80 contributors to its editorial columns during a recent year. That included regular and occasional writers. On the other hand, several persons with Western Newspaper Union write comments that appear in hundreds of weeklies that purchase material from that syndicate. Many magazines have one person writing all their editorials—on a part-time basis.

The size of a daily newspaper's editorial page staff is not geared directly to any other thing about the paper, except capacity to pay the writers' salaries. Although it may give a hint, circulation is not always a reliable key. For example, the *Hartford Courant*, with circulation of approximately 90,000, has four editorial writers; the New York *Daily News*, with the country's largest newspaper circulation, has two. The quotability of a publication's editorials—for instance, the number of times that a paragraph or two are included in a roundup of "What Editors Said" or an editorial reprinted in full by other journals—does not provide an accurate clue for estimating how many individuals contributed to its editorial columns. Dr. Douglas S. Freeman, whose opinions were republished widely, worked alone as editor of the Richmond *News Leader* until he retired in 1949.

In an effort to ascertain how typical editorial page staffs worked, this author sent questionnaires to a number of better known United States newspapers. Forty dailies replied. They reported a total of 160 editorial page workers, or an average of exactly four for each paper. These figures break down as follows:

Number of Full-Time Editorial Writers	Number of Newspapers	Percentage of All Newspapers Queried
1	4	10.0
2	6	15.0
3	5	12.5
4	9	22.5
5	7	17.5
6	7	17.5
7	1	2.5
8	1	2.5

When Professor Roscoe Ellard, then at the University of Missouri, studied 65 "strong" editorial pages during 1937, he found that their staffs averaged considerably less than three writers to a paper. He reported in "How to Read Editorials," in *Education Against Propaganda, Seventh Year Book of the National Council for the Social Sciences* (1937), that only 15 papers had four or more editorial writers. The more recent survey showed 25 dailies had four or more staff members working full-time.

When broken down by circulation groups, the more recent survey showed:

Classification by Circulation	Number of Newspapers	Maximum Staff	Minimum Staff	Average Staff
Under 200,000	17	6	1	3.4
200,000 to 500,000	18	9	1	4.2
Over 500,000	5	7	2	4.6
All papers	40	9	1	4.0

Only two papers—*The New York Times* and the *New York Herald Tribune*—reported more than six editorial staff members, the highest listed by any papers with daily circulations under 200,-

480

ooo. Two tabloids each reported two full-time editorial writers and both had circulations of more than 500,000. These tabloids solved the problem of small staffs by using less space than the conventional eight-column page and by discussing, as a rule, a single topic in a particular day's editorial comment.

A survey of 98 members of the National Conference of Editorial Writers printed in *The Masthead* (Winter, 1950–51) also showed that as a general rule the number of editorial staff members rises with circulation. These statistics follow:

Circulation	Average Number of Writers
Less than 25,000	1
25,000 to 50,000	1.2
50,000 to 100,000	1.9
100,000 to 175,000	3.3
175,000 to 300,000	4.3
More than 300,000	4.8

A geographical analysis in the same study showed that the largest editorial page staffs were in the Middle Eastern and Southwestern states. The lowest region in number of editorial page staff members was the Northwest, followed by the Southeastern and Central areas.

A few gifted writers, working alone, have won their papers' editorial pages wide recognition, but in most cases results are better when there is a larger staff with more time and opportunity for thought and research. Many (although not all) metropolitan dailies and a few exceptional papers in smaller communities have editorial page staffs large enough to insure that the opinion-forming job can be done adequately. The majority of dailies and virtually all weeklies, however, depend upon one or, at most, two editorial writers. Their efforts are not included in any list of strong editorial pages unless the writer is one of the brilliant exceptions.

These general conclusions also apply to the magazine field. As was pointed out in Chapter Three some of the largest circulation magazines deliberately have let their editorial pages atrophy. The influence that they yield comes from a judicious selection of non-fiction articles which can be more stimulating than poorly done editorials. Other mass circulation magazines purchase editorials from non-staff members or turn the job over to an experienced writer on a part-time basis. Little of this applies to the specialized trade press, as was pointed out earlier in this chapter.

Common ownership of a group of publications with standardized, syndicated editorials presents another complication for opinion pages. Practically all editorials on international and national subjects and, in some cases, even those of regional interest are supplied from a central office. Such group editorializing is sound only when the comments are of equal interest in, for example, an Eastern steel metropolis, a Southern state capital, or a Western community interested primarily in farm products. Strictly limited are the topics that include common aspects of industry, politics, and agriculture. While managements of groups of papers frequently supply syndicated editorials and provide a single editorial writer on each paper, this attempted solution is not always a happy one.

Should we hire some outside help?

Should editors tap the abilities of reporters who have special background information and permit them to write editorials in their own fields? Or should such reporters simply supply the facts and let the regular editorial page staff handle all the writing assignments?

In daily newspaper offices, two conflicting camps exist. Some of the country's more prominent editors line up on each side of this argument.

The New York Times, as cited earlier, makes the most extensive use of specialists among its reporters. Charles Merz, its editor, does not hesitate to request an editorial from a labor reporter or science writer who has the "inside story" well in mind along with the printed news. Some reporters contribute a single editorial during a year; others supply copy whenever a news development in their special field requires comment.

J. M. North, editor of the *Fort Worth Star-Telegram*, explained the arrangement on his paper as follows:

> Various members of the staff do, from time to time, contribute editorials on subjects with which they are qualified to deal—sometimes when requested, other times voluntarily. Some of the men on our Farm and Ranch News, a tabloid section published monthly as a Sunday feature, frequently contribute editorials on farm topics, soil conservation programs, etc. A staff writer who handles aviation will do an editorial on some phase of this subject.

Washington correspondents, reporters in state capitals, and men on regular runs submit editorials on many dailies. On the *Los Angeles Times*, the paper's political editor occasionally wrote on that subject and a staff reporter who specialized on the *Times*' campaigns such as smog control or water supply contributed editorials tied in with the subject he was treating. On the *Chicago Daily News*, Sydney Harris, a columnist, was the paper's most frequent part-time contributor during a recent year.

The *Minneapolis Star* has tapped the academic resources of its community and one of its two part-time editorial writers for years was a professor of economics at the nearby University of Minnesota. The other contributor was the man responsible for all copy, other than editorials, that went on the page. Other papers in college towns have used faculty members on a less permanent basis.

The Portland *Oregonian*, during the early post-war years, utilized as contributing editorial writers two of Portland's nationally known authors—Stewart H. Holbrook and Richard Neuberger. Holbrook wrote on all phases of forestry, an especially important topic for any Pacific coast publication, and Neuberger discussed politics, a subject he knew from first-hand experience as a one-time member of the state legislature.

Some newspapers that accepted outside help on editorials were not adverse to printing contributions, under a by-line, from prominent individuals in the community. After all, the problem varied from town to town and the editors solved it as they thought would be most advantageous to their own publications.

Those dailies that permit occasional contributions to the editorial columns offer a way toward becoming a full-time staff member. Some editors have a paternal interest in finding competent reporters or copydesk workers who may be able to help out with an infrequent contribution. At first, possibly only the idea or a paragraph or two will be incorporated into the published version. As the writer becomes more adept with the opinion-making style, he may have his efforts published with only copyreading changes. Then, if a vacancy occurs, he has a chance of being offered an opportunity to graduate from the news room into the editorial writing staff.

Editors on some prominent newspapers utilize their own editorial page staffs exclusively for editorials. To mention just a few of the papers that do this, the list includes the New York *Daily News*, Philadelphia *Evening Bulletin*, *Philadelphia Inquirer*, Baltimore *Evening Sun*, *Atlanta Constitution*, *Detroit Free Press*, Louisville *Courier-Journal* and *Times*, *Des Moines Register* and *Tribune*, and *San Francisco Chronicle*.

As a vigorous spokesman for this point of view, Forrest W. Seymour, then Des Moines editor, wrote:

We have no part-time editorial writers. I do not have much use for that practice. Oh, other people on the staff—copyreaders and makeup editors, for example, may write an *occasional* editorial, but occasional only. When we want the thinking and experience of other people on the staff—our Washington correspondents, our farm editor, etc.—a member of our regular editorial writing staff communicates with these persons, gets and absorbs the necessary knowledge

484

and writes the editorial himself. I frequently assign a man to such a task.

Mark Ethridge of the Louisville *Courier-Journal* and *Times* said his papers did not have any part-time editorial writers and explained that "almost all of the work is done here, even though the information might come from the labor reporter or the Washington correspondent."

EIGHTEEN

Crusades,

courage, and

contest awards

IF THE UNITED STATES PRESS IS TO BE TRULY GREAT, IT HAS TO BE more than a business for dispensing news stories. It has to display the courage to be responsible to the society of which it is an essential part. Professor Zechariah Chafee, Jr., of Harvard University, a long-time student of mass communications, called it "a weighty and difficult moral responsibility to adjust the demands of a profitable business to the demands of an educational enterprise of the highest importance."

Occasionally an editor or publisher has to face up to the hard choice between a courageous, responsible editorial stand to support the general welfare despite a potential business loss, on one side, and a wishy-washy position guaranteed to antagonize no one, on the other. Except for visionary idealists with few financial obligations, it is never an easy decision. Yet surprisingly often, considering the costs, newspaper and magazine directors stand up and are counted for responsible (and, if need be, deficit) journalism.

Crusades are what you make them

Crusades, where publications flex their muscles in an effort to move public opinion, have been praised as the "Big Berthas" of journalism. And they have been denounced as crass exhibitionism seeking to build circulation. Both are correct. Robert J. Blakely,

486

then with the *St. Louis Star-Times*, put it this way in the 1951 Don R. Mellett lecture:

In itself a "crusading" newspaper is neither good nor bad. That depends in a large part upon its motivations. There are newspapers that "crusade" for ulterior reasons—to build up circulation or to grind an axe rather than to sharpen the sword of justice. These are contemptible. They injure the innocent. They rarely accomplish beneficial results that endure, always stopping short when the cream of sensationalism has been skimmed and never pressing to where they touch the really powerful and dangerous elements of the community. They discredit the free press and make suspect the sincere crusade. And there are newspapers which do not "crusade" because they are slothful and cowardly.

But to me the free press reaches its zenith in a good newspaper looking for a fight in a good cause in its own avenues and alleys. Few personal satisfactions can match the knowledge that one is making one's community a better place in which to live. Given this primary motivation, what does it matter that a newspaper is accused of trying to build circulation? A newspaper cannot be solvent without adequate circulation. Without solvency it cannot be strong. Without strength it cannot be free. And where is there a better harmony of private and public interests than in a newspaper that is strong because it is purposeful, that uses its strength and its freedom to buttress each other?

Critics of crusading generally attack from two fronts: (1) it hurts too much—financially, and (2) the job takes so long that very few publications really carry it through.

A number of editors and publishers have been discouraged and heart-broken in their efforts to build a better community when the public was apathetic, the advertisers antagonistic, and subscribers hesitant to buy a "radical" paper. Few have told the story quite as bluntly and forcefully as did Harry B. Haines of the *Paterson* (N.J.) *Evening News* years ago. After a career as a crusader, he explained why he was changing his policy in *Editor and Publisher* (October 11, 1930):

Crusading is a rich man's game, especially in a community the size of Paterson. You lose advertising, you lose circulation, you even lose prestige. People begin thinking you have a personal axe to grind, and that the publisher himself is working for some ulterior motive. And when you have thwarted the plans of scheming politicians and have saved the city or county millions of dollars—what happens? No one gives a damn! The friends appreciate the service you have done for a few minutes, and then forget it immediately and completely. But the enemies you have made never forget. No, and neither do their brothers, sisters, fellow lodge members and everybody else connected with the culprit or culprits. The good will you generate in a crusade is short and fleeting, and the ill-will lasts forever.

I have discovered that the people hate a crusader and love a pussy-footer. Since I adopted my new policy of barring crusading, everything is running along smoothly and without any fuss or bother. I used to have a string of politicians a block long waiting outside this office to argue and threaten and express their contempt or elucidate their ambitious plans. Now it is quiet. Everything is routine. Everybody slaps you on the back and says you're a good fellow. We just shut our eyes to everything, and then everybody's happy.

That feeling of disillusionment, frustration, and despair has been shared by practically all newspaper and magazine crusaders. The answer to these emotions appears in the following paragraph by Reed Sarratt of the Baltimore *Evening Sun* from *The Masthead* (Spring, 1950):

The easiest and most comfortable way to run an editorial page is to print pleasant, bright, safe, inoffensive pieces. But any editor or editorial writer who looks the facts in the face on the critical and controversial problems of our time is going to come to some unpopular conclusions. If the newspaper is fulfilling its responsibility to its community as it should, it will express unpopular points of view forthrightly and fearlessly. Cream puffs won't do the job of brickbats.

Stressing this same viewpoint, a statement of the principles for the National Conference of Editorial Writers declared that the function of American journalism, especially of editorial writers, is "to help the average citizen to better understanding and to truth." That, as any experienced journalist knows, can be a difficult, arduous, and soul-searching assignment.

In the early 1700's in the first crusade of American journalism, James Franklin fought yellow fever vaccination and gained enough circulation to establish his new paper, the *New-England Courant*, on a sound basis. Others have crusaded for the same motives during the intervening two and a half centuries. Series on sex abnormalities, drug addiction, and causes of divorce have attracted curious readers to many a sensational metropolitan daily. A whole category of magazines cater to this same titillation-seeking audience.

Mike Gorman, who won a special Lasker award in 1948 for arousing public interest in mental hospitals through articles in the *Daily Oklahoman*, discussed it this way in *Nieman Reports* (April, 1949):

Too many newspapers start off with a Hollywood-trumpeted expose—complete with promotional ads and pictures of their star reporter—then fold as soon as the original series appears. . . . The opening blast, I have learned from bitter experience, is merely five per cent of the battle. It's the follow-through—the constant pounding away over a period of months, even years—that gets the job done. In the same way the advertising huckster makes you like that soap, love that soap, finally buy that soap, the reporter has to make the reader like the idea, get indignant about the idea, and then get off his posterior and do something about the idea.

An outstanding illustration of a long-range crusade is the decades-long battle of the *New York World-Telegram and Sun* to obtain clean waters for the millions of bathers who spend summer weekends at New York metropolitan area beaches. The paper began its fight in 1931. The weapons, according to Murray Davis who directed the crusade, were "facts presented in news stories, editorials that backed up these stories, cartoons, and unquestioned support from all editors."

Shortly after the stories on pollution began to be printed, a shocked deputy commissioner of sanitation asked the paper for the results of its sampling of water at various beaches. His request was honored by the editors and the commissioner laid the foundations for building the Ward's Island sewage disposal and treatment plant, which was opened five years later. A second plant followed in about seven years.

Davis got copyreaders to pass stories saying the beaches were being polluted by raw sewage from metropolitan comfort stations and bathrooms. Later, he used the word "toilet." This corrected the general misinformation that sewage was the same as garbage.

More than 15 years after the newspaper began its battle, Davis started translating the findings, which previously had been told in terms of 100 cubic centimeters, into the meaningful "large mouthful of water." That graphic description convinced the health commissioner, who then praised the campaign. His department swung whole-heartedly behind the beach pollution clean-up. The *World-Telegram and Sun* moved its battleground and during the 1950's, the paper sought to persuade suburban communities to follow the metropolis' example in eliminating pollution.

Numerous crusades to uncover political corruption went on for years before officials were convicted. Well-known illustrations are the New Orleans *Times-Picayune* and *States* battle against the machine of Huey Long and his successors during the 1930's, the *Kansas City Star* and *Times* overthrow of the Pendergast gang during the 1940's and the *Tulsa Tribune's* expose of excessive expenditures by Oklahoma county officials during the 1950's.

How investigative reporting, backed by demands for official action, brought a healthier society is shown by the campaign of the *Whiteville* (N.C.) *News Reporter* and the *Tabor City* (N.C.) *Tribune* "against the Ku Klux Klan, waged on their own doorstep at the risk of economic loss and personal danger, culminating in the conviction of over 100 Klansmen and an end to terrorism in their communities." The quotation is from the 1953 Pulitzer award citation, the first given to weeklies for public service since the first prizes were presented in 1917. Again in 1955, a Pulitzer prize went for such an expose—to the *Columbus* (Georgia) *Ledger* for complete news coverage and "fearless editorial attack" on widespread corruption in nearby Phenix City, Alabama.

When an explosion on March 25, 1947, ripped through the labyrinth of tunnels near the town of Centralia, Illinois, and killed

"YOU GAMBLED BUT I PAID"

DANIEL R. FITZPATRICK drew this cartoon as part of the St. Louis Post-Dispatch's campaign for mine safety after 111 miners were killed in a 1947 explosion at Centralia, Illinois.

111 coal miners, the *St. Louis Post-Dispatch* gave the story full treatment of reporting in depth, editorial comment with vigor, and graphic cartoons by Daniel R. Fitzpatrick. Results included a Pulitzer prize to the paper for "public service," removal of the state director of mines, and defeat of the Illinois governor by Adlai Stevenson in the 1948 campaign.

This was achieved through stories after stories, many on the front pages as the investigation into corruption unfolded, editorial after editorial, and cartoon after cartoon. Irving Dilliard, editorial page editor of the *Post-Dispatch*, told about it as follows:

> It was not a week-end sensation with us. We didn't fold up and go home after a few days. When Mr. Pulitzer [*Post-Dispatch* publisher] found out that not enough newspapers were being sent to Centralia, he directed a supplement be prepared, and all the news stories and cartoons were put together in a supplement—20 pages of roto and color. And it was widely circulated free of charge throughout the mine area for the information of the people.
>
> Then we went to work to improve safety in the mines. Governor Green [of Illinois] had pledged before he took office—before he was elected governor—that the mine statute would be enforced to the letter of the law. But he forgot that, as well as a good many other things, after he became governor. It remained for the miners to look out for themselves or to be protected as the newspapers might protect them.

These fights for a law-abiding democracy neatly demonstrated what James S. Pope of the Louisville *Courier-Journal* once advocated for the responsible, conscientious editor everywhere—a man who "spots and cauterizes civic germs, regardless of the enemies gained, before the infection takes root," rather than one who waits for the right moment before crusading on a spectacular scale. They also show that the press need not abdicate to congressional committees with television audiences, or to book writers.

Another contribution to public service by newspapers and magazines is interpretation, whether it be issue-by-issue or a series when some topic looms upon the news horizon. *The New York Times*, daily or Sunday, is unsurpassed on interpreting current news. Look at any issue and you will find at least several good examples of interpretive news coverage. Other daily papers and magazines consistently do a conscientious job. To cite only two conspicuous examples in the magazine field, a 1953 Sigma Delta Chi award went to *Look* for a series on religion's role in contemporary United States life, which the judges considered "a most timely contribution to public service," and the *Ladies' Home Journal* won the 1954 Benjamin Franklin Magazine Award for "the most distinguished and meritorious public service" with ten articles and supporting editorials on how communities had solved such local problems as teen age gangs, school bond elections, and adoption counseling. The business and trade press performs some of its most useful service through printing specialized information of interest to readers. For example, one business paper reported, despite the anguished protest of carpet manufacturers, that a defect in a new line had been discussed at a convention of dry cleaners. The manufacturers wanted to take their chances on not correcting the flaw. The news story forced them to revise their operations and within a year a newly designed carpet was on the market that could be cleaned without difficulty. Here was a service to the business interests it served as well as to the consumers, few of whom ever saw the publication. Hundreds of dailies, weeklies, and monthlies quietly give their readers the news scorecard, which admittedly is less spectacular than investigative reporting, but none the less important.

An effective battle formation invariably is one that utilizes basic reporting, whether it is interpretive or investigative, plus vigorous editorials and cartoons. Over and over again, as cited earlier in this chapter, an effective crusade has combined informative news stories and persuasive editorial arguments. This does not mean that news stories should be slanted to match editorial policy. Far from it!

Joseph Pulitzer, whose journalistic laurels rest to a great degree on effective and forceful crusading, completely reversed the *New York World's* editorial stand on a child labor amendment when his reporters in the South sent up news dispatches that tore away the basis for the *World's* position. The daily shifted its editorial support; it did not kill or modify the news dispatches.

During the 1952 presidential campaign, when some newspapers and magazines let the hand that wrote the editorials copyread the news stories, managing editor Turner Catledge issued a 1,250-word memorandum to *The New York Times* political staff. He explained that the directive was intended to "help safeguard the *Times* from incautious reporting, writing or editing of political news." His concluding advice was:

The editorial page is no concern of *Times* reporters and news editors. It might be stressed conversely that bending too far in the other direction in an effort not to give any semblance of favoring the paper's candidate is also to be avoided. The rule—and this *is* a hard and fast one—is the same as they give the umpires: "Call them as you see them."

When reporters call them as they see them, even if they are far out in right field, then the critics have little basis on which to blame the press. A chief trouble is that writers do not always call them that way and other people who saw the same ball game complain.

Adolph Ochs and Joseph Pulitzer left credos

"Where the press is free, and every man able to read, all is safe," wrote Thomas Jefferson considerably more than a century ago. For contemporary times, the answer unfortunately is not quite that simple and optimistic. Of course, the press must remain free. Newspaper and magazine suppressions in Europe and Asia during the Twentieth Century have inevitably presaged totalitarian or tyrannical governments. Freedom has survived only in those countries where the press was free. The United States is close to the

Jeffersonian goal of "every man able to read." But that is not enough. The press, including owners and workers, has to display a high order of courage. The rise of one-newspaper communities and mass-circulation magazines has reinforced the need for the journalist's "professional conscience" which was once defined as "love of truth combined with zeal for the people's cause."

Two great publishers have left credos as a heritage for present day publishers, editors, and writers. One, Adolph S. Ochs, was concerned primarily with the news in *The New York Times;* the other, Joseph Pulitzer, was interested more in aligning his papers on the side of public welfare, that is, in crusading.

First printed on the editorial page of August 19, 1896, under the heading, "Business Announcement," Ochs' statement included this oft-quoted paragraph:

It will be my earnest aim that *The New-York Times* give the news, all the news, in concise and attractive form, in language that is parliamentary in good society, and give it as early, if not earlier, than it can be learned through any other reliable medium; to give the news impartially, without fear or favor, regardless of any party, sect or interests involved; to make the columns of *The New-York Times* a forum for the consideration of all questions of public importance, and to that end to invite intelligent discussion from all shades of opinion.

When he stepped down from active control of the *New York World* April 10, 1907, Joseph Pulitzer sent its staff a statement that still is the platform of the remaining Pulitzer newspaper, the *St. Louis Post-Dispatch.* Printed daily on the *Post-Dispatch* editorial page and embedded deeply in the minds of its staff members, the statement reads:

I know that my retirement will make no difference in its cardinal principles; that it will always fight for progress and reform, never tolerate injustice or corruption, always fight demagogues of all parties, never belong to any party, always oppose privileged classes and public plunderers, never lack sympathy with the poor, always remain devoted to the public welfare, never be satisfied with merely printing news; always be drastically independent; never be afraid to attack wrong, whether by predatory plutocracy or predatory poverty.

Many are the daily and weekly newspapers, mass-circulation and specialized magazines, trade and business publications that see their responsibilities as striving for the Ochs and Pulitzer goals. They try to present the news "without fear or favor" while remaining unafraid "to attack wrong, whether by predatory plutocracy or predatory poverty." That all the press does not respond to the challenge reflects more the height of the standards than the shortcomings of newspaper and magazine owners and workers.

Among the dailies that hold fast to these responsibilities, the *Milwaukee Journal* usually is rated highly. An explanation for this is found, in part, in the following quotation from "Milwaukee's Dutch Uncle" by David Wittels, which appeared in the *Saturday Evening Post* of September 20, 1947:

The *Journal* is Milwaukee's self-appointed civic conscience. It patrols Milwaukee and the greater part of Wisconsin with club poised to conk malefactors of all kinds, as well as any politician who dares lift his head to take a hungry look at public funds. And Milwaukee, unlike most cities, listens to its conscience. Because the *Journal* is against gambling, even bingo games at church socials and firemen's picnics are practically taboo in Milwaukee.

Many newspapers make spasmodic crusades against gambling, but at the same time most of them carefully print horse-race entries, selections and results in full, to keep the trade of the betting fraternity. The *Journal* is more consistent. It never prints selections or "dope," and never prints entries or mutual prices, except for that American classic, the Kentucky Derby. . . .

The *Journal* began its career of self-appointed civic conscience when a stubborn, bulldog type of man named Lucius (Lute) W. Nieman took it over sixty-five years ago. Soon afterward more than seventy people were killed when a hotel advertised as fireproof burned to the ground. While the city's seven other dailies tisk-tisked piously over the unpredictable and tragic vagaries of fire, the *Journal* charged that the hotel was "a known firetrap" and blasted the owners and city authorities for greedy, criminal negligence. Milwaukee's almost religious devotion to high safety standards dates from that exposure.

Many comparable examples of publications that serve as a "self-appointed civic conscience" are reported regularly in the files of *Editor and Publisher, Nieman Reports, Printer's Ink, Publisher's Auxiliary*, other professional and some mass-circulation magazines. A valuable assignment for anyone interested would be to scan recent issues of these publications for additional case histories.

Infrequently, publications themselves write about these plus signs of their professional conduct in their own columns. They should do it oftener. Here are two examples, one from a large metropolitan daily and the other from a weekly, that attracted attention when they were first printed.

Newspapers, Cancer, and Cigaret Ads

Stocks of big tobacco companies lost approximately 5 per cent of their value Wednesday on the New York Stock Exchange. The drop was directly related, as one company recognized by issuing a statement on the subject, to a story that appeared that morning in the news column of this and other leading newspapers throughout the country.

This story quoted some physicians who reported at a New York scientific convention that there is a definite connection between cigaret smoking and the incidence of lung cancer in men. Similar but less definite reports have been given in the past and have been printed in this and other newspapers. Dr. Van Dellen, our health editor, has treated the subject a number of times during the last three or four years.

Tobacco companies have some of the largest advertising budgets in the country, devoted largely to pushing the sale of cigarets. The next time someone tells you that advertisers dictate or influence the editorial policies of newspapers, ask him about cigarets and cancer.

—*Chicago Daily Tribune*

The Ad We Didn't Choose to Run

A New York advertising agency submitted to us last Friday a large television advertisement for inclusion in this week's issue of the *Gazette*. The ad makes, in our opinion, blatant and distasteful assertions; it infers that the seven-year-old child feels a "deep loneliness" and a sense of "humiliation" unless his parents provide a television set for the home; and it quotes Angelo Patri, "Authority on Child Guidance," as saying: "Youngsters today need television for their morale as much as they need fresh air and sunshine for their health. . . . It is practically impossible for boys and girls to hold their own with friends and school mates unless television is available to them. . . . To have television is to be 'cock o' the walk.' Not to have it, well, that is unthinkable." With all due respect to Mr. Patri and all possible disrespect to the ad writer responsible for this unusual piece of copy, the Gazette's publishers, by Saturday morning agreed that since they believed the advertisement might do a vast disservice to the children of eastern Greenwich, to their parents and, incidentally to area television retailers, that they would choose not to print it. Later that day a telegram arrived from the advertising agency cancelling the ad, a denouement which caused us to think that other weekly newspaper publishers had reacted similarly. This incident reemphasizes, we believe, that happy fact that specious, misleading advertising can work only to the detriment of the product so advertised. P.S. And, by the way Mr. Patri, don't you *really* think that a keen sense of values, an understanding of man's social obligations, and what an appreciation of religion can do for him are more important to a child's morale than a television set? Of course you do!

—*The Village Gazette*, Old Greenwich, Connecticut

Speaking about the job of the non-metropolitan daily's editor, Charles A. Sprague of the *Oregon Statesman* of Salem, Oregon,

498

offered this advice at the 1952 California State Editors Conference:

In the field of news-gathering and transmission, newspapers have competition from the new media of radio and television, each with its values, each with its limitations. The newspaper though should remain the major medium for interpreting the news and making it meaningful to the people, and for helping in the formation of public policy. Publishers should point their papers definitely in this direction. This will require that the editor be restored to eminence in the newspaper hierarchy and given the status and the reward which the importance of his office warrants.

Today's editor should throw himself zestfully into his job, multiplying what talents he has and employing them freely and fearlessly in the fight against ignorance, fear, hypocrisy, kluxism, and fuzzy thinking. He should not hesitate to tackle dragons abroad and crackpots and rascals at home. He should aim at the mass audience and not fire until he sees the whites of their eyes—then let them have it. If he does this he will win a place in whatever Valhalla is reserved for good ex-editors, and have a heap of fun as he goes along.

Most students of the United States press agree that the publication's conscience generally has improved as many publishers and editors have become more humble with mounting responsibilities in communicating information and guiding public opinion. Now they realize that radio broadcasting and televising news will not replace the printed word. Thus they can concentrate on modifying the press' techniques of news presentation to meet an electronic age. The news weeklies, opinion magazines, and major segments of the business and trade journals ride in the same boat; their existence is unthreatened but innovations should make them more effective.

Prizes are one pay-off

For the overwhelming majority of publishers, editors, and writers who accept their professional responsibilities and do their jobs as they believe they should be done, the rewards consist of infrequent

499

praise from their colleagues, local citizens, and occasional office-holders. To a select few come prizes, awards, and plaques in recognition. Among the widely recognized competitions are those for the Pulitzer prizes, Sigma Delta Chi citations, and Benjamin Franklin magazine awards.

Besides allocating funds for establishing a journalism school at Columbia University, Joseph Pulitzer in his will provided for a series of annual prizes, the first of which were made in 1917.

In the light of the cited traditions of Pulitzer and Ochs, it was not unexpected that the late *New York World* and the *St. Louis Post-Dispatch* led all other newspapers in prizes for meritorious public service, and that *The New York Times* correspondents repeatedly won at least one of the reporting awards year after year.

Before Roy Howard purchased it in 1931, the *World* had won three Pulitzer prizes for public service and the *Post-Dispatch* received five from 1937 to 1952. And the paper might have won even more if the second Joseph Pulitzer had not hesitated to enter *Post-Dispatch* crusades during the 1930's. Before the reporting awards were regrouped in 1948, *Times* reporters had won or shared five Pulitzer prizes for general reporting, nine for correspondence, and one special citation in 1941 for the public educational value of its foreign news reports. Under the new arrangement, its correspondents continued to win greater recognition than any other daily.

Newspapers have won Pulitzer prizes for such varied activities as: *Canton* (Ohio) *Daily News* in 1927 for its "brave and effective fight" on municipal corruption during which its editor, Don R. Mellett, was assassinated; the *Bismark* (N.D.) *Tribune* in 1938 for helping restore the Dust Bowl's self-confidence; *Los Angeles Times* in 1942 for reaffirming by court action the right of United States newspapers to comment on judicial proceedings after verdicts had been entered, despite the fact that appeals were pending; *The New York Times* in 1944 for a national survey of American history courses for freshmen in 36 colleges and universities; and the earlier-cited *St. Louis Post-Dispatch* coverage of the Centralia disaster and the two North Carolina weeklies' fight against the Ku Klux Klan.

In the editorial prizes, the late Henry J. Haskell of the *Kansas City Star* was the only individual to win twice, in 1933 and again in 1944. When Donald M. Murray won in 1954 with a series of more than 100 editorials on the "new look" in national defense, he was the fourth *Boston Herald* writer to receive a Pulitzer prize for distinguished editorial writing. Other *Herald* winners were Frank Buxton in 1924, F. Lauriston Bullard in 1927, and John H. Crider in 1949. The *Herald* thus lead all other papers.

Editorial awards have gone for a single, much-quoted editorial as, in 1923, William Allen White's short "To an Anxious Friend" which defended a free press; in 1936, George B. Parker's "Censorship, You—and Us" which appeared in all Scripps-Howard papers; in 1946, Hodding Carter's "Go For Broke" which asked tolerance between races; in 1950, Carl M. Saunders' plea in the *Jackson* (Michigan) *Citizen Patriot* for designation of Memorial Day as an occasion for prayers for peace; in 1952, Louis La-Coss' editorial entitled "Low Estate of Public Morals" in the *St. Louis Globe-Democrat*; in 1955, Royce Howe's analysis in the *Detroit Free Press* of an unauthorized strike.

Prizes also have been awarded series of editorials, such as Murray's more than 100 on national defense in the *Boston Herald*, Haskell's three series on economic conditions at home and abroad which won in 1933, and Geoffrey Parsons' editorials in the *New York Herald Tribune* where, as the 1942 citation said, "political affiliation was completely subordinated to the national welfare and a newspaper firmly led its party to higher ground."

Pulitzer prizes for reporting have gone for a wide diversity of news stories. Walter Duranty's coverage of the Soviet Union in the 1930's won one and so did series of articles from the same country after World War II by Brooks Atkinson of *The New*

York Times, Eddy Gilmore of the Associated Press, Paul W. Ward of the Baltimore *Sun,* Edmund Stevens of the *Christian Science Monitor* and Harrison E. Salisbury of *The New York Times.* There were exclusive stories such as Arthur Krock's interview with President Franklin D. Roosevelt in *The New York Times* on what the executive proposed to do during his second term; and Anthony Leviero's disclosure of conversations at Wake Island between President Harry S. Truman and General of the Army Douglas MacArthur printed in *The New York Times.* Examples of investigative reporting included Bert Andrews' series on the State Department's loyalty inquiry in the *New York Herald Tribune;* Edwin O. Guthman's series in the *Seattle Times* that provided information clearing University of Washington Professor Melvin Rader of Communist charges; Alvin Scott Mc-Coy's stories in the *Kansas City Star* that led to the resignation of C. Wesley Roberts as Republican National Chairman; and George de Carvalho's exposé in the *San Francisco Chronicle* of "ransom" extortion from Chinese with relatives in Red China. Interpretive reporting was represented by William L. Laurence's series on the atomic bomb for *The New York Times;* and Austin C. Wehrwein's "Canada's New Century" in the *Milwaukee Journal.* Colorful, graphic spot news reporting included such examples as Meyer Berger's story for *The New York Times* of a veteran who went berserk in Camden, N.J., and killed 13 persons; the coverage of a bank robbery and capture of the bandit, by the entire staff of the *Providence* (R.I.) *Journal* and *Evening Bulletin;* and Don Whitehead's reporting for the Associated Press of President-elect Dwight D. Eisenhower's 1952 trip to the Korean battle fronts.

Unlike the Pulitzer prizes, the bronze medallions of Sigma Delta Chi, professional journalistic fraternity, are awarded for magazine and radio journalism as well as newspaper excellence. The fraternity's citations started modestly in 1935 with a $50 cash award for significant, original research in journalism to Professor Oscar Reigel of Washington and Lee University for his book, *Mobiliz-*

ing for Chaos (Yale University, 1934). In 1940, the fraternity added an annual award for distinguished service to journalism but the wide contemporary range of recognition was authorized in 1949.

Public service citations have gone to numerous large dailies and such other papers as the specialized *Wall Street Journal*, for an interpretation of what a change in RKO management meant, and the *Moose Lake* (Minnesota) *Star-Gazette*, a weekly that battled to keep county records open because its editor, James R. Etzell, felt "a newspaper, and I include small town newspapers, must print all the news if we are to retain our democratic heritage." In the magazine field, *Collier's* won two consecutive public service medallions while the same magazine's writers won reporting awards for four consecutive years. *Look* won two consecutive public service citations; its series on various religious creeds was mentioned in both.

Two Pulitzer prize winners were among the editorial writers honored by Sigma Delta Chi—John Crider of the *Boston Herald* and Virginius Dabney of the *Richmond Times-Dispatch*. Dabney won twice, the second time with his widely reprinted "We Choose Eisenhower," published during the 1952 campaign when the traditionally Democratic daily shifted parties. Other editorial winners include Bradley L. Morison of the *Minneapolis Tribune*, Robert M. White II of the *Mexico* (Missouri) *Ledger*, John N. Reddin of the *Milwaukee Journal*, and Robert H. Estabrook of the *Washington Post and Times Herald*.

Some Sigma Delta Chi reporting awards were for exclusive stories, such as those by Richard L. Wilson in the *Des Moines Register* and *Tribune* on a 1945 Federal Bureau of Investigation report on Harry Dexter White which was sent to the White House (this story also got a Pulitzer prize) and Kingsbury Smith's exchange of questions and answers with Joseph Stalin in 1949 for International News Service. Carl T. Rowan, a Negro born in the South, wrote an interpretive series on "Jim Crow" schools for the

Minneapolis Tribune which the judges in 1954 said "did a calm job of news reporting which could nurture understanding of the issues without inflaming passions" and he won again in 1955 with an interpretive series, "This Is India." Chalmers M. Roberts of the *Washington Post and Times Herald* won with a discussion of the national capital's growth which presented a master plan for development.

Criticism of both Pulitzer prizes and Sigma Delta Chi medallions has centered on what some have called the "monopoly" of some organizations. Critics have asked if these annual journalistic selections reflected, in truth, a real cross-section of performance by the United States press. In any such argument, however, none has denied the high integrity and professional competence of the winners. The dispute was over whether others did not do an equally impressive job.

The University of Illinois launched the Benjamin Franklin magazine awards in 1954, thus adding a recognition exclusively for magazines. *Ladies' Home Journal* was cited for the most distinguished and meritorious public service in printing ten articles and supporting editorials on community public activities. John Bartlow Martin won an award for "original reporting in which serious obstacles had to be overcome" with a four-part series in the *Saturday Evening Post* on the Jackson, Michigan, prison riots. William H. Whyte, Jr., got a citation for "the best writing depicting life, culture, or institutions in the United States" with a series in *Fortune* entitled "The Transients." *Redbook* won a 1955 public service awards for another series. The Alsop brothers, syndicated columnists for newspapers, received the "original reporting" citation for "We Accuse!" in *Harper's Magazine,* in which they defended Dr. J. Robert Oppenheimer against security charges—their article was expanded later into a book of the same name (Simon and Schuster, 1954).

While these three sets of awards are generally known, members of the press recognize that many other competitions reward writers and their publications. Among these are the Heywood Broun Award of the American Newspaper Guild, bronze plaques and certificates presented by *Industrial Marketing* for editorial excellence among business papers, the Headliners' Club awards, Sidney Hillman Foundation prizes, Inland Daily Press Association Awards for outstanding community service, University of Missouri Honor Awards for Distinguished Service in Journalism, Overseas Press Club Awards, and the George Polk Memorial awards for "distinguished reporting" presented by Long Island University.

To thousands of newspaper and magazine workers who never win a prize, medallion, citation, or plaque, there are other satisfactions. Those who contribute the most may never be known outside their own communities but they have earned and receive the respect of their fellows.

Some have helped worth while causes. For instance, *The New York Times'* Neediest Cases Fund and the *New York Herald Tribune's* Fresh Air Fund each raise more than a quarter of a million dollars annually. Other publications may contribute as much, if not more, proportionately, to their communities.

Many journalists have endorsed ideas and projects that made their towns and regions better places in which to live. And many have provided the news, explanations, and interpretations that are essential to a sound public opinion.

Index